Russia's Balkan entanglements
1806–1914

This book examines the reasons for the Russian involvement in the Balkan peninsula and attempts to explain the connections that drew the Russian government into entanglements that were not only dangerous to its great power interests but contained emotional commitments that were difficult to control. The wars, waged at a high human and economic cost, limited the resources that could be spent on internal development and, in particular when they ended in defeat, led to domestic unrest and, after 1856 and 1917, to drastic internal change.

Russia's Balkan entanglements
1806–1914

BARBARA JELAVICH

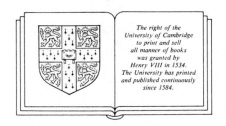

The right of the
University of Cambridge
to print and sell
all manner of books
was granted by
Henry VIII in 1534.
The University has printed
and published continuously
since 1584.

CAMBRIDGE UNIVERSITY PRESS

CAMBRIDGE

NEW YORK   PORT CHESTER   MELBOURNE   SYDNEY

Published by the Press Syndicate of the University of Cambridge
The Pitt Building, Trumpington Street, Cambridge CB2 1RP
40 West 20th Street, New York, NY 10011, USA
10 Stamford Road, Oakleigh, Melbourne 3166, Australia

First published 1991

Printed in the United States of America

Library of Congress Cataloging-in-Publication Data
Jelavich, Barbara, 1923–
Russia's Balkan entanglements, 1806–1914 / Barbara Jelavich.
p.   cm.
Includes bibliographical references.
ISBN 0-521-40126-7
1. Balkan Peninsula – Foreign relations – Soviet Union.   2. Soviet
Union – Foreign relations – Balkan Peninsula.   3. Eastern question
(Balkan)   4. Soviet Union – Foreign relations – 19th century.
I. Title.
DR38.3.S65J45   1991
949.6 – dc20
90-20036
CIP

British Library Cataloguing in Publication Data
Jelavich, Barbara
Russia's Balkan entanglements, 1806–1914.
1. Russia. Foreign relations with Balkan countries,
history   2. Balkan countries. Foreign relations with
Russia
I. Title
327.470496

ISBN 0-521-40126-7 hardback

Contents

List of maps and illustrations   *page* vii

Preface   ix

I Rights and obligations acquired: The advance to
     the Black Sea, the Danubian Principalities,
     and the Serbian revolution   1

   The Danubian Principalities; the Russo–Turkish War, 1806–12   2

   The Serbian revolution   9

   Russian interests in the Balkans after 1815   24

     Economic interests   25

     Geopolitical considerations   27

     Ideology: Autocracy and Orthodoxy   32

II Rights and obligations defended and extended: The Greek
      revolution and the Russo–Turkish War, 1828–9   42

    The Greek revolution   49

    The Russo–Turkish War   75

III The defense of the status quo: The Crimean War   90

     The Eastern Question, 1831–53   94

     The Crimean War   115

IV Balkan involvements continued: The Bulgarian question
      and the Russo–Turkish War, 1877–8   143

    Russia's Balkan policy, 1856–75   147

v

Contents

Russian–Bulgarian connections 159

The Russo–Turkish War and the Congress of Berlin 170

Russian–Bulgarian relations, 1878–87 178

V Final steps: The Belgrade link and the origins
of World War I 197

Russia and the Balkans after 1905 200

  Economic interests 201

  Geopolitical considerations 203

  Ideology and politics 206

Russian–Balkan relations, 1894–1914 210

Russia and Serbia 235

Russia, Serbia, and the origins of World War I 248

Conclusion: A century of Balkan involvement: Gains and losses 266

Bibliography 277

Index 285

Maps and illustrations

MAPS

1.	The expansion of Serbia, 1804–1913	23
2.	The Ottoman Balkans, 1815	25
3.	Europe in 1815	45
4.	The expansion of Greece, 1821–1919	55
5.	The Straits	98
6.	The expansion of Romania, 1861–1920	149
7.	The Treaty of San Stefano; the Treaty of Berlin	175
8.	Bulgarian territorial changes, 1878–1919	179
9.	The Balkan states, 1914	249

ILLUSTRATIONS

1.	Alexander I	43
2.	Karl Vasil'evich Nesselrode	47
3.	Ioannis Capodistrias	48
4.	Nicholas I	91
5.	The Battle of Inkerman	139
6.	Alexander II	144
7.	Alexander Mikhailovich Gorchakov	145
8.	The Battle of Plevna	174
9.	Alexander III	182
10.	Nicholas Karlovich Giers	183
11.	Nicholas II	198
12.	Sergei Dmitrievich Sazonov	226

Preface

In the century between 1806 and 1914 Russia was drawn into six wars. Of these, five were due to its deep involvement, based on treaty rights and established traditions, in Balkan affairs; only one, the Russo–Turkish War of 1828–9, brought a clear victory both on the battlefield and at the peace table. A second, fought between 1806 and 1812, had to be ended quickly when the Russian armies were withdrawn to meet a threatening French invasion. The third, the Russo–Turkish War of 1877–8, resulted in a military victory, but a subsequent European congress drastically limited the advantages gained. Of the remaining two, the Crimean War was both a military and a political disaster; participation in World War I brought down the tsarist government and ended in a peace settlement in which the Bolshevik regime was forced to surrender large territories that had been part of the Russian state for a long period. These wars, waged at an extremely high economic cost, limited the amount that could be spent on internal development and, in particular when they ended in defeat, led to domestic unrest and after 1856 and 1917 to drastic internal change.

The purpose of this study is to examine the reasons for the Russian involvement in the Balkan peninsula and to attempt at least partially to explain the connections that drew the Russian government into entanglements that were not only often in contradiction with its great-power interests, but contained emotional commitments that were difficult to control. The emphasis is on the unique relationship that many Russian statesmen felt that they had with the Orthodox Balkan people, one that they believed was shared by no other state. At the same time an explanation is offered about why Balkan national leaderships did not reciprocate these feelings but were extremely happy to exploit Russian willingness to come to their assistance.

Preface

The following pages do not comprise a history of the Eastern Question, that is, the international controversies caused by the decline of the Ottoman Empire, or a detailed analysis of the many crises connected with this most lengthy and dangerous of the European controversies in the nineteenth century. Instead Russian policy is discussed in connection with the major Balkan national movements of each period. Chapter I describes the peace settlements following the Russo–Turkish Wars of 1768–74 and 1806–12. These agreements, extending the Russian territory to the Black Sea and the Pruth River, gave the Russian government certain definite rights in regard to the Balkan Christian population. This chapter pays particular attention to Russia's close relationship with the Danubian Principalities and its attitude toward the Serbian revolution of 1804. Chapter II covers the Russian involvement in the Greek revolution, the major European diplomatic controversy of the 1820s, and the Russo–Turkish War of 1828–9. The main subject of Chapter III is the Crimean War, which arose directly from the Russian association with the Balkan Christians and the rights apparently gained in the peace treaties. Russo–Bulgarian relations are the central theme of Chapter IV, which deals with the Balkan rebellions of 1875–7, the Russo–Turkish War of 1877–8, and the subsequent estrangement after 1885. Chapter V emphasizes Russian policy toward Serbia and the events leading to World War I. In the Conclusion, the Russian connection with the major events in these Balkan national revolutions is reviewed to determine the causes of Russian involvement and the degree to which the government lost or benefited by the association. Less attention is given in this narrative to the relationship with the Danubian Principalities, a subject that has been discussed by the author in another book, *Russia and the Formation of the Romanian National State, 1821–78*. No attempt is made to cover Albanian or Montenegrin events. Russia had little to do with the Albanian national movement; the often comic relationship with Montenegro led to only a few serious international incidents.

The spelling of personal names and geographic terms causes certain problems in any study of Russia and the Balkans. In general, standard systems of transliteration have been used except where another spelling is in general usage in English language publications. It is thus, for example, Giers not Girs, Izvolsky not Izvolskii, Hartwig not Hartvig, and Jomini not Zhomini. Many common first names, such as Alexander, Peter, Michael, Paul, and Nicholas, have been anglicized, as have the names of all rulers. Similarly, geographic place names are in the form used most commonly in diplomatic histories and in the documentation. The dates given in the text are in the Gregorian, or New Style, calendar, which in the nineteenth century ran twelve and in the twentieth century thirteen days ahead of the Orthodox Julian, or Old Style, calendar. Both dates are included in the footnotes when they appear on the documents cited or when they are necessary for clarity. All of the direct quotations retain the spelling of the source.

This study is based on research in the Bavarian State Archives, Munich; the Ethnographic Museum, Sofia; the Hariciye Arshivi, Istanbul; the Haus-, Hof-, und Staatsarchiv and the Kriegsarchiv, Vienna; the Institute for Balkan Studies, Thessaloniki; the Public Record Office, London; the State Archives and Foreign Ministry Archives, Bucharest; the State Archives of Serbia and Foreign Ministry Archives, Belgrade; and the Wilson Center, Washington, D.C. The author would like to acknowledge the kind assistance given by the staffs of these institutions. She wishes also once more to thank Serge Giers for allowing her to use the papers of his grandfather. Although the Russian Foreign Ministry archives have not been open for research, this narrative has profited from the use of the publications of the Institut Slavianovedeniia i Balkanistiki in Moscow. Some sections of this book are based on articles which the author has previously published; they are cited in the footnotes. The material that appears on pp. 49–65 is reprinted here with the permission of Notre Dame Press.

This book has benefited greatly from the comments and criticism of Professors David M. McDonald, University of Wisconsin, Norman Rich, Brown University, Paul W. Schroeder, University of Illinois, and Mark, Peter and Charles Jelavich, all of whom have read the manuscript. The author would like to thank in particular Professor M. Jeanne Peterson and Dean Morton Lowengrub of Indiana University for their support and the Office of Research and Advanced Studies, Indiana University, for research and travel grants. She wishes also to acknowledge the expert assistance of her Cambridge editors, Louise Calabro Gruendel, Helen Greenberg, and Frank Smith, and of Debbie Chase, who typed the final manuscript.

CHAPTER I

Rights and obligations acquired: The advance to the Black Sea, the Danubian Principalities, and the Serbian revolution

During the eighteenth century, a period when its prime attention had of necessity to be directed toward events in Central and Western Europe, the Russian state nevertheless acquired extensive territories to the south and came to share with the Ottoman Empire control of the Black Sea. In 1783 the Crimea was annexed and Georgia came under Russian protection. During the wars of the French revolution and Napoleon, the advance was continued. In 1812 in the Treaty of Bucharest Russia received Bessarabia and control of the navigable channel of the mouth of the Danube. The forward policy in the Caucasus was continued during the reigns of Paul and Alexander I. After wars with Persia (1804–13) and with the Ottoman Empire (1806–12), Russia forced these two states to accept its Caucasian conquests.

Russia, firmly entrenched on the Black Sea coast, found its position in the Near East buttressed by the settlement negotiated in Vienna in 1815 that restored the European balance of power temporarily disrupted by the Napoleonic conquests. During the next decades Russian security was ensured not only by its dominant military power but also by its alliance with its conservative neighbors, Austria and Prussia. With their common policy of the defense of the territorial and political status quo established in 1815, the three states, by cooperating, ensured a long period of peace in Central Europe. The weak point in the relationship was to be the conflicting aims of Russia and Austria in the Balkan peninsula, where by 1815 the Orthodox empire had assumed binding connections and obligations, both in its own interests and ultimately to the advantage of the Christian population.

Russian involvement in and penetration of the Balkan peninsula commenced with the reign of Peter the Great at the beginning of the eighteenth century. Although Peter did indeed call upon the Balkan Christians to rise in support of his army, the emphasis in Russian policy at this time and throughout the eighteenth century was on strategic concerns. During the next years when Peter's successors continued his policy of expansion southward, Russia usually acted with the Habsburg Empire, which had a similar interest in weakening Ottoman power. This cooperation resulted in significant Russian gains. Although a war waged in alliance with Austria in 1736–9 brought meager results, the conflict of 1768–74 was concluded by the extremely advantageous Treaty of Kuchuk Kainardji. During these wars the Russian government established direct relations with three Balkan peoples: the Romanians of the Danubian Principalities of Moldavia and Wallachia; the Serbs, in particular during the Napoleonic period; and the Greeks, whose national development will be discussed in a later chapter. Of first importance were the connections developed with the Danubian Principalities because of their prime strategic position in the wars with the Ottoman Empire. Relations with these provinces were intimately interwoven into the successive conflicts with the Russian Ottoman neighbor and with France.

THE DANUBIAN PRINCIPALITIES;
THE RUSSO–TURKISH WAR, 1806–12

Russia first became involved in the affairs of these provinces during the reign of Peter the Great. At this time the Danubian Principalities of Moldavia and Wallachia were separate states, enjoying an autonomous position under native princes. Despite their rights of self-government, their rulers were naturally tempted to use any opportunity to break away from the declining Ottoman Empire. In April 1711 Peter made an agreement with the Moldavian prince, Dimitrie Cantemir, that assured him of local support. In July, however, Peter was defeated and both provinces were subsequently brought more firmly under Ottoman control. The princes were henceforth appointed from prominent Greek families, usually associated with the Phanar district of Constantinople.[1] The Phanariot period in Romanian history brought extreme economic pressure on the native

---

[1] The Ottoman government regularly appointed Greek officials to high state posts. Since many of them lived in the Phanar district of Constantinople, which was also the residence of the patriarch, this group was known collectively as *Phanariots*.

population and political turmoil. Despite the unfortunate beginning of the association, the Russian government retained its interest
in the fate of the Principalities; these lands, after all, lay on the direct
route to Constantinople. They were important as staging areas from
which to launch attacks on the Ottoman Empire and as a source of
supplies for the army. In the period from 1711 to 1812 Russia and
the Ottoman Empire engaged in five wars, with much of the fighting carried on in the Principalities.

Although Russian troops occupied Moldavia in 1736 in the course
of another war with the Ottoman Empire, it was not until the
accession of Catherine the Great in 1762 that political intervention
was inaugurated. After warfare was resumed in 1768, Russian armies
again entered the Principalities and a fleet was sent from the Baltic
to the eastern Mediterranean. In both areas the Russian government
called for the assistance of the Christian population against the
Porte.[2] Russian agents were successful in promoting a local uprising
in the Peloponnesus in 1769, but it was suppressed with little
difficulty. In the Principalities the native aristocracy, the boyars,
cooperated with the Russian officials with the hope that they could
improve their political position, perhaps even win their independence. Although these desires were not fulfilled, the peace brought
certain improvements in their status.

The Treaty of Kuchuk Kainardji, signed in 1774, is the most
important document for the subsequent history of Russian–Balkan
relations.[3] Since its text specifically called for the annulment of all
previous agreements, it is the starting point for the establishment of
the Ottoman treaty obligations toward Russia that were to be so
important for the future. The agreement, in addition to the section
on the Principalities, dealt with the major issues in contention
between the signatories. Of direct advantage to Russia was the
Ottoman cession of the lands between the Bug and Dniester rivers
and Caucasian territory; the Crimea was also declared independent.
In addition, Russian ships were to have the right to sail freely in the
Black Sea and through the Straits, and Russian merchants were to

[2]The term *Porte* or *Sublime Porte* was used in European diplomatic correspondence
to designate the Ottoman government. Specifically, it referred to the building in
Constantinople containing the principal Ottoman offices of state.
[3]An English translation and a discussion of the treaty can be found in Thomas
Erskine Holland, *A Lecture on the Treaty Relations of Russia and Turkey from
1774 to 1853* (London: Macmillan and Co., 1877). The text is printed on pp. 36–55.
See also E. I. Druzhinina, *Kiuchuk-Kainardzhiiskii mir 1774 goda* (Moscow:
Izdatel'stvo Akademii nauk SSR, 1955).

enjoy the same commercial privileges that had previously been granted to France and Britain. The Russian government could also appoint consuls in the major Ottoman cities. For Russian relations with the Balkan Orthodox the significant section of the treaty was Article VII, which gave St. Petersburg certain vaguely defined rights in connection with these people. Because of the importance that the controversial nature of this article assumed in future European diplomacy, it is quoted in full.

> The Sublime Porte promises to protect constantly the Christian religion and its churches, and it also allows the Ministers of the Imperial Court of Russia to make, upon all occasions, representations, as well in favour of the new church at Constantinople, of which mention will be made in Article XIV, as on behalf of its officiating ministers, promising to take such representations into due consideration, as being made by a confidential functionary of a neighbouring and sincerely friendly Power.

Henceforth, the Russian government repeatedly cited this section of the treaty to justify its intervention in the affairs of the Ottoman Balkan Christians. Confusion existed over the exact interpretation of this article, in particular over the question of what response the Russian diplomats were entitled to make should the Ottoman government not live up to its promise "to protect constantly the Christian religion and its churches."

Other sections of the treaty referred specifically to the Greek and Romanian lands whose inhabitants had been involved in the war. In regard to the islands of the Greek Archipelago, the Ottoman government in the second of the five sections of Article XVII agreed:

> That the Christian religion shall not be exposed to the least oppression any more than its churches, and that no obstacle shall be opposed to the erection or repair of them; and also that the officiating ministers shall neither be oppressed nor insulted.

Article XVI reflected the enormous Russian interest in the Principalities. Of the ten points in this section, the most important was the last:

> The Porte likewise permits that, according as the circumstances of these two Principalities may require, the Ministers of the Imperial Court of Russia resident at Constantinople may remonstrate in their favour, and promises to listen to them with all the attention that is due to friendly and respected Powers.

This article also provided for amnesty for those who had joined the Russian forces, tax relief, permission for emigration, and the free exercise of the Orthodox religion. The princes were allowed to send accredited representatives to Constantinople.

The treaty, which thus gave Russia specific rights of intervention, preceded a period during which the Porte, acting with St. Petersburg, issued a series of declarations and made agreements that widened considerably both the autonomous rights of the Principalities and the Russian supervision. In September 1787, Russia, joined later by Austria, once again went to war against the Ottoman Empire, with the principal objective of obtaining an extension of territory and perhaps the creation of an independent Romanian buffer state. Other European events, however, forced Catherine to make peace before a decisive military victory could be achieved. The Treaty of Jassy (Iaşi) of 1792 did, nevertheless, allow Russia to annex the lands between the Bug and Dniester rivers, a change that made it a neighbor to Moldavia. No alteration was made in the conditions pertaining to the Principalities.

During Catherine's reign these provinces had an important place in the various partition schemes considered at this time. Among these the so-called Greek Project has received the most attention. This plan was developed in an exchange of letters between the empress and Joseph II of Austria in 1782. In this division of the Ottoman Empire Russia was to annex directly Black Sea and Caucasian lands; Austria was to obtain Oltenia (western Wallachia), Bosnia, Hercegovina, Istria, Dalmatia, and part of Serbia. In addition to the territorial acquisitions, Russia was to benefit from the establishment of two puppet kingdoms: a resurrected Byzantine state, which was to include Bulgarian, Greek, and Macedonian lands and be ruled by Catherine's grandson; and a Romanian kingdom, called Dacia, to be composed of Wallachia, Moldavia, and Bessarabia, and given an Orthodox prince. Venice, although surrendering Istria and Dalmatia, was to be compensated with Crete, Cyprus, and the Peloponnesus. France would receive Syria and Egypt. Although the plan was never carried through, certain aspects were to reappear in other partition discussions. The acquisition of the Principalities, either as part of a partition scheme or a direct understanding with the Ottoman Empire, remained a possible Russian alternative policy until 1812.

Before her death in 1796 Catherine was not able to realize her most ambitious projects. Her son Paul, on his accession, reversed the expansionist policy of his mother and attempted instead to seek an accommodation with the Porte with the aim of replacing France as the predominant influence in Constantinople. This goal, which included the maintenance of Ottoman territorial integrity, was also to become one of the possible solutions to Russia's involvement in the area in the future. During Paul's reign, however, Balkan and Eastern affairs became almost a sideshow in comparison with the events taking place elsewhere in Europe. Nevertheless, when Napoleon in 1798 first took Malta and then invaded Egypt, the area became again a war arena. With France now the main menace to its interests, the Ottoman government in 1799 negotiated a treaty with Russia containing a secret clause that allowed the Russian fleet to pass freely through the Straits of the Bosphorus and the Dardanelles during the war. Previously, it had been the established Ottoman policy to close the Straits to foreign ships of war. At the same time a joint Russian–Ottoman expedition captured the Ionian Islands from France. The two allied powers then established the autonomous Septinsular Republic under Ottoman sovereignty but Russian protection.

In March 1801 Alexander I succeeded his father. Through the first years of his reign, he continued the policy of cooperation with the Ottoman Empire. Russia made peace with France in 1801, followed by a similar action by the Porte in the next year. Although the Ottoman Empire enjoyed a period of peace between 1802 and 1806, it had to face rebellions by local notables (ayans) in various sections of its lands. At this time the most serious action was led by Pasvanoglu Osman Pasha from his center in Vidin on the Danube. His supporters, a collection of bandits, rebellious janissaries, and political opportunists, devastated the surrounding countryside. Wallachia was severely affected. In this period of continued Ottoman domestic turmoil the Russian government, although still seeking to maintain the empire's territorial integrity, was able to increase its treaty rights in regard to the internal affairs of the Principalities. In 1802 the Porte issued an imperial decree confirming and widening the privileges of the provinces. The princes, chosen for a term of seven years, could be appointed and removed only with Russian approval. Article IV directed them "to take into consideration the representations that the Russian envoy will make to them."[4] Other documents enlarged and defined previous enactments in the same direction of

[4]Dimitri A. Sturdza et al., *Acte şi documente relative la istoria renascerei României* (Bucharest: Carol Göbl, 1900), I, pp. 259–63.

increasing the autonomy of the Principalities in regard to the Porte but enlarging Russian rights of intervention.

These agreements were to be the direct cause of the next conflict between Russia and the Ottoman Empire. In 1805 Russia and France were again at war. In 1806 the Ottoman government, at this time with good relations with France, removed the princes of Wallachia and Moldavia, who were Russian candidates. Although the Porte almost at once reversed its decision, Russian troops were sent into the Principalities. This action, which we will see repeated in other crises between the two states in the future, was naturally regarded as an act of war by the sovereign power; a formal declaration was issued in December. Russia was thus drawn into a major conflict as a direct result of its agreements in regard to a Balkan people. Of course, the war also involved issues connected with the Russian relationship with France.

Until 1812 the Russian objectives included not only the annexation of the Principalities, but wider goals as well. In his conversations with Napoleon at Tilsit in 1807 Alexander I also discussed the question of the partition of Ottoman lands, although no decisions were reached. However, during a meeting at Erfurt held the next year, it was agreed that Russia would annex the Principalities. From 1807 to 1812 peace negotiations were carried on, which failed largely because the Porte would not cede the provinces. In 1811, faced with a breakdown in its relations with France, the Russian government reduced its demands to the acquisition of Moldavia. Finally, in May 1812 the two powers signed the Treaty of Bucharest. Article IV gave Moldavian territory to the Pruth River to Russia, a cession that left the vital Kilia Channel at the mouth of the Danube River in Russian hands. Article V provided for the reconfirmation of the previous agreements concerning the privileges of the two provinces, that is, the treaties of Kuchuk Kainardji and Jassy, as well as the agreement of 1802. It also made provision for the payment of taxes and tribute. Thus, except for the loss of the Bessarabian territory, the Principalities remained, as before, under Ottoman suzerainty and Russian protection.

From 1806 until 1812, when the Russian army was withdrawn to meet the French invasion, Russian officials were in control of the Principalities. One of their chief objectives was to secure supplies for the support of their troops. Since these were often obtained by violent methods, the Russian occupation became increasingly resented by the population. The costs of the occupation also had to be paid, so that, as an authority on the question has written, "during the war more than half of the Principalities' income went to supply the Russian army. . . . By the end of 1809 almost all of the working cattle and wagons in the Principalities were being used to move supplies for the army."[5]

After 1812, even with the departure of the Russian army, the situation remained difficult. The provinces had been impoverished by the war and the costs of occupation. Moreover, the region was now returned to the control of Phanariot rulers, who continued their previous extortionate policies. In this period the animosity of the native Romanian leadership turned chiefly against the Phanariot princes and their Russian backers; the peasants, who paid the costs of the oppressive political conditions, resented chiefly the social and economic burdens under which they were placed.

In their attitude toward the Principalities, as we have seen, Russian officials during the reigns of Catherine, Paul, and Alexander I adopted varying policies ranging from the direct annexation of the provinces to the control of them through agreements with the Porte. To justify their attempts at domination, they often spoke about Ottoman oppression and the need to protect Orthodox Christians. In fact, the Principalities were, at least in a juridical sense, autonomous; an Ottoman administrative system was not in place, nor was an Ottoman army in occupation except in time of war. Political oppression resulted from the policies of the Orthodox Christian Phanariot princes, who were, of course, appointed by the Ottoman Empire but who were responsible for the internal conditions in the country.

Despite its deep involvement in the affairs of the Principalities, the Russian government did not have to face a native national movement or the issue of the establishment of an independent Balkan state. Both of these elements were to arise in connection with the Serbian revolution, the first genuine national revolt with which Russia had to deal. Because of its significance, the Russian relationship with this revolution will be examined in detail. Although this revolt did not draw Russia into war, it nevertheless resulted in the negotiation of treaty obligations in 1812 and the acquisition by the Russian government of rights and obligations toward another Balkan people. It also led to the establishment of a state that was at times in the future to have a very close relationship with St. Petersburg.

[5]George F. Jewsbury, *The Russian Annexation of Bessarabia, 1774–1828: A Study of Imperial Expansion* (Boulder, Colo.: East European Monographs, 1976), p. 52.

Rights and obligations acquired

THE SERBIAN REVOLUTION

In sharp contrast to the close ties with the Principalities, before the beginning of the nineteenth century there had been few direct links between Russia and the Serbs under Ottoman control.[6] In fact, the chief Russian interest had been shown in the condition of the Serbs of the Habsburg Empire. There, under pressure from the Catholic church, the Orthodox Metropolitanate at Sremski Karlovci had called on Russia for material and spiritual aid. In 1722 Peter the Great directed the Russian synod to respond to this appeal; ecclesiastic establishments in Moscow and Kiev also sent assistance. This cultural influence led to a Russification of the Habsburg Serbian educational and religious institutions. Their literary language became the so-called Slavo-Serbian, deeply influenced by the Russian vocabulary. Despite this relationship with the Habsburg Serbs and the support given to Orthodoxy there, Russian political interest was not extended over the frontier. In fact, throughout the eighteenth century the Russian government usually conceded that Serbia and the western Balkans were within the unofficial Habsburg sphere of influence.

For their part, the Serbian leaders in the Ottoman lands were equally ignorant about Russia. Concerning his mission to St. Petersburg in 1804, the Serbian notable Prota Matija Nenadović wrote:

> So went Columbus and his crew on the blue seas to find America and to acquaint it with Europe; so today we are travelling on the quiet Danube to find Russia, about which we know nothing, not even where it is, but have only heard tell of it in our songs, and to acquaint Serbia with Russia![7]

In discussing Russian relations with the Serbian revolt, it is important to emphasize that, unlike the Principalities, the Serbian lands were under direct Ottoman administration, and they were garrisoned by Ottoman troops. In the eighteenth century, in addi-

---

[6]The principal documentary collections on the Russian attitude toward the Serbian revolution are *Pervoe serbskoe vosstanie 1804–1813 gg. i Rossiia* (Moscow: Izdatel'stvo nauka, 1980, 1983), 2 vols. (cited hereafter as *PSV*) and Ministerstvo inostrannykh del SSSR, *Vneshniaia politika Rossii XIX i nachala XX veka: Dokumenty Rossiiskogo ministerstva inostrannykh del.* (Moscow: Gosudarstvennoe izdatel'stvo politicheskoi literatury, 1960ff) (cited hereafter as *VPR*). See also Lawrence P. Meriage, *Russia and the First Serbian Revolution, 1804–1813* (New York: Garland Publishing, Inc., 1987).

[7]Prota Matija Nenadović, *The Memoirs of Prota Matija Nenadović* (Oxford: Oxford University Press, 1969), p. 97.

tion to the control by the suzerain power, the Serbs fell under the influence of the Greeks of Constantinople. In the eighteenth century, along with their political control of the Principalities, Phanariot Greeks were able to obtain strong positions in other sections of the Ottoman Empire. In Serbia they were able to dominate the religious institutions. Most important, in 1766, the Serbian Patriarchate of Peć was abolished and the institutions attached to it were placed under the authority of the Greek-controlled Constantinople Patriarchate. In the next years the Serbian church was Hellenized, with the high offices held by Greeks. This situation resulted in the rise of strong anti-Phanariot feelings in the Serbian lands, which were to last well into the nineteenth century.

As regards the European great powers, the Habsburg Empire had previously exerted the greatest influence in the Serbian lands. Not only had its armies represented a liberating force, but its lands, particularly Croatia-Slavonia and other border districts, held a predominantly South Slav population of Croats, Serbs, and Slovenes. Most important for this narrative was the presence of a concentrated Serbian Orthodox population along the monarchy's southern border. As could be expected, in the long years of warfare many Serbian families fled over the border to escape the Ottoman authorities. The Habsburg government could employ the services of these people. The border areas were difficult to control; brigandage and lawlessness were major problems. To establish settled conditions, the Habsburg authorities formed military colonies consisting primarily of Serbian but also Croatian families. In return for military service the Serbian settlers were guaranteed free exercise of their Orthodox religion and control of their local administration. In 1630 a charter was issued regulating the conditions on the Military Frontier. A large concentration of Serbs thus came to inhabit areas directly adjacent to the Serbian-inhabited lands of the Ottoman Empire.

The Serbian presence in the Habsburg Monarchy was made more significant by the establishment of Orthodox religious centers. In 1689 the patriarch of Peć, Arsenije III Crnojević, called upon the Serbs to rise in support of an invading Austrian army. When the Habsburg forces were compelled to withdraw, Arsenije and about 30,000 families accompanied the army. With Habsburg recognition, they organized a Serbian Orthodox Metropolitanate at Sremski Karlovci. In 1737, as a result of a similar series of events, another patriarch, Arsenije IV, led a similar but smaller migration. The Habsburg Monarchy thus acquired an Orthodox religious center that was to hold both spiritual and secular associations for the Serbs.

These close ties were to be important at the beginning of the Serbian revolt.

The Serbian revolution, which commenced in early 1804, was not at first a national liberation movement aiming at independence, but rather a revolt of the local notables under their leader, Karadjordje Petrović, against the violent actions of a group of janissaries who were in fact challenging the authority of the sultan. The Serbian goal was the implementation of promises concerning their status that had previously been given by Sultan Selim III. Since they were aware that they needed foreign support, the leaders turned first to the Habsburg Monarchy. The connections with the Habsburg Serbs, the geographic proximity, and the remembrance of the many wars that had been conducted on their territory between the monarchy and the Ottoman Empire led them to hope for assistance. In return, they offered to place their country under the jurisdiction of a Habsburg prince. At this time and throughout the rebellion the Habsburg government, absorbed in the struggle with Napoleon, consistently refused to assume obligations in Serbia, even when it was also urged to act by Russia.

During the first period of the revolution the Serbian aim was a reconciliation with the Porte on the basis of an Ottoman assurance of certain autonomous rights. The first requests for assistance from Russia were for support for this goal. Leontije, the Greek-national metropolitan of Belgrade, hoped to use the offices of the Constantinople Patriarchate to present the Serbian case to the Porte. At the same time, the Russian ambassador at Constantinople, Andrei Iakovlevich Italinskii, who was sympathetic to the Serbian position, was asked to aid in this effort. In May 1804 the first direct appeal was made to St. Petersburg. It took the form of a Serbian petition to the tsar sent through Italinskii; Alexander I was asked to mediate with the Porte to secure for Serbia the same conditions that applied at that time in the Ionian Islands, Moldavia, and Wallachia, that is, local autonomy and Russian protection. Even more important, in September 1804 a three-man delegation, headed by Nenadović, set out from Serbia for St. Petersburg with petitions for the tsar. The stated aim of the mission was to secure Russian intervention to reconcile the Serbs and the Ottoman government. It was emphasized that the revolt was against those who themselves did not obey the sultan; it was not a challenge to the sovereign. The desire was again expressed that Serbia receive a status similar to that of the Ionian Islands; the appointment of a Russian consul in Belgrade was also requested.

With a preponderant control established in the Principalities and in alliance with the Ottoman Empire, the Russian government was unlikely to regard the Serbian revolt as anything but inconvenient. Without agents in Serbia proper, the Russian officials gained what little information they had about conditions in the country through their agents not only in Constantinople but also in Vienna, Bucharest, and Jassy. The first reports from these sources depicted the uprising as little more than a minor rebellion. The general Russian reaction was thus negative; there was certainly no interest in a weakening of Ottoman control over the region, and concern was shown that the revolt could lead to a general Balkan uprising at a time that was detrimental to Russian interests.

Although the Nenadović mission did not succeed in its basic aims, it did lead to an increase of Russian interest in Serbian conditions and to a few small concessions. At first, the Russian attitude was negative. If there was to be a mediation, the government preferred that Austria act. The Serbian delegation thus received calming advice. Although its members did not see Alexander I, they were received twice by the foreign minister, Prince Adam Czartoryski. He promised to place their petition before the tsar, but he warned that "Serbia and Russia are very far apart and we are in friendship with the Turks."[8] He advised that the Serbs should deal directly with the Porte.

Despite this generally negative reply, Czartoryski recommended to Alexander I that money be sent to the rebels, and he instructed Italinskii to urge the Porte to meet the Serbian requests. The ambassador was to emphasize that the Serbs would be happy to submit to their legitimate monarch. The foreign minister, however, believed that the Ottoman officials should not be informed of the Serbian visit to St. Petersburg; they were already suspicious of Russian intentions and possible connections with the revolt.[9] From this time on the Russian government did send some financial and military assistance, and its intervention at Constantinople increased. It also looked more favorably on the Serbian request for an autonomous status with Russian protection.

In June 1805 another Serbian delegation went to Constantinople, where it stayed at the home of the patriarch.[10] The discussions did

---

[8]Ibid., p. 114.
[9]Czartoryski to Italinskii, January 3/15, 1805; Czartoryski to Italinskii, May 4/16, 1805, *PSV*, I, pp. 80, 119–21.
[10]Italinskii to Czartoryski, no. 147, Buyukdere, June 2/14, 1805, ibid., I, pp. 129–30.

not proceed well; the Porte would not grant the Serbian demands for autonomous rights. Fighting thus continued during the winter of 1805–6. With the failure of the negotiations the Serbian leaders again appealed to both Vienna and St. Petersburg. In response, the Russian government instructed Italinskii to advise the Porte "as an intimate ally" not to use military force against the Serbs, but instead to combat French aggression.[11] The Serbian demands for an autonomous regime were also supported: They should receive an administrative system similar to that in the Principalities, but with a native rather than a Phanariot prince as the head of state. Should the Porte doubt that the Serbs would fulfill their obligations in the future concerning the payment of taxes and the provision of troops, then Italinskii could suggest, as if coming from him, that "the imperial court would not reject guaranteeing the new order of things" if the Ottoman government issued an official act confirming Serbian privileges. Such an action would attach the Serbs irrevocably to their "legitimate sovereign." They had genuine grievances caused by the local misgovernment. After all they had suffered, they could not easily surrender, but would fight to the last extremity rather than accept a return of the former regime. Even if the Porte secured a military victory, all that it could accomplish would be the ruin of a "brave and faithful" people. In delivering this advice, Italinskii was instructed that he could cooperate with the Austrian representative in Constantinople, whose government had also received Serbian appeals, but that it would be preferable if the Serbian question were settled by an exclusive Russian intervention. In any case, Alexander I, the ambassador was told, could not be indifferent to the fate of Serbia "because of the similarity of origin and of religion which exists between it and the peoples of Russia."

Although Russian interest in Serbian events had thus increased, the major concern was still with France, which had meanwhile become an Adriatic power. Following the French victory at the battle of Austerlitz, the Habsburg government was forced to accept the conclusion of a punitive peace. In the Treaty of Pressburg of December 1805 Austria ceded Venetia, Istria, and the Dalmatian coast, including Kotor, to France.[12] The establishment of a French strong-

---

[11] See the two despatches of Czartoryski to Italinskii of February 3/15, 1806, ibid., I, pp. 207–11.

[12] The Russian concerns over the French presence on the Adriatic coast are clearly seen in Czartoryski's memorandum to Alexander I of January 11/23, 1806. Here he proposed that the Russian government attempt to win the support of the

hold here placed Serbia close to territories under French control and made it a strategic center. The Russian government henceforth had to be concerned that the Serbian rebels, if their demands were not satisfied, might seek French protection, which indeed they did.

With these considerations in mind, Italinskii on March 31, 1806, sent a note to the Porte whose main intention was to warn the Ottoman government about the French danger.[13] In the final section, which referred to both the Principalities and Serbia, the Porte was advised not to take military action against the Serbs, but to concentrate its forces in those places that were menaced by the French presence, such as Bosnia and Albania. In urging a peaceful solution to the revolt, the note nevertheless reflected the circumspection with which the Russians, as well as the Austrians, were treating the Serbian question. For instance, the text stated: "It is as much the desire to submit to their legitimate sovereign as the danger from which they are menaced that has led the Serbs to address themselves" to the tsar.

The Russian efforts were soon to fail. As a weak state, open to great-power pressure, the Ottoman Empire was bound to be affected by changes in the European balance of power. The great French military victories in Europe inevitably influenced its attitude. After peace was restored in 1802, the French representatives began a determined and finally successful drive to regain their former position of supremacy in the Ottoman capital. The constant Russian pressure to increase its influence in the Principalities naturally caused major concern among the Ottoman officials; France could exploit this friction. It was thus as a result of French urgings as well as in reaction to the Russian occupation of the Principalities that the Ottoman government declared war on Russia in December 1806. With this action the attitude of both Russia and the Ottoman Empire toward the Serbian revolt changed radically. Whereas previously the Russian government had urged a negotiated settlement on moderate terms, it now wished the revolution to continue.

Meanwhile, the Serbian attempts to obtain a satisfactory agreement with the Porte were meeting with more success. Their position

Greeks and "the other Christian people who inhabit Albania, Bosnia, Serbia, and who because of the similarity of their religion have always shown attachment to the court of Russia. Czartoryski to Alexander I, St. Petersburg, January 11/23, 1806. Sturdza, *Acte şi documente*, I, pp. 453–72. He had the greatest expectations for the Serbs and Montenegrins. Czartoryski to Alexander I, St. Petersburg, January 11/23, 1806, ibid., pp. 458–65.

[13]Italinskii to the Turkish government, March 19/31, 1806, *VPR*, III, pp. 95–9.

was improved after a series of important victories, including the capture of the fortress of Smederevo in 1805 and culminating in the taking of Belgrade in December 1806. Under these circumstances the Porte was more willing to reach an understanding with a new Serbian delegation, under Peter Ičko, that arrived in Constantinople in July 1806. In September, Ičko returned home with an agreement that met the basic Serbian desires. It was confirmed as the basis for a permanent settlement by a Serbian assembly held in October. Although most of their demands had been met, the outbreak of war between Russia and the Ottoman Empire offered the Serbian leaders an alternate opportunity.

At war with France and the Ottoman Empire, the Russian government needed the assurance of Serbian cooperation. Russia at this time had an army in the Principalities and a fleet in the Adriatic. Russian soldiers had landed on the Dalmatian coast and were cooperating with the Montenegrins. Serbia thus held a key position between the two Russian points of occupation; fears of possible Serbian cooperation with France had been previously expressed. In order to strengthen its relations with the Serbs, the Russian government sent Filipp Osipovich Paulucci to Belgrade in June 1807 with instructions to judge the situation and ascertain the Serbian desires. He could also offer the Serbs money and arms.[14] Since little was known about conditions in Belgrade, he was to make a standard intelligence report on the Serbian military strength and on "the degree of their attachment" to Russia. He was first to make contact with Metropolitan Leontije and the local military commander, making known to them

the dangers to which the Serbian nation would expose itself in submitting to the Porte or in abandoning itself to the insidious offers of France. You will assure them at the same time that they can always count on the assistance of Russia, whose inhabitants are of the same extraction and profess the same religion as they do.

Not only did Paulucci carry out his instructions, but he made a formal convention with the Serbian leaders, who already had abandoned negotiations with the Porte in favor of continued fighting with the goal of obtaining complete independence. The first article of the document placed Serbia under direct Russian protection:

The Serbian people most humbly beg H[is] I[mperial] M[ajesty] to appoint a capable governor who will bring order to the people, administer the Serbian land,

[14]Budberg instruction to Paulucci, Bartenstein, May 11/23, 1807, ibid., III, pp. 583–6.

and devise a constitution in consonance with the customs of the people. The promulgation of the constitution should be done in the name of H.I.M. Alexander the First.[15]

Although Paulucci was not authorized to make this agreement, and it never came into effect, its general spirit did reflect the Russian program for Serbia.

Unfortunately for the Serbian revolutionary cause, its leaders, in opting for Russia and independence, had made the wrong choice. In June 1807 France defeated Russia at the battle of Friedland; a truce was then concluded, and Napoleon and Alexander met at Tilsit. The agreement signed there in July primarily dealt with general European problems, but Napoleon agreed to mediate a peace between Russia and the Ottoman Empire. In August their representatives concluded the armistice of Slobozia. Although the tsar did not approve its terms, two years of uneasy peace followed during which the negotiations continued. In these the major Russian objective was, as we have seen, the acquisition of the Danubian Principalities. As regards Serbia, the same goals of autonomy and Russian protection remained. With the emphasis on securing peace on favorable terms, the Russian officials were obviously not going to make Serbian independence a prime objective.

While these discussions were proceeding, the Russian government initiated in Serbia the same policy that was already causing problems in the Danubian Principalities – direct interference in the internal affairs of the state. For the Serbs, as for other Balkan people, the requested protection and assistance meant primarily military aid against the Ottoman Empire. For the Russian officials cooperation involved, in addition, the reordering of the internal administration to conform to Russian ideas of administration and the securing of a regime favorable to Russian interests. In August 1807 Constantine Konstantinovich Rodofinikin, an agent of the Russian army, arrived in Belgrade, where he immediately involved himself in Serbian politics. Karadjordje by this time was facing domestic problems and increasing criticism of his leadership. Only one of the numerous Serbian notables, he came into conflict with others of his kind who opposed the transfer of too much power to his hands. To satisfy the opposition, he had in 1805 agreed to the establishment of a governing council composed of other prominent notables, but in 1808 he proclaimed himself hereditary ruler. After his arrival, Rodofinikin

[15]Quoted in Michael Boro Petrovich, *A History of Modern Serbia, 1804–1918* (New York: Harcourt Brace Jovanovich, 1976), I, p. 55.

cooperated with Karadjordje's opponents. During this period, disenchanted by the lack of concrete assistance from Russia, Karadjordje sent appeals to Austria and France, but without success.

In addition to its inclusion in the negotiations involving the Porte, the status of Serbia was also discussed by French and Russian diplomats after the conclusion of the Treaty of Tilsit.[16] In talks in St. Petersburg in March 1808 the French ambassador, Armand de Caulaincourt, and the Russian foreign minister, at that time Nicholas Petrovich Rumiantsev, reviewed various alternate solutions for Serbia, including the formation of an autonomous government under French or Russian protection or under an Austrian archduke. Even the possibility of independence was considered, or, should the Ottoman Empire be partitioned, the assignment of both Serbia and Macedonia to Austria. The possible dissolution of the empire was, however, rejected at the second meeting between Alexander I and Napoleon, held at Erfurt in September 1808. Although it was agreed that Russia could take Wallachia and Moldavia, no further partition plans were agreed upon; Serbia would thus continue to remain under Ottoman sovereignty.

Henceforth the Serbian fate was to be determined by Western and Central European events rather than by successes or failures on the Balkan battlefields. Changes taking place in Constantinople were also of significance. In 1807 and 1808 a period of crisis preceded the ascent of Mahmud II to the throne. During this time of domestic weakness the Porte was willing to grant the Serbs wide autonomy, but the parties could not agree on the exact terms. In August 1809 the situation improved for the Porte, and the Ottoman armies resumed the offensive. The Serbian forces were able to obtain some military supplies and money from Russia and to achieve limited victories.

Meanwhile, the negotiations between the Russian and Ottoman delegates were proceeding slowly. The Russian demands still included the cession of Moldavia and Wallachia and concessions for the Serbs. The international situation, however, deteriorated for Russia. In February and March 1812 Napoleon negotiated alliances with Prussia and Austria. The increasing dangers on the European front, the French and Austrian actions in particular, led Alexander I to consider seriously using the Balkan Christians against both these powers. In April 1812 he instructed Vice-Admiral Paul Vasil'evich Chichagov, the commander of the Russian army of the Danube, to

[16]Ibid., I, pp. 60–1.

attempt to win over the South Slavs of Austria as well as of the Ottoman Empire.[17] Given the military situation at the time, he believed that it was most important

to utilize in our favor the military spirit of the people of Slavic origin, such as those of Serbia, of Bosnia, of Dalmatia, of Montenegro, of Croatia, of Illyria, who once armed and organized militarily, can contribute greatly to our operations.

The tsar also favored using the Hungarians. Chichagov was further instructed to use any means possible to incite the Slavic populations: "For example, you could promise them independence, the erection of a Slavic kingdom, monetary rewards for the most influential men among them, decorations and titles suitable for the chiefs and the troops."

These measures were never put into practice. With relations with France deteriorating and faced with a possible invasion, the Russian leaders recognized that peace would have to be made with the Ottoman Empire. In the final negotiations leading to the conclusion of the Treaty of Bucharest, the Russian representatives reduced their demands not only in relation to the Principalities but also in regard to their requirements for Serbian autonomy.

In the discussions on Serbia the Porte continued to hold to its previous position of opposing wide concessions to the rebels. Ghalib Effendi, the chief plenipotentiary, objected: "If autonomy is granted to the Serbians, who share the same faith as the Russians, other Orthodox Christians will seek to benefit from this measure by seeking similar concessions."[18] Ghalib also expressed the Ottoman view that the revolt was an internal problem, not subject to outside intervention. Nevertheless, in the final treaty, Article VIII made provision for Serbia.[19] These stipulations were to be so important in the future that almost the entire article is quoted:

The Sublime Porte, therefore, grants to the Servians a general Pardon and Amnesty, and they shall in no way be molested for their past actions. The Fortifications which may have been erected as a result of the War, in the Countries inhabited by them, and which did not formerly exist, becoming henceforth useless, shall be destroyed, and the Sublime Porte shall resume possession as formerly of all the Fortresses, Palankas, and other fortified Places which have always existed, with the Artillery, Munitions, and other War Materials, and shall establish Garrisons

[17]Alexander I to Chichagov, no. 87, St. Petersburg, April 19, 1812, Sturdza, *Acte şi documente*, I, pp. 1014–17. See also *Mémoires de l'Amiral Tchitchagoff, 1767–1849* (Leipzig: A. Frank'sche Verlags-Buchhandlung, 1862), pp. 51–108.

[18]Quoted in Meriage, *Russia and the First Serbian Revolution*, p. 209.

[19]Edward Hertslet, *The Map of Europe by Treaty* (London: Butterworths, 1875), III, p. 2032.

therein, as it may think fit. But in order that those Garrisons shall in no way annoy the Servians contrary to the Rights of the Subjects, the Sublime Porte, moved by a feeling of clemency, will settle with the Servian Nation the necessary securities. It will grant to the Servians, at their request, the same advantages which are enjoyed by its subjects of the Islands of the Archipelago and other Countries and will make it feel the effects of its high clemency in making over to them the administration of their internal affairs, in fixing the whole of their Tributes, in receiving them from their own hands, and will, in short, settle all these matters with the Servian Nation.

These terms, although ensuring some benefits to the Serbs, were far from meeting even their minimum expectations. Moreover, without active Russian support Ottoman compliance was in doubt. From June 1812, when the French armies invaded Russia, until March 1814, when an allied force entered Paris, Russian attention had to be concentrated on the battlefields of Europe. The situation was a catastrophe for Karadjordje. The Russian armies that had been operating in Serbia, as well as in the Principalities, were withdrawn to meet the French invasion. Serbian resources after so many years of fighting were at an end. With no other distractions the Ottoman army could devote its full attention to the reconquest of Serbia. In July 1813 the Ottoman campaign commenced; in October Karadjordje, Leontije, and other prominent leaders escaped across the Danube into the Habsburg Empire. With the entrance of the Ottoman troops into Belgrade, the first Serbian revolution came to an end.

The Ottoman military victory did not, of course, solve the basic problems in the Ottoman–Serbian relationship. Despite the adoption by the Porte of a policy of conciliation and the departure of most of the Ottoman soldiers, major difficulties remained. The revolution had embittered the local Christian–Muslim relations; outnumbered, the Muslims wanted protection for the future. With similar fears, the Serbian leaders were unwilling to render themselves defenseless either by the return of the fortresses they had captured to Ottoman possession, as required by the treaty, or by the surrender of personal weapons. Moreover, Serbian resistance to Ottoman maladministration continued, this time under a new leader. In April 1815 Miloš Obrenović led a short-term rebellion that was soon successfully concluded. By this time the war in Europe had ended, and the Porte could expect that the Russian government would insist upon the implementation of Article VIII.

During the years when the war in Europe was absorbing the full Russian attention, Italinskii could not stop the Ottoman reconquest of Serbia. He did, however, continue to advise conciliation and oppose military action.[20] The ambassador was also instructed to warn the Ottoman government that the tsar would not be indifferent to violations of Article VIII. The argument used was: "It is by good deeds that the Porte should reconquer the love and fidelity of the Serbs."[21] In October 1813 Italinskii was informed that Alexander I was greatly concerned about the fate of Serbia. It appeared to him as if the Ottoman Empire had "the atrocious plan of putting to the sword all the inhabitants above seven years of age";[22] he could not remain indifferent to such calamities. Although the Russian government recognized that the Treaty of Bucharest had indeed placed the Serbs under Ottoman control, it was expected that a settlement would be achieved through negotiation.

In September 1812 a Serbian delegation of five members arrived in Constantinople to continue discussions.[23] Until then the Serbs had not been informed of the exact provisions of Article VIII, or even that their interests had been at least partially protected in the treaty. At this time Italinskii gave the Ottoman foreign minister, upon his request, a copy of the article; he, in turn, communicated it to the Serbian representatives. During this visit the deputation did not get in touch with the Russian ambassador. The Ottoman objections to foreign intervention were thus met.

The negotiations did not proceed smoothly. Italinskii reported the Serbian reluctance to surrender the fortresses as specified in the treaty.[24] He did not intervene in the discussions unless the stipulations of Article VIII were in question; he also wanted to reassure the Ottoman ministers and to calm their suspicions that Russia was behind the Serbian resistance. The Russian desire not to be involved in Balkan entanglements as long as the war with France was in progress was clearly shown in the instructions sent to Italinskii in July 1813.[25] He was told that Alexander I had decided not to intervene in the negotiations since, on the one hand, the Serbs were

---

[20]Italinskii to Chichagov, no. 33, Buyukdere, September 7/19, 1812, *PSV*, II, pp. 271–3.

[21]Rumiantsev to Italinskii, October 9/21, 1812, ibid., II, pp. 276–7.

[22]Nesselrode to Italinskii, Teplitz, September 21/October 3, 1813, ibid., II, pp. 342–3.

[23]Italinskii to Rumiantsev, no. 21, Buyukdere, October 18/30, 1812, ibid., II, pp. 281–3.

[24]Italinskii to Nesselrode, no. 2, Buyukdere, February 1/13, 1813, ibid., II, pp. 294–8. See also Kiriko to Nedoba, May 11/23, 1813, and Kiriko to Rumiantsev, Bucharest, June 21/July 3, 1813, ibid., II, pp. 312, 319–20.

[25]Rumiantsev to Italinskii, St. Petersburg, June 30/July 12, 1813, ibid., II, pp. 326–7. See also Nesselrode to Italinskii, no. 151, July 31/August 11, 1813, ibid., II,

proving recalcitrant and would not accept what had been given them in the treaty, and, on the other hand, the Ottoman government was not expected to agree to the Serbian terms. This decision, however, did not mean that Russia would sacrifice "to the Turks the safety [*salut*] of that brave and loyal nation," but would support it when the right time came.

A similar message was sent in September by Karl Vasil'evich Nesselrode, at this time secretary of state, to Teodor Ivanovich Nedoba, the Russian agent in Semlin:[26] The war in progress at that time would decide the fate of Europe; Russia could not send aid to Serbia. Moreover, the Treaty of Bucharest placed limits on the protection that Russia could offer the country. Serbian resistance was to be encouraged, however, until events would permit Russia to offer "powerful assistance." Meanwhile, the Russian government was willing to give asylum to the Serbs who had fled their country; negotiations were carried on with the Habsburg government on this matter. As a result, Karadjordje, Leontije, and other prominent men did emigrate, at least for a short period, to Russia.

Once the war in Europe ended, the Serbian leaders had hopes of attracting renewed outside assistance. In this endeavor Nenadović in December 1814 went to Vienna, where the Congress was in session, with a petition again asking for Alexander's intercession with the Porte and the other powers; the Serbian representative continued to stress the religious tie, and he saw Russia as the best source of support, although appeals were also addressed to the other governments.[27] The Russian advice remained the same: The Serbian leaders should seek a reconciliation with the Porte. Russia would stand behind them, but patience was advised. The Serbian delegate received similar recommendations from the other diplomats he visited.

The Nenadović mission, although it did not bring the outside intervention that the Serbs desired, did encourage the Russian leaders to think about the questions raised. Although Ottoman issues were not a part of the discussions at Vienna, two documents were

---

pp. 327–9; Nesselrode to Shtakelberg, Paris, May 22/June 3, 1814, and Nesselrode to Nedoba, Paris, May 22/June 3, 1814, *VPR*, VIII, pp. 17–18, 19.

[26] Nesselrode to Nedoba, Teplitz, September 17/29, 1813, *PSV*, II, pp. 337–9.

[27] Nenadović told Nesselrode: "Our Serbian hope is in Russia, our protector, and maybe soon our deliverer; if we are delivered it will be thanks to Russia and if we remain destroyed and made into Turks that too will be attributed to Russia." Nenadović, *Memoirs*, pp. 199–200. See also the Nesselrode Memorandum to Alexander I, December 25, 1814/January 6, 1815, *VPR*, VIII, p. 156.

drawn up at this time that reflected the official Russian view. The first, a memorandum of February 15, gave the reasons why Russia was supporting the Serbian cause:[28]

> The emperor is the natural protector of Christians of the Greek Oriental rite placed under Ottoman domination, just as the emperor of Austria and his very Christian Majesty [the king of France] are it for the Roman Catholics living in the Orient. . . . All the stipulations with the Porte bestow on him the right to watch over the maintenance of their prerogatives in several parts of the Ottoman Empire, and the emperor of Russia exercises that [right] of protecting them actively in placing them under his immediate jurisdiction through the services of his agents.

The Treaty of Bucharest had reaffirmed the previous treaties and had assured the Serbs "a full and complete amnesty, together with some alleviations of their primitive condition." The Porte was not living up to its agreements.

> The emperor of Russia has thus incontestably the right to protest against the violations committed by the Porte; he has in addition that of interesting himself in the fate of Christians in general. Finally, he is obliged by his religion and his conscience to support the Serbs strongly [*prendre fait et cause*].

A second memorandum of the same date repeated these arguments.[29]

Meanwhile, negotiations continued in Constantinople. There Italinskii continued to put strong pressure on the Porte to conciliate the Serbs, warning that the discussions should be brought to a conclusion

> as the most sure means of avoiding in the future unpleasant [*fâcheuses*] discussions on the deviations from the Treaty of Bucharest in regard to the Serbians at a time when it could be imagined that Russia did not wish to occupy itself with the maintenance of stipulations drawn up in their favor.[30]

Russian intervention, it was argued, was based on "a solemn treaty, the most precise stipulation, the most explicit."

Because of this determined Russian attitude and its own domestic interests, the Ottoman government hastened to act. Although it argued that it was not bound by the Bucharest stipulations since the Serbs had not accepted them, it nevertheless recognized that an

---

[28]Memorandum on Serbia, Vienna, February 3/15, 1815, ibid., VIII, pp. 193–5.

[29]Razumovskii circular note to the participants in the Vienna Congress, February 3/15, 1815, ibid., VIII, pp. 197–9.

[30]Italinskii note to the Turkish government, Constantinople, September 18/30, 1815, ibid., VIII, pp. 528–30.

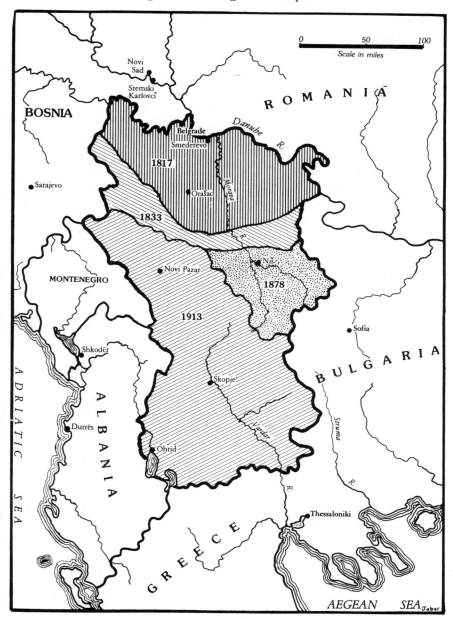

Map 1. The expansion of Serbia, 1804–1913.

arrangement would have to be made.[31] Negotiations were thus carried on between the Serbian representatives and Marashli Ali Pasha, the vezir of Rumelia. The final terms, agreed upon in November, granted Serbia a semiautonomous position. Miloš Obrenović was recognized as supreme prince [*knez*]; a National Chancery of twelve notables was to serve as the highest court of the land. The Serbs were allowed to collect their own taxes and to keep their guns; a general amnesty was given to those who had participated in the revolution.

This settlement, of course, left much still to be decided. It could not be expected that the Serbian leaders would accept what was in fact an indeterminate status. Discussions on the terms of Serbian autonomy were to continue until another agreement was made in 1830. Meanwhile, the controversies continued, and Russia had more reasons to complain about violations of Article VIII. Serbian internal politics under Miloš were not stable. When Karadjordje returned in July 1817, the prince had him killed and sent his head to the sultan. Without a consul in Belgrade, the Russian government still suffered from a lack of direct information on the area.

RUSSIAN INTERESTS IN THE BALKANS AFTER 1815

By 1815, as we have seen, Russia had been involved deeply in the events in the Balkan peninsula for over a century. In the next hundred years that region was to play an even more important role in Russian foreign relations. The solution to the Eastern Question, that is, to those problems attendant upon the increasing weakness of the Ottoman Empire and its apparent impending dissolution, were to become vital issues for the Russian leadership. The state was to be drawn into four wars – in 1828, 1853, 1877, and 1914 – because of the prime strategic importance of the area and the Russian relationship with the Balkan Christian population, already established through the treaties that have been discussed previously. Before proceeding to an examination of the background of these conflicts, which form the major portion of this narrative, it is necessary to study in greater detail the reasons why the Russian government remained so involved in Balkan events throughout the nineteenth century. The economic, strategic, and ideological ties will be examined separately.

[31]Italinskii to Nesselrode, no. 116, Constantinople, November 17/29, 1815, ibid., IX, pp. 8–10.

Map 2. The Ottoman Balkans, 1815.

Economic interests

Of the three elements to be considered, the economic issues received
the least attention in the diplomatic correspondence. Although Russia's comparative backwardness was to be a major cause of its loss of
the Crimean War, the Russian leadership placed more weight on the
strategic and political aspects of its policy than on the economic

25

costs or benefits. When Russian ministers warned, as they often did, about the financial disaster that would accompany involvement in a war, their arguments were usually overriden by other considerations. If economic advantage had been a truly deciding factor, Russia would not have entered any of the wars of the next century.

The chief problem here was the fact that in this period the Balkan peninsula, in fact the entire Ottoman Empire, and Russia had parallel economic systems. Both areas were primarily agricultural; neither produced the goods nor provided the raw materials that the other could use. When Russia entered the industrial age at the end of the nineteenth century, its products could not compete with those of the West, in particular with those of Britain, France, Germany, and Austria. The country also did not have the financial resources to invest in Eastern enterprises. As far as the utilization of Balkan resources was concerned, it was primarily British and French, and later German, entrepreneurs who exploited, for instance, the oil of the Romanian lands and the mines of Serbia. The struggle for markets and sources of raw materials thus did not usually play a significant part in Russian policy in the area.

One aspect of Russian economic development, however, needs special emphasis. After the acquisition of the lands to the Black Sea, the Russian government made great efforts to settle the territory and develop its agricultural economy. By the 1830s and 1840s the export of grain, especially wheat, grown in the area and shipped out through the Black Sea ports played a major role in the Russian economy and in maintaining a favorable balance of trade. Odessa became the chief Russian port for exports. The significance of this development, of course, is that Russian interests required that the Black Sea and the Straits remain open for merchant ships and peaceful trading. Events that interrupted shipping, such as the Greek revolution of the 1820s and the Turkish–Italian War of 1911, could mean economic disaster.

As far as foreign relations was concerned, Russian commercial interests did not always coincide with those of its foreign policy. As we shall see, throughout the nineteenth century Britain was the chief Russian adversary, yet at the same time this country was an excellent customer for Russian agricultural exports. Moreover, Russia never developed a significant merchant marine; its ships carried only about 10 percent of the total Russian trade. The British navy, of course, dominated the seas and could interfere with this shipping at any time. It is thus difficult to make easy generalizations on the effect of economics on foreign policy.

Rights and obligations acquired

One additional aspect of the question should be mentioned. Quite obviously, Russian landowners profiting from Black Sea trade should have favored actions in foreign affairs that promoted their interests. It is, however, difficult to find direct evidence in the diplomatic documentation that Russian landowners were indeed able to influence policy decisively one way or another, or that individual Russian statesmen in fact made decisions reflecting their economic leadership when they were also great landowners. The direction of Russian foreign relations was usually in the hands of men who emphasized other aspects of the national interest of their country. Throughout this century, it must be remembered, Britain, whose policy was affected by commercial and imperial concerns, was often derided as "a nation of shopkeepers."

Geopolitical considerations

After 1815, with the destruction of French military predominance, Russia, with its army of 800,000 men, was in the eyes of contemporaries the strongest single power. The subsequent cooperation of the Russian, Prussian, and Austrian governments ensured that, unlike the period of the wars of the French revolution and Napoleon, Central Europe would not be a battlefield, nor would an enemy army have easy access to the Russian interior. The partition of Poland, accomplished at the end of the eighteenth century and confirmed at Vienna in 1815, gave Russia an additional territorial buffer on its most vital frontier.

Britain, the country that over the course of the century became the major Russian opponent, although the world's greatest naval power, did not have a strong army. The confrontation of the two powers occurred along a long band of territory stretching from the Pacific waters of the Far East to the eastern Mediterranean and the Baltic Sea, with major conflicts arising over Chinese affairs and the control of Afghanistan, as well as over the fate of the Ottoman Empire. For Britain the Ottoman lands were of principal significance because the main routes to its imperial domains ran through the area. Their importance increased with the replacement of sailing ships with steamships, which made shorter routes necessary, and the opening of the Suez Canal in 1869. Because of these considerations, British statesmen usually supported the maintenance of the Ottoman Empire and the integrity of its lands. For most of the nineteenth century they opposed the creation of independent Balkan states because they feared they would be Russian puppets.

In facing the British opposition, the Russian leaders had chiefly to be concerned about certain areas of their country. As long as the alliance with Prussia and Austria held, Russia did not need to fear an overland invasion. The British army was barely sufficient to hold down its empire and Ireland. In the past it had fought only with continental allies and had been generous with subsidies. Where Russia was open to attack was at those points where a predominant navy could overwhelm a coastal defense and send in a landing party. Thus for Russia throughout most of the nineteenth century the Black Sea area was its most vulnerable region. The immense dissatisfaction of the Caucasian people with the Russian conquest also meant that British naval forces could perhaps count on assistance here, as well as from an Ottoman state under Russian pressure.

Because of their emphasis on Black Sea defense, the Russian ministers were always most concerned about the fate of the Balkan and Caucasian lands directly adjacent to the Black Sea, particularly the Romanian and Bulgarian territories, and about the status of the Straits. For Russia the Straits question was almost always considered in a defensive sense. The narrow waterway was indeed the key to the Russian house, but householders need keys to keep intruders *out*, not to enable them to leave their homes. The Russian objective was thus usually to establish a system that would ensure that the British and French fleets would be excluded from the Black Sea, either by an agreement with the Ottoman Empire, an international treaty, or possession of the Bosphorus. Russian control of *both* the Bosphorus and the Dardanelles was not considered a possible objective before World War I.

The fate of the Ottoman lands and the Balkan people naturally figured prominently in Russian world strategic plans. With the demonstration of Ottoman weakness shown in the repeated military defeats and the increasing internal anarchy evident at the end of the eighteenth century, Russian statesmen, like those of the other great powers, naturally considered what would happen should the Ottoman Empire collapse. They recognized that no single government could decide the fate of the region; they knew that, in the past, all of the great powers had at one time or another been concerned about Russian advances into Ottoman territory. At this time and throughout the nineteenth century, the Russian leaders considered three possible solutions to the problems posed by Ottoman weakness. First, they could seek to preserve the empire, but dominate the Ottoman government and thus all of its territories; second, they could cooperate with other states and partition the Ottoman lands;

third, they could, at least as far as the Balkan area was concerned, sponsor the establishment of autonomous and independent national regimes and then either cooperate with them or attempt to dominate them. No matter what policy was adopted, it was recognized that the reaction of the other governments would have to be considered.

As far as the first alternative was concerned, this possibility was also considered, in fact preferred, by the French and British governments, the chief rivals in the Ottoman capital. In the coming years the representatives of the three powers fought for a predominant voice in the councils of the sultan; each had its clients and friends. When one embassy achieved a prime influence, the other two tended to join against it. The weakness and corruption at the center allowed this system to remain in effect until the collapse of the empire in 1922.

Throughout most of this period, domination of the Ottoman government and preservation of its territorial integrity was the preferred Russian policy; the advantages of having a weak neighbor in a vulnerable region were thoroughly understood. Influence over Ottoman decisions could be ensured by the presence of threatening Russian armies on the Balkan and Asian frontiers and the use of treaty stipulations as weapons. These advantages were, however, not always decisive. As we have seen, in the eighteenth century the French position in Constantinople was strong; in the next century sea power and its basic strategic interest in Ottoman integrity gave Britain an often predominant influence.

In regard to the second alternative, the partition of the empire, this subject was a constant source of speculation and negotiation.[32] French and British interest was primarily concentrated on North African and Arab lands, Syria and Mesopotamia in particular. The Balkans were chiefly of interest to Russia and the Habsburg Empire. Here the various plans discussed by representatives of the two states involved both questions of direct annexation and the establishment of spheres of influence. Typical of the many partition schemes considered was the Greek project of Catherine the Great and the discussions between Russian and French representatives surrounding the Treaty of Tilsit. In general in considering partition schemes, the Russian government showed a primary interest in the eastern Balkans, that is, in the fate of the Danubian Principalities and the

---

[32]For some of the many plans proposed for the partition of the Ottoman Empire, see T. G. Djuvara, *Cent projets de partage de la Turquie, 1281–1913* (Paris: Librairie Félix Alcan, 1914).

Bulgarian lands, which lay on the road to Constantinople and bordered on the Black Sea; Habsburg concerns centered in the west on Bosnia, Hercegovina, and Serbia.

The third alternative policy, the establishment of separate autonomous or independent Balkan governments closely associated with St. Petersburg, is of particular importance to this study. The great advantage that the Russian government had in dealing with the Balkan subjects of the Ottoman Empire was the existence of ties that were not duplicated by other powers. The overwhelming majority of the Christian people were Orthodox; most of the diplomatic reports of the time estimated their number at approximately 12 million. In addition, the Serbs and Bulgarians were, like most Russian citizens, Slavs, with languages relatively close to Russian. Although the Slavic connection was to become important after 1856, it was the Orthodox tie that was to be particularly significant prior to that time. This link was to allow the Russian government to claim a special position in regard to the Balkan people and to play a role in the national development of the area different from that of the other great powers. As will be shown subsequently, the formation of the modern states was accomplished not only because of Russian military actions, but also with the involvement of Russian officials in the establishment of the first national governments. The role of Russia in the internal affairs of the Principalities and Serbia has already been discussed. Here treaty rights had been used both to assist in the formation of autonomous regimes and to attempt to ensure Russian control over them.

As already explained, the Russian government in the period under consideration did not believe that it alone could decide the fate of the Balkan people or the major issues in the Eastern Question. It knew that the interests and attitudes of the other powers had to be considered. British concerns have already been outlined, but the Habsburg Empire, France, and later united Germany and Italy also had national objectives.

Of these states, the Habsburg Empire, with its immediate geographic proximity, was most directly involved in Balkan developments. Moreover, like the Russian tsars, the Habsburg rulers also felt that they had a duty to defend Christianity, but with an emphasis on the Catholic rather than the Orthodox church. Vienna had twice experienced Ottoman sieges, in 1529 and 1683; many Austrians, and other Europeans too, felt that the great service of the Habsburg state had been the defense of Christianity against what was judged to be an Ottoman crusade to subjugate Christian Europe. Thereafter the long Ottoman–Habsburg border – far greater in extent than the Russian–Ottoman frontier in Europe – was the scene of constant unrest and conflict. The Habsburg government had to be at all times aware of Balkan developments.

For the Habsburg Empire the most important settlement with the Ottoman Empire was the Treaty of Karlowitz (Sremski Karlovci) of 1699, which set the boundary at the Sava–Danube line. This border, with certain alterations, such as the annexation of Bukovina in 1775, remained permanent until 1908, when the monarchy acquired Bosnia and Hercegovina. Although in the eighteenth century Austria had cooperated with Russia in actions against the Ottoman Empire, in the nineteenth century the Habsburg leaders, with some exceptions, usually regarded a further conquest of Balkan lands as only weakly appealing. Lacking a direct Orthodox or Slavic connection with the Balkan revolutionary leaderships, they did not have the same emotional involvement in Balkan affairs as did many of their Russian counterparts. Without close links to any Balkan movement, the Habsburg government after 1815 was to adopt a largely negative policy toward Ottoman developments. Sharing with Britain the fear that the establishment of autonomous or independent national states in the Balkans would lead to eventual full Russian control, Habsburg statesmen usually became strong advocates of the defense of the status quo.

The French influence was to be of a different character. Like Britain, France was an imperial power and was to seek to annex Ottoman territories, in particular in North Africa, and to show a strong interest in Lebanon. The state was also, particularly in the middle of the nineteenth century, to act to support its claim to be the protector of the Catholics in certain sections of the Ottoman Empire. French imperial pressure, however, was not felt in the Balkans. Here the Habsburg Empire stood as the chief supporter of Catholic interests; after 1815 that state and Russia were the powers with the major interest in the fate of the Ottoman Balkan lands. In contrast, the enormous influence that France was to wield in the nineteenth century rested chiefly on ideological considerations, that is, on the association of that state with the liberal and national doctrines of the French revolution. Cooperation with France also gave Balkan national leaderships an alternative to conservative, autocratic Russia. It should be emphasized too that in the nineteenth century Paris set the standard for style and manners. Russian aristocrats and Balkan revolutionaries alike regarded the French capital indeed as the city of light. Balkan leaders, even those sympathetic to and closely associated with tsarist Russia, usually saw the future for their country in the adoption of French, not Russian, ways of life.

In considering the policy to take toward events in the Balkans, Russian statesmen thus had to consider carefully not only their own interests in the Black Sea region, but also those of other powers, in particular Britain and the Habsburg Empire. The great nightmare of Russian diplomacy was that an issue would arise that would draw together all of the European powers into a coalition against Russia. Throughout the century the memory of 1812 stayed strongly in Russian minds. As we shall see, this danger threatened to recur in connection with various crises in Balkan affairs.

Ideology: Autocracy and orthodoxy

Although the Russian geopolitical considerations resembled those of the other great powers, the Russian government had certain interests that were unique or that it shared only with the conservative monarchies of Europe. First, Russia was an autocracy. The final decisions in foreign policy, as in other aspects of state life, were made at least in theory by the tsar. Throughout most of the century the Russian rulers, like their European counterparts, took a direct personal interest in foreign affairs and in the military. Not only did the five tsars in power before 1914 – Alexander I (1801–25), Nicholas I (1825–55), Alexander II (1855–81), Alexander III (1881–94), and Nicholas II (1894–1917) – believe in the defense of conservative principles in their own country, but both Alexander I and Nicholas I made it a part of their foreign policy, and it was the basis of their alliance system. Under these circumstances, the attitudes and convictions of the individual tsars were of great importance. In general, all of the rulers in question upheld conservative values, but in the spirit of Enlightened Despotism. Each believed that he had received his power from God and that, in turn, he was responsible to God for the welfare of the Russian people. The conviction that final decisions must somehow reflect this divine sanction, in turn, influenced each ruler's attitude. The importance that religious issues played in the relationship with the Balkan people can be explained at least in part by these convictions. Like the Protestant rulers of Britain and other European monarchs, Orthodox tsars expected to be defenders of the faith.

In addition, and closely connected with the conservative orientation, each tsar inherited a moral code that was again typical not only of Russia, but of the general outlook of most European monarchs. Of the values that a ruler was expected to reflect in his own conduct, two, honor and duty, stood very high. For the Balkan relationship, the concept of honor was to be of particular importance. Not only did a monarch need to conduct his personal life on a high plane, but his given word was a sacred bond. In practical terms in foreign policy, this conviction was carried over into the negotiation of treaties. As will be shown, the tsars were repeatedly faced by Ottoman violation of treaties that they believed gave Russia specific rights in regard to the Balkan Christians. *Honor* forced the Russian rulers to regard the defense of treaty rights as a *duty*. This attitude was to influence deeply Russian policy throughout the years under consideration.

With the possible exception of Nicholas II, the tsars were all assisted by capable ministers and advisers, and they usually based their decisions on the recommendations of these men. As a group those associated with foreign relations, either as officials in the foreign ministry or as members of the embassy or consulate staffs, were well educated and cosmopolitan in attitude. The majority had traveled widely and were well acquainted with all aspects of European cultural and political life. Usually moderate and judicious, they seldom stood for adventurous or dangerous courses of action. In fact, they often acted as brakes on the impetuous action of tsars.

In the post-1815 years the Russian rulers and their ministers had to deal with two revolutionary principles, liberalism and nationalism. As far as the first ideal was concerned, they were principally against the introduction of liberal institutions by revolutionary means. As regards the question of nationalism, the Russian attitude was divided. There was certainly no approval of the romantic-revolutionary definition of "national" as inferring an identity of language, historical background, and unique customs. After all, Russian tsars were by bloodline German princes. Until the end of the century the Russian government contained a large number of men from families of foreign origin. For example, of the three foreign ministers in office between 1814 and 1896, K. V. Nesselrode, A. M. Gorchakov, and N. K. Giers, only Gorchakov was both Slavic and Orthodox. Until the end of the century the rulers and their advisers conversed and wrote principally in French. The Russian state that they governed was, of course, multinational and became more so as the century progressed. In foreign relations this condition meant that Russian statesmen could not stand clearly and openly for the idea of the nation-state. They obviously could not recognize that the Poles, for instance, had any implicit right to a national organization. It is important to note that the state's multinational character was seldom acknowledged in the words or attitudes of the leadership. Tsars and their officials alike spoke as if Russia was a cohesive unit in their declarations on foreign policy.

Despite the varied background of the Russian leadership, a Russian national spirit did exist that had some elements in common with the radical revolutionary movements of the time. Certainly, Russian society did share in a common past history, similar customs and beliefs, and an intensely patriotic devotion to the defense of state interests. In the future, as we will see, the tsars and their associates would repeatedly make use of phrases such as "the positive interests of Russia," "the honor of the Russian name," and "the true interests of Russia." Although there were indeed differences between Russian nationalism and the ideas that propelled the leaders of nationalities with irredentist goals, such as, for instance, the Greeks, Serbs, Bulgars, Italians, and Germans, it had much in common with the convictions of the citizens of other multinational complexes, such as the Habsburg Empire, and of Britain and France with their vast colonial possessions.

Moreover, variations of nationalism did affect Russian judgment on foreign policy questions. Many of the Balkan people under Ottoman rule, that is, the Serbs, Bulgars, and Montenegrins, but not the Greeks, Romanians, Albanians, and Turks, were Slavs. Before 1914 three major movements emphasized the Slavic heritage of the Russian people and the links to the other European Slavic peoples. Thus Slavophilism during the reign of Nicholas I, Panslavism during those of Alexander II and Alexander III, and Neoslavism before 1914, through their influence on public opinion among the educated sections of Russian society, did play a role in foreign policy in both a positive and a negative direction. These movements will be discussed in relation to the events they influenced, but it should be noted here that each reflected a generally paternal attitude toward other Slavic peoples. Like the Russian officials themselves, those influenced by Slavic themes tended to look upon the Balkan Christians as a primitive people who needed firm if friendly guidance.

Although conservative and Russian national themes are important in this narrative, they are overwhelmed in significance in the first half of the nineteenth century by the role of Orthodoxy in determining Russian Balkan policy. Because religion is so important, it might be well to examine in closer detail the exact position of

Russia in relation to the Balkan religious organizations.[33] It was a question that was to cause much misunderstanding and controversy throughout the period under study. First, it is important to emphasize that, unlike the Western political systems, Ottoman citizens, according to the millet system, were divided along the lines of religion rather than nationality, geography, or other considerations. The Ottoman rulers made few major attempts to convert the Christians, but, under the principle of separate and unequal, they could not enjoy the same privileges as the Muslims. The Christian people were thus allowed to continue in their faith, but they were subject to numerous restrictions. Moreover, since religion and politics were seen as one, Ottoman officials regarded the head of the Balkan Orthodox, the patriarch of Constantinople, as both a spiritual and a secular leader. These duties, assumed by the Patriarch Gennadius after the Ottoman capture of Constantinople in 1453, gave the Patriarchate civil powers and duties that it had not held under the Byzantine Empire, where the civil authority dominated the religious institution. The patriarch thus became in fact the ruler of a Christian political unit within the Muslim empire.

The major spiritual and cultural connection between Russia and the Balkan people was this religious tie, but the relationship was complicated. The Russian Kievan state had accepted Christianity through Constantinople in the tenth century. At first the Russian church was directly controlled from Constantinople; its metropolitans were named and consecrated by the patriarch. The period of Mongol domination, commencing in the first half of the thirteenth century, loosened the ties with Constantinople and increased the prestige of the Russian church. The capture of the imperial city in 1453 by the Ottoman Turks, of course, was a major event for both the Greek and Russian institutions. Although the authority of the patriarch over the Balkan Orthodox was subsequently strengthened, his ability to influence Russian affairs weakened. Gradually the Russian rulers began to take over the religious authority in their lands. With the conquest of the Balkan kingdoms, only the king of Georgia and the grand prince of Moscow were independent Orthodox rulers. Even though, at least in theory, the Russian church was

---

[33]For this subject see in particular Steven Runciman, *The Great Church in Captivity: A Study of the Patriarchate of Constantinople from the Eve of the Turkish Conquest to the Greek War of Independence* (Cambridge: Cambridge University Press, 1968), and the first chapter of John Shelton Curtiss, *Church and State in Russia: The Last Years of the Empire, 1900–1917* (New York: Columbia University Press, 1940).

simply one of the Metropolitanates of the Patriarchate, it was in fact autocephalous even before the fall of Byzantium. The grand prince appointed the metropolitans after an election by a church council. In 1470 Ivan III declared that the Patriarchate did not have authority over the Russian institution, but in practice the metropolitans continued to seek confirmation from Constantinople. It was only in 1598, during the reign of Theodore I, that the Russian church became a Patriarchate, with its head numbering last in the list of Orthodox patriarchs.

In subsequent periods the position of the Russian Patriarchate was not to be affected as much by the relationship with Constantinople as with the Russian rulers who continued the Byzantine tradition of affirming state control. In 1721 Peter the Great abolished the Russian Patriarchate and introduced a new organization. The church was placed under the direction of a Holy Synod, headed by a lay official, the Ober Procurator, who was appointed by the tsar. Under traditional rules the Russian church should have come once again under the authority of Constantinople, but in practice the metropolitan of Moscow held the most influential position among the Russian clerics. Another blow to the authority of the church occurred during the reign of Catherine the Great, when the empress confiscated church lands, particularly those belonging to the monasteries. This action made the church more dependent financially on the state.

The relationship of the Russian rulers with the Constantinople Patriarchate had another important aspect. Although after the Ottoman conquest the Patriarchate played a major role in the political life of the empire, the Orthodox world still suffered from the lack of an acknowledged Orthodox secular authority to whom the faithful could turn for support and protection. Claims that the Russian rulers were the legitimate heirs of Byzantium were put forward during the reign of Ivan III, who in 1472 married Zoe Paleologus, a niece of the last Byzantine emperor, who had died during the siege of Constantinople. Ivan also took the title of tsar and autocrat and incorporated the Byzantine double-headed eagle into his family's crest. Byzantine ceremonials, including the rites accompanying the coronation, were similarly adopted.

These events, combined with declarations of various Russian Orthodox dignitaries, were in the future to lead to a misunderstanding of Russian policy among some European observers and to the belief that the Russian rulers seriously claimed the heritage of Byzantium and believed that Moscow was the "Third Rome." To support this belief the words of the monk Philotheus of Moscow have been most often quoted. In 1511 in an address to the tsar he declared:

> ... instead of Rome and Constantinople ... Now there shines through the universe, like the sun in heaven, the Third Rome, of thy sovereign Empire and of the holy synodal apostolic Church, which is in the Orthodox Christian faith. ... Observe and see to it, most pious Tsar, that all the Christian empires unite with thine own. For two Romes have fallen, but the third stands, and a fourth there will not be; for thy Christian Tsardom will not pass to any other, according to the mighty word of God.[34]

This quotation, whose content can be duplicated from other sources, implied, of course, that the Russian rulers were the spiritual and secular leaders of Christendom and, as a logical corollary, that they should exert political control in the sense of seeking the reestablishment of another Roman or Byzantine Empire. In the future these concepts were indeed to be appealing to certain extreme sections of Russian opinion, but, and even more important, they were to be used by Russia's political opponents, who exploited such declarations to attempt to show that Russia in the nineteenth century had embarked upon a dangerous expansionistic program. Such goals, as will be repeatedly demonstrated, were far from the thinking of any Russian ruler in the period under consideration.

Moreover, such concepts, implying Russian spiritual and political domination over Balkan lands, were never acceptable to the Balkan Christians or their central leadership, the Patriarchate of Constantinople. They naturally felt the need for a powerful secular protector who would provide military and financial assistance; they were willing to use a subservient vocabulary implying all sorts of wonderful characteristics to Russian tsardom in order to gain this aid. Nevertheless, even during the period when Russian state power was indeed impressive, most Balkan Orthodox religious leaders and their followers, certainly among the Greeks and Romanians, did not concede a predominant position to Russian Orthodoxy. To them the primary Orthodox center remained Constantinople. Moreover, many in the hierarchy shared the common European view that Russia was backward and barbaric. Their conviction of superiority was reinforced by the remembrance that Russia had, after all, re-

---

[34]Runciman, *The Great Church in Captivity*, p. 324. Patriarch Jeremias II made a similar declaration: "Since the first Rome fell through the Appollinarian heresy and the second Rome, which is Constantinople, is held by the infidel Turks, so then thy great Russian Tsardom, pious Tsar, which is more pious than previous kingdoms, is the third Rome ... and thou alone under heaven art now called Christian Emperor for all Christians in the whole world," ibid., p. 331.

ceived Christianity through Byzantium; the Church Slavonic used in Russian services came through Bulgaria. The Holy Places of Christianity were in the Ottoman domains and under the authority of the Eastern Patriarchates. For the Greeks, who held the major church positions, the past was extremely important. Ancient Greece and Byzantium had made enormous contributions to European civilization; Russia had added comparatively less to the common heritage. The language of the New Testament was Greek; Greek influences were strong in early Christianity.

This attitude was characteristic of the Constantinople Patriarchate in particular. It must be remembered that notwithstanding any Russian ideas about the Third Rome or claims to superiority in the Orthodox world, the Balkan Christians did in fact have a political as well as a religious leadership in the Patriarchate. Moreover, this office claimed to be ecumenical, that is, that it had authority over all the Orthodox, whether in Russia, the Balkans, or elsewhere. The patriarchs considered themselves in no manner, spiritually or temporally, under Russian control. In fact, over the centuries since the fall of Constantinople, the Patriarchate, as part of the Ottoman administrative system, had meshed its policies well with those of the Muslim overlord. Its chief opposition had been directed not against the sultans and their officials, but against any Catholic or even Protestant threats to its religious jurisdiction.

By the eighteenth century another important development had taken place. The Patriarchate was at this time dominated by Phanariot Greeks, the same group who also provided the princes for the Danubian Principalities. The Phanariots not only held the central position in Constantinople, but they also took control of the Serbian, Bulgarian, and Romanian churches, which were henceforth administered by clerics of another national background and language. Since what education was available in these lands was provided by the church, Greek cultural dominance was established. As we will see, among the first actions taken by the national leaderships in the nineteenth century was the attempt to throw off this ecclesiastical dictatorship. As a result, the unity of the Balkan Orthodox, which the Russian government fostered, was continually endangered.

These intra-Orthodox quarrels naturally involved Russian officials. It is important to emphasize that the Russian government never controlled the Constantinople Patriarchate; in fact, their goals often conflicted. The Patriarchate, with a long tradition of cooperation with the Porte, usually wished to maintain the status quo;

Orthodox unity was favored, but only under its direction and not that of the secular great power. It did want Russian assistance, but not political protection or domination. The Greek bishops were well aware of the fate of the Russian church. The Ottoman sultans under most circumstances allowed the Orthodox to run their own religious affairs without interference; in contrast, in Russia the church was in clear subordination to the state.

Given this situation, the Russian government worked best with the Constantinople center when its policy was the maintenance of the status quo and cooperation with the Porte, which was the patriarchal position. The church also needed Russian assistance in times of crisis, such as during the Greek revolution. However, the Russian policy of supporting increased autonomy for the Balkan regions was often opposed, since it could involve the establishment of a separate national ecclesiastical authority and a weakening of the jurisdiction of Constantinople. In the many disputes that arose during the century between the Patriarchate, on the one hand, and either the Porte or the Balkan national churches, on the other, the Russian government could never dictate a solution. At best, Russian officials, usually the ambassador at Constantinople, could attempt to mediate a compromise satisfactory to the contending parties.

For the purposes of this study the significance of both the Russian and the Balkan attitudes lay in the fact that they introduced a great deal of confusion into tsarist policy. As we have seen, stipulations regarding the Orthodox were a part of the Russian treaty system. Moreover, successive tsars were apparently convinced that they had a right and duty to defend both the spiritual and secular interests of the Balkan Christians even before they received specific rights in treaties with the Ottoman Empire. It should be strongly emphasized that the official attitude was paternal, not messianic. Russian leaders did not have world missions or grand designs. They had instead duties and responsibilities, which, when linked to the Russian geo-political interests, were bound to involve the country deeply in Balkan affairs.

In this regard it is important to note that the Russian government not only had specific treaty rights but also that, by the beginning of the nineteenth century, Russian officials and the tsars themselves had adopted a vocabulary that assumed that Russia did indeed have wide rights of protection in regard to the Balkan Christians. For instance, a general instruction written by Nesselrode in May 1815 declared that, in endeavoring to conserve peace with the Ottoman Empire, the Russian representatives should not lose sight of the relationships of protection and religious and political affinity that H.I.M., like his august predecessors, is pleased to maintain with the Wallachians, the Moldavians and the Greeks in general.

That salutary influence sanctioned by the treaties, rightly and as shown by experience, should be considered as a moral force which has always worked in favor of Russia and paralyzed the hostile designs of the Ottoman Empire.[35]

A memorandum on Serbia drawn up to be circulated at the Congress of Vienna stated:

Summoned by the conformity of religion to consider himself as the natural protector of the Christians of the Greek Oriental rite, according to the system adopted by all the sovereigns in regard to those of their respective communions placed under Ottoman domination, H.I.M. the emperor of all the Russians has always at heart to shelter the Serbians from all tyrannical persecution . . . and he believes himself obligated by the critical nature of the circumstances and by the imminent danger that faces the Serbian nation to take it under his protection.[36]

By the end of the Napoleonic Wars the Russian leadership had so often used rhetorical phrases with this content that the assumption was strong that Russia did indeed have an internationally recognized special relationship with the Balkan Orthodox and one that went considerably beyond the wording of the treaties. Moreover, once it was taken for granted that a Russian right existed, it soon became a question of whether that did not also involve an obligation. For instance, if the Ottoman government gave certain assurances in regard to Serbia in the Treaty of Bucharest, was it not a Russian obligation to make certain that these were carried out? And, a step further, were the Russian honor and the tsar's personal honor involved? As we will see, in the future these questions drew the Russian government into dangerous entanglements.

Another problem also existed. No attempt was made to define the exact nature of the protection that Russian leaders claimed; did it involve simply spiritual and religious matters, or did it include political intervention? In Russian eyes, it certainly covered political life, and under Ottoman conditions a religious protectorate carried a political connotation. Moreover, Russian statesmen believed that their protégés needed Russian advice and assistance. Without adequate information on Balkan internal affairs, they assumed that all the people lived in extremely primitive conditions and that they were not capable alone of establishing their own institutions, in fact

[35]Nesselrode instruction to Shtakel'berg, Vienna, May 13/25, 1815, *VPR*, VIII, pp. 344–6.
[36]Razumovskii memorandum on Serbia, Vienna, February 3/15, 1815, ibid., VIII, pp. 197–9.

that they were children who needed the paternal guidance of the benevolent Russian protector. This attitude toward lands and peoples existing outside of the magic circle of European civilization was, of course, shared by all the great powers.

By 1815 the treaty basis had been established for the next century of Russian–Balkan relations. In the first part of the eighteenth century Russian interests had been primarily strategic and military. Russian leaders had called upon Balkan people to rise to aid them in the accomplishment of their military plans. Cantemir's response to Peter's initiatives and the Greek rebellion during Catherine's reign, for instance, resulted in disaster for the people concerned with no Russian attempts at reparation. Later in the century the Russian military presence, combined with increasing Ottoman weakness, enabled the Russian government to play a stronger role in intervening in the affairs of the Christian subjects of the Ottoman Empire. The greatest interest was first shown in the affairs of the Principalities whose lands lay on the direct route to the Ottoman capital. These provinces, with autonomous governments, came increasingly under Russian control through a series of agreements made by the Porte under Russian pressure. Although Russia was not able to annex the area, by 1802 it had a de facto protectorate over the governments.

By the end of the eighteenth century the status of other Balkan Christians was similarly dealt with in Russo–Turkish agreements. Most important was to be Article VII of the Treaty of Kuchuk Kainardji, which was henceforth to be used to justify the claim that Russia had a special relationship with the Balkan Christians, legally recognized in an international agreement. The key phrase here was the Ottoman promise "to protect constantly the Christian religion and its churches." The question was soon to arise of what the Russian rights or obligations would be should Ottoman agents massacre Balkan Christians. The clauses in the agreements relative to the Romanians, the Greeks, and, after the Treaty of Bucharest, the Serbs brought up similar questions. The next century was to show the confusing role that the combination of strategic, religious, and political factors was to play in Russian foreign policy. It was also to demonstrate that the links with the Balkan Orthodox brought dangers as well as benefits to the Russian state.

CHAPTER II

Rights and obligations defended and extended: The Greek revolution and the Russo–Turkish War, 1828–9

When Alexander I rode into Paris in March 1814 at the head of his troops, he was the ruler of a country at its height of influence and power. Well aware of this situation, the leaders not only of vanquished France, but also of victorious Britain and Austria, looked with apprehension at a tsar whose declarations often filled them with dismay and distrust. Alexander had come to the throne in 1801 after the assassination of his father. A young man of twenty-three, he had not had time to gain the experience needed for his position. The product of a troubled childhood, he had been affected by the split between Paul and his grandmother, Catherine the Great, who directed his education. Her influence meant that he had become acquainted with the doctrines of the Enlightenment and the body of ideas that lay at the basis of the French revolution. During the first part of his reign it appeared that he would adopt a reform program; his early advisers pushed him in this direction. The devastating conflict with Napoleon, however, shifted his thinking in other directions. His early education, nevertheless, had lasting effects. He kept a tendency to think about problems in general terms, and he was fond of lofty declarations of principles intended to embrace all humanity. He was, on the positive side, cosmopolitan in his attitudes and European in his frame of reference. Although a Russian patriot and deeply convinced of his God-ordained task of bringing happiness to his people, he was not a chauvinist, nor did he support programs of imperial expansion.

Around the time of the French invasion of Russia, he appears to have undergone a profound emotional crisis. He later declared:

Figure 1. Alexander I.

The burning of Moscow enlightened my soul, and judgment of God on the fields of ice filled my heart with a faith which I had never so deeply before experienced. . . . I was filled with a deep and mature conviction to devote myself and my government only to Him and to the furtherance of His honor. Since that time I have been another man; to the salvation of Europe from destruction I owe my salvation and liberty.[1]

The shift that occurred at this time toward a religious emphasis in Alexander's thinking was to result in a closer relationship not with the official Russian Orthodox institutions, but with outside circles that emphasized personal mystical experience. He was henceforth increasingly to apply a moral and religious vocabulary to political

[1]Quoted in Karl Stählin, *Geschichte Russlands* (Graz: Akademische Druck, 1961), III, pp. 238–9.

life and to use words and phrases, for instance "empire of evil," "satanic spirit," "presence of evil," "salvation," and "occult means," when dealing with events, such as violent revolutions, of which he did not approve. He also applied strict moral strictures to his own conduct, explaining, "I feel that I am the depository of a Sacred, Holy Task, and I neither must nor can compromise it."[2] In 1823 he declared: "Providence has not put eight hundred thousand soldiers at my order to satisfy my ambition, but to protect religion and justice, and to preserve those principles of order on which human society rests."[3]

Despite these and similar declarations Alexander I in his practical actions showed a keen awareness of Russian national interest and European realities. Certainly, at the Congress of Vienna he gained an advantageous settlement for Russia; Finland (in 1809) and Bessarabia (in 1812) had already been annexed. In 1815 Russia received the greater part of the former Duchy of Warsaw. These lands were to form a separate political unit, the Congress Kingdom of Poland, with the tsar as king. The territory was thus under de facto Russian control. The organization of Central Europe into small states under the primary direction of the Habsburg Empire was also to the Russian advantage. The Habsburg government too favored the division of the German and Italian lands. The vulnerable Russian western frontier was thus protected.

Having achieved this settlement, it was to the interest of the Russian government to maintain the status quo in regard to both the territorial divisions and the internal order in the states. It should be emphasized that Alexander I was not a true reactionary; he did favor reform under certain conditions. He approved of the introduction of constitutional government in the Ionian Islands in 1803, in Finland in 1809, and in France and Poland in 1815. What he was to condemn strongly was the overthrow of a legitimate government by force and violence, in his mind an essential element in most of the reform movements of his time.

Although Russia was clearly the strongest European power in 1815, Alexander I certainly had no ambition to rule Europe alone. Instead he wished to bring the European powers together in associations to protect the settlement and ensure political stability. In 1815 the Quadruple Alliance of Britain, Austria, Prussia, and Russia was already in existence; it was primarily directed against France until

[2]Quoted in Patricia Kennedy Grimsted, *The Foreign Ministers of Alexander I* (Berkeley: University of California Press, 1969), p. 39.
[3]Ibid., p. 44.

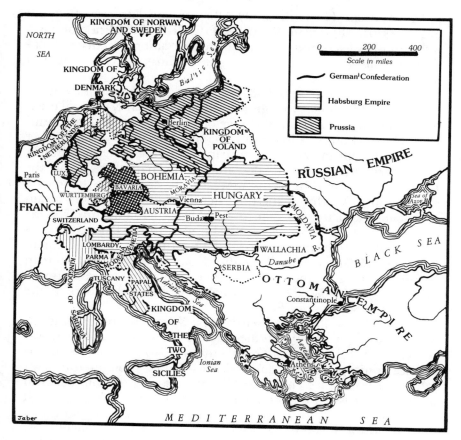

Map 3. Europe in 1815.

1818, when that power joined the alignment. In addition, the tsar secured the agreement of most of the rulers to another document, the Holy Alliance. In this statement of principles the signators declared "their fixed resolution, both in the administration of their respective States, and in their political relations with every other Government, to take for their sole guide the precepts of that Holy Religion, namely the precepts of Justice, Christian Charity, and Peace."[4] Despite the tsar's enthusiastic endorsement, the signators accepted the declaration out of consideration for Alexander I, but it had no

[4]Edward Hertslet, *The Map of Europe by Treaty* (London: Buttersworths, 1875), I, pp. 317–20.

practical effects. The term "Holy Alliance" was later used to designate the close alignment of Russia, Prussia, and Austria that, with interruptions, lasted until 1853, to be renewed after 1871, a combination that was to function better in general European affairs than in the Eastern Question.

After 1815 Alexander I had two principal advisers, neither of whom held the title of foreign minister.[5] The first, Karl Vasil'evich Nesselrode, was to remain in charge of Russian foreign affairs until 1856. He was born in Lisbon in December 1780 of a Catholic father and a Protestant mother. He was baptized in the Anglican church, and he remained with this denomination. His father was in the Russian service, but his posts were abroad. Nesselrode attended a gymnasium in Berlin at the time that his father was the Russian representative at the Prussian court. After graduating in 1796, he became at the age of sixteen a midshipman in the Baltic fleet. His subsequent career was very successful; he became an aide-de-camp to Paul. Thereafter, he entered the diplomatic field and held posts in Berlin, the Hague, and Paris. In 1811 he was named secretary of state, rising in 1816 to the headship of the Foreign Ministry with the title of First Secretary of State.

This background was reflected in Nesselrode's attitudes and actions. Like many of those in the Russian service at this time he was conservative and cosmopolitan; his marriage to the daughter of the finance minister, Dmitrii Aleksandrovich Gurev, brought him closer to other conservative circles. He did not place a definite personal imprint on Russian foreign affairs; he was certainly no Metternich

---

[5]For the career and ideas of Alexander I and all of his foreign ministers, see Grimsted, *The Foreign Ministers of Alexander I.* Of the two men of importance discussed in this chapter, Nesselrode and Capodistrias, the first has not received an adequate biographical treatment. Part of his career is, however, discussed in Harold N. Ingle, *Nesselrode and the Russian Rapprochement with Britain, 1836–1844* (Berkeley: University of California Press, 1976). A selection of documents from his family archive is published in A. Nesselrode, ed., *Lettres et papiers du chancelier comte de Nesselrode, 1760–1856,* 11 vols. (Paris: A. Lahure, 1904–11). For Capodistrias and his relationship with the Greek revolution there is a great deal more material, including the biography by C. M. Woodhouse, *Capodistria* (London: Oxford University Press, 1973), and his article "Kapodistrias and the Philiki Etairia, 1814–1821" in Richard Clogg, ed., *The Struggle for Greek Independence* (Hamden, Conn.: Archon Books, 1973), pp. 104–34; and two books by G. L. Arsh, *Eteristskoe dvizhenie v Rossii* (Moscow: Izdatel'stvo nauka, 1970) and *I. Kapodistriia i grecheskoe natsional'no-osvoboditel'noe dvizhenie, 1809–1822* (Izdatel'stvo nauka, 1976). Very important for this study is Capodistrias's memoir, "Aperçu de ma carrière publique, depuis 1789 jusqu'à 1822 in *Sbornik imperatorskogo russkogo istoricheskogo obshchestva,* III (1868), pp. 163–292.

Figure 2. Karl Vasil'evich Nesselrode.

or Bismarck. Serving under two strong-willed tsars, he proved an able instrument for enacting their desires. He did, nevertheless, have convictions of his own, and he did express his ideas. He had only a limited knowledge of Russian; he could not write it with ease, a characteristic, of course, shared by his contemporaries in the diplomatic service.

The second figure of importance was Ioannis Capodistrias. Born in Corfu in 1776 of an aristocratic Greek Orthodox family, he experienced directly many of the events described previously. He first

Figure 3. Ioannis Capodistrias.

studied in Padua and became a doctor, but he soon turned to politics. From 1797 to 1799 the Ionian Islands were under French control. After their capture by Russia and the Ottoman Empire and the establishment of the Septinsular Republic, Capodistrias was very active in local political life; he took part in the formulation of the constitution of 1803. Supporting the Russian protectorate, he believed that the islands were best off under Russian protection until they could achieve independence. When in 1807 France took control again, Capodistrias left and in 1809 entered the Russian service. By 1812 he had become a close confidant of the tsar, and he attended the Congress of Vienna.

Rights and obligations defended and extended

Although Capodistrias was to show sympathy to concepts of constitutional government and national states, he also favored Russian expansion. For instance, he did not approve of the terms of the Treaty of Bucharest; he thought that Russia should annex Wallachia and Moldavia. He also supported the use of the Russian claim of protection over the Balkan Orthodox to increase political control in the region. His major interest, however, remained Greek affairs. As we will see, he was associated with Greek circles in Russia, and he followed Ottoman events with close interest. He, however, advised a conservative, cautious, and careful policy for his fellow countrymen, since he believed that education and cultural development should precede a struggle for independence.

THE GREEK REVOLUTION

Capodistrias's concern over Greek events directly reflected Russian Balkan interests. Certainly, of all the great powers involved in Eastern affairs, Russia had the closest relationship with the Greeks of the Levant.[6] The strongest link was, of course, the common Orthodox

[6]The section on the initial phases of the revolution in this chapter, pp. 49–65, has been published under the title "Tsarist Russia and Greek Independence," in John T. A. Koumoulides, ed., *Greek Connections: Essays on Culture and Diplomacy* (Notre Dame: University of Notre Dame Press, 1987), pp. 75–101. This material is reprinted here with the kind permission of Notre Dame Press. The most important documentary collection for Russian diplomacy during the time of the Greek revolution is Ministerstvo inostrannykh del SSSR, *Vneshniaia politika Rossii XIX i nachala XX veka: Dokumenty Rossiiskogo ministerstva inostrannykh del* (Moscow: Izdatel'stvo nauka, 1980), series 2, IV–VI (XII–XIV), covering March 1821 to December 1826 (cited hereafter as *VPR*). The documents in Anton von Prokesch-Osten,*Geschichte des Abfalls der Griechen vom Türkischen Reiche im Jahre 1821 und der Gründung des Hellenischen Königreiches*, 6 vols, (Vienna: Carl Gerold's Sohn, 1867), should also be consulted. For a general study of the revolution see Douglas Dakin, *The Greek Struggle for Independence, 1821–1833* (London: B. T. Batsford, Ltd., 1973). Russian policy is discussed in I. S. Dostian, *Rossiia i Balkanskii Vopros* (Moscow: Izdatel'stvo nauka, 1972); A. V. Fadeev, *Rossiia i vostochnyi krizis 20kh godov XIX veka* (Moscow: Izdatel'stvo Akademii nauk SSSR, 1958); and O. B. Shparo, *Osvobozhdenie Gretsii i Rossiia, 1821–1829* (Moscow: Izdatel'stvo mysl', 1965). For the role of the other great powers, see: for Austria, Paul W. Schroeder, *Metternich's Diplomacy at Its Zenith* (Austin: University of Texas Press, 1962); for France, Edouard Driault, *Histoire diplomatique de la Grèce de 1821 à nos jours* (Paris: les Presses universitaires de France, 1925), vol. I on the years 1821 to 1830; for Britain, Charles Webster, *The Foreign Policy of Castlereagh, 1815–1822* (London: G. Bell and Sons, Ltd., 1947), and Harold Temperley, *The Foreign Policy of Canning, 1822–1827* (London: Frank Cass & Co., Ltd., 1966); and for all of the powers, G. L. Arsh, I. S. Dostian, V. I. Sheremet,

faith that it alone among these states shared with the Greek nation. The Patriarchate of Constantinople was, as we have seen, under Greek control; Russian dealings with this institution thus passed through Greek hands.

Russians and Greeks were also brought together by other than religious affiliation. During the eighteenth century, with common land and sea borders, Russia and the Ottoman Empire were drawn into an ever closer relationship. In dealing with the Porte, the Russian diplomats were regularly in touch with Greeks in their role as Ottoman officials, in particular in their functions as interpreters or secretaries. Enjoying the leading political position among the non-Muslim citizens of the empire, Greeks also held certain high offices, the most important of which were the governorships of Wallachia and Moldavia. Thus when Russian diplomats dealt with the affairs of these provinces, the most important of the Balkan regions for them, they negotiated with rulers from Greek families who might or might not be Russian protégés.

Common economic links also joined Russians and Greeks. At the beginning of the nineteenth century Greek merchants dominated the commercial life of the Ottoman Empire; their ships had taken over the carrying trade in Russian grain, and they had the right to fly the Russian flag. As Greek commerce continued to prosper, the colonies of merchants increased; in Russia, Odessa became a center of Greek activity. Because of their prominence in Eastern trade and in the life of the empire, the Russian government appointed Greeks as its consuls throughout the Balkans, but particularly in Greek-inhabited lands.

Such religious, political, and economic ties led often to close personal relations. Phanariot families contributed members to the Russian army and bureaucracy; many married into the Russian aristocracy. It should, however, be noted that despite this situation, Russian officials were primarily in touch with those Greeks who were prominent in Ottoman affairs, either as church officials, members of the bureaucracy, or merchants and bankers, all of whom had their center in Constantinople. Russian statesmen had less knowledge of and fewer links with the Greeks of the Peloponnesus or the mainland.

and V. N. Vinogradov, *Mezhdunarodnye otnosheniia na Balkanakh, 1815–1830 gg.* (Moscow: Izdatel'stvo nauka, 1983). In addition, see the papers published in *Les Relations greco–russes pendant la domination turque et la guerre d'indépendance grecque* (Thessaloniki: Institute for Balkan Studies, 1983), and Eberhard Schütz, *Die europäische Allianzpolitik Alexanders I. und der griechische Unabhängigkeitskampf, 1820–1830* (Wiesbaden: Otto Harrassowitz, 1975).

Another important relationship existed. After the conquest of the Black sea lands the Russian government was eager to populate the region with Christian settlers, often with the aim of replacing the local Muslim inhabitants. Immigration from Europe was strongly encouraged, and special privileges were given to foreign settlers. Greek immigration commenced in the reign of Catherine. After 1812 Greeks also settled in Bessarabia in Kishinev, Khotin, Ismail, Kilia, Reni, and Akkerman, all close to the Ottoman border. This situation was to aid in the initial phases of the preparations for the Greek revolution.

As a great power embarked upon a period of imperial expansion, Russia had already in the eighteenth century shown a great deal of interest in the Greek-inhabited lands. Catherine's Greek Plan and the Russian-instigated rebellion in the Peloponnesus have already been mentioned. The Treaty of Kuchuk Kainardji, of course, affected the Greek political and economic position. At the beginning of the new century the Russian government also became directly involved in Greek events through its occupation of the Ionian Islands. By 1821 it had thus gained a special position in regard to the Greeks, based in particular on its Black Sea commerce, its right of intervention in the Danubian Principalities and the Greek islands, and its general relationships with the Balkan Orthodox.

When this situation is considered, it is easy to understand why Russia became a center of Greek conspiracy and why revolutionary leaders were able to involve so many who were in the Russian service. The most important conspiratorial society, the Philiki Etairia (the Friendly Society), was organized in Odessa in 1814 by three Greek merchants. From its founding the Etairia aimed at gaining official Russian support, and its hopes were high. After all, in the past Russian leaders had talked a great deal about protecting Orthodox Christians; Alexander I was believed to be sympathetic to the Greek cause. In recruiting agents and supporters, the society had no hesitation about using the Russian name freely and encouraging the illusion that the movement enjoyed imperial favor.

Well aware that it needed a leader of European stature, the Etairia in 1817 turned to Capodistrias, the most prominent Greek national in the Russian government. Recognizing the dangers in the situation, Capodistrias rejected the offer and evidently informed the tsar. After his second refusal in 1820 the society turned to Alexander Ipsilanti, a general in the Russian army and an aide-de-camp to the tsar. When he accepted, plans for action were accelerated. The center of the conspiracy was an estate near Kishenev where the Etairia assembled arms and men; money for the rebellion was collected throughout southern Russia. The local governors – General Alexander Fedorovich Langeron, with his headquarters in Odessa, and General Ivan Nikitich Inzov in Bessarabia – were apparently aware of these activities. Exactly what Capodistrias knew or what he told the tsar is difficult to ascertain, but certainly neither Alexander I nor his minister approved of the specific plan for rebellion formulated by the Etairia and its friends at this time.

Although the goal was Greek independence, the Etairia chose the Danubian Principalities as the location of its first action. These provinces were adjacent to the southern Russian lands that served as the headquarters for the organization of the revolt and that had a large Greek population. The commanding position of Phanariot Greeks as governors of Wallachia and Moldavia, and the presence of Greeks in other influential positions, were also significant in this decision. In addition, an agreement was made with the Romanian leader, Tudor Vladimirescu, who in January 1821 commenced an insurrection that had primarily social and economic objectives.[7]

However, most important, despite the previous negative attitude, the Etairia leaders were convinced that Russia would indeed intervene once the revolt started. They expected a violent Ottoman reaction; the resultant atrocities would both stir up Russian sentiments and involve treaty stipulations. Russian armies would then be forced to march. Thus on March 8, 1821, after crossing from Bessarabia into Moldavia, Ipsilanti announced in his proclamation on the Greek uprising: "Act, oh friends, and you will see a Mighty Empire defend our rights."[8] He also addressed an appeal to the tsar, hoping to turn this declaration into a reality.

Despite the expectations of the Greek leaders, the revolution was the wrong rebellion, at the wrong time, and in the wrong place. The Russian government had an Eastern program, which had resulted in the conclusion of the treaties previously mentioned, but it also had a far more important Western policy. At the time of the rebellion,

---

[7]For Vladmirescu's revolt, see the documents in *Revoluţia din 1821 condusă de Tudor Vladimirescu: documente externe* (Bucharest: Editura academiei republicii socialiste România, 1980); the Russian reaction is discussed in Barbara Jelavich, *Russia and the Formation of the Romanian National State* (Cambridge: Cambridge University Press, 1984), pp. 16–31.

[8]Richard Clogg, ed., *The Movement for Greek Independence, 1770–1821* (London: Macmillan, 1976), pp. 201–3. See also Prokesch-Osten, *Geschichte des Abfalls der Griechen*, III, pp. 55–8.

Alexander I was cooperating closely with the rulers of Prussia and Austria to preserve stability and the status quo. In their eyes the chief menace to European peace and tranquility were the revolutionary manifestations that became increasingly evident after 1815. The revolts that occurred in 1820 caused particular alarm among the conservative leaders. In January a rebellion broke out in Spain and another in August in Portugal. In July a similar movement forced King Ferdinand I of the Kingdom of the Two Sicilies to accept a constitution. Meeting in Troppau in October, the representatives of Austria, Russia, and Prussia came to an agreement on their right to intervene should a legitimate government be overthrown by revolutionary action. Assembling again at Laibach (Ljubljana) in January 1821, they approved an Austrian military action in Naples to restore Ferdinand; during the meeting, on March 10, news arrived of a revolt in Turin.

At both Troppau and Laibach Alexander I, working closely with the Austrian chancellor, Clemens von Metternich, enthusiastically supported the actions taken to end the rebellions in the Italian peninsula. Deeply concerned about similar outbreaks throughout Europe, which could have repercussions in Russia, the tsar had come to believe that a revolutionary central committee had been organized that was actively engaged in stirring up revolutions wherever possible. He thus saw a common thread linking all of the movements to one controlling center. When the news of the revolts in the Danubian Principalities reached him at Laibach, his strong reaction could be predicted. After the Vladimirescu uprising, Nesselrode on March 7 sent an instruction to the Russian ambassador at Constantinople, Grigorii Aleksandrovich Stroganov, expressing his disapproval and emphasizing that at Troppau and Laibach the "allies had firmly decided to oppose a common dike against the flood of revolutions which threatens once more to convulse Europe."[9] The reaction to Ipsilanti's action was to be even stronger; the Etairia leader's proclamation calling upon the Greeks to rise up against tyrants and to fight for liberty was not apt to appeal to a conservative ruler bent upon suppressing revolts in other areas. Alexander condemned Ipsilanti's conduct, struck his name from the army list, forbade him from ever returning to Russia, and informed him clearly that "he could not count on any aid, nor even on any mark of interest on our part, as long as he misguided his com-

[9]Nesselrode to Stroganov, no. 1, Laibach, February 23/ March 7, 1821, *VPR*, XII, pp. 36–8.

patriots and led them to inevitable misfortunes."[10] The tsar's reaction was reflected also in a letter written by Capodistrias from Laibach to a close friend:

The emperor has highly disapproved of those [means] which Prince Ipsilanti appears to wish to employ to deliver Greece. At a time when Europe is menaced everywhere by revolutionary explosions, how can one not recognize in that which has broken out in the two principalities the identical effect of the same subversive principles, the same intrigues which attract the calamities of war and a military occupation to one of the peninsulas and in the other – the most dreadful plague yet of demogogic despotism.

If such indeed was "the origin and character" of Ipsilanti's revolt, then, Capodistrias concluded, "all is lost for the unfortunate Greeks."[11]

The attempt to start a revolution in the Principalities was soon to end in a total disaster. Although the Etairia was able to attract about 5,000 men to its side, the Greek movement soon came into conflict with that of Tudor Vladimirescu. Deprived of support from local Romanians as well as from the great powers, Ipsilanti faced certain defeat. The decisive battle was fought at Drăgăşani on June 19; by the end of the month, the last Greek bands had been crushed and Ipsilanti had fled into the Habsburg Empire. At the commencement of the rebellion the Ottoman army had entered the Principalities, where it was to remain for sixteen months.

The defeat of the Etairia did not, of course, mark an end to the revolution. By early April revolts had broken out in other Greek regions, particularly in the Peloponnesus and the islands. Although the Etairia was involved here too, it did not play as important a role in the events. Moreover, since Russia did not have a fleet in the Mediterranean and since its borders were no longer directly adjacent to the centers of rebellion, the Russian diplomats of necessity had to cooperate with other states, in particular France and Britain, both seapowers, in dealing with the affairs of the Greek lands. Henceforth Russian attention centered primarily on events in the Principalities, the threats to Black Sea commerce, and the apparent violation of certain treaty rights, in particular those in regard to the protection of Orthodox Christians. The center of negotiations at this time became Constantinople.

In the Ottoman capital Stroganov, despite his personal sympathy for the Greek cause, had assured the Porte of the Russian dis-

---

[10]Nesselrode circular despatch, Laibach, March 18/30, 1821, ibid., XII, pp. 70–1.
[11]Capodistrias to A. S. Sturdza, private letter, Laibach, March 18/30, 1821, ibid., XII, pp. 72–3.

Map 4. The expansion of Greece, 1821–1919.

approval of revolutionary activity even before precise instructions arrived. Thereafter, he undertook the difficult double task of attempting to reassure Ottoman officials and at the same time urging moderation and caution in suppressing the rebellion. He understood the fears that had been aroused in Constantinople:

Vladimirescu in his proclamations speaks of the sovereignty of the sultan and presents himself uniquely as the rectifier of the wrongs that Wallachia has suffered from the iniquitous administration of the boyars, united with the princes. Ipsilanti on the contrary, with a fatal impudence that has compromised all his nation and extended a veil of mourning over Constantinople, has given the signal for a war of religion and has sworn to die or to exterminate the tyrants which have oppressed Greece for four centuries.[12]

It was also difficult for the Ottoman officials not to suspect a Russian hand in the events. They had reports on the activities of the Etairia in southern Russia and on the enthusiasm with which the news of the revolt was received there. Their suspicions were, of course, encouraged by the British ambassador, Lord Strangford, who used the opportunity to further British interests.

The revolution caught the Ottoman government at a difficult time. Its military forces were deeply engaged in attempting to suppress the rebellion of Ali Pasha. A member of a prominent Albanian family, he had first risen to hold high posts in the Ottoman service, but had subsequently established an independent political base at Janina and had defied the Constantinople authorities. Most Ottoman officials were convinced that the Russian government was using the opportunity to back a Greek revolt. Moreover, in both the Principalities and the Greek lands the rebels had massacred hundreds of Muslim civilians. In the Peloponnesus the Muslim inhabitants had been forced to take refuge in the fortified cities. This combination of Christian revolt, suspicion of Russian intrigue, and the killing of Muslims resulted in a violent reaction, whose manifestations the Ottoman government could not completely control. Throughout the empire Muslims rose against Christians and looted and destroyed church and private property. Pressure was put on the Porte to act decisively in what was rapidly becoming a religious war.

In Constantinople the anger of the government and the public turned in particular against the Phanariot Greeks, who now lost their former posts in the Ottoman administration. Prominent Greeks, including high officials, were accused of treason and executed. As far as relations with Russia were concerned, the most provocative act occurred on Easter eve, April 22, when the eighty-four-year-old Patriarch Grigorios V was hanged at the door of his church by a band of janissaries. Bishops, priests, and other Orthodox Christians in Constantinople died at the same time. The patri-

---

[12]Stroganov to Nesselrode, no. 20, April 10/22, 1821, ibid., XII, pp. 113–16. See also Stroganov to Nesselrode, no. 4, February 10/March 3, 1821, ibid., XII, pp. 23–8.

arch's body, after having been dragged through the streets and eventually dumped in the Bosphorus, was rescued and shipped to Odessa, where it was buried with high honors.

Other actions taken by the Porte similarly increased Russian–Ottoman tension. In their hunt for Greek refugees and arms, Ottoman officials began to search all ships sailing through the Straits, but they took special measures in regard to those flying the Russian flag since these could be of Greek ownership. Moreover, Greek pirate ships, which soon came to control the Aegean, were able to halt food deliveries to Constantinople. To meet their own needs, Ottoman officials required ships passing through the Straits to sell any grain that they might be carrying to government stores. These and other measures affected Russian commerce, and they violated the stipulations of commercial agreements. The Russian government was thus faced with the dilemma that its commerce was being severely restricted by Ottoman attempts to suppress a revolt that the tsar too deplored.

However, it was not economic but religious and humanitarian issues that primarily affected Russian–Ottoman relations. In their negotiations with Ottoman diplomats, the Russian representatives regularly accompanied their denunciation of the revolt with the advice that it be met not only with firmness, but also with justice, moderation, and administrative reform. The initial Russian policy was summarized in the tsar's instruction to Stroganov of April 12: Alexander I would never encourage insurrection, but the Porte should know that the "victims of events" would find in the Russian mission "the assistance always owed to misfortune and even more natural yet when this misfortune falls upon a nation which is united to us by the sacred ties of a common faith."[13] With this emphasis on Orthodoxy, the execution of the patriarch came as a rude shock both to the religious sensibilities of the Russian leaders and to Russian prestige among the Christian people of the East. Stroganov on April 23 delivered a strong protest about the deaths of the patriarch and the bishops, calling particular attention to

the method of their execution, the day chosen for that – a solemn and sacred day for all the rites of the Christian religion, that the Sublime Porte by Article VII of the Treaty of Kainardji *had promised to protect constantly* – these deplorable actions are scarcely proper to win back a population already desperate and fearing a bloody reaction.[14]

[13] Alexander I to Stroganov, Laibach, March 31/April 12, 1821, ibid., XII, pp. 93–4.
[14] Note delivered by Stroganov to the Turkish government, April 11/23, 1821, ibid., XII, pp. 118–19.

Other treaties besides Kuchuk Kainardji had been violated. Although Stroganov had initially accepted the fact that the Ottoman government would have to occupy the Danubian Principalities, he opposed the entrance of an army in May, an action that was carried through without adequate consultation with the Russian embassy. Throughout April, May, and June the Russian government through its ambassador in Constantinople continued to put pressure on the Porte, particularly in regard to those questions on which it felt that it had a legal right to intervene, such as the internal affairs of the Danubian Principalities, the interruption of Black Sea commerce, and the treatment of the Greek Orthodox, who were obviously not being "protected." In his instructions to his representatives at the European courts the tsar continued to condemn the rebellion, but he also denounced the methods used in its suppression. A Russian circular dispatch of July 4 declared:

> The emperor is *fully justified* in demanding that the Turkish government *protect* the exercise of the Christian religion, the persons of its ministers, the inviolability of its temples; that it not at all carry devastation and death into the principalities of Wallachia and Moldavia, and that for the inhabitants of these countries, as for those of the islands of the Archipelago and the rest of Greece, it observes a just and constant distinction between innocence and crime.[15]

As reports of acts of violence against Orthodox Greeks poured into his embassy, Stroganov personally became convinced that his government should take a stronger stand. He believed that the honor of the Russian mission was at stake and that unless Russia acted, its government would appear weak or in complicity with the acts of terror being committed.[16]

The ambassador's increasingly belligerent attitude was paralleled by a modification in the views of Alexander I, who left Laibach in May. At about this time the tsar received word of the killing of the patriarch. Once back in St. Petersburg, away from the influence of Metternich, he began to listen more to the arguments of those who for religious, diplomatic, or humanitarian reasons called for a policy of intervention. In fact, many prominent sections of Russian opinion backed this viewpoint, ranging from the military and imperialist circles, which wished to continue the program of Catherine the Great, through the ardent supporters of Balkan Orthodoxy, to the

[15]Nesselrode to Golovkin, St. Petersburg, June 22/July 4, 1821. Prokesch-Osten, *Geschichte des Abfalls der Griechen*, III, pp. 101–4.
[16]See Stroganov to Nesselrode, no. 35, April 27/May 9, 1821, *VPR*, XII, pp. 132–3, and Stroganov to Nesselrode, no. 50, May 29/June 9, 1821, ibid., XII, pp. 162–5.

liberal left, the future Decembrists, who saw in this revolution a struggle for the liberation of a people whom they identified with the Greeks of their classical education. The Russian nationalists, religious circles of various views, and Philhellene liberals criticized official policy.

Meanwhile, the relationship of Stroganov with the Ottoman officials became even more strained. The Porte now asked for the extradition of Greeks who had fled into Russia, a demand that received a firm refusal. In addition, the Ottoman government not only stopped commercial vessels flying the Russian flag, but also a warship carrying a postal flag that had been sent for the ambassador's use. The crisis between the two states reached its height in July, when Stroganov received an instruction, dated June 28, transmitting to him a strong note to the Porte, but with the authorization to modify its terms if he saw fit.[17] When delivering this message to the Ottoman government on July 18, Stoganov insisted forcefully on the fulfillment of its terms within its eight-day time limit. The document was written by Capodistrias and reflected his views on Eastern affairs; the emphasis was on the protection of Orthodoxy rather than on the suppression of revolution:

> . . . the cause which Russia pleads is a European cause. . . . The Sublime Porte has given Christendom the alternative of asking whether it can remain an unmoved witness of the extermination of a Christian people, whether it can tolerate continual insults to its religion, whether it can acquiesce in the existence of a state which threatens to disturb that peace that Europe has bought at the price of so many sacrifices.[18]

The specific demands included the restoration of damaged Orthodox property; the protection of the Christian religion; an assurance that a distinction would be made between the innocent and the guilty; the reestablishment of internal tranquility and reforms to ensure its maintenance; and the acceptance of Russian cooperation in organizing the internal affairs of the Danubian Principalities. Should the Porte not accept these terms, the note threatened, Russia would find itself obliged to offer the Greek rebels "asylum, because they would be persecuted; protection, because they would be entitled to it; assistance, jointly with the whole of Christendom, because it [Russia] could not surrender its brothers in religion to the mercy of a blind fanaticism."

---

[17]See the two despatches to Stroganov from St. Petersburg on June 16/28, 1821. Prokesch-Osten, *Geschichte des Abfalls der Griechen*, III, pp. 89–95.
[18]Note delivered by Stroganov to the Turkish government, July 6/18, 1821, *VPR*, XII, pp. 203–7.

Of these demands, two – the just treatment of Greeks who were not in rebellion and the recognition of the Russian treaty rights in regard to the domestic affairs of the Principalities – were regarded as most important. None of the terms, however, were accepted within the time limit. On July 27 Stroganov received an oral reply from the Ottoman officials that they had not had time to prepare an answer, but that one would arrive in three days.[19] The ambassador, an adherent of a strong stand, then broke off relations between the states and departed for Odessa as soon as the weather permitted.

The Ottoman failure to comply with the terms of the Russian ultimatum should have been followed by the Russian government's consideration of a military action – if not a declaration of war, at least an occupation of the Danubian Principalities. However, despite the firm tone of the Russian note, Alexander I was not prepared to adopt extreme measures without the assurance of support from the other European powers, in particular his close allies, Austria and Prussia. Although the ultimatum's phrasing had implied that the Russian government spoke in the name of Christendom, it had, of course, no authorization to do so. Nevertheless, efforts had been made to win support for the Russian position in regard to the Orthodox Balkan Christians and the maintenance of treaty stipulations. What Alexander I now sought was the assent of the powers for Russia to assume the role in regard to the Ottoman Empire that Austria had taken in Italy. There, acting as the agent of the Alliance, an Austrian army was suppressing revolutionary activity and aiding in the restoration of the previous political order. Alexander did not, it will be noted, want a European mediation or intervention; he sought instead a mandate to deal with the Porte alone, but he wanted the backing of Christian Europe.

Even before the delivery of the ultimatum, in the dispatch of July 4, the Russian position had been stated and the support of the European courts requested.[20] The emphasis remained on the defense of Orthodoxy, but revolutionary activity would not be condoned. The statement also showed Alexander's deep concern lest the European alliance be endangered:

However, we repeat it in the name of the Emperor, Russia will never act either on the basis of its exclusive interests nor without cooperating with the powers with which the transactions which constitute the guarantee of general peace unite it.

[19]Stroganov to Nesselrode, no. 75, July 15/27, 1821, ibid., XII, pp. 224–6.
[20]Nesselrode to Golovkin, St. Petersburg, June 22/July 4, 1821. Prokesch-Osten, *Geschichte des Abfalls der Griechen*, III, pp. 101–4.

What it [Russia] asks, on the contrary, of these powers is that they inform it without evasion of their intentions, their wishes, and the means which they judge the most proper to assure the prosperity of the East, if the Turkish government . . . itself provokes events which it matters to it the most to avoid.

The Russian army, the document concluded, was ready to march to repel aggression or to aid in the achievement of any plan that the European governments might agree upon:

But, today as previously . . . the Russian armies would march, not to move the frontiers of the Russian Empire forward or to give it a preponderance to which it does not aspire, but to restore peace, to strengthen the equilibrium of Europe . . . and to bring to the countries which compose European Turkey the blessing of a happy and inoffensive political life.

The Russian actions and declarations neither intimidated the Ottoman government nor won the support of the European powers. For Alexander I the reaction of Austria and Britain was of principal significance, but their leaders, Metternich and the British foreign secretary, Lord Castlereagh, were suspicious of the Russian intentions. They feared that, despite all the fine words about the defense of Christianity, Russian policy aimed in fact at the domination of the East, which neither could allow. Meeting in October in Hanover, they agreed upon a common policy. In the future the British government was to refuse all cooperation of the type that Alexander was requesting. Metternich, in contrast, was to appear more accommodating, but he would always make his conditions for support so complicated that the tsar would hesitate to act. At the same time that the two governments were attempting to deter Russia from military action, they pressed the Porte to grant some of the principal Russian demands. Metternich summarized them as, first, the restoration of the churches that had been destroyed; second, a guarantee of the protection of the Ottoman Christians; third, the maintenance of a distinction in the treatment of the guilty and the innocent in the Greek rebellion; and, fourth, the evacuation by the Ottoman army of the Principalities and the restoration of the previous administrative system.[21] These conditions were acceptable to both Britain and Austria.

After the breaking of relations with the Porte and the failure to receive adequate support from any European government, Alexander had to decide whether he dared risk war under these conditions. Certainly, none of his demands had been met. Moreover, after the death of Ali Pasha in January 1822, the Ottoman army was free

[21]Webster, *The Foreign Policy of Castlereagh*, pp. 379–80.

to turn its full strength against the Greek rebels. Reports of atrocities and massacres mounted, with the worst occurring on the island of Chios in April 1822. Within Russia influential circles continued to press for action. Among the diplomats not only Capodistrias and Stroganov[22] urged a militant attitude, but also the ambassadors, Karl Osipovich Pozzo di Borgo in Paris, Khristof Andreevich Lieven in London, and Iurii Aleksandrovich Golovkin in Vienna. The generals, Paul Dmitrievich Kiselev, Aleksei Petrovich Ermolov, and Ivan Ivanovich Dibich, were similarly for war. Alexander I, however, although he listened to varying opinions, remained attached to his European policy, and he continued to regard the Greek revolt as a manifestation of the general revolutionary spirit. In August 1821 he expressed his reservations to Capodistrias about a war with the Ottoman Empire. He feared that "the directing committee of Paris will triumph, and no government will remain standing. It is not in my intentions to let the field free for the enemies of order."[23] In September he told the British ambassador, Sir Charles Bagot, that he agreed with Castlereagh's opinion that a war "would assist the game of the revolutionists in every country in Europe, to whom and to whom alone the late events are to be attributed."[24] This attitude was shared by others, including the minister of finance, D. A. Gurev, and Nesselrode, who had opposed the ultimatum and did not think that war would bring the glorious results that some expected.

Alexander's determination to maintain the European alliance and his fears about a general European revolution led him to continue through the fall and winter of 1821–2 to seek a solution through diplomacy. A military intervention was never excluded, but the tsar continued to shrink from taking such a decisive step without the assurance of at least Austrian support. In February 1822, responding to Metternich's proposals for a settlement of the crisis, he sent Nesselrode's nomination, Dmitrii Pavlovich Tatishchev, as a special envoy to Vienna.[25] At the same time the other courts were informed

---

[22]In September Alexander I wrote to Nesselrode from Italy that he had just spoken with Stroganov. It was possible that, once back in St. Petersburg, the ambassador might advise war. Nesselrode was to make clear to him "the true interests of the European alliance" and the tsar's fixity of purpose. Alexander to Nesselrode, September 12, 1821. A. Nesselrode, ed., *Lettres et papiers du chancelier Comte de Nesselrode*, VI, pp. 124–5.

[23]Capodistrias, *Aperçu de ma carrière publique*, pp. 268–9.

[24]Webster, *The Foreign Policy of Castlereagh*, p. 373.

[25]See the instruction of Alexander to Tatishchev, February 5/17, 1822, *VPR*, XII, pp. 426–8.

of the specific Russian demands, some of which went beyond those of the July ultimatum. As before, the Russian statement lacked precision, but in essence it repeated the earlier proposals: The Russian government wished to act with the Porte and agree on measures that would ensure the Balkan Christians a "happy and peaceful" existence; they were to be guaranteed the free exercise of their religion, security of their persons and property, a just legal system, and a general pacification of their lands.[26]

At the same time that negotiations were proceeding in Vienna, both the Austrian and British governments attempted to persuade the Porte to meet some of the Russian demands, in particular to remove its army from the Principalities. When it became apparent that this pressure was not working, Metternich did make some concessions to the Russian arguments. Although Lieven's discussions with Castlereagh were not so successful, the British government remained willing to accept the four basic Russian demands, as previously formulated by Metternich.

Unable to gain the support of the powers for a Russian war against the Ottoman Empire to be waged in the name of Europe, Alexander in May sent Tatishchev on a second mission to Vienna. In this month the Ottoman Empire commenced the evacuation of the Principalities. Alexander's instructions to Tatishchev reflected his preoccupation with the danger of revolution and his decision to avoid a war:

> I do not wish at all to attack the sovereignty of the Porte. All that I desire is that the system that it adopts allows Russia and its allies to cooperate with it in order to preserve the insurgent provinces from the curse of revolution. This service, as indispensable to Europe and to the Ottoman Empire itself as to our co-religionists, constitutes the true protection that Russia should exercise and assigns to it at the same time its nature and limits.[27]

Thereafter, the Russian government divided its demands into two categories: First, those that dealt with general pacification and specifically Greek matters were to be solved in agreement with the European governments; second, those that concerned the Principalities or Russian treaty rights would be negotiated directly between St. Petersburg and Constantinople.

Alexander's decisions in the spring of 1822 marked the collapse of Capodistrias's plans and the end of his influence on national policy.

---

[26]Instructions to the Russian representatives in Vienna, Berlin, London, and Paris, February 6/18, 1822, ibid., XII, pp. 430–8.
[27]Instruction of Alexander to Tatishchev, May 14/26, 1822, ibid., XII, pp. 507–10.

Throughout the previous months the British and Austrian governments had quite correctly singled him out as the major proponent of a military solution. Metternich consistently made him the chief culprit for the crisis. The British ambassador, Sir Charles Bagot, reported in January 1822: "The labour and intrigues of Count Capo d'Istria to bring on the war are inconceivable . . . and his enormous presumption still makes him think that he can guide the politics of Russia and lead the revolutions of Greece at the same time."[28]

Certainly, of all the high Russian officials, Capodistrias was closest to Greek events and most eager that Russia intervene to stop the massacres. Conservative himself, he always placed his arguments on a basis that would appeal to the tsar, emphasizing the religious ties and the treaty stipulations that, he argued, gave Russia a right to intervene. The Greeks, according to his views, were resisting annihilation and not engaging in revolutionary activity.[29]

In addition, Capodistrias, well aware that Russia could not win the backing of the European governments, consistently favored an independent policy in Eastern affairs. He opposed the appeal for a European mandate, arguing that Russia should not accept any outside mediation or interference in its relations with the Ottoman Empire. The support of other powers should be requested only to gain their assent to Russian demands, which should be formulated on the basis of independent decisions. Capodistrias also pressed for forceful measures, convinced that past experience had demonstrated that moderation and reason would not succeed in Constantinople, where these attributes were looked upon as signs of weakness. Russian prestige, he believed, was being severely damaged by the country's reluctance to adopt a strong policy; Russian treaties were being

[28]Webster, *The Foreign Policy of Castlereagh*, p. 387. Bagot had reported the previous October on Capodistrias's attitude: "He seems to me to be labouring night and day . . . to produce a state of things in which he hopes to find the rest of Europe at the opening of the Spring, if not allied with Russia in a war against the Porte, at least committed to give their sanction to Russia engaging in it single-handed." Ibid., p. 383.

[29]Capodistrias's views are given in the material already cited and in the following documents: Capodistrias to Nikolai, private letter, June 22/July 4, 1821, *VPR*, XII, pp. 192–4; report of Capodistrias to Alexander I, July 29/August 10, 1821, ibid., XII, pp. 242–5; memoir of Capodistrias for Alexander I, August 9/21, 1821, "Second agenda sur les affaires d'Orient," ibid., XII, pp. 256–61; Capodistrias report, October 11/23, 1821, ibid., XII, pp. 327–9; Capodistrias to Lieven, private letter, November 27/December 9, 1821, ibid., XII, pp. 371–6; Capodistrias report for Alexander I, May 1/13, 1822, ibid., XII, pp. 500–3.

violated, and the achievements of three wars and fifty years of diplomacy were being wiped out.

As far as concrete steps were concerned, Capodistrias in the summer of 1821 advised the occupation of the Principalities. In the first months of 1822 he supported the sending of a mission to the European courts, but only with the goal of winning their approval for a Russian military action. When his choice of Stroganov as the special envoy to Vienna was rejected in favor of Tatishchev, he understood that he would henceforth have little influence on Russian policy in regard to Greek affairs. The decision in May not to go to war reduced him to despair. In a letter to Lieven of May 29, 1822, he expressed his bitter disappointment and noted that future dispatches would demonstrate that

all that we have said for a year on the great interests in the East is considered today by the imperial ministry as cancelled [*non avenu*], and that a new era is commencing with a new system. I am not able to be [a part of] either the one or the other. And the emperor agrees. . . . I love above all the good of the service and the glory of the emperor. If it is by the new system which has just been adopted that Russia is able to save its interests in the East and to assure on a solid basis the general peace and the alliance which is the guarantee of it, certainly, I would blame it on my headstrong attitude that I have not been able to understand the arrangements by which that double aim is going to be attained. . . . [I have taken a] resolution to consider myself as dead for the part of the service which is conducted under a system contrary to that which we have followed until the present . . . one man more or less changes nothing as regards the nature and force of circumstances. And it is that force which will prevail. Do not doubt it.[30]

Capodistrias remained in office for a short time, but he did not involve himself in Eastern affairs. In August he left for Switzerland, which was to be his headquarters until he was summoned to Greece in 1828 to be the first president of the modern nation.

Alexander's decision to put the major emphasis in Russian policy on the preservation of the European alliance and the suppression of revolution was shown again at the Congress of Verona, which opened in October 1822. Since that conference dealt primarily with the revolt that had broken out in Spain in 1820 and the plan for a French intervention, the Greek situation received little attention. The subject was dealt with on one day; Tatishchev, who was accompanying the tsar, in a declaration that was inserted in the protocol presented the Russian standpoint. He strongly denied any Russian complicity in the rebellion: "That disastrous revolution" he stated,

[30]Capodistrias to Lieven, private letter, May 17/29, 1822, ibid., XII, 30, pp. 515–16.

"is the work of sects which brought the same calamity on Spain and on Portugal, which provoked it last year in Italy, and which are ready to bring it about again wherever it seems to them that there is the slightest hope of success."[31] Russia did, however, have legitimate grounds for complaint about the actions of the Porte. After reiterating the accusations made over the past months, Tatishchev gave three conditions for the Russian renewal of relations with the Ottoman Empire: (1) the pacification of Greece, to be carried out either by negotiation between the powers and the Ottoman government or by a series of acts showing that the Porte respected "a religion placed by the letter of treaties under the protection of Russia,"[32] (2) the complete evacuation of the Principalities and the naming of new princes, and (3) a repeal of the measures that hindered commerce and free navigation on the Black Sea.

Meanwhile, however, a change had occurred in the British leadership that was to have a strong influence on negotiations over Greece. In August 1822 Castlereagh committed suicide and was followed by George Canning as foreign secretary. Canning, like his predecessor, was not in favor of an active British intervention, and he too was concerned about possible Russian advances at Ottoman expense. He did, however, allow some measures that were to the Greek advantage. In March 1823 he recognized the Greek rebels as belligerents, a move taken in the interest of British commerce, which was suffering from pirate attacks. In 1824, in another action favorable to the revolution, the British government did not interfere when a loan was raised in London. Although there was much corruption in its administration, it did bring British subjects and Greek rebels together. Canning was also strongly influenced by pressure from British Philhellenes, who now saw in the modern Greeks the heroes of their classical education. When the enormously popular romantic poet Byron died at Missolonghi in 1824, this intense concern and passionate interest were given an additional impetus.

Sentiment aside, pragmatic British concerns over the Russian danger to Ottoman integrity remained strong. The British statesmen, like the Ottoman and Austrian, at first had seen a Russian hand in the rebellion. Even after these fears subsided, the suspicion remained that the Russian government was attempting to provoke a

---

[31] Russian declaration at the Congress of Verona, November 9, 1822. Prokesch-Osten, *Geschichte des Abfalls der Griechen*, III, pp. 437–50.

[32] Ibid., p. 440. See also Nesselrode note to Metternich, Montmorency, Wellington, and Bernsdorff, Vienna, September 14/26, 1822, *VPR*, XII, pp. 581–3.

war that, at best, would result in the establishment of a Greece that would be under a Russian control similar to that in the Principalities, or, at worst, the complete destruction of the Ottoman Empire. With these views in mind, a very careful watch was maintained over Russian activities. The British government wanted a negotiated settlement both of the Ottoman and Russian specific differences and of the Greek question. The British ambassador, Lord Strangford, was given instructions to influence the Porte to agree to the Russian conditions and to restore diplomatic relations. A wider settlement could then be discussed in Constantinople. There Britain would have more influence, and the continental alliance, and thus Russia, would have less.

The entire course of negotiations over Greece was made more uncertain with the deterioration of conditions in that country. Given a choice, the great powers in 1821 would have welcomed a swift Ottoman suppression of the revolt, followed by a period of reform in the Greek lands. However, although some successes were indeed achieved, the Ottoman army could not win a decisive victory. With only a weak navy, and dependent on an army that had to maintain supply lines over a difficult terrain, the Ottoman government was unable to defeat the rebel groups who were operating in familiar territory and using guerrilla tactics.

The Greek forces too were facing immense problems. The rebellion was carried on by armed bands under local leaders in actions that lacked a strong central organization. Moreover, bitter conflicts had developed among the various factions, in particular among the representatives of the Greeks of the islands, Constantinople, and the mainland. The Ottoman armies were indeed stopped, but a condition of civil war weakened the Greek forces. By the end of 1824 a military stalemate existed: Neither side could expect a full victory. Unable to control the situation, the sultan at this time called in his vassal, Mehmet Ali of Egypt, an extremely ambitious and independent leader who had at his service an effective army and navy. The entrance of the Egyptian troops into the conflict and their subsequent victories, including the occupation of Crete and the Peloponnesus, changed the entire strategic outlook in the Mediterranean and caused the British, French, and Russian governments to reassess their positions on the Greek revolt.

The Russian leadership in particular was in a difficult situation. A strong stand had been taken in 1821 and relations had been broken with Constantinople. Since that time the Ottoman government had continued military actions against the Greeks, soldiers and civilians alike, and it had adopted measures that, in the Russian view, violated the previous treaties. At the same time, Alexander I continued to denounce the revolutionary nature of the Greek events. Repeated Russian declarations emphasized, on the one hand, that Russia could not accept an Ottoman suppression of the rebellion that would result in an extermination of the Greek population, and, on the other hand, that it could not condone Greece falling into the hands of men "all of whose efforts tend only to the subversion of the social order."[33] These apparently conflicting positions were difficult to reconcile.

Given the decision not to go to war in 1821, the Russian government was, in fact, left with few diplomatic options. The ideal solution remained, as before, the application of the congress system to the Greek crisis: The five great powers would meet, decide on a settlement for Greece, and mandate the enforcement to Russia. By using either the threat of war or actual war, the Russian government could then secure both satisfaction for its individual claims against the Porte and settle the Greek question. It was, however, recognized that the political organization and the territorial extent of the future Greek state would have to be determined by the powers acting together, since their interests were so closely tied to the settlement.

Unfortunately for Russian policy, effective European cooperation could not be obtained. Britain had already withdrawn from the continental alliance system and was not participating in the congresses; it certainly did not want a conference on the Greek question. Instead it urged a renewal of Russian–Turkish relations, which would allow Constantinople to become the center of future negotiations on the major issues separating the two states. Holding the predominant naval power in the Mediterranean and with a strong influence within the Ottoman government, British leaders felt that their interests could be best defended in this manner. The continental powers similarly were not enthusiastic about cooperative action. Alexander I preferred to work with the Habsburg Empire, but Metternich continued to hold a negative attitude toward active intervention in Eastern affairs. Prussia generally followed the lead of Vienna in Balkan matters, but it was careful also to conciliate St. Petersburg. France, with interests in Egypt and the Mediterranean, did not wish to antagonize the Ottoman Empire over Greek issues. Nevertheless, the four continental governments were willing to accept some kind

---

[33]Nesselrode instruction to Alopeus, Pozzo di Borgo, and Tatishchev, April 4/16, 1825, ibid., XIV, pp. 126–31.

of collective mediation. They were in favor of conciliation and negotiation, but they were very suspicious about the Russian insistence on measures of enforcement to back up any decisions reached. It was clear to the powers that if force were employed, it would be the Russian army that would march. No government trusted the Russian motives.

For their part, the Russian leaders recognized these fears. In declarations over the next years they repeatedly denied that they sought any additional special privileges or territorial acquisitions. They placed an emphasis on the need to correct treaty violations and to secure the pacification of Greece, a condition essential for stable Ottoman–Russian relations. On the basis of past experience they did not think that the Porte would cede on any issue unless the threat of force was implicit. In a despatch of 1827, Nesselrode expressed an opinion widely held not only in Russia, but also in other Western courts: "It is as a result of a political and religious principle that Orientals come to terms only when it is absolutely necessary, but, in return, the day when that necessity appears, the transaction is carried out."[34]

Throughout this crisis the Russian government acknowledged that it could not determine a Greek settlement unilaterally. Not only were other states involved, but it was not certain that Russia alone could compel the Greek rebels to accept its terms for a settlement, which were, of course, autonomy and not the independence that was the goal of the revolution. A conference of the powers and a joint mediation would be an advantage here too. If the European states adopted a single program and agreed that force could be used, then both the Greek leaders and the Porte would see the necessity of compliance. It should be strongly emphasized that the European intervention was to involve only those matters that in Russian eyes had a European significance, that is, the pacification of Greece and some aspects of the problem of the interruption of trade caused by the events. Questions concerning treaty relations between Russia and the Porte were still reserved for bilateral negotiation.

The major Russian initiative toward a settlement of the Greek crisis was contained in a memoir of January 21, 1824.[35] It recommended that three Greek principalities be organized: The first, in eastern Greece, would be composed of Thessaly, Boeotia, and Attica;

[34]Nesselrode to Lieven, St. Petersburg, January 9/21, 1827, Prokesch-Osten, *Geschichte des Abfalls der Griechen*, V, pp. 9–18.
[35]Memoir to the Austrian, British, Prussian, and French governments on the pacification of Greece, January 9/21, 1824, *VPR*, XIII, pp. 308–14.

the second, of western Greece, Epirus, Etolia, and Akarnania; and the third, of the Peloponnesus and perhaps Crete. The political arrangements would be similar to those of the Danubian Principalities: Each section would be autonomous, under the suzerainty of the Porte, but with the guarantee of the allied courts.

The Russian proposal was discussed at an ambassadors' conference in St. Petersburg in June 1824.[36] The British representative, although without instructions, attended, an action for which he was later rebuked. The two sessions were disappointing to the Russian hosts; the participants did not have the necessary authority to allow them to act decisively, nor did they agree with the Russian program.

Not only could Russia not gain support from the continental states, but also the British opposition to a great-power settlement became even stronger. On May 31, 1824, the Paris newspaper *Constitutionnel* published the Russian project. The proposals elicited an immediate and violent response in the Greek camp. The Greek aim of independence had not been accepted, and there had been no attempt to consult with Greek representatives. Fearing, as did the great powers, that the Russian intent was to place Greece in a position of subjection to Russia, similar to the condition of the Danubian Principalities, the Greeks turned to Britain. In July 1825 in the so-called Act of Submission, a majority of the revolutionary groups asked for British protection.[37] Thereafter the British government could give this Greek action as a reason not to participate in any further sessions of the St. Petersburg conference, at least until a Russian ambassador returned to Constantinople.

Although the Russian government recognized that it could not secure British cooperation, it still hoped that it could gain the consent of the continental states to another formal meeting to discuss a Greek settlement based on the Russian memoir.[38] In the negotiations the chief point of conflict remained the Russian insistence on the necessity of accepting the fact that coercive measures might have to be used should either the Porte or the Greek rebels refuse to accept a settlement decided upon by the powers. The Russian government proposed that if the Ottoman government remained adamant, the powers should suspend diplomatic relations;

---

[36]Lebzeltern report on the conference, St. Petersburg, June 21/July 3, 1824, Prokesch-Osten, *Geschichte des Abfalls der Griechen*, IV, pp. 84–90.
[37]See Dakin, *The Greek Struggle for Independence*, pp. 161–6.
[38]Nesselrode instruction to Pozzo di Borgo and Alopeus, December 18/30, 1824, *VPR*, XIII, pp. 657–8.

if the Greeks returned a negative answer, they should be informed that the allied courts would not protect them.[39]

In March 1825 another official session of the St. Petersburg conference was held.[40] Attended by representatives from France, Prussia, Austria, and Russia, it again resulted in an unsatisfactory conclusion that left the Russian government with a feeling of "regret and sorrow." It was now clear that a collective démarche in Constantinople was not possible. Nesselrode, in a circular of April 16, expressed his government's dilemma:[41] Russia faced the alternatives of either declaring war or, if remaining at peace, of sacrificing the four years of moderate policy that had been adopted in deference to the European alliance. The rights acquired in the treaties were also at stake. In May the meetings of the conference were suspended.

By August, after further negotiations, the Russian government decided not to reopen the St. Petersburg conference soon. Alexander I was left with a feeling of frustration and bitterness, particularly against Austria, at this failure to secure a collective action. A circular despatch justifying this decision and reflecting Russian discontent stated that only Prussia had adopted a satisfactory position.[42] The other states had refused to meet the basic questions at issue, that is, that if the powers did not act, they would face either the destruction of the Greeks or their administration by a "democratic and revolutionary authority." Moreover, the Russian position won over the last half century was endangered:

> The emperor in fact cannot allow that Russia, while not ceasing to give proof of the most pure intentions, be exposed to unjust suspicions, nor that it become of its own free will the instrument of the ruin of an influence that it has legitimately acquired and of which the original titles are before the eyes of the universe. The interests of the empire further do not permit our august master to change the bases of his former relations with Turkey in a manner to place in a perpetual state of suffrance its rights, its treaties and the commerce of its meridional provinces.[43]

Although the attempt to secure a collective intervention failed, Strangford had meanwhile been able to gain concessions on com-

[39]Note to the diplomatic representatives of Austria, Prussia, and France in St. Petersburg, February 12/24, 1825, ibid., XIV, pp. 63–7.
[40]Protocol of the conference of the plenipotentiaries of Russia, Austria, Prussia, and France, St. Petersburg, March 1/13, 1825, ibid., XIV, pp. 82–5.
[41]Nesselrode to Alopeus, Pozzo di Borgo, and Tatishchev, April 4/16, 1825, ibid., XIV, pp. 126–31.
[42]Nesselrode to Tatishchev, Alopeus, and Pozzo di Borgo, *réservé*, August 6/18. Ibid., XIV, pp. 229–34.
[43]Ibid., XIV, p. 232.

mercial questions from the Porte that were sufficient to allow the Russian government to send Matvei Iakovlevich Minciaky (Minchaki) with the title of commercial attaché to Constantinople in February 1824. The British ambassador continued to have difficulties in his discussions with the Ottoman officials concerning Greece and the Principalities. In June, however, he felt that he had secured the fulfillment of the basic Russian conditions after the Porte agreed to the reduction of its military force in the Principalities to the level preceding 1821.[44] As a result, Russia did indeed officially reestablish diplomatic relations. Alexander Ivanovich Ribeaupierre (Ribop'er) was named as ambassador, but his departure was delayed.[45] Since at this time the Russian government still hoped for a collective action in Constantinople, Minciaky, appointed chargé d'affaires, was instructed to attempt to secure the agreement of the Porte to a friendly intervention by the four continental powers. The envoy was also to continue to negotiate on the unsettled problems of the Principalities and Serbia.[46]

Minciaky, a man of Greek background and interests, was not optimistic about the chances of successful negotiations with the Porte: Its armies had won victories, and it could count on the support of Mehmet Ali. Minciaky believed that only an armed intervention would lead to a settlement of the Greek question.[47] The conferences had only shown that the other powers did not have similar interests. Instead, in Eastern affairs, Britain, Austria, and the Ottoman Empire were joined in a natural alliance against Russia in order

> to prevent a rupture, to diminish the consideration and influence of Russia, to destroy its moral force which rests on public opinion, to break the links of a reciprocal attachment that religious similarity have formed for centuries between Russia and the Greeks, to paralyze the legitimate protection that it exercises over the Wallachians and Moldavians, and to bring about their ruin by a patience without limits. . . .[48]

Although relations had been resumed with the Porte, the general Russian position in the Near East, in particular as regards the Greek lands, had in fact deteriorated. Russian influence there had virtually disappeared. One of the great difficulties faced by the Russian

---

[44]Strangford to Nesselrode, Constantinople, June 29, 1824, Prokesch-Osten, *Geschichte des Abfalls der Griechen*, IV, pp. 105–14.

[45]Nesselrode to Said, St. Petersburg, August 25, 1824, ibid., IV, pp. 117–18.

[46]Nesselrode to Minciaky, August 16/28, 1824, *VPR*, XIII, pp. 587–94.

[47]Minciaky to Nesselrode, no. 28 secret, June 8/20, 1825, ibid., XIV, pp. 190–4.

[48]Ibid., XIV, p. 191.

leaders in this crisis was the fact that they really did not know what was going on in the very areas they were attempting to protect. In April 1825, Nesselrode sent an appeal to Minciaky requesting information on Greece and containing a rather amazing statement for a power that did claim to have the right to settle Greek affairs:

We do not possess any information worthy of trust either on the true forces of the insurrection in Greece, or on the extent of its resources, or on the character of the men who govern it, or on the general disposition of the mass of the people, or on the ways to make understood and appreciated there the overtures of peace, or even on the individuals who could support us with the most zeal and effectiveness in the accomplishment of that benevolent enterprise.[49]

In contrast to Russia, which had only a consul in Zante and Minciaky in Constantinople, Britain, France, and Austria all had important sources of information.

In December 1825 Alexander I died and was succeeded by Nicholas I, a man of a much more decisive character. Since the succession was in question, an interregnum offered the opportunity for a rebellion – the Decembrist revolt. The program of this movement, like that of most of the Balkan conspiracies, including the Greek revolution, called for the introduction of constitutional government. Although at this time Russia acquired a tsar with more determination and will than his predecessor, he was to have, if anything, stronger views on the dangers of revolutionary agitation.

Meanwhile, the situation in the Greek lands had declined during 1825. In February Mehmet Ali's son Ibrahim, after occupying Crete, landed with an army in the Peloponnesus. Reports circulated that he intended to keep the area, remove the Greeks, and colonize it with Egyptians. Ibrahim's actions, together with other aspects of the Greek crisis, had implications damaging to both Russia and Britain, which, despite the previous break in their negotiations, found that they needed each other. Canning's preferred policy was to compel the Porte to make concessions and to accept British mediation. Should this goal not be reached, he was willing to cooperate with Russia, an action that would also prevent the tsar from acting alone and weaken the diplomatic ties between St. Petersburg and Vienna. Negotiations between Canning and the Russian ambassador, Lieven, commenced even before the death of Alexander I.

Nicholas I at the beginning of his reign inaugurated a period of successful and forceful diplomacy. Like the British, the Russian diplomats saw advantages in mutual cooperation. The attempt to

[49]Nesselrode to Minciaky, *réservé*, April 4/16, 1825, ibid., XIV, pp. 143–9.

secure a united European intervention had failed; the Russian government was aware that it could not act in total isolation in Eastern affairs. Association with the strongest sea power would allow it to exert greater pressure on the Porte not only concerning the Greek revolt, but also on other matters at issue.

The accession of the new tsar also provided the opportunity for a British initiative.[50] Using the rumors concerning Egyptian intentions as the justification, Canning sent the Duke of Wellington to St. Petersburg at the head of a mission to attend the coronation. The British government, which had previously opposed the use of force in the Greek question, was now willing to consider a limited naval action against Ibrahim designed to cut communications between Egypt and Greece. It was hoped that this step, which would make a complete Ottoman victory impossible, would lead to negotiations toward the establishment of an autonomous Greek state. Once in the Russian capital Wellington proved to be less than an astute negotiator, and he allowed the Russian diplomats to guide the discussions. He also appears not to have understood the implication of the terms that he accepted.

The Convention of St. Petersburg, signed on April 4, 1826 by Nesselrode, Wellington, and Lieven, who came to St. Petersburg for the occasion,[51] concerned Greece only: The two powers were to mediate with the objective of establishing an autonomous, tribute-paying state with full control over its own internal affairs. Many important details, including the territorial limits of the nation, were to be determined later. The question of enforcement was left very vague. It was agreed that should the attempts at mediation fail, both signators would continue to regard the basis of the settlement for Greece to be as stated in the Protocol, but they would seek to put it into effect "by their intervention, be it in common or separately, between the Porte and the Greeks, and they will seize all favorable opportunities to make their influence felt with the two parties in order to bring about that same reconcilation on the agreed basis." The phrase "in common or separately" was to be used by Russian diplomats later to justify unilateral actions.

In another section, and one that was to limit future Russian gains, both signators accepted a self-denying restriction:

---

[50]Nesselrode to Minciaky, March 5/17, 1826, ibid., XIV, pp. 422–5.
[51]Russian–British Protocol on Greece, St. Petersburg, March 23/April 4, 1826, ibid., XIV, pp. 449–50.

. . . in this same arrangement H.I.M. and H.M. [His Britannic Majesty] will not seek, neither the one nor the other, any augmentation of territory, any exclusive influence, any advantage of commerce for their subjects that those of any other nation cannot equally obtain.

The Convention concluded with an invitation to the other powers to adhere to the agreement. In a circular despatch, Nesselrode argued that Russia and Britain were the states best suited to arrange matters in the Levant. Their actions paralleled the Russian, Prussian, and Austrian agreement on the Italian problems and the Russian and French cooperation in regard to Spain; Russia had no wish to weaken the bonds that joined it to the continental powers with which it had worked for ten years.[52]

The terms of the Convention were regarded as a victory in St. Petersburg. The agreement provided for cooperation with Britain, and it did not exclude a Russian use of coercion. The background was thus in place for the next steps in Russian diplomacy: the delivery of an ultimatum to the Porte and, in 1828, involvement in a war with the danger of a British intervention lessened. The Convention also marked a diplomatic revolution. In the Greek question Russia was now to stand with Britain, and soon France, and be in opposition to the Habsburg Empire, with which it had been on close terms during Alexander's reign. Metternich was sharply critical, denouncing the entire transaction in harsh words: "All in this system is absurd, and of an incontestable absurdity."[53]

THE RUSSO-TURKISH WAR

The new firmness in Russian policy was demonstrated not only in the rapprochement with Britain, but also in the vigor shown in addressing those problems closest to Russian interests in the Near East, in particular the implementation of the past treaties. The Russian government now directed its attention to events in the Principalities and Serbia, and here cooperation with Britain, or with any other power, was not considered. Treaty violations were to be corrected through bilateral Russian–Turkish negotiations exclusively.

The status of the Principalities, because of their central geographic position, remained of chief concern. The Russian govern-

---

[52]Nesselrode to Alopeus, Pozzo di Borgo, and Tatishchev, March 30/April 1, 1826, ibid., XIV, pp. 459–62.
[53]Quoted in Temperley, *The Foreign Policy of Canning*, p. 393.

ment was not satisfied that all of the Ottoman military forces had left the region, and it was felt that the agreements regarding the nomination of the princes had been violated. Again, with no representatives in Bucharest or Jassy after the breaking of the diplomatic relations with the Porte in 1821, it did not have adequate information on local affairs. The situation there was in fact changing to the advantage of the Romanian population.

Conditions in the Principalities during the first year after the revolution had indeed been difficult. An Ottoman army was in occupation; most of the units remained for sixteen months, with the cost of their upkeep borne by the local inhabitants. However, on the positive side, the Ottoman attitude toward the Phanariots and to their predominant position in the Principalities had changed sharply. Using this favorable opportunity to get rid of the Greek influence, two delegations of Romanian boyars, one each from Moldavia and Wallachia, went to Constantinople to request the appointment of native governors and an administration under local control. Agreeing to these proposals, the Porte in July 1822 named two members of the delegations to the supreme position: Ioan Sturdza for Moldavia and Grigore Ghica for Wallachia. This action, although favorable to Romanian interests, was denounced by the Russian government. It had not been consulted in accordance with the treaties, and it thus refused to accept the nominations. Despite the advantages for the Romanian population in the removal of Phanariot control, the Russian diplomats added this action to their list of charges against the Ottoman Empire.

The Russian officials also regarded the situation in Serbia as unsatisfactory, although they paid less attention to this province than to the Principalities or the Greek lands. Without a consul in Belgrade, they also lacked information on events there. Moreover, after 1815 the Porte made an effort to secure peaceful conditions in Serbia so that Russia would have no excuse for interference. Prince Miloš and his supporters, however, wanted not only the fulfillment of the concessions already granted, but further steps toward full autonomy. Miloš also wished the position of prince to be recognized as hereditary in the Obrenović family. He was aware that if he expected to secure further advances, he would need the support of a great power and that Russia was the only possible choice.

Meanwhile, in Constantinople the Russian representatives did take some steps to the Serbian advantage. In August 1815 Nesselrode instructed Italinskii to point out to the Ottoman government that the signs of unrest apparent in Serbia were not caused by Russia, but by the actions of the Ottoman administrators and their failure to carry out previous promises. The ambassador was to discuss the situation and to argue that the prompt pacification of Serbia was "the most certain means of avoiding in the future awkward (*fâcheuses*) discussions on the deviations from the Treaty of Bucharest committed by the Porte in regard to the Serbs at a time when Russia could not be concerned with maintaining the stipulations drawn up in their favor."[54] In the next years the Russian representatives were instructed to maintain good relations with the Porte, but to insist on the observance of the treaties. Frequent warnings were delivered about the failure to fulfill the provisions of Article VIII.[55]

In April 1820 Miloš sent a delegation to Constantinople not only to negotiate on the basis of Article VIII, but also to attempt to gain additional privileges. He was particularly interested in securing full autonomy, fixing the amount of the tribute, and extending Serbian administration to the six districts that had been included in the Serbian territory before 1812 but that were at the time under direct Ottoman rule. A second delegation followed with further requests, such as the recognition of Miloš as hereditary prince, but without the issue of the enlarged territory. This mission soon ran into major problems. When it was in Constantinople, the Greek revolt commenced. Since the Porte was convinced that the Serbs were involved in a general conspiracy, it broke off the negotiations, removed the delegates from the patriarch's residence, where they were staying, and put them under arrest in the palace.

Throughout the initial phase of the Greek crisis, even when its relations with the Porte were broken, the Russian government put strong pressure on the Serbian leadership to do absolutely nothing. As we have seen, it did not want a Balkan rising. Miloš was warned not to raise any new claims and to be patient; the Serbian representatives should show deference to the Porte. As Nesselrode advised, "It is in giving such gages of respect and devotion to the suzerain power and in showing an equal confidence in the advice of

[54]Nesselrode to Italinskii, Paris, August 4/16, 1815, *VPR*, VIII, pp. 459–60.
[55]See Italinskii to Nesselrode, no. 117, Constantinople, November 17/29, 1815, ibid., IX, pp. 11–12. Stroganov memorandum to the Turkish government, December 2/14, 1816, ibid., X, pp. 323–31; Stroganov memorandum to the Ottoman foreign minister, January 23/February 4, 1817, ibid., IX, pp. 419–28; Stroganov to the Turkish government, March 12/24, 1817, ibid., IX, pp. 490–1; Stroganov note to the Turkish government, September 15/27, 1817, ibid., IX, pp. 674–6.

the protecting power" that the prince could fulfill his proper role at the time.[56]

Once diplomatic relations were reestablished, the Russian government, pleased with Miloš conduct, intervened with the Porte in the Serbian interest. The Serbian delegates were still under arrest. Minciaky was instructed to urge the Ottoman ministers to reward Serbian fidelity with the granting of all the privileges guaranteed by the Treaty of Bucharest.[57] He was also to warn them of the danger of further alienating the Serbs. Such actions would encourage the revolutionary elements, and they might follow Greece into rebellion. At the same time, Minciaky was to caution the Serbian representatives about the dangers of revolt and to advise them to remain faithful to the Porte; "that fidelity alone can assure it [the nation] the special protection of the emperor and sooner or later win it the most valuable advantages, while a revolt would only draw upon the entire nation unfailing misfortunes and have it abandoned forever by Russia."[58]

Minciaky personally opposed an intervention with the Porte in favor of the Serbs, since he felt that such an action would arouse suspicions of Serbian–Russian collaboration.[59] His main efforts, reflecting his personal concerns, were directed toward the Greek question. He certainly did not succeed in moderating the Ottoman attitude. When the Ottoman foreign minister spoke with the Serbian delegates, he accused them of looking abroad for aid when they should see in the sultan their "only and unique" protector. The Ottoman position remained that it "would never permit strangers to interfere in the affairs of the empire" and that it would defend its frontier "to the last drop of blood." If the Serbian government showed any opposition, an Ottoman army would be sent against it.[60]

In February 1826 Nesselrode drew up a memorandum for the tsar that is significant because it outlined general Russian policy and foreshadowed the decisions regarding the Ottoman Empire implemented in 1829.[61] The document basically recommended a change of course in Eastern affairs. Hitherto Russia had avoided unilateral action or the use of force. Cooperation with other powers had been

[56]Nesselrode to Minciaky, May 17/29, 1823, ibid., XIII, pp. 113–15. See also Nesselrode to Pini, secret, August 4/16, 1822, ibid., XII, pp. 565–6.
[57]Nesselrode to Minciaky, no. 6, April 4/16, 1825, ibid., XIV, pp. 153–4.
[58]Ibid., XIV, p. 154.
[59]Minciaky to Nesselrode, no. 14, March 22/April 3, 1825, ibid., XIV, pp. 110–11.
[60]Minciaky to Nesselrode, no. 48, Buyukdere, July 14/26, 1825, ibid., XIV, pp. 218–21.
[61]Nesselrode memorandum for Nicholas I, February 16/28, 1826, ibid., XIV, pp. 393–400.

preferred. The failure of this policy, Nesselrode argued, was shown in the continuance of the problems relating to the Principalities, Serbia, and Greece. Should coercive measures be adopted, he did not think that Russia had to fear an intervention by a single European power or a coalition as long as only limited goals were pursued. Thus the destruction of the Ottoman Empire was not to be a Russian objective; such a result could be achieved only with the cooperation of other powers, but all opposed it. The possession of Constantinople, the great territorial prize, involved similar considerations. Since Russia could not hope to win the city for itself, Nesselrode asked: "Of all the powers that can occupy the Bosphorus and possess Constantinople, is not the Porte the one from which Russia will always have the most means of assuring deference?" The Russian government should thus concentrate on making certain that the Porte would never again violate its treaties with Russia and that it should

demand that it be surrounded by consideration and respect at Constantinople, that it make a noble and constant usage of its rights of protection in regard to the countries in favor of which they have been stipulated, that the way be found to assure Greece of a prosperous existence and a perfect commercial liberty, that finally a prompt and complete transaction end forever the negotiations that it [Russia] has carried on with the Porte since 1816, and bring to an end the causes of discord and war that such questions never cease to present.[62]

Thus by 1826 Nesselrode had come to support the use of force, an alternative that he had argued against in 1821. However, although he felt that Russia was fully justified in using coercion, he advised that a last démarche be attempted.

A course of action in conformity with the Nesslerode recommendations was adopted at the time that Wellington was in St. Petersburg.[63] The text of an ultimatum to the Ottoman Empire was drawn up and then shown to the British delegate. He was not, however, informed when it was sent on March 17. The document, dated April 5, contained three main demands: The Principalities were to be returned to the conditions existing prior to the 1821 revolt; the imprisoned Serbian deputies were to be released, and negotiations were to be conducted on the basis of Article VIII; and Ottoman plenipotentiaries were to be nominated who would meet with Russian representatives someplace on their common border to settle the

[62]Ibid., XIV, p. 398.
[63]Nesselrode to Minciaky, March 5/17, 1826, ibid., XIV, pp. 411–17.

other questions in dispute. The ultimatum had a six-week time limit.[64]

Despite their nature and manner of delivery the Ottoman government had little choice but to accept these demands. The ultimatum arrived during a period of domestic chaos in Constantinople. In June 1826, recognizing the disastrous state of the Ottoman military, Mahmud II abolished the janissary corps, previously the main strength of the army but by this time a political danger. For a period the state would be without an adequate military defense. Under these circumstances, the Porte accepted the terms of the ultimatum and sent a delegation to the border city of Akkerman. There it received the text of the Russian proposals; they were to be accepted as they stood, with changes allowed only in the wording. It was made clear that a refusal would bring a Russian declaration of war. Although the Ottoman delegates attempted to use delaying tactics, the Porte was in no position to reject the Russian conditions. Since the terms of the Convention of Akkerman, concluded on October 7, 1826, defined Russian relations with the Principalities and Serbia until the Crimean War, a review of its text deserves particular attention.[65]

The main body of the Convention provided for a settlement of the issues that involved Russia and the Ottoman Empire exclusively. Here the contention of the Russian government that all it desired was a confirmation of what it had already been granted in other treaties and special conventions was indeed confirmed. The agreement made no mention of Greek affairs. The terms of the Treaty of Bucharest were reconfirmed; questions in regard to the Danubian and Asiatic frontiers were settled; the previously granted privileges of Moldavia, Wallachia, and Serbia were acknowledged; and the disputes concerning commerce and navigation were resolved. The most significant portions of the agreement, however, were the two Separate Acts that greatly widened Russian rights, in particular in regard to the Principalities.

The Separate Act for Moldavia and Wallachia defined more precisely changes to be made in their internal administration. The princes were henceforth to be elected from among the Romanian

---

[64]Minciaky to the Turkish government, March 24/April 5, 1826, ibid., XIV, pp. 451–3. On the negotiations see Nesselrode memorandum to Vorontsev and Ribeaupierre, June 1/13, 1826, ibid., XIV, pp. 500–2; Nesselrode to Minciaky, Moscow, August 15/27, 1826, ibid., XIV, pp. 576–9; Nesselrode to Vorontsev and Ribeaupierre, Moscow, September 13/25, 1826, ibid., XIV, pp. 591–5.

[65]The texts of the Convention of Akkerman and the Separate Acts are printed in Hertslet, *Map of Europe*, II, pp. 747–59.

boyars by the traditional councils, or divans, composed of the most influential men; their nomination had to be approved by both the Russian and Ottoman governments. The Convention also designated the terms of office and conditions of tenure for the princes. For the future the most important section was the one that dealt with administrative reform. Citing the injury that had been caused to the country by the previous disorders, the princes and the divans were directed "to take the necessary measures to improve the condition of the Principalities confided to their care, and those measures shall form the subject of a general regulation for each province, which shall be put into immediate execution."[66]

The Separate Act for Serbia was shorter and simpler. Nevertheless, it marked an advance in that not only was the Porte to fulfill the stipulations of Article VIII, but it was to negotiate on other Serbian demands. The Russian government was also to be informed of the progress of the discussions and to be given a copy of the final agreements. In a memorandum interpreting the Convention, Nesselrode commented that the conditions, if executed,

should set limits to the desires of the Serbs and recompense their submission to the Porte, as well as their docility in following the councils of Russia. They have placed their fate in the hands of their august protector, and their waiting will not be at all in vain.[67]

Throughout 1826, while conducting separate negotiations with the Porte, the Russian government continued the discussions with the other powers over the Greek question. The Convention of St. Petersburg ensured British cooperation, but the Russian statesmen preferred a wider participation.[68] The March agreement, it will be remembered, invited the adherence of other powers. The Habsburg Empire, followed by Prussia, refused because both opposed the use of coercion in any form. The French government, however, joined Britain and Russia. Forces of national interest and Philhellenism influenced its decision. Deeply involved in Mediterranean affairs, it certainly could not refuse to participate in an agreement regulating conditions in the region.

The Treaty of London of July 6, 1827 was similar to the St. Petersburg Convention, but with some additions that strength-

[66]Ibid., II, p. 757.
[67]Nesselrode instruction to Ribeaupierre, November 12/24, 1826, *VPR*, XIV, pp. 650–6.
[68]Nesselrode to Alopeus, Pozzo di Borgo, and Tatishchev, March 30/April 11, 1826, ibid., XIV, pp. 459–62.

ened the provisions for intervention.[69] An additional article, imprecise in its wording, provided that if the Porte after a month did not accept mediation by the allies, then the signators would send representatives to Greece, thus establishing a direct link with the rebels. If either party, the Porte or the revolutionary Greek leadership, refused a preliminary armistice, "the High Powers will, jointly, exert all their efforts to accomplish the object of such Armistice, without, however, taking any part in the hostilities between the Two Contending Parties."[70] Arrangements were also made for the establishment of a joint blockade to prevent Mehmet Ali from supplying his army in the Peloponnesus. With the conclusion of the Convention of Akkerman and the Treaty of London, the Russian position appeared very strong. Direct pressure could be exerted on Constantinople on those matters that concerned Russia and the Porte exclusively; major allies had been secured for the pacification of Greece.

This favorable situation, however, was soon to deteriorate. First, a significant change occurred in the British government. In August 1827 Canning died, and was followed in office first by Lord Goderich and then, in January 1828, by Wellington. This administration had to deal with major domestic issues, such as Catholic emancipation and parliamentary reform. At the same time another crisis arose in Greece. In accordance with the decisions taken in connection with the Treaty of London, an allied squadron had established a blockade. In October 1827, in the course of its activities, it encountered a Turko–Egyptian fleet stationed in the Bay of Navarino. Shots were fired and a battle ensued. The Ottoman fleet was completely destroyed, with a loss of fifty-seven vessels and 8,000 men. The incident was greeted with enthusiastic approval by the Russian government, which hoped that the Porte would now be forced to negotiate a settlement on Greece.[71] The tsar gave decorations to the commanders of the squadrons. The interim administration in office in Britain could do little, but Wellington, once in power, made his opposition clear. Although he had previously negotiated the Convention of St. Petersburg, he at this time stepped back from the policy of cooperation with Russia and the use of coercion in the negotiations

[69]Hertslet, *Map of Europe*, I, pp. 769–74.
[70]Ibid., I, p. 773.
[71]Nesselrode circular despatch, St. Petersburg, November 12/24, 1827, Barbara Jelavich, *Russia and Greece during the Regency of King Othon, 1832–1835* (Thessaloniki: Institute for Balkan Studies, 1962), pp. 133–40.

over Greece. The same negative attitude was taken by Metternich, who regarded Navarino as a catastrophe.

The battle had also the immediate effect of bringing into question the validity of the Convention of Akkerman. The Ottoman Empire, with very good reason, regarded Navarino as an act of war. In December the sultan issued an imperial rescript, designed for domestic circulation, to the Ottoman provincial administrators who were meeting in Constantinople.[72] Its contents were subsequently used by the Russian government to justify its declaration of war, but the statements were in fact basically correct. The document singled out Russia as having been "at all times the sworn enemy of Islam . . . its government had in the past forty to fifty years repeatedly carried out hostile acts." As far as a settlement of Balkan problems was concerned, the rescript declared that although the terms of the Akkerman agreement had been accepted in order to win time to prepare for war, they had nevertheless for the most part been carried out. The attitude toward the Greek crisis was very pessimistic. The powers were pressing for a settlement, but even if the Porte granted more privileges to the islands, the Peloponnesus, and the area around Athens, the Greeks would not accept these as final. Moreover, the Greek population of Anatolia and Rumelia would demand similar rights. Since these areas contained a large Muslim population, whose fate would be placed in jeopardy, concessions could not be made. The empire would have "to fight for its faith and its national existence."

The Russian government at this point faced a diplomatic impasse. The lines of understanding with London had broken down; the Porte obviously would not accept the subservient relationship implicit in the Akkerman agreement. Moreover, the Russian diplomats no longer had a means of negotiating directly with the Ottoman government. In December 1827, in compliance with the terms of the Treaty of London, the ambassadors of Britain, France, and Russia broke off relations with the Porte and handed over the care of their affairs to the Dutch embassy. At this time both the Russian and Ottoman governments accepted the fact that a war was inevitable.

With this decision taken, the Russian government had to begin serious preparations not only for military action, but also on the

---

[72]Imperial rescript issued to the ayans meeting in Constantinople in December 1827, Prokesch-Osten, *Geschichte des Abfalls der Griechen*, V, pp. 140–4.

diplomatic front.[73] The correspondence with the other governments placed an emphasis on the Russian insistence that the treaties be observed, including those stipulations concerning "the Christian peoples that these same treaties place under the protection of H.I.M."[74] Assurances were given, similar to those in the St. Petersburg Convention, that Russia did not seek territorial conquests or exclusive advantages and that the other powers would be consulted on all matters having to do with Greece.[75] In Nicholas's manifesto on the declaration of war in April 26, 1828, he gave the breaking of treaties as the reason for his action and declared that Russia was fighting for "the honor of the Russian name, the dignity of the empire, the inviolability of its rights and that of our national glory."[76] The Balkan Christians were not mentioned.

The Russian action had the support of none of the other European powers. The British foreign secretary, Lord Dudley, specifically emphasized in his correspondence that Russia had gone to war for goals separate and exclusive to itself and that there had been no consultation with its partners in the Treaty of London of 1827. He also took particular note of the Russian assurances that there would be no conquests or special advantages taken and that the Ottoman Empire would not be destroyed. The British government was also concerned over the question of indemnities, which Russia intended to demand.[77]

During the Russo–Turkish War the relationship established by the Treaty of London was nevertheless maintained. The allied powers kept a strict separation of the issues involving Russia and the Ottoman Empire alone and those connected with a Greek settlement. A conference of the ambassadors of Britain, France, and Russia, meeting in London, discussed both the type of administration that Greece should have and the extent of its future territories. Lieven was assisted in the negotiations by Adam Fadeevich Matuszewicz (Matushevich), who was sent as a special envoy for this specific purpose.

---

[73]Nesselrode to Lieven, St. Petersburg, December 25/January 6, 1827, ibid., V, pp. 145–56.

[74]Nesselrode to Lieven, St. Petersburg, February 14/26, 1828, ibid., V, pp. 169–76.

[75]Nesselrode to Lieven, St. Petersburg, December 25/January 6, 1827, ibid., V, pp. 145–56.

[76]Nicholas I manifesto, ibid., V, pp. 216–17.

[77]Dudley to Lieven, Foreign Office (F. O.), March 7, 1828, ibid.,V, pp. 165–9. See also Lieven to Dudley, London, February 11/23, 1828, ibid., V, pp. 163–5, and Dudley to Lieven, F. O., March 25, 1828, ibid., V, pp. 230–5.

While Russian attention was concentrated on the war with the Ottoman Empire, the British and French were in a position to exert their influence in Greece. A French expeditionary force landed in the Peloponnesus and forced an Egyptian evacuation. The British government had direct connections with the revolutionary leadership. British as well as other European Philhellenes were involved in both the military and political activities in the Greek lands. The Russian government had no similar basis of support. In January 1828 Capodistrias assumed his position as the first president of Greece, but despite the suspicions of the other powers, he was in no sense a Russian figurehead. Nevertheless, his assassination in October 1831 removed from the Greek scene the one important political figure with a strong tie to the Russian government.

When embarking on the war with the Ottoman Empire in April 1828, the Russian leaders had not expected to encounter major difficulties. They had in February ended a war with Persia, which had commenced in 1825, with the advantageous Treaty of Turkmanchai. Contrary to expectations, two Balkan campaigns were necessary to win a victory. They were, of course, fighting without allies, and they could not call for a general uprising of the Balkan Christians because they feared the reaction of the other powers. Among the assurances given at the commencement of hostilities was the promise to maintain tranquility in Serbia and not to offer "exaggerated" expectations to the Danubian Principalities.[78] Particular care was taken to calm Habsburg anxieties. Thus General Ivan Ivanovich Dibich, the Russian commander-in-chief, wished the Serbs to remain quiet, since any activity could excite "the jealousy of Austria." He believed that they could best assist in the war by concentrating their forces so that Ottoman troops would be held in Bosnia and that they should be ready to repulse an invasion.[79]

Despite the decisiveness of the final victory – Russian troops in August 1829 entered Adrianople, which put them within striking distance of Constantinople – the Russian government recognized that it could not make a peace that would destroy the empire. Not only were the Russian leaders acutely aware of the European consequences of any attempts in this direction, but they had given specific assurances previously that drastically limited their possible gains, particularly in Europe. As a result, the Treaty of Adrianople of

---

[78]Nesselrode circular, St. Petersburg, April 14/24, 1828, ibid., V, pp. 227–30.
[79]Extract of a letter from Diebitsch to Langeron, Jassy, February 17/29, 1829, ibid., VI, 46.

September 14, 1829, provided for a moderate peace.[80] As far as direct gains were concerned, Russia received the Danube Delta and territory in Asia, as well as an indemnity. In regard to the Balkan Christians, the chief attention was, as before, devoted to strengthening the Russian position in the Principalities and providing for reforms in their administration. Article V restated the validity of previous agreements, but a Separate Act enumerated in detail additional privileges. Most important, the provinces were freed from the previous requirement that they provide grain, sheep, timber, and other supplies to the Ottoman Empire. Article VI pertained to Serbia, with the most important section providing for the restitution of the six districts in dispute to "that faithful and devoted nation." In Article X the Ottoman government accepted the stipulations of the Treaty of London and also of an additional agreement, concluded in London on March 22, 1829, establishing an autonomous Greece. Other provisions of the treaty dealt with questions such as trade and commerce and details relating to the conclusion of the war.

The treaty in its entirety represented a definite approach by the Russian government to its future relationship with the Ottoman Empire. In this time of crisis Nicholas I had appointed a committee to examine this question. Its report appeared after the signing of the treaty, but the conclusions reached were similar to those that dictated the moderate nature of the settlement and, in fact, to those of Nesselrode's memorandum of February 1826. Russia, the report advised, should not attempt to destroy the Ottoman Empire. Instead it should work for its preservation, but under predominant Russian influence. A Nesselrode circular of May 1830 expressed this attitude well:

A new era in our relations with the Ottoman Porte should date from the treaty of Adrianople. It depended entirely on us whether to occupy former Byzantium. Its fate and that of the empire of which it is the capital has been in our hands. However, instead of overthrowing that empire Our August Monarch decided to follow only the noble impulsion of his generosity in making use of the victory. But as you know, the moderation of His Imperial Majesty conforms in this serious situation with the true interests of Russia. . . . If we have allowed the Turkish government to continue to exist in Europe, it is because that government, under the preponderant influence of our superiority, suits us better than any of those which could be set up on its ruins. If we have left out of the Treaty of Adrianople those stipulations which would have deleted the Porte from the list of powers, it is because the clauses of this act, although marked by a visible magnanimity, ap-

---

[80]Hertslet, *Map of Europe*, II, pp. 813–31. On the war and the treaty see Vitalii Ivanovich Sheremet, *Turtsiia i Adrianopol'skii mir 1829g* (Moscow: Izdatel'stvo nauka, 1975).

peared to us sufficient to assure us the influence of which we speak, sufficient to demonstrate to the Porte that, nevertheless, any serious difference with us would be a sentence of death [*l'arrêt de sa chute*], in order to convince it that if it still is able to live, it will be only the life the emperor is in some manner pleased to allow it.[81]

The Greek question was settled by the representatives of France, Britain, and Russia, meeting in London without Greek participants. The London Protocol of February 3, 1830 established Greece as an independent, not autonomous, state with restricted boundaries and placed it under the protection of the three powers. Despite the fact that the Greek revolutionary leaders had previously shown a preference for constitutional regimes, the powers, in the interest of stability, established a monarchy, and one without constitutional limitations. The throne was initially offered to Leopold of Saxe-Coburg. When he refused, the position went to Prince Othon (Otto), the second son of the Philhellene King Ludwig I of Bavaria. The new ruler was only seventeen and a Catholic.

Although Russia had won the war and obtained an advantageous peace, the Eastern crisis of the 1820s had certainly shown the dangers of the Balkan connection to Russian state interests. Before 1812 the major concern had been the expansion of the Russian boundaries southward and westward; the Russian government had wished to annex Moldavia and Wallachia before fears over a French invasion had forced it to settle for Bessarabia only. However, once the favorable European settlement of 1815 had been achieved, Alexander I had correctly understood that Russian interests called for the maintenance of the status quo as regards both the territorial settlements in the Bucharest and Vienna treaties and the conservative regimes of the post-Napoleonic era. The Greek revolution was, of course, a revolt against a legitimate sovereign and, with its goal of full independence, it sought to upset the territorial balance in the Near East. In relation to these questions the tsar could easily condemn the entire action and call upon the Ottoman government to restrain its rebellious subjects. In contrast, other elements of the revolution brought into play those ties that connected Russia with Balkan Orthodoxy. The hanging of the patriarch, for instance, could not be ignored, nor could the indiscriminate reprisals taken against Greek civilians. In addition, other measures adopted by the Porte to stop the revolt violated Russian treaty rights, in particular the measures to restrain

[81]Nesselrode to Potemkin, secret circular, St. Petersburg, April 28/May 10, 1830, Jelavich, *Russia and Greece*, pp. 137–46.

Black Sea trade and the actions in the Principalities. Aside from the Greek issues, the Porte had also not fulfilled the obligations undertaken in the Treaty of Bucharest in regard to Serbia.

Alexander I, Nicholas I, and their advisers, as we have seen, did not want to go to war over these issues. They were primarily concerned with the situation in Europe. They had no further claims on the Ottoman Empire, and they recognized that they could not settle Eastern matters alone. Yet personal and national honor, Orthodox connections, and treaty stipulations were brought into question. In describing the motives behind the ultimatum of March 1826, Nesselrode spoke of the heritage left by Alexander I and the necessity of finding a solution to the conflict that involved

the positive interests of Russia which are compromised; it was the most explicit stipulations of its treaties which were infringed; it was finally its dignity, it was the noble sentiments of Emperor Alexander which were misunderstood and by the length of time during which the Turks had abused his moderation and by the silence which they have kept on his last démarches.[82]

These reasons lay not only behind the negotiations leading to the Convention of Akkerman, but also behind the declaration of war in April 1828 when the Porte failed to adhere to the letter and spirit of this agreement. The problem of European opposition to a Russian unilateral action had been largely solved by agreement with France and Britain over Greece and by the strict limits on future gains that the Russian government announced before going to war. Austria and Prussia, allies on other European matters, did not threaten the Russian position as long as its goals remained moderate.

The Treaty of Adrianople did not bring Russia great material rewards. The costs of this conflict to the state in money and manpower were high. Whether the gains were worth the losses is open to question. Although some territory was acquired and an indemnity levied, the treaty did little more than strengthen and reaffirm the Russian right of interference in the affairs of Wallachia, Moldavia, and Serbia and reestablish the previous commercial relationships. Although Russia now clearly had more rights in regard to some Balkan Christians, it also had increased obligations. Article X provided for Greek autonomy, but it cannot be said that Greece owed its ultimate independence to the war. The French and British military and naval presence there was by this time so strong that no other arrangement was practical. In fact, for Russia the Greek settlement

[82]Nesselrode to Tatishchev, St. Petersburg, May 26/June 7, 1826, Prokesch-Osten, *Geschichte des Abfalls der Griechen*, IV, pp. 274–6.

represented a strategic loss. In the future it was to be the sea powers that exerted the strongest influence in the independent state.

The great achievement of the war was the predominant position that Russia now held in Constantinople. By the time of the peace-making, Russian policy had become that of maintenance but domination of the Ottoman government. The stipulations of the treaty on Russian rights in regard to the Balkan Christians could in the future become a means of pursuing this prime objective; they could be a weapon against the Porte. Used in this manner they could also be instruments of Russian domination over the internal regimes of the Principalities and Serbia, provinces in which the Russian government had clear rights of intervention. The future would tell whether the Russian leadership would use the treaties in a constructive manner to assist in the development of native institutions in the Balkan states or as a means of increasing Russian influence in the Ottoman Balkan lands. During the 1820s the relationship of Russia to the Balkan Christian people had certainly become closer as a result of the Greek revolution and the Russo–Turkish War. This condition was to lead to new conflicts with the Porte and cause renewed anxiety among the great powers about Russia's true intentions.

CHAPTER III

The defense of the status quo:
The Crimean War

In the first years of his reign Nicholas I, as we have seen, had to deal with an internal rebellion and a major Eastern crisis. In the next years, although he faced no dangerous domestic opposition, the Eastern Question continued to cause concern. The Russian policy was to remain that adopted at the end of the Russo–Turkish War: the maintenance of the territorial integrity of the Ottoman Empire but a strong influence over its government. As regards the Balkan Christians, Russia would continue to play an important role in their development both through the protectorates and through pressure on the Porte. How difficult it was to maintain this policy against great-power rivals and internal Balkan challenges was to be repeatedly demonstrated in the next two decades. Nicholas's abilities as a leader and the soundness of his foreign policy decisions were to be thoroughly tested.

Although in many ways a contrast to his predecessor, Nicholas I, nevertheless, shared Alexander's conviction that the political system in Russia responded to the needs and conditions of Russian society, and that the tsar held his position on divine authority and was in turn responsible to God for the dutiful fulfillment of his imperial responsibilities. Nicholas I came to the throne at the age of twenty-nine with firmly set ideas that he did not basically modify throughout his reign. With a military background he sought for simplicity and precision in his policy. Adopting military values, he saw his reign in terms of service and regarded duty as the highest of virtues. Prussia was the country to which he felt most strongly attracted; his happy marriage to the eldest daughter of Frederick William III reinforced his sympathies and was to affect Russian foreign policy.

Figure 4. Nicholas I.

His visits to England left a generally favorable impression, but he did not particularly like its constitutional government. His dislike of France was influenced by that country's reputation as a center of revolutionary conspiracy for all of Europe and by the 1830 and 1848 revolts that brought about a change of leadership. Nicholas I could never accept on equal terms a ruler who came to power by revolutionary means. The fact that his own accession to the throne had been the occasion of a rebellion reinforced his attitude, although, as we have seen in the case of the Greek revolution, he would in some instances accept results obtained by violent means. Continuity was maintained during his reign by the fact that he was served by only one foreign minister, Nesselrode, whom he inherited from his brother.

The concepts upon which his reign was based – devotion to autocratic political principles, the Orthodox faith, and the interests of Russia – all were part not only of his domestic but also of his foreign policy. The support of the first principle, autocracy, explains his attitude toward revolutionary movements that endangered legitimate monarchs. He denounced the Greek revolt in these terms, and he was to support the sultan against another rebel, Mehmet Ali of Egypt. His European policy aimed at securing the collaboration of other governments to suppress revolutionary activities that threatened the conservative order.

The second consideration, Orthodoxy, was of particular importance for the Russian relationship with the Balkan people. Here Nicholas I took his responsibilities seriously, as was shown in his declaration to Karl Ludwig von Ficquelmont, the Austrian ambassador in St. Petersburg:

> I am on earth the only ruler who professes the Eastern rite; I must regard that position as a mission from heaven that imposes on me the duty to protect the church to which I belong; I must employ in favor of my coreligionists, if they need me, all the resources of power that God has given me. I will never neglect my duty.[1]

In addition to his specific relationship with the Orthodox, the tsar believed that the Christian nations together represented a moral unity and that they should cooperate, particularly when their faith was endangered.

The third concept, involving Russian nationalism, in contrast to the previous terms is more difficult to define. Nicholas I was certainly strongly against the national components of the revolutionary movements of the day, all of which involved at least to some degree the idea of popular sovereignty, a principle that the tsar abhorred. He certainly did not, for instance, believe that the Hungarians or Poles were entitled to an independent state; he supported the Habsburg government when it was challenged by its minorities. Within Russia all signs of national dissent were suppressed, with the Poles seen as the major danger to the state. However, in contrast, those who justified Nicholas's reign used arguments that were part of the ideology of European nationalism. They too emphasized the

---

[1] Ficquelmont to Buol, private letter, Vienna, May 24, 1853. Winfried Baumgart, ed., *Akten zur Geschichte des Krimkriegs*, series I, *Österreichische Akten zur Geschichte des Krimkriegs* (Munich: R. Oldenbourg Verlag, 1980), I: 1, pp. 153–5. The series of three volumes will be cited hereafter as *AGK*, I. For an analysis of Nicholas's views see Nicholas V. Riasanovsky, *Nicholas I and Official Nationality in Russia, 1825–1855* (Berkeley: University of California Press, 1967).

uniqueness and special position of their country in history. They also defined specific Russian qualities, in particular, loyalty to the tsar and devotion to the Orthodox church. In a sense, Russia was depicted as a great family ruled by the firm but kind hand of a benevolent father. With these convictions in regard to their own country, Russian officials could feel justified in applying them to Balkan affairs, and it explains at least in part the often patronizing attitude that they adopted when dealing with Balkan regimes.

These basic principles of Nicholas's reign aroused, of course, much opposition. On the left, those with liberal or social programs both within and without Russia saw the tsar as the representative of those concepts that they rejected. Since all Balkan revolutionary movements were liberal and national, this situation complicated the Russian activities in the peninsula. However, the arguments from the right, in particular from those who wanted a more assertive policy, were to be even more significant for foreign affairs. Among these, the writings of the Slavophils were to be especially important because of their influence on future Panslav thought, even though their numbers and influence were small during Nicholas's reign. In opposition to those who extolled Western culture and the reign of Peter the Great, the Slavophils were primarily concerned with studying and defining the Russian character. Sharing some of the beliefs of those who supported approved official views, they emphasized what was unique about the Russian past. They praised in particular the Orthodox religion and what they saw as a particularly Russian communal spirit as embodied in the peasant and the commune (the *mir*). Representing a philosophic outlook, not a political school, they were primarily interested in specifically Russian conditions; they thus paid less attention to non-Russian Slavs, about whom they knew comparatively little. Their ideas, although not connected to a definite political movement or organization, were disliked by the tsar because of their implications for both domestic and foreign policy. He wrote concerning the activities of two Slavophils, Ivan Sergeevich Aksakov and Iurii Fedorovich Samarin:

> Under the guise of compassion for the supposed oppression of the Slavic peoples . . . there is concealed the idea of rebellion against the legitimate authority of neighboring and, in part, allied states, as well as the idea of a general unification which they expect to gain not through God's will but through disorder, which would be ruinous for Russia.[2]

[2]Quoted in Michael Boro Petrovich, *The Emergence of Russian Panslavism, 1856–1870* (New York: Columbia University Press, 1956), pp. 25–6.

Although Nicholas was to face serious Eastern crises, his chief concern was over the progress of the revolutionary movement in Europe, which produced in 1830 and 1848 upheavals that threatened Russian interests as the tsar defined them. The first wave of activity commenced in France in July 1830, when the Bourbon ruler Charles X was overthrown and replaced by Louis Philippe of the contending house of Orléans. In September a revolutionary conspiracy resulted in a revolt against the Dutch King William; its aim was the separation of the Belgian provinces from the Kingdom of the Netherlands. Far more serious from the Russian perspective was the outbreak of a major rebellion in the Russian-controlled Congress Kingdom of Poland. This revolt was difficult to suppress, and it aroused a great deal of sympathy in Western Europe.

Despite its ultimate failure, the Polish revolt and its diplomatic consequences were to have an important effect on Russian foreign policy. Particularly significant was to be the subsequent influence of Polish émigrés on European revolutionary movements. Hereafter a major center for Polish conspiracy became Paris, where Prince Adam Czartoryski, the former minister of Alexander I, established at the Hôtel Lambert an organization with extensive ties to the European governments as well as to other revolutionary groups. Polish emissaries were to appear in the next years in the Ottoman Empire in regions that the Russian government considered its proper sphere of control, in particular, Serbia, Wallachia, and Moldavia.[3] The attitude of Nicholas I toward revolutionary movements and his specific actions in Poland made Russia henceforth the bugbear of European liberals and socialists. The complications from this association for Russian policy will be amply demonstrated.

THE EASTERN QUESTION, 1831–53

A similar revolutionary situation developed in the Ottoman lands. By the early 1830s Mehmet Ali was becoming increasingly a danger to the Porte and to the Russian policy of the status quo. As we have seen, he had come to the aid of his sovereign and had played a significant military role in the Greek revolution. After the establish-

---

[3]On Czartoryski's activities see Hans Henning Hann, *Aussenpolitik in der Emigration: die Exildiplomatie Adam Jerzy Czartoryskis, 1830–1840* (Munich: R. Oldenbourg Verlag, 1978), and Robert A. Berry, "Czartoryski's Hôtel Lambert and the Great Powers in the Balkans, 1832–1848," *The International History Review*, VIII: 1 (1985), pp. 45–67.

ment of independent Greece, he could not, of course, annex the Peloponnesus, but he did receive Crete as payment for his services. Deprived of a promised province, he demanded Syria as a replacement. When its cession was refused, he began a revolt in 1831, and he achieved a major victory over the Ottoman army at the battle of Konya in December 1832. Sultan Mahmud II was now in a desperate situation; his vassal could cause the downfall of his empire. Although he appealed to the European powers, only the Russian government responded. In February 1833 a Russian squadron and about 14,000 troops appeared in the Straits. This assistance, together with British and French diplomatic intervention, forced Mehmet Ali to sign the Peace of Kutahia, which did, however, give him Syria.

This crisis also enabled Russia to strengthen its relations with the Porte. In May 1833 Nicholas I sent Aleksei Fedorovich Orlov as his personal emissary to Constantinople. At this time the sultan too favored an understanding. In July, Orlov negotiated the Treaty of Unkiar Iskelessi. On the surface a mutual defense pact with an eight-year duration, it had a secret annex that limited the Ottoman obligations to Russia in case of hostilities "to closing the strait of the Dardanelles, that is to say, to not allowing any foreign vessels of war to enter therein under any pretext whatsoever."[4] The agreement and its secret clause, which was known immediately, caused immense concern to the British government. Not only did it seem to ensure a predominating influence for the Russian representatives in the Ottoman capital, but fears were expressed that the provision for a wartime closure of the Straits would not apply to Russian warships. The balance of political influence in Eastern affairs appeared to have been radically altered.

In the next years under the energetic leadership of Lord Palmerston, the British government, cooperating at first with France, attempted to reverse what it considered its deteriorating position at Constantinople. Great efforts were made to encourage Ottoman reform, with the goal of making the state strong enough so that it would not once again need to call for Russian assistance to quell internal rebellion. Efforts to improve the military were similarly supported. The British statesmen were also concerned about the development of the empire as a market for their goods and as a source of raw materials.

Despite British fears, there is little evidence that Nicholas I in-

[4]Text in J. C. Hurewitz, *Diplomacy in the Near and Middle East* (Princeton, N.J.: Princeton University Press, 1956), I, pp. 105–6.

tended to use the new treaty relationship to establish an exclusive domination at Constantinople. In fact, he was soon to act in an opposite direction. His chief concern was the maintenance of the political and territorial status quo throughout Europe and the suppression of revolutionary activities. With this aim in mind he wished to renew and strengthen the bonds of the Holy Alliance, which had become weakened during the Greek crisis. The Treaty of Münchengrätz of September 1833 was negotiated chiefly to ensure cooperation between Russia and Austria in Europe, but it also had provisions for Eastern affairs. The two signatories agreed that they would oppose further Egyptian expansion, but should the Ottoman Empire collapse, they would cooperate to establish a new order based on the balance of power. In October Prussia adhered to this agreement in the Berlin Convention. The three powers were thus once again in harmony over both their Eastern and Western objectives.

The Egyptian problem, however, refused to go away. With a strong territorial base centered on the Red Sea and including Egypt, Crete, and Syria, and with close relations with France, Mehmet Ali appeared to be in an advantageous position. However, Mahmud II, smarting under the previous humiliation, was bent on subduing his disobedient subject. At the end of April 1839 he opened a new Eastern crisis when he sent his army against Egypt.[5] Not only was his military force defeated, but his fleet went over to the enemy. In this disastrous situation Mahmud II died and was succeeded by Abdul Mejid, who was sixteen years old. Once again the empire appeared to be at the point of dissolution.

Although it appears that Nicholas I was not averse to repeating the actions of 1833 and going to the aid of the sultan, he was dissuaded by other advice. Nesselrode in his reports warned that the great powers would not allow Russia to settle Eastern affairs alone and that instead an international solution, and one that kept the Straits closed, should be sought. Accepting this position, Nicholas I

[5]For the Eastern crisis of 1839–41 and its general background see V. A. Georgiev, *Vneshniaia politika Rossii na Blizhnem Vostoke v kontse 30- nachale 40-kh godov xix v.* (Moscow: Izdatel'stvo Moskovskogo universiteta, 1975); Harold N. Ingle, *Nesselrode and the Russian Rapprochement with Britain, 1836–1844* (Berkeley: University of Calfornia Press, 1976); P. E. Mosely, *Russian Diplomacy and the Opening of the Eastern Question in 1838 and 1839* (Cambridge, Mass.: Harvard University Press, 1934); V. I. Sheremet, *Osmanskaia imperiia i zapadnaia Evropa vtoraia tret' xix v.* (Moscow: Izadat'stvo nauka, 1986); Harold Temperley, *England and the Near East: The Crimea* (London: Longmans, Green, 1936).

agreed that he should attempt to work with the British government as he had during the Greek crisis. The tsar's dislike of Louis Philippe as a ruler who came to power through revolutionary action and his conviction that Paris remained a center of dangerous conspiracy played a part in his decisions too. He hoped that he could use this new crisis to divide France and Britain. His policy was aided by the fact that the British government was indeed worried about French actions in Spain and Belgium as well as in Syria and Egypt.

The task of coming to an arrangement with Britain was entrusted to Filipp Ivanovich Brunnow, who traveled to London in September 1839 and again in December. He gave assurances that Russia would not renew the Treaty of Unkiar Iskelessi in 1841 when it was due to expire, but would seek instead a collective agreement endorsing the principle of the closure of the Straits. In July 1840 Russia, Britain, the Habsburg Monarchy, and Prussia, but not France, reached an understanding on the settlement of the Turkish–Egyptian conflict and the status of the Straits. In September, British and Ottoman forces joined in a successful campaign against Egypt. Faced with a coalition of powers, France too accepted a European decision on Egypt. It was agreed that Mehmet Ali would rule only in Egypt but that his position would be hereditary in his family.

With the powers in agreement on the closure of the Straits, the Convention of 1841 was concluded with little controversy. This treaty placed the Straits, which were legally part of Ottoman territory, under international control. The powers agreed to conform to

the ancient rule of the Ottoman Empire, according to which passage of the Straits of the Dardanelles and of the Bosphorus is always to be closed to Foreign Ships of War, so long as the Porte is at peace.[6]

The agreement had no time limit; Unkiar Iskelessi lapsed. By accepting an international regulation of the status of the Straits, the Russian government thus abandoned any attempt to settle the question by means of a bilateral understanding with the Porte on the lines of the former treaty. By this time, of course, Nicholas I and his advisers had recognized that they could not impose a unilateral solution to the problems connected with the Eastern Question. They had already limited their ability to act alone by the understandings with Austria and Prussia. Nicholas I was in the future to attempt to negotiate a similar agreement with Britain in the expectation of

[6] Edward Hertslet, *The Map of Europe by Treaty* (London: Butterworths, 1975), II, pp. 1024–6.

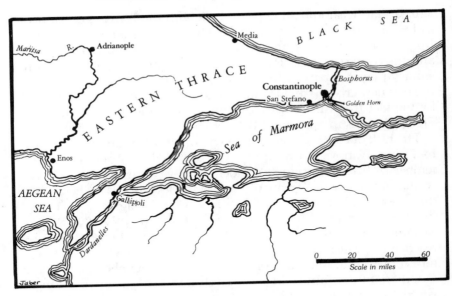

Map 5. The Straits.

another Eastern crisis. His aim here was to isolate France by drawing Britain into close cooperation with the continental coalition.

In the 1830s the Russian energies, as we have seen, were devoted principally to upholding Ottoman integrity against its main challenger, Egypt, a Muslim power. A similar attitude was adopted toward the Christian Balkan states. At this time and during the next decade the Russian diplomats worked for the fulfillment of the treaty stipulations, but they did not support a widening of the autonomous rights or the territory of the Balkan governments. As before, they attempted to ensure that Russian influence would be strong if not predominant in the centers of political power, and they were concerned about signs of revolutionary activity.

At this time, as before, Russia placed a primary emphasis on its position in the Principalities. The provinces lay on the Russian border, and they were on the direct road to Constantinople. When campaigns were undertaken or contemplated against the Porte, these lands were a source of supplies and transport equipment for the army as well as a point for the concentration of troops. It was thus to Russian advantage to ensure that prosperous and stable conditions be established once their predominating position was recognized. It must be remembered that until 1854 the Russian government had more influence over the fate of the provinces than did the suzerain Ottoman Empire.[7]

Fortunately for the Principalities, the chief official of the Russian occupation, General P. D. Kiselev, was a responsible and gifted administrator. Governing the Principalities from November 1829 to April 1834, he supervised the introduction of an Organic Statute for each of the provinces. These administrative regulations, drawn up by Russian officials and Romanian representatives, had certain features that were progressive for the time and place. Following accepted political principles, there was a separation of powers, with the executive headed by a prince elected for life from a special assembly of boyars. The legislative branch was composed of an assembly of thirty-five in Moldavia and of forty-two in Wallachia; it was empowered to pass laws, but they could be vetoed by the prince. The assemblies had control over the budgets, but they could not dismiss the princes.

These highly restrictive documents left the great boyar families in a predominant position. The major change in the Romanian ruling group was the elimination of the Greek Phanariot element that had occurred as a result of the revolt of 1821. The provinces were thus at this time administered by Romanian conservative landowners, some of whom had a close relationship with the Russian government. Highly placed Russian officials intermarried with families in the Principalities, and many Romanian boyars continued to enroll in the Russian service.

The Russian troops left the Principalities in 1834 after the Ottoman payments on the war indemnity had been completed. The first princes were chosen not by the assemblies, but by the Ottoman Empire and Russia, and only for seven years. Thereafter the protecting power rather than the Porte remained the major political factor in Romanian life. In fact, national elements in the Principalities were often to turn to Constantinople to protest Russian interference. In this period the Russian officials did indeed make their presence felt. Russian control was exerted through the consulates in Bucharest and Jassy, where the agents were instructed to supervise internal developments closely. As in other areas, the Russian representatives had their supporters as well as their opponents.

Although it can be argued that in supervising the introduction of the Organic Statutes the Russian government did act in the interest

---

[7]This section is based on Barbara Jelavich, *Russia and the Formation of the Romanian National State, 1821–1878* (Cambridge: Cambridge University Press, 1984), pp. 31–42.

of the Principalities, in another matter its actions were not consonant with that of a protector. The Treaty of Adrianople had ended the Ottoman right of preemption of the agricultural products of the Principalities. Grain from this area, which could now be sold on world markets, at this time came into competition with the produce of southern Russia. In possession of the mouth of the Danube, the Russian authorities allowed it to silt up, so that goods transported on the river had to be transhipped before they could proceed by way of the Black Sea to European markets. The cost of this operation gave the Russian Black Sea ports an advantage over Galatz and Braila and raised the price of Romanian products. This action affected in particular Britain, the chief market for both Romanian and Russian wheat.

The heavy-handed nature of the Russian protectorate was bound to have negative consequences. Although Russia had adherents among the boyars, some of whom were genuinely grateful for past Russian intervention against the Porte or saw their conservative neighbor as a protector of their own special position, it was to be another group that was to provide the future leadership of the country. The problem for the Russian government was not to come so much from the older generation as from its successors. Wealthy boyar families were able to send their children abroad to be educated; Paris thus became a center for privileged Romanian youth. Here they picked up the popular revolutionary ideas of the age. In a sense, Nicholas I was not wrong in regarding Paris as a hotbed of revolution and subversion. Like others of their generation, these young men were deeply affected by national and liberal programs, and, in particular, by the Polish struggle against Russian rule. Many of them also came to see the Russia of Nicholas I as the embodiment of backwardness and reaction.

Opposition to Russian influence also arose in Serbia, although the situation was in many ways different in a country with a contrasting economic and social order. Without a native aristocracy of large landowners or a long tradition of autonomous rule, the province was administered by local notables whose families were often in competition with each other. The prince, Miloš Obrenović, like his predecessor Karadjordje, was simply a member of a prominent family with a strong home base. He thus did not enjoy the advantage often associated with membership in a historical territorial nobility or a European royal family.

Although Serbia, like the Danubian Principalities, had become a Russian protectorate, it was very difficult for St. Petersburg to exert here the type of control that it did in Bucharest or Jassy. Most important, Serbia was located in a remote area, not on the Russian route to Constantinople. Moreover, as has been emphasized, the Habsburg ties were more immediate and direct. Serbia and the monarchy shared a long border; Habsburg Serbs were politically active both at home and in Serbia. Most significant was the fact that Russia not only did not have an army in occupation, but it did not even have a consulate in Belgrade until 1837. In dealing with Serbian affairs the Russian government often sent emissaries to Belgrade, but its influence was exerted primarily through the embassy in Constantinople directly on the Porte.

As was the case in regard to the Principalities, the Russian diplomats were determined to ensure that the obligations undertaken by the Ottoman government in regard to Serbia in the treaties of Bucharest, Akkerman, and Adrianople were fulfilled. In addition to the other provisions, Article VI of the Treaty of Adrianople called for the return to Serbia of the six districts that had been held before 1813. This question, together with the details of the political order to be introduced in Serbia, was discussed by representatives of the Ottoman Empire and Serbia. The Ottoman government in Belgrade dealt with the Serbian government, which also sent special delegates to Constantinople. The new conditions were introduced through special decrees in 1830 and 1833.

Russian participation in the negotiations came primarily through the intervention of the Russian ambassador in Constantinople, Ribeaupierre, who took part in the discussions. As previously in Serbia, and also in the Principalities, the Russian government did not want a strong executive whom it could not control; it thus pressed for the establishment of a council of notables that could act as a check on arbitrary actions by the prince and allow an element of Russian interference.

In 1830 Serbia finally achieved a fully autonomous position in the Ottoman Empire and Miloš gained his objective of having the position of prince recognized as hereditary in the Obrenović family. The settlement also provided that an assembly of elders was to govern with him. The Ottoman presence was limited to the possession of six garrison fortresses; Muslims living in Serbia were to sell their property and leave. Many points in the settlement were not immediately carried out. The Russian government was preoccupied by the Polish rebellion of 1830 and then by the crisis caused by Mehmet Ali. Finally, impatient with the slowness of the final negotiations over the transfer of the six provinces, Miloš proclaimed their union in June 1833. The final work by the border commissions was completed in 1834.

The establishment of institutions of self-government was to take longer to achieve. Unlike the Principalities, where the political order was determined by Russian officials working with selected Romanians, the Serbian administration was primarily established by the Serbs themselves, although with some Russian and Ottoman participation. Despite the protectorate established in the treaties, the Russian government was not able to exert effective control. Most important was the fact that Serbian autonomy had been won after two insurrections in which Russia played a very small part. Perhaps even more significant was the character of Miloš Obrenović. A strong and crafty leader, he desired to retain the autocratic powers that he had assumed, and he did not want to have to submit to the interference of a foreign power. Moreover, in the development of the administrative system of the newly autonomous state, he did not need the services of Russian officials. Although the Serbs in Serbia proper did not have a trained cadre of administrators – the overwhelming majority, including Miloš, being illiterate – they could use the services of the educated Serbs from the Habsburg Monarchy, who indeed did provide the first generation of state officials.

The rise of opposition to the autocratic prince and the imported officials did, however, offer the Russian government opportunities for some interference. Unable to control the prince, it pressed for the establishment of the council already provided for in an Ottoman decree of 1831. The Russian officials also wanted the formulation of something like the Organic Statutes introduced in the Principalities. Faced by the necessity of fulfilling the stipulations of the Ottoman decree, Miloš in 1835 granted the Presentation Constitution, approved by an assembly of about 4,000, which remained, however, in effect only a short time. Since it had not been consulted during its formulation, the Russian government opposed its introduction.

The Russian officials were also not involved in the negotiations over church affairs despite their previous ostentatious concern over Balkan Orthodoxy. With the acquisition of an autonomous political status by the state, the Serbian church sought the reestablishment of the position that it had enjoyed before the abolition of the Patriarchate of Peć. The new arrangements were worked out by representatives of the Patriarchate and the Serbs, with the participation of the Porte. In September 1831 the patriarch issued a concordat that granted the Serbian church a position of autonomy but not independence. The bishops were henceforth to be chosen from the Serbian clergy; the bishop at Belgrade would have the title of metropolitan. The church was to be governed by a synod composed of members of the hierarchy.

In the next years a thorough reform of the church institutions was undertaken. It is interesting to note that the greatest accomplishments were achieved under the direction of Metropolitan Peter Jovanović, who held office from 1833 to 1859. Born in the Habsburg Empire, he was educated in the Serbian gymnasium and theological seminary in Sremski Karlovci. His background was thus Austrian, not Russian. In his reorganization of Serbian ecclesiastical affairs, he took the Serbian church in the Habsburg Empire as his model.

Although the treaties did indeed give Russia a special position, the Serbian government was soon presented with alternatives for support due to the establishment of a number of consulates in Belgrade in the 1830s. In 1836 the Habsburg representative, Antun Mihanović, became the first consul assigned to Serbia. At the same time, the Russian government appointed Gerasim Vasil'evich Vashchenko as consul with duties in regard to Serbia, but assigned him to Orsova in the Habsburg Empire and placed him under the jurisdiction of the consulate-general in Bucharest. In May 1837 George Lloyd Hodges became the first British agent, followed by A. Duclos for France in November 1838. Henceforth the British and, at times, the Habsburg consulates became centers of opposition to Russia.[8]

Since the independence of the prince could not be curbed, the Russian government pressed harder for the introduction of a council. It was expected that Russian agents could work with the Serbian notables who resented Miloš and wanted to limit his authority. This group, which sought the formulation of some sort of document that would establish on a firm basis the administration of the country and that would limit the power of the executive, became known as the Constitutionalists. With similar aims the Russian government in October 1837 sent Vasilii Andreevich Dolgoruki to Belgrade. When he failed to influence Miloš, the negotiations were transferred to Constantinople, where the Russian ambassador, at this time Apollinarii Petrovich Butenev, was able to put pressure on the Porte. The new regulations for Serbia were thus drawn up by the Russian ambassador and the Ottoman officials. The result of their efforts, the so-called Turkish Constitution, was proclaimed by the Ottoman government in December 1838; it was to form the basis of the Serbian government until 1869.

[8]See Stevan K. Pavlowitch, *Anglo–Russian Rivalry in Serbia, 1837–1839* (Paris: Mouton, 1961).

The Russian diplomats thus obtained the type of document that conformed to their wishes. The most important section called for the establishment of a council of notables of seventeen men. Despite this victory, a period of political instability followed, whose final outcome was not to the Russian advantage. In June 1839 Miloš was forced to abdicate; a regency ruled until his son Michael arrived in Belgrade in March 1840. The first reign of Prince Michael lasted only until 1842, when he too was forced to leave. In September 1842 a special assembly elected Alexander Karadjordjević, the son of the leader of the first revolution. The Russian government refused to accept this choice, since it had been made without Russian participation. The Porte, however, agreed to the change. In a strong intervention, St. Petersburg sent K. A. Lieven as a special emissary to Belgrade and then to Constantinople to attempt to persuade the sultan to annul the election.

Finally, in June 1843 a second election was indeed held, with both Lieven and Vashchenko present, which brought the same result. In September the Russian government finally recognized Michael. The Constitutionalist period in Serbian history, although it was brought into being in part by Russian opposition to Miloš, did not create a favorable atmosphere for Russian influence. Although they could play among the factions in Serbian politics and attempt to organize a Russian party, the Russian agents could not control the government. Moreover, many aspects of Serbian politics began to acquire characteristics that could only be regarded as dangerous by the protecting power.

In this period, it will be remembered, the Russian government was standing for the maintenance of Ottoman integrity. Neither the tsar nor his officials were in favor of independent national movements, out of Russian or European control, that threatened Ottoman territory. Yet it was exactly at this time, in 1844, that the Serbian minister, Ilija Garašanin, drew up a national program, the *Načertanije*, that called for the unification of all the lands claimed by Belgrade.[9] This

[9]In the *Načertanije* Garašanin expressed his mistrust of Russian motives, writing that "the more independently Serbia is administered, the less confidence she will enjoy among the Russians. . . . Russia does not permit a small state such as Serbia to prescribe terms to her. She demands that her advice be listened to unconditionally as if they were orders and those who wish to serve her must yield themselves to her completely." The Načertanije can be found in Dragoslav Stranjaković, "Kako je postalo Garašaninovo 'Načertanije'," *Spomenik* (Belgrade: Srpska kraljevska akademija, 1939), XCI, pp. 65–115. For Garašanin's biography see David MacKenzie, *Ilija Garašanin: Balkan Bismarck* (Boulder, Colo.: East European Monographs, 1985).

period was also marked by the arrival in Belgrade of delegates from the Polish emigration who acquired considerable influence in the Serbian government. Moreover, when it became apparent that Russia would not aid Serbian national expansion, and when friction over domestic problems continued, the Serbian leadership sought increasingly to obtain French assistance. Russia's often hectoring attitude and its refusal to support national aims thus caused the same reaction in Serbia that we have previously seen among progressive Romanian elements; those Serbs and Romanians who sought to see their country advance looked to Paris as the center of European enlightenment and progress.

In Greece, the third Orthodox country in which the Russian government had an acknowledged interest in combatting competing foreign, that is, British and French, influence, its position was even more difficult. It will be remembered that at the time that the Russian army was fighting in the Balkans, the Western sea powers were strengthening their influence in Greece. Thereafter, Russia joined these states in signing the London Protocol of February 3, 1830, which established Greece as an independent state under a foreign prince. Since the first ruler, Othon, was underage, he came to Athens accompanied by a regency of three Bavarian officials. The powers also gave him a mercenary army of about 3,500, mostly German, soldiers. After the death of Capodistrias the country had fallen into anarchy. Given the political disputes of the time, it would have been difficult to form a national army from the disputing guerrilla bands that had fought in the revolution.

As far as Russian involvement was concerned, Greek affairs in the 1830s were a relative side issue, at least compared to the interest shown in the Danubian Principalities, Serbia, and the fate of the Ottoman Empire as a whole. Nevertheless, the Russian officials were determined to play an active role in the future of the kingdom.[10] As far as the internal order was concerned, the Russian government had four major goals: the establishment of a conservative monarchical regime; the protection of the position of the Orthodox church; the ensurance of a stable balance of influence among the protecting powers; and, finally, the maintenance of the territorial status quo, at least until the time came when Russia could benefit from further changes. In all four categories the Russian position was to be challenged in the next years.

---

[10]This section is based on Barbara Jelavich, *Russia and Greece during the Regency of King Othon, 1832–1835* (Thessaloniki: Institute for Balkan Studies, 1962).

In regard to the first question, the Russian government was well satisfied with the absolute monarchy established in 1830, although it apparently expected that some sort of constitutional act would be prepared. In an instruction of January 1833 to Gabriel A. Katacazy, the newly appointed representative in Athens, Nesselrode directed the envoy to urge the regency to take firm control of the country: "It is necessary that it begins by exercising the royal power *on its own authority, to its full extent,* and that it does not have the appearance of subordinating that power to the will of the nation."[11] When it is remembered that the revolutionary leadership had drawn up and enacted three constitutions, none of them calling for a monarchy, it can be understood why Greek opposition to the conservative regime soon arose.

The Russian government was, however, more interested in the strengthening and reorganizing of the Greek Orthodox church than in the political institutions. It was not happy about the Catholic faith of the new king, although it supported his appointment with the hope that he would convert to Orthodoxy either before assuming the throne or at least before his majority in 1835. When this did not happen, the attempt was made to secure at least the firm assurance that Othon's children or his successor, if he had no direct descendants, would be Orthodox. The religious question was the chief point of conflict between the Russian government and Othon until his overthrow in 1863.

The Russian officials were not only dissatisfied with the religion of the monarch, but they were also disturbed by the reorganization of the church carried out by the Bavarian regents.[12] Recognizing that an independent state could not have a church organization subordinate to an institution under foreign control, the regency separated the Greek church from the Patriarchate of Constantinople. The new organization was the work of a synod of bishops, including the leading Greek theologian, Theokletos Pharmakidis, and the Bavarian regent, Georg von Maurer, who was a liberal and a Protestant. They took as their models the Orthodox church in Russia and the Catholic church in Bavaria, both of which were under firm state control. The Greek church was henceforth to be administered by a Holy Synod, whose head was under oath to obey Othon. At the same

---

[11]Instruction to Katacazy, January, 1833, ibid., p. 57.
[12]See Charles A. Frazee, *The Orthodox Church and Independent Greece, 1821–1852* (Cambridge: Cambridge University Press, 1969).

time, a reform of the monasteries resulted in the dissolution of around 412, with only about 150 remaining.

Nicholas I was extremely displeased by these measures. He felt that the changes should have been made in consultation with Russian representatives and with the patriarch. In general, the Russian government preferred to maintain the authority of the Constantinople Patriarchate over Balkan Orthodoxy. The action was also strongly criticized in Greece; many did not like the manner in which the reform had been carried through or the break with the Patriarchate, which did not accept the new arrangements until 1850. The dissatisfied tended to turn to the Russian consulate for support, and they were the strongest base for Russian influence in Athens.

As far as the third point is concerned, the balance of influence between the three protecting powers, Russia was in the weakest position. From the military standpoint it was, of course, not able to compete with the sea powers, who in a crisis could and did control the Greek islands and the mainland harbors. Moreover, the Russian insistence on conservative political principles and the territorial status quo was contrary to the desires of most of the politically active Greeks. Nevertheless, an influential Russian, or Nappist, Party was organized, which was based, however, on an internal contradiction. As could be expected, those who emphasized the Orthodox basis of Greek society turned for support to Russia, the obvious center of Orthodox power and influence. However, this party was to enter into conspiracies directed at the overthrow of the monarch, and it also came to stand for a policy of territorial expansion not supported by St. Petersburg.

In fact, it was in this category, the question of the territorial future of the Greek state, that the foundation was set for future conflict. No Greek nationalist was content with the Greece of the 1830s, which contained only a quarter of the ethnic Greeks. Their ideal was incorporated in the *Megali Idea*, or Great Idea, which in its widest interpretation called for the re-creation of the Byzantine Empire. The immediate aims were the acquisition of the neighboring Greek islands, with Crete as the most important, and expansion into Thessaly. The Byzantine ideal, which was well known in St. Petersburg, put the small Greek state into possible contention with Russia for the Ottoman heritage, in particular for Constantinople. Because of their policy of upholding the Ottoman Empire, both the Russian and British governments were strongly opposed to the wider program of the Greek nationalists.

In the first years of Othon's reign the basic Greek legal and administrative institutions were introduced; here the parallel with the Danubian Principalities and Serbia should be noted. In Greece, however, the principal influence was exerted by the Bavarian regents, working with Greek advisers. In the subsequent period political life revolved around the activities of three parties, the British, French, and Russian, all of which had connections with the respective embassies. There was no royal or Bavarian party. The small size and poverty of the Greek state made government a difficult affair. Moreover, all three parties intrigued against each other and competed for influence over the government. The absolute authority vested in the king and some of the actions of his Catholic and Bavarian advisers also caused friction. In 1843 a military coup, organized by the British and Russian parties, at least partly in opposition to the French party's influence, which was predominant at the time, succeeded in forcing Othon to agree to the granting of a constitution.[13] The conspirators made free use of the Russian name, and Katacazy was evidently deeply involved.

The reaction of Nicholas I could be predicted. Like his brother in 1821, he was faced with a Greek rebellion organized against a legitimate ruler. He strongly denounced the revolt and recalled his representative in disgrace. Russian partisans had actively supported just the type of rebellion that the tsar had found so reprehensible in the rest of Europe. Nesselrode, reflecting this attitude, condemned "the conduct of men who, obligated by their duty and their oath to defend their sovereign, had perfidiously betrayed him or in a cowardly manner had abandoned him.[14] The tsar's reaction was stronger:

> What has happened in that country is infamous . . . the universal treason, the complete isolation in which the king found himself, the insolence with which they treated him – the violence which they did to him, cannot be condemned in strong enough terms, or dishonorable enough. Therefore I have commenced by throwing out my minister, yes, by *throwing* him *out*, for after conduct like this, so contrary to my wishes and my principles, he cannot remain any more in my service.

During the revolt Othon had agreed to the summoning of a constitutional convention. Although the tsar deplored the decision – "I would have left or have killed myself" – he nevertheless agreed that Othon would have to proceed with the constitution because "a

---

[13]For more details on the revolt see Barbara Jelavich, *Russia and the Greek Revolution of 1843* (Munich: R. Oldenbourg Verlag, 1966).
[14]Bray to Ludwig I, no. 1, St. Petersburg, October 7/19, 1843, quoted in ibid., p. 32.

royal promise can never be given in vain, no matter what the means are by which it has been obtained."[15] However, during the discussions about the constitution, the Russian representatives were instructed to maintain an attitude of expectancy and not cooperate in the making of the document.[16] As a result, the chief influence came from the Western missions. The constitution finally adopted was conservative and resembled that of the July Monarchy of Louis Philippe. In it the Russian desires were met in one important respect: Article 40 stated that the successor to the throne must be Orthodox. Nevertheless, a revolution had occurred, leading to the introduction of a constitutional government, with an elected chamber and an appointed senate. Subsequently, the political situation was to develop to the interest of the French party and to the further weakening of Russian influence.

Despite the difficulties described, the Russian government was able to maintain its favorable position in the Balkans acquired as a result of the treaties of Bucharest and Adrianople, and its good relationship with Britain and the Habsburg Monarchy. Although points of friction existed among these states on certain matters, they were in agreement on keeping the status quo in the Near East. In contrast to the situation here, Russian policy was to face severe reverses in Europe as a result of the revolutions of 1848-9.

Under Nicholas I, as has been previously emphasized, Russian attention was primarily concentrated on Western and Central Europe. There the goal was to protect the settlement of 1815 as regards not only territorial distribution but also the regimes in power. The central Russian alliance system, the Holy Alliance, rested on the common political principles shared by Prussia and the Habsburg Monarchy as well as on their agreed-upon foreign policy objectives. In January 1848, with the outbreak of rebellion in Sicily, Nicholas's objectives in Europe became severely endangered. In February, Louis Philippe was overthrown; in March the revolutionary wave engulfed the Russian allies. Frederick William IV conceded to the revolutionary demands; Metternich was forced out of office, and Vienna fell under the control of a revolutionary leadership. Al-

---

[15]Bray to Ludwig I, no. 2, October 12/24, 1843, quoted in ibid., pp. 33-4.
[16]The Bavarian ambassador in St. Petersburg reported that Nicholas I did "not wish in any way to agree to the making of a *constitution,* of which he condemns the principle and the origin, regarding, besides, any participation whatsoever in this work as a source of grave responsibility, for which he refuses to be answerable." Bray to Ludwig I, no. 4, St. Petersburg, October 20/November 2, 1843, quoted in ibid., p. 35.

though Russia remained unaffected by the movement, Nicholas I by the end of March found himself without allies and faced by a potentially explosive situation.

Although there was little that the Russian government could do about the situation in the rest of Europe, it could act in the Balkans, where it became principally concerned with the events in the Danubian Principalities. Signs of revolutionary activity appeared in both Moldavia and Wallachia. The prince of Moldavia, Michael Sturdza, was able to handle the situation, but Wallachia was soon in full rebellion.[17] In June a revolutionary leadership, composed primarily of young men with strong French connections, took power with a program aimed more against the Russian protector than the Ottoman suzerain. The Russian government thus found itself directly challenged in a region that it regarded as vital for its own interests.

Nevertheless, no immediate action was taken against the Wallachian revolution. In July, however, a Russian force entered Moldavia. From this position events in the Habsburg Empire as well as in Wallachia could be observed. The Russian government was particularly concerned about the establishment of a revolutionary regime in Budapest, which had connections with prominent Polish émigrés. In September, after an agreement with the reluctant Ottoman Empire, both Russian and Ottoman troops entered Wallachia and caused the downfall of the revolutionary regime. In May 1849 the two states signed the Convention of Balta Liman, an agreement that marked the height of Russian domination of the Principalities. The princes were henceforth to be chosen for terms of seven years by Russia and the Ottoman Empire. The assemblies were replaced by councils, or divans, whose members were to be chosen by the princes with the assent of the Porte. Russian troops remained in occupation only until 1851, although the Convention provided for their return in case events in the future required a renewed Ottoman and Russian intervention.

After the suppression of the revolt in Wallachia, the Russian government was able to use its position in the Principalities as a base from which to operate against the Hungarian revolution. In May 1849 the young Habsburg emperor, Franz Joseph, called upon the tsar to aid him in restoring his authority in his domains. The subsequent Russian intervention resulted in the crushing of the

---

[17]For the Russian position see Barbara Jelavich, "The Russian Intervention in Wallachia and Transylvania, September 1848 to March 1849," *Rumanian Studies*, IV (1979), pp. 16–74.

Hungarian revolt in August. It is interesting to note that at the time that the Russian military forces operating in the Ottoman and Habsburg lands were suppressing the revolution in the Principalities, Russian officials were receiving delegations from the Romanians and Serbs of the Habsburg Empire requesting assistance against the highly nationalistic Hungarian movement. The Serbs of Vojvodina were, in turn, backed by the Serbs of Serbia proper.

Although the situation in Central Europe was reestablished to Nicholas's satisfaction, the revolutions were to have a lasting effect. The coming to power of Louis Napoleon, the nephew of the great Russian opponent, was to cause major problems in the future. The defeat of the Hungarian revolution also led to an immediate crisis in Eastern affairs. Thousands of refugees fled into the Ottoman Empire. When the Habsburg government, backed by Russia, demanded their extradition, the Porte, supported by Britain and France, refused. In the course of this incident, the British fleet entered the Straits in violation of the 1841 agreement, but it withdrew immediately.

By midcentury Russia was in a secure and powerful position. In a report dated November 1850, Nesselrode summarized the achievements of the twenty-five years of Nicholas's reign and concluded: "Since 1814 the position of Russia and of its sovereign has not been either more favorable (*belle*) or more noble (*grande*)."[18] He particularly emphasized the tsar's role as the opponent of revolution and the defender of the monarchical idea, the principle of order, and the European balance of power: "Everywhere where thrones totter, or undermined society gives way before the pressure of subversive doctrines, the powerful hand of Your Majesty makes itself obvious or felt."[19]

In the section on the Eastern Question, Nesselrode placed his emphasis on the tsar's relationship with the Ottoman Empire: "The proximity of that state, in the situation of comparable inferiority which our previous conquests have left it, offers, under present circumstances, the most favorable arrangement for our commercial and political interests." In pursuance of this policy, Russia, "the power that was formerly regarded as the natural enemy of Turkey

---

[18]Report presented by Nesselrode to Nicholas I on the twenty-fifth anniversary of his reign, St. Petersburg, November 20, 1850. A. de Nesselrode, ed., *Lettres et papiers du chancelier Comte de Nesselrode, 1760–1856* (Paris: A. Lahure, n.d.), X, p. 10. This series will be cited hereafter as Nesselrode, *Lettres et papiers*.
[19]Ibid., X, p. 3.

has become its strongest support and its most faithful ally; two times, in an interval of six years, beset by the ambition of a rebellious vassal, the Ottoman Empire has seen itself menaced by an almost inevitable dissolution; two times it has owed its salvation to the decisive intervention of Your Majesty."[20] Russia had, however, avoided getting a territorial guarantee that would bind the tsar for the future.

What is notable about this report is the lack of any discussion of the condition of the Balkan Christians under Ottoman rule or of Russia's rights and duties toward them, questions that were soon to become major international issues. Mention was made only of independent Greece and how the tsar had saved the country from "the inevitable ruin to which the Egyptian sword menaced it."[21] The Russian influence in the establishment of a monarchical government and in placing "in harmony the religious faith of the monarch with that of his subjects" was similarly praised.[22]

The report also reflected the emphasis placed at this time on good relations with Britain and the breaking of that government's cooperation with France, which Nesselrode judged as "so hostile" to Russian interests and "so fatal for the situation of conservative governments."[23] Certainly, by this time Nicholas I had indeed made numerous efforts to maintain a close relationship with London, particularly in matters relating to the Ottoman Empire and the Eastern Question. What he sought was an agreement, resembling that made at Münchengrätz with the Habsburg Empire, that would ensure that in another Eastern crisis Russia and Britain would work together. More than that, he wanted provision made that some prior understanding would be reached on the fate of the Ottoman lands should it appear that the empire was indeed facing dissolution. The aim here too was the isolation of France.

As we have seen, until this time the tsar had exerted himself to maintain Ottoman integrity. As the years passed, with the increasing dangers to the sultan both from the Christian national movements and from Muslim regional centers such as Egypt, the Russian leaders had to consider the fact that it might be impossible to maintain the unity of the lands. Well aware that in Eastern affairs Russia could face a coalition of powers fearful of its advantages in the area and knowing that he could not impose a solution alone, Nicholas I attempted to come to more precise arrangements with Vienna and London about the future. Without a definite precon-

[20]Ibid., X, p. 6.   [21]Ibid., X, pp. 1-2.   [22]Ibid., X, pp. 4-5.   [23]Ibid., X, pp. 6-7.

ceived plan, he was willing to consider many possible solutions, including the establishment of independent states, the division of the area into great-power spheres of influence, and straight annexations of territory. His approaches to Austrian and British diplomats at various times illustrated both his concern and his lack of a determined course of action.

An example can be found in the conversations that Nicholas I had with Ficquelmont, the Habsburg ambassador in St. Petersburg, in September 1844. During these the tsar emphasized that the monarchy and Russia should make a more precise agreement on the future in case a catastrophe arose. He suggested that Austria should take Constantinople and, in fact, the entire Balkan heritage: "I shall never cross the Danube . . . and everything between this river and the Adriatic ought to be yours."[24] Britain could annex Egypt and divide the Greek islands with France. At this time and later he indicated that he would not consent to a revival of the Byzantine Empire, which was, it will be remembered, the Greek national program, nor would he allow France or Britain to control Constantinople. He also warned that if the Habsburg Empire did not join with him, Russia would have to act alone. In other talks the tsar and his diplomats repeated similar themes, in particular concerning Constantinople, the negative attitude toward Greek aspirations, and that Austria could be the Turkish heir.

Even more important, and in many ways more controversial, was the tsar's attempt to obtain an understanding with the British government. In June 1844 Nicholas visited Britain, where he discussed these problems with the prime minister, Sir Robert Peel, and the foreign secretary, Lord Aberdeen. In these discussions there was general agreement that the attempt should be made to hold the empire together, but to consult should it indeed collapse. Later Nesselrode summarized the conversations in a note that was sent to Aberdeen and the tsar and approved by both.[25] This exchange apparently gave the Russian leaders the feeling that they had an understanding with Britain that the governments would act together in a crisis.

The last important discussions took place after Russia and France

---

[24] The Ficquelmont interviews are summarized in G. H. Bolsover, "Nicholas I and the Partition of Turkey," *Slavonic Review*, XXVII (1948), pp. 126–8.
[25] The Nesselrode memorandum is printed in Vernon John Puryear, *England, Russia, and the Straits Question, 1844–1856* (Berkeley: University of California Press, 1931), pp. 439–42.

had become embroiled in a conflict over religious rights in the Ottoman Empire. In January 1853 Nicholas I commenced a series of conversations with Sir Hamilton Seymour, the British ambassador in St. Petersburg, with Nesselrode also participating. In these talks the tsar expressed his desire for an understanding with Britain to deal with the expected collapse of the empire, but he did not present a specific plan. What he did, however, was to enumerate what he would not accept: There was to be no revived Byzantine Empire, nor did he wish to see the Balkan peninsula divided into "little republics, asylums for the Kossuths, Mazzinis and other revolutionists of Europe."[26] He thought that Serbia and Bulgaria might receive governments similar to those of the Danubian Principalities; Egypt and Crete would go to Britain. It is interesting to note that the tsar was fully confident that he could represent the opinions of Vienna: "When I speak of Russia, I speak of Austria as well; what suits the one suits the other; our interests as regards Turkey are perfectly identical."[27]

Despite Nicholas's apparent conviction that he was addressing a friendly audience, neither the British nor the Habsburg diplomats accepted his words at their face value. It seemed instead as if the tsar was preparing for an aggressive move against the Ottoman Empire; his declarations were thus greeted with deep suspicion. The official British reply to the overtures was that the government did not see that there was an immediate crisis; a dissolution of the empire could come in 20, 50, or 100 years, and any understanding would have to involve the Habsburg Empire and France. Britain, however, would not make any agreements concerning the fate of the Ottoman Empire without prior consultation with Russia. The document also contained a phrase about the Russian position: "that exceptional protection . . . although it was without doubt imposed by duty and sanctioned by treaties."[28] Nesselrode's answer also mentioned the tsar's "traditional rights of protection."[29]

The discussions initiated by Nicholas I during his reign, particularly those that took place immediately prior to the Crimean crisis,

---

[26]Quoted in Bolsover, "Nicholas I and the Partition of Turkey," p. 142.

[27]Quoted in ibid., p. 142.

[28]Russell to Seymour, secret and confidential, Foreign Office, February 9, 1853. Andrei Medardovich Zaionchkovskii, *Vostochnaia Voina*; *Prilozheniia* (St. Petersburg: Ekspeditsiia zagotovleniia gosudarstvennykh bumag, 1908), I, pp. 359–62. This volume will be cited hereafter as Zaionchkovskii, *V.V.: Prilozheniia*.

[29]Verbal note, Nesselrode to Seymour, February 21, 1853, ibid., I, pp. 362–5.

were to have their effect. It did seem as if the tsar was preparing the ground for an aggressive move against the Ottoman Empire. No other government shared his views on the coming demise of the "sick man." The British and Habsburg statesmen, on the contrary, favored actions to defend its integrity. With the memory of the national revolts of 1848–9 still fresh, the Habsburg government wanted no disturbances of the status quo in the Balkans. The British diplomats, although with differing approaches to the problem, remained apprehensive about Russia's links with the Balkan Orthodox and its ability to put pressure on the Porte.

THE CRIMEAN WAR

Although the Russian government was unable to obtain the specific understandings that it wished, it certainly sailed into the Eastern crisis of 1853 with the conviction that Britain would consult with the Holy Alliance and that France was isolated. These illusions were compounded by the highly optimistic reports that Brunnow, now ambassador in London, sent regarding the attitude of the British government, in particular about the personal opinions of Lord Aberdeen. Should a major dispute arise, it appeared that Russia need only fear the reaction of France. If war came, it would involve France and the Ottoman Empire against Russia, which would have the active or passive support of Austria, Prussia, and Britain.

Relations with France were made worse by a dispute, itself of relatively minor significance, that involved wider issues for both countries. The advent of another Bonaparte to power in 1848 had, as we have seen, caused great uneasiness in St. Petersburg. Since this action violated the treaty of 1814, which denied the throne of France to this family, Nicholas I was willing to organize a European intervention, but he found no supporters among the powers. Considerable ill will was also caused between the nations by the question of titles; the tsar refused to address the French ruler, as was customary, as *"mon frère,"* (my brother), but only as *"cher ami"* (dear friend). The establishment of the Second Empire in December 1852 caused further uneasiness. The Napoleonic name was associated in the Russian mind with French imperial conquests and general war.

The quarrel over the control of certain Holy Places in Jerusalem, the first event leading to the outbreak of the Crimean War, involved Orthodox and Catholic clerics who came into conflict over the possession of certain rights based on past practice and on definite agreements. They also appealed to their great-power patrons.[30] The French backing of the Catholic claims came about primarily because of Napoleon's need for the church's support at home; Nicholas I, as we have seen, was consistently an ardent champion of Orthodox rights. The exact nature of the conflicting claims are not important for this narrative, but they involved such matters as which faith should have the right to repair the cupula of the Church of the Holy Sepulchre and which should be given the keys to the Church of the Nativity in Bethlehem, an action that signified possession.

In this dispute it was the French who took the first steps. During the years of the French revolution and Napoleon, some of the Catholic rights had been allowed to lapse. There were then very few French pilgrims, particularly in contrast to the increasing number of Orthodox visitors. It was only at the time of Louis Napoleon that this question became an issue in French politics. In 1851 the French ambassador in Constantinople intervened in the conflict, basing his position on the Capitulation of 1740. His claim to a French right of intervention, it should be noted, was limited to Catholic ecclessiastics and property, not to the Catholic subjects of the Porte as a whole.

As could be expected, the Russian government reacted at once in defense of the Orthodox. The Porte thus found itself caught between the two powers. The French could use a naval threat, but the Russians had their larger army on the Ottoman border. In 1851 Nicholas I wrote the sultan requesting that the status quo be kept and the French demands rejected. In February 1852 an imperial decree, or *firman*, was issued to this effect, and the sultan sent assurances to the tsar. However, this act was never officially proclaimed, and in December 1852 another firman surrendered to the French demands. The Catholics now received the coveted keys. In answer to the Russian complaints, the foreign minister, Fuad Pasha, argued that France had a treaty, whereas Russia did not.

---

[30]For the Russian role in the origins and diplomacy of the Crimean War, see in particular John Shelton Curtiss, *Russia's Crimean War* (Durham, N.C.: Duke University Press, 1979); Alexander Genrikhovich Jomini, *Etude diplomatique sur la Guerre de Crimée*, 2 vols. (St. Petersburg: Librairie de la Cour Impériale H. Schmitzdorff, 1878); Norman Rich, *Why the Crimean War? A Cautionary Tale* (Hanover, N.H.: University Press of New England, 1985); Anne Pottinger Saab, *The Origins of the Crimean Alliance* (Charlottesville: University Press of Virginia, 1977); Paul W. Schroeder, *Austria, Great Britain, and the Crimean War* (Ithaca, N.Y.: Cornell University Press, 1972); E. V. Tarle, *Krymskaia Voina*, 2 vols. (Moscow: Izdatel'stvo Akademii Nauk SSSR, 1944); and A. M. Zaionchkovskii, *Vostochnaia Voina, 1853–1856* cited previously.

The entire episode was extremely unsettling to Nicholas I. His attitude toward Napoleon III and toward Paris as a revolutionary center made him deeply suspicious of French actions. It seemed as if this country would now assume a prime influence in Constantinople, where, the Russian diplomats recognized, a new generation was in control. The era of reform, which started with the issuance of the Gülhane decree in 1838, had brought a more progressive group of officials to power whose links with France were clear. There was also the possibility that the Porte would use the French connection to get rid of Russian and Orthodox influence.

Some also saw the episode and the crisis that was to follow as a Napoleonic tactic. The Eastern Question had not been a part of the settlement of 1815; it was the one area where the Holy Alliance bonds, in particular the links between Vienna and St. Petersburg, were often fragile. Should a crisis arise, Napoleon III might use the occasion to form a coalition against Russia. Some Russian statesmen, including Nesselrode, worried that, in order to prove himself equal to his famous ancestor, Napoleon might act to cause the collapse of the Ottoman Empire. Although France would not be able to secure the entire heritage, it might obtain lands such as Morocco, Tunis, Egypt, Palestine, Syria, or Crete, or even compensation in Europe, such as Belgium, Savoy, or the Rhine frontier.[31]

By late 1852 it appeared that the conflict was at a deadlock. Since the Porte had apparently caved in before French threats, the Russian government was determined to act in the same manner. In deciding upon a firm course, its leaders felt fairly secure, convinced that both Vienna and London were obligated to consult with St. Petersburg in the event of an Eastern crisis. Three actions were decided upon: First, the Porte was to be assured that should the disputes over the Holy Places lead to war with France, Russia would come to its aid; second, two army corps were mobilized to back up this strong position; and, third, a special mission was sent to Constantinople to secure the Russian demands. Nesselrode advised this move in order to impress upon the sultan the seriousness of the situation.

When deciding on this course of action, the Russian government did not inform either Britain or the Habsburg Empire of its details, although it expected the cooperation of both states. With regard to the monarchy, Russia was at this time giving full support to Habsburg efforts to stop an Ottoman invasion of Montenegro. In Feb-

[31] See Nesselrode to Brunnow, private letter, no. 5, St. Petersburg, January 2, 1853, Zaionchkovskii, *V.V.: Prilozheniia*, I, pp. 365–7.

ruary 1853, at the height of this crisis, Nicholas I wrote to Franz Joseph, assuring him that if the Ottoman Empire declared war, it would be as if it had also been declared on him.[32] The tsar certainly expected a similar trusting attitude on the part of his ally in the dispute with France.

The choice of Prince Alexander Sergeevich Menshikov as special emissary to the Porte was made by the tsar and not by Nesselrode, who preferred Prince Orlov. The envoy had the reputation of being closely associated with conservative Orthodox circles and with sharing the views of Nicholas I. His instructions, which gave him considerable latitude, directed him to settle the Holy Places dispute by securing the promulgation of the firman of February 1852, which settled the question of the possession of the keys to the church in Bethlehem and the repairs to the church of the Holy Sepulchre according to Russian and Orthodox desires.[33] In addition, he was to obtain solid guarantees to ensure that a similar situation did not arise in the future through the negotiation of a solemn engagement or convention (a *sened*) having the force of a treaty, which would make the Russian rights clear. Menshikov was given for this purpose the text of a draft treaty of seven articles.[34] He was also empowered to conclude a secret defensive alliance in case the Ottoman government felt threatened by France, an agreement that was to be limited in duration and to apply only to the situation at hand.[35] In return for the assurance of Russian military aid, the Porte was expected to conclude the desired settlement of the Holy Places controversy.

At this time and later, the tsar and his advisers were evidently convinced that they were demanding no new privileges, but only written assurances similar to those in French possession of their legal rights. To strengthen his position, Menshikov was given the authority to deliver an ultimatum and to leave should he not be able to negotiate an agreement. He was also allowed to alter his instructions as he saw fit. The goal of the Menshikov mission was thus to ensure the continuation of the successful policy that the Russian government had carried out since Adrianople: the maintenance of the status quo in the Near East and thus the territorial integrity of

[32]Nicholas I to Franz Joseph, St. Petersburg, February 11/23, 1853, ibid., I, pp. 368–9.
[33]Menshikov's instructions can be found in nine documents printed in ibid., I, pp. 369–82.
[34]The draft convention is in ibid., I, pp. 382–5.
[35]The text of the secret, separate agreement is in ibid., I, pp. 385–6.

the Ottoman Empire, but with a strong Russian influence in Constantinople.

It is interesting to note that at the time of the sending of the mission, Nicholas I was considering that war might come and, as a result, the Ottoman Empire might collapse. Among the alternate possibilities for its replacement, he did indeed consider an independent Serbia and Bulgaria, but also the annexation of the Principalities and Bulgarian land as far as Kustendil by Russia. He recognized that such a settlement would have to take into account the interests of all the other powers, but his prime concern was obviously with protecting Russian strategic interests.[36]

After his arrival in Constantinople on February 28, Menshikov worked for the implementation of his instructions. With the view held commonly on the proper way to handle Ottoman ministers, he adopted a harsh tone. He demanded and secured the removal of Fuad as foreign minister and his replacement by Rifat, whom the Russians regarded as more compliant. However, if pressure and intimidation were to decide the question, the Russian envoy was soon to meet his match when on April 5 Stratford Canning, now Lord Stratford de Redcliffe, returned as British ambassador.

Although Stratford did in fact follow his instructions, which were to advise moderation to the Ottoman government, British policy in fact began to shift as the significance of the Menshikov demands became more apparent and British as well as French statesmen were forced to confront exactly what was meant by the word "protection." Thus, although Brunnow continued to send optimistic despatches from London about the British attitude, that country was gradually moving into the position of becoming the strongest defender of Ottoman interests against what appeared to be a Russian threat to the territorial and political integrity of the Muslim empire. Thus what started out as a confrontation between Russia and France over religious rights in Palestine gradually turned into a Russian–British conflict over Russia's relationship with the Orthodox in the empire. Stated in this manner, Britain became the chief Russian adversary despite the tsar's illusions about his relationship with London. This question also had a grave disadvantage for Russia in that it brought together Britain and France, two powers with severe differences elsewhere. Nicholas's policy of attempting to isolate France was thus endangered, a situation that affected Russian general interests in Europe.

[36]Notes by Nicholas I on the Eastern Question, 1853, ibid., I, pp. 357–8.

The quarrel over the specific rights of Orthodox and Catholics in regard to the Holy Places was soon settled. On the advice of Stratford, the Ottoman government separated these issues from the more general questions that had meanwhile arisen. A settlement was in fact negotiated between Menshikov and the French ambassador without much difficulty; on these questions the Russian government was willing to make some concessions. The major issue, and the one that was the basic cause of the Crimean War, nevertheless remained. Menshikov's instructions, it will be remembered, called for guarantees for the future in the form of a document, having the force of a treaty, that would clearly state the Russian rights in regard to the Orthodox. The achievement of such an agreement became the main objective of Menshikov's further negotiations.

In the subsequent discussions the arguments focused principally on exactly what Article VII of the Treaty of Kuchuk Kainardji signified and what rights of protection in regard to the Balkan Christians it allowed the Russian government. It must first be recalled that Article VII had been singularly ineptly formulated. Containing two different concepts, it first ensured that "the Sublime Porte promises to protect constantly the Christian religion and its churches," and, second, it allowed "the Ministers of the Imperial Court of Russia to make, upon all occasions, representations, as well in favor of the new church at Constantinople, of which mention will be made in Article XIV, as on behalf of its officiating ministers, promising to take such representations into due consideration, as being made by a confidential functionary of a neighboring and sincerely friendly Power."[37] After 1774, as we have seen, this treaty was made the basis for further understandings that did define specific Russian rights and responsibilities. In the Treaty of Kuchuk Kainardji itself and in subsequent agreements, the Russian government did indeed receive definite rights of protection in the Danubian Principalities and Serbia; it shared in the three-power protectorate of Greece. Where the waters became murky was over questions in regard to the populations of Bulgaria, Macedonia, Bosnia, Hercegovina, Albania, and the Greek-inhabited lands still under Ottoman rule. It should be noted that although Kuchuk Kainardji referred to Christians in general, the Russian government at this time claimed only the right to speak for the Orthodox, leaving the protection of the Catholics to Austria and France.

[37] Holland, *Treaty Relations*, p. 41. For the various interpretations of the treaty see Temperley, *The Crimea*, pp. 467–9.

Aside from the exact wording of the treaties, it is important to emphasize that the Russian attitude was also based on the subsequent use and interpretation of the text. Certainly, diplomats of all countries, not just Russia, had freely employed expressions that implied a recognition of Russian rights of protection. Some, as well as the Russian diplomats, had believed that Article VII did give Russia the right to make representations should the Sublime Porte not protect the Christian religion. Although the issue had arisen often, for instance, during the Greek revolution, it had never been clearly spelled out what the Russian rights and obligations were should the Ottoman government act unjustly or with violence toward its Christian subjects.

Nicholas I and his diplomats argued along one line. Thus on December 15, 1853, in a letter to Queen Victoria, Nicholas declared:

. . . it is clear that this treaty confers upon us and has always conferred upon us the right to watch over the effective protection of our coreligionists in Turkey.

It is thus that for three-quarters of a century Russia and the Porte itself have constantly understood it. To maintain this interpretation of its original concept and, since the Porte invalidates it, to confirm it by a new engagement, that is the objective of my efforts and the aim that I must pursue at all hazards, because it concerns here a point vital for the existence as well as for the honor of Russia, for which no sacrifice costs too much to safeguard both.[38]

For Nicholas I the issue of treaty rights was extremely important. As we have seen, throughout his reign he had strongly supported the European treaty system and the fulfillment of the letter and spirit of international agreements. As an autocrat of the old school, he saw his personal honor and that of his nation as involved in the upholding of a treaty relationship that he was convinced existed and that he believed necessary for the prestige and security of Russia.

The tsar's interpretation of Kuchuk Kainardji was argued strongly by his diplomats and apparently shared by them. Thus the Russian ambassador in Vienna, Peter Kazimirovich Meyendorff, wrote to Nesselrode:

. . . [the Porte] contests with Russia the right to protect and watch over the liberty of the Orthodox cult in Turkey. . . . What would have been in fact the aim and the meaning of the stipulations of Kainardji, if it is not to grant to Russia that right that is being challenged today after 80 years when we have constantly exercised it? If England, after having conquered a Catholic power, let us say Spain, would have obtained from it in a treaty of peace the promise of freedom of religion for the Spanish Protestants, and supposing that there had been millions of them, would she [England] not be considered to have the right to watch over the strict fulfillment

[38]Nicholas II to Queen Victoria, December 3/15, 1853; Zaionchkovskii, *V.V.: Prilozheniia,* II, pp. 204–5.

of that promise, and still Catholicism is not more hostile to Protestants than Islam to the Christian religion. . . . Russia, it seems to me, asks only for the right of protection and surveillance, and there is nothing there that is wrong, for what does a promise signify if the one which receives it is not able to check on it and if necessary to demand its accomplishment?[39]

The Russian interpretation of Article VII was the basis of the three proposals that Menshikov introduced during the successive stages of the negotiations: the draft treaty contained in his instructions; the draft sened of May 5, 1853; and the final draft note of May 20. Because of their importance to this narrative, the crucial sections of each will be quoted.

The preamble of the proposed treaty stated that the tsar and the sultan, in order to preserve peace and harmony and to strengthen their relations, had resolved on "the conclusion of a special convention, having the force and validity of a treaty and destined to better explain and make precise the terms and the meaning of Articles VII, VIII, XIV and XVI of the treaty concluded in the year 1774 at Kuchuk Kainardji and confirmed by subsequent treaties and that of Adrianople." The first article, directly related to this declaration, recalled the wording of Article VII:

> The Imperial Court of Russia and the Ottoman Sublime Porte, desiring to prevent and to remove forever any reason for disagreement, for doubt, or for misunderstanding on the subject of the immunities, rights, and liberties accorded and assured *ab antiquo* by the Ottoman emperors in their states to the Greek-Russian-Orthodox religion, professed by all Russia, as by all the inhabitants of the principalities of Moldavia, Wallachia, and Serbia and by various other Christian populations of Turkey of different provinces, agree and stipulate by the present convention that the Christian Orthodox religion will be constantly protected in all its churches, and that the ministers of the Imperial Court of Russia will have, as in the past, the right to make representations on behalf of the churches of Constantinople and of other places and cities, as also on behalf of the clergy, and that these remonstrances will be received as coming in the name of a neighboring and sincerely friendly power.[40]

The relevant section of the draft sened of May 5 was much simpler: Article I stated:

> No change shall be made in the rights, privileges, and immunities that the churches, the pious institutions and the Orthodox clergy have enjoyed or are in

---

[39]Meyendorff to Nesselrode, Vienna, October 7/19, 1853. Otto Hoetzsch, ed., *Peter von Meyendorff; Ein russischer Diplomat an den Höfen von Berlin und Wien: Briefwechsel* (Berlin and Leipzig: Walter de Gruyter & Co., 1923), III, pp. 82–3. Cited hereafter as Meyendorff, *Briefwechsel*.

[40]Draft of a convention with the Porte, St. Petersburg, January 28, 1853, Zaionchkovskii, *V.V.: Prilozheniia*, I, pp. 382–5.

their possession *ab antiquo* in the states of the Ottoman Sublime Porte, which is pleased to assure these to them forever on the basis of the *strict status quo* existing today.[41]

The second article of this document provided that any concessions made to other Christian faiths should also be "considered as belonging also to the Orthodox cult."

The final Russian offer, contained in the note of May 20, softened the form but not the basic content of the demands:

The Orthodox cult of the Orient, its clergy, its churches, and its possessions, as well as its religious establishments, will enjoy in the future without any injury, under the aegis of His Majesty the Sultan, the privileges and immunities that have been assured to them *ab antiquo*, or that have been granted to them on different occasions by Imperial favor, and in a principle of high equity they will participate in the advantages accorded to other Christian rites, as well as to the foreign legations accredited to the Sublime Porte, by convention or special arrangement.[42]

Throughout the negotiations the Ottoman position remained virtually unchanged. It was willing to issue declarations on its own account recognizing the religious rights of its citizens, but it refused to agree to the conclusion of a special arrangement with one power. The Ottoman standpoint was clearly expressed in a note of May 10, 1853:

. . . the Sublime Porte is entirely disposed to observe scrupulously the religious immunities which all the subjects of the Sublime Porte enjoy . . . even though the intentions of the Russian government may be friendly, but should a government make with another government a *sened* on such a delicate question . . . it is evident to all in general that it is not only entirely contrary to the rights of governments, but that it destroys the foundation of sovereign independence.[43]

It is interesting to note that this negative attitude toward Menshi-kov's demands also reflected the views of the Constantinople Patriarchate. Although all Orthodox, lay and clerical alike, strongly favored Russian intervention against a Catholic threat, both the patriarch and the synod opposed allowing Russia any kind of official protectorate. They did not want any outside power intervening in their affairs. They were also well aware that the Orthodox church within the Russian empire did not have a position similar to

[41]Note of Menshikov to Rifat, April 23/May 5, 1853, with enclosed draft sened, ibid., I, pp. 407–10.
[42]Draft of a note proposed by Menshikov to the Porte, May 8/20, 1853, ibid., I, pp. 434–6.
[43]Official note of the Porte, April 28/May 10, 1853, ibid., I, pp. 417–18.

the one they enjoyed: A strengthening of the Russian position could thus lead to a diminution of their own authority.

The Russian demands, clearly stated in Menshikov's proposals, together with the Ottoman refusal to accept their basic premises, confronted the representatives of the other powers, in particular those of Britain and France, with a major problem. Although they had indeed in the past been very free in using expressions suggesting that Russia did have a "special position" in relation to the Ottoman Orthodox, they feared that the acceptance of any of the Russian proposals would in practice hand over effective control of the Ottoman Empire to St. Petersburg. They were now more concerned with the practical consequences than with the Russian theoretical justifications. The general opinion was thus close to that expressed earlier by Lord Palmerston:

> The Kainardji treaty contains indeed a promise to protect the Christian religion generally and to attend to Russian representations as to the Greek church at Constantinople, but that is very different from giving Russia a right of interference in all matters spiritual and temporal in which Greek subjects of the Sultan are concerned.[44]

Nicholas and his advisers were, of course, well aware of these objections. The Russian counterarguments were that they were only seeking in written form the privileges that they in fact enjoyed, that they had always held the right of protection, and that they had not used it to challenge the authority of the Porte over its own lands. Indeed, as we have certainly seen, Russian tsars had usually urged upon the Balkan Christians the duty of obeying their legitimate monarch. The Russian representatives also denied that they were seeking a political rather than a spiritual protectorship; what they had in mind was instead a "religious patronage." Given the Ottoman millet system, with its identification of religion and politics, most diplomats understood that such a separation could in fact not be made.

Unable to fulfill the objectives of his mission, Menshikov, following his instructions, issued an ultimatum and, when its terms were not met, he left Constantinople on May 21. From this time on, by slow stages over a ten-month period, Russia and the Western sea powers moved toward a military confrontation. With the increase in tension the British and French fleets moved to Besika Bay, an

---

[44]Quoted in Temperley, *The Crimea*, p. 469. The French reaction was similar. Kiselev despatch, no. 349, Paris, August 1, 1853, Zaionchkovskii, *V.V.: Prilozheniia*, II, pp. 12–18.

Ottoman roadsted near the Dardanelles, in early June. At the beginning of July, in an action that we have seen in previous crises between Russia and the Ottoman Empire, the Russian army entered the Principalities. Despite the fact that the occupation was a hostile act, the Russian government declared that it wished to avoid an "offensive war." The aim was to obtain "a material guarantee" and to counter the move of the Western fleets, which constituted a "maritime occupation." At the same time, strict limits were placed on the Russian actions. A Nesselrode circular despatch thus declared:

In occupying the Principalities for a time, we disavow beforehand any idea of conquest. We do not intend to obtain any increase in territory. Knowingly and voluntarily we will not seek to excite any uprising among the Christian populations of Turkey.[45]

Even after the break between Russia and the Ottoman Empire, the diplomats cooperated to attempt to find a formula that would satisfy both contending powers. At this time and throughout the next years Vienna was the center for negotiations. Here in July the Habsburg foreign minister, Karl Ferdinand von Buol-Schauenstein, with the cooperation of the British, French, and Prussian representatives, drafted the Vienna Note, which was intended to meet the objections of both the Porte and the Russian government. The declaration was designed to be signed by the sultan and sent to St. Petersburg. The significant section stated:

If the Emperors of Russia have at all times evinced their active solicitude for the maintenance of the immunities and privileges of the Orthodox Greek Church in the Ottoman Empire, the Sultans have never refused again to confirm them by solemn acts testifying their ancient and constant benevolence toward their Christian subjects. . . . The undersigned has in consequence received orders to declare by the present note that the Government of His Majesty the Sultan will remain faithful to the letter and the spirit of the Treaties of Kainardji and Adrianople relative to the protection of the Christian religion, and that His Majesty considers himself bound in honor to cause to be observed for ever, and to preserve from all prejudice either now or hereafter, the enjoyment of the spiritual privileges which have been granted by His Majesty's august ancestors to the Orthodox Eastern Church and which are maintained and confirmed by him; and, moreover, in a spirit of exalted equity, to cause the Greek rite to share in the advantages granted to the other Christian rites by convention or special arrangement.[46]

[45] Nesselrode circular despatch on the occupation of the Principalities, June 20/July 2, 1853, ibid., II, pp. 5–9.
[46] Text of the Vienna Note, ibid., II, pp. 52–3. English translation in Curtiss, *Russia's Crimean War*, pp. 567–8.

This statement met the Russian desires; it rested on the obligations contained in previous treaties, and the assurances were given in the name of the sultan. The Russian government thus accepted it on August 5, but with the stipulation that the Porte was not to make further conditions. When the Ottoman reply did indeed demand alterations that St. Petersburg could not accept, this attempt to secure a settlement also failed.

Meanwhile, the Ottoman ministers had become well aware of their favorable diplomatic position. In this crisis, it appeared that both Britain and France were aligned with them against Russia. The temptation to use this unusual opportunity was strong. On October 4 an Ottoman declaration of war was issued; the Russian occupation of the Principalities was the justification. At the same time the British and French fleets, which had been stationed at Besika Bay, moved into the Straits. On November 30 the Russian navy in the Black Sea destroyed an Ottoman fleet at the battle of Sinope. Finally, on March 28, 1854, Britain and France declared war.

In his manifesto at the beginning of the hostilities with the sea powers, the tsar emphasized the Orthodox origins of the struggle:

> From the very beginning of our Dispute with the Turkish government, we solemnly announced to our Faithful Subjects that a feeling of justice had alone induced us to reestablish the injured Rights of Orthodox Christians, subjects of the Ottoman Porte.
>
> We have not sought, nor do we seek, to make conquests, or to exercise in Turkey any supremacy whatever which was of such a nature as to exceed the influence belonging to Russia by virtue of existing treaties. . . .
>
> Ready to confound the audacity of the enemy, shall she deviate from the sacred aim assigned to her by Divine Providence? No! Russia has not forgotten God! It is not for worldly interests that she has taken up arms; she fights for the Christian Faith, for the defense of her co-religionists oppressed by implacable enemies.[47]

In the spring of 1854 the Russian government thus found itself in exactly the position that it had made great efforts to avoid previously: It faced a coalition of France, Britain, the Ottoman Empire, and eventually Piedmont over an issue connected with the Eastern

---

[47]Russian Manifesto Relative to the War with Great Britain, France, and Turkey, St. Petersburg, April 11/23, 1854, Hertslet, *Map of Europe*, II, pp. 1205–6. The same religious theme was contained in other declarations of the tsar. For instance, in June he wrote to King Frederick William IV of Prussia: "It remains to me now only to fight, to conquer or to perish with honor, as a martyr for our holy faith." Nicholas I to Frederick William IV, private letter, Peterhof, June 17/29, 1854. Theodor Schiemann, *Kaiser Nikolaus* (Berlin and Leipzig: Walter de Gruyter & Co., 1919), IV, pp. 429–31.

Question, and one for which it could not expect to receive the enthusiastic support of its Holy Alliance partners. How little Nicholas I could rely on the Habsburg Empire was soon to be demonstrated, and the attitude of Vienna was crucial. In order to win, the Russian army needed a free passage across the Danube, over the Balkan Mountains, to Constantinople. The Habsburg army could, of course, menace this line of attack; as Nesselrode wrote in May 1854, Austria "holds the sword of Damocles suspended over our head."[48] The Russian army could not advance in the Balkans unless it was assured of a friendly attitude on the part of the Habsburg forces concentrated in Transylvania and Galicia.

Even more important, once the war involved the sea powers, the Habsburg position, as well as that of the German states, was of even greater significance. This conflict opened the Baltic and the Far East as additional areas of combat. Russia also needed troops to ensure that there would be no rebellions in the Polish lands or the Caucasus. With insufficient forces to deal even with these threats, it was absolutely essential that the Habsburg and German areas remain at least neutral. In the discussions throughout this period the Russian goal was to obtain a clear assurance of Habsburg neutrality, not a war alliance. In the effort to continue what he thought was his close association with the Habsburg court, Nicholas I made repeated attempts to induce its representatives to cooperate with him. Although the Russian public declarations in this crisis emphasized that there was to be no attempt to change the status quo in the Near East, the tsar was evidently convinced that the war would encourage the Christian nationalities to rise spontaneously, an action that would result in the dissolution of the empire. In his approaches to Austria he therefore also attempted to negotiate something like a partition of influence agreement.

At first, Nicholas I appears to have been as optimistic about the Austrian attitude as he had previously been about the British. He was firmly convinced that the Holy Alliance ties remained strong. Moreover, he expected Habsburg gratitude. He had not only sent his troops against the Hungarian revolution in 1849, but he had supported the Austrian position in the recent controversy over Montenegro. What the tsar did not adequately consider at this time were the difficulties of the Habsburg position in relation to both the Western

[48]Nesselrode to Meyendorff, St. Petersburg, May 24, 1854, Nesselrode, *Lettres et papiers*, XI, pp. 61–3.

powers and the Balkan national question. As a multinational Catholic state, the Habsburg Empire had in fact much the same interests as Britain and France in the Eastern Question, although not in general European issues. It certainly did not wish to see a weakening, much less an ending, of Ottoman control over the Balkan peninsula. A great Russian diplomatic or military victory over the Ottoman Empire was thus not desired. As in previous similar crises, the Habsburg leaders believed that they could not compete with Russia in winning the support of the Balkan nationalities. Moreover, the national issue had implications for their own country; the memory of 1848 was still alive. Should the Habsburg Empire take a position favoring Russia against the Western states, the danger existed that France would use the opportunity to encourage Italian rebellion.[49]

Despite the difficulties in the situation, Nicholas I and his advisers placed great emphasis on securing a clear understanding with the Habsburg Empire, particularly after the breakdown of relations with the Porte and the increasing tension with the sea powers. In return, they offered a share in influence in the Balkan peninsula. In a letter of May 30, 1853, Nicholas I wrote to Franz Joseph, informing him that he intended to occupy the Principalities and suggesting that Austria could act similarly in Serbia and Hercegovina.[50] On July 2, as the Russian army was entering the Principalities, the tsar sent another letter in which he expressed his concern about what would happen in the Balkans should the conflict become a general war involving France and Britain as well as the Ottoman Empire.[51] He then expected that the Christian population would revolt, and neither the Porte nor the Western states would be able to suppress the movements. Thus, even without Russian encouragement or participation, Ottoman control in Europe would be ended. Under

[49]On January 7, 1854, the French foreign minister, Edouard Drouyn de Lhuys, remarked to the Austrian ambassador in Paris, Joseph Alexander von Hübner: "France with Austria is a conservative power, France at war with Austria is a revolutionary power." J. A. von Hübner, *Neuf Ans de souvenirs d'un ambassadeur d'Autriche à Paris, 1851–1859* (Paris: Librairie Plon, 1905), I, p. 198.

[50]In his reply, Franz Joseph wrote that great care should be taken regarding the question of occupying Serbia. Nothing should be done that was openly hostile to the Ottoman Empire, because that might cause France to cooperate with the revolutionaries. Franz Joseph to Nicholas I, private letter, Vienna, June 15, 1853. *AGK*, I: 1, pp. 195–6.

[51]Nicholas I to Franz Joseph, Peterhof, June 20/July 2, 1853. Zaionchkovskii, *V.V.: Prilozheniia*, II, pp. 243–4.

these circumstances the tsar wished the Habsburg government to make its views and intentions known. He again gave assurances that Russia desired no conquests; in fact, its armies, after occupying the Principalities, would not cross the Danube. However, the future had to be considered. Returning to his previous plans for the partition of the empire, Nicholas I suggested that each Balkan region – Moldavia, Serbia, and Bulgaria, for instance – should be given its independence but placed under joint Russian–Habsburg protection. Constantinople could be made a free city and the forts on the Bosphorus and Dardanelles destroyed.

After the Ottoman declaration of war in November and the heightening of the crisis, Nicholas sent Prince Orlov to Vienna in January 1854; again the objective was to secure a declaration of Austrian neutrality.[52] The situation had now changed. Despite the previous assurances, Orlov informed the Austrian ruler that the Russian army might cross the Danube; a general rising of the Christian population was then expected. The Russian envoy repeated the previous suggestion that independent Balkan states be established under a joint protectorship.

These proposals did little more than increase the Austrian apprehensions and distrust of Russian motives. The Habsburg government could not fulfill the Russian desires without guarantees that Ottoman territorial integrity and independence would be maintained, that Russian troops would not cross the Danube, and that the occupation of the Principalities would not last too long – in other words, conditions that the Russian government could not accept. In addition, at this time, in view of their fears concerning potential French actions in Italy, the Habsburg statesmen could not afford to take any definite steps that would make it appear that they were acting in close cooperation with Russia.[53] Their objective was to secure an agreement between Russia and the Ottoman Empire, such as that contained in the Vienna Note of the previous July.

In these negotiations the Austrian fears about the consequences of Russian-sponsored Balkan national movements were clearly appar-

---

[52] Orlov's reports on the meetings are in Orlov to Nicholas I, private letter, Vienna, January 23/February 4, 1854; and Orlov to Nesselrode, nos. 1 and 2, Vienna, January 22/February 3, 1854, ibid., II, pp. 262–70.

[53] For instance, a diplomat remarked to Hübner in Paris that an Austrian occupation of Serbia and Bosnia could result in the loss of Lombardy. Hübner to Buol, Paris, November 13, 1853, ibid., II, pp. 176–7.

ent.[54] The Habsburg statesmen simply did not trust the Russian declarations, particularly when they involved the establishment of Balkan states. They distrusted the offers of a joint protectorship because they were convinced that Russia would always have a stronger influence with the Orthodox. Their greatest concern, however, was what would happen if the Russian army crossed the Danube. Like the Russians, they felt that a spontaneous uprising would occur and, if it were successful, it could not be suppressed later. They were worried in particular that the northern provinces of the Ottoman Empire, those adjacent to the Habsburg Empire and the Danube, would rise in rebellion. Convinced that independent Balkan states would be either satellites or allies of Russia, they could not allow the Danube to become a "Russian river" or the lands on their southern border to be organized under Russian supervision. Under these circumstances plans were made in February 1854 to occupy Serbia if necessary. The aim was to prevent an extension of the Russian protectorship of the Principalities westward through Serbia and Bosnia to Montenegro. As far as Serbia was concerned, it was to keep its autonomous privileges but to remain in the Ottoman Empire.[55]

In the next months Russia's relations with its Holy Alliance partner deteriorated swiftly. Deeply concerned about the Russian presence in the Principalities, aware of the implications of a possible Russian victory over the Ottoman Empire, and fearful of French actions in Italy, the Habsburg Empire moved into a position of neutrality, but one that was inimicable to Russia. In June 1854, in order to lessen the dangers on the Balkan front, the Habsburg government demanded that Russia withdraw its troops from the Principalities, and it concluded an agreement with the Porte. The Russian government, under the circumstances, had little choice; when the withdrawal was completed, Austrian and Ottoman forces moved in. This action, together with the Habsburg ultimatum of December 1855, which forced Russia to the peace table, left lasting and bitter memories in Russian minds.

[54]For the Habsburg attitude toward the Russian proposals at this time, see the reports on the two ministerial conferences held on January 23 and 31, 1854. *AGK*, I; 1, pp. 521–4, 551–4; and Buol to Franz Joseph, Vienna, January 16, 1854, and Buol to Esterházy, no. 3, Vienna, March 5, 1854, ibid., I: 1, pp. 505–7, 640–1.

[55]On the question of a possible occupation of Serbia and the plans made for it, see Buol to Coronini, Vienna, July 18, 1853; Buol to Coronini, February 2, 1854; Franz Joseph to Coronini, Vienna, February 2, 1854; and Buol to Esterházy, Vienna, April 17, 1854, ibid., I: 1, pp. 258–60, 557–8, and 558–60, I: 2, pp. 114–16.

At the beginning of the crisis Nicholas I had been convinced that he shared common interests with Franz Joseph; his letters were affectionate and intimate. For instance, on November 26, 1853, after the Ottoman declaration of war, the tsar wrote an emotional justification of his actions, ending with the words: "Let me again embrace you tenderly and tell you that my friendship for you is and will be unalterable and that it is deep in my soul, that I am for life, my very dear friend, your faithful and devoted brother, friend and ally."[56] In July 1854, stung by the Habsburg policies, Nicholas I told the Austrian envoy, Count Valentin Ladislaus Esterházy, that Franz Joseph had completely forgotten what he had done for him and that "the confidence which had existed until now between the two sovereigns for the happiness of their empires being destroyed, the same intimate relations could not exist any more."[57] The implications of this break for Vienna were not to be fully apparent for another decade.

As the Habsburg officials feared, there were some Russian plans to exploit the Balkan situation. Although Field Marshal Ivan Fedorovich Paskevich, in command of the Russian army, opposed the use of Balkan volunteers paid and organized by Russia, the possible value of a Christian revolt was discussed in the fall and winter of 1853–4. The tsar and his advisers, convinced that a rebellion would break out spontaneously once Russian troops crossed the Danube, developed plans on the basis not of organizing or sponsoring a revolt, but of handling the situation in a manner of benefit to Russia. The difficulties and dangers were made clear in a note written by the tsar at the time that attempts were being made to persuade the Habsburg government to accept an arrangement on the Balkans. At this time Nicholas I was concerned that British policy might change, and that instead of supporting Ottoman integrity, its government would sponsor the emancipation of the Christians. British leadership in this movement was obviously contrary to Rus-

---

[56]Nicholas I to Franz Joseph, Gachina, November 14, 1853, Zaionchkovskii, *V.V.: Prilozheniia*, II, pp. 250–1.

[57]Esterházy to Buol, no. 60A, St. Petersburg, June 24/July 6, 1854, *AGK*, I: 2, pp. 247–9. Nicholas I wrote to King Frederick William IV at the time of the Russian withdrawal from the Principalities his opinion about the Austrian emperor: "He wished to break the most affectionate (*tendre*) ties that I had believed solidly established between us; he did it in the most base (*noire*), the most callous (*sensible*) manner for my heart. The rest does not concern me any more; it is he who will give an account to God. It remains to me only to do my duty, as long as it pleases God to leave me at the head of Russia." Nicholas I to Frederick William IV, Alexandria, August 14/26, 1854, Schiemann, *Kaiser Nikolaus*, IV, pp. 434–5.

sian interests. To combat this "infamous plan," Nicholas I suggested that Russia should declare openly its support for the independence of the Christian states and call on the European powers to join in the achievement of this "sacred aim."[58]

In reply Nesselrode drew up a report that was an excellent summation of the difficulties of the Russian position in regard to the Balkan people.[59] The minister too expected an unprovoked uprising once the Russian army crossed the Danube. He was, however, extremely pessimistic about the outcome. Without Russian aid he expected that the Ottoman army would crush any rebellion. Since Russian military strength was barely sufficient to hold the Principalities, such assistance could not be given. Moreover, any Russian call for Christian independence would jeopardize the diplomatic negotiations that were going on. The Russian government had hitherto declared that it did not seek the downfall of the Ottoman Empire. It had given assurances at the time of the occupation of the Principalities that revolts would not be encouraged. If it now declared that it had as an aim to free the Balkan Christians, the other powers would remain extremely suspicious about the true Russian intentions.

The strong point in Nesselrode's report was, however, its clear statement of the relationship of conservative, autocratic Russia to national revolutionary movements. The minister pointed out that the traditional Russian position had been to oppose national causes, such as the Polish, Hungarian, and Italian movements, as well as those in the Danubian Principalities and among the Caucasian mountaineers. It would thus be difficult for Russia to call upon the European nations to support Balkan insurrection. In fact, the Porte could use similar tactics and proclaim the independence of the Circassians and other Muslim peoples under Russian rule. The Western powers could aid these people by sea. The revolutionary side of the question also had to be considered. The conservative forces in Europe would be alienated by any change in the Russian policy of opposing revolutionary activities.

Nesselrode, nevertheless, recognized that if the war entered a more active stage, and if the Christians rose, even without Russian encouragement, then Russia would have to become involved. Such an action would lead to the collapse of the Ottoman Empire, a state that at the time, however, showed no sign of disintegrating.

[58]Nicholas I notes, Zaionchkovskii, *V.V.: Prilozheniia*, II, pp. 321–2.
[59]Nesselrode memorandum, with annotations by Nicholas I, November 8, 1853, ibid., II, pp. 322–6.

In his comments on Nesselrode's report, Nicholas I signified his agreement with most of the arguments. Obviously, a campaign in the Balkans could not be commenced until spring; a declaration on emancipation would be best made when the Russian army crossed the Danube. At this time the tsar made clear that he and his advisers, as had also been the case during the Greek rebellion, did not really know much about the Balkan Christians. At this late date Nicholas I decided that he did not want to support any Balkan uprising until reliable information had been obtained on "the degree of confidence that we are able to base on the disposition of the Christian provinces and on the aid which they are able to offer in the case of the next operations. That should precede everything, and there is no time to lose to carry this out."

In December, in implementing the tsar's instructions, Nesselrode wrote to Meyendorff about a possible crossing of the Danube in the coming campaign and made clear the weakness of the Russian knowledge of Balkan conditions:[60]

> You understand that at the moment when, forced by circumstances, we see ourselves obliged to pass to the offensive, to cross over the Danube, it is important for us to know to what point it will be permitted to us to count on the cooperation of the Christian populations under the control of the sultan; unfortunately, they will be in that eventuality the only ally which remains for us. It has thus appeared indispensable to the emperor to gather from now on some more exact and more detailed ideas, above all on the true dispositions of these peoples; on the effect that the war, which just broke out between us and the Porte, has produced on them; on the chiefs which would place themselves at the head of this movement; finally on the kind of aid that it is possible to give them while awaiting the moment when they will find it in our military operations.

Meyendorff shared Nesselrode's concerns about the Balkan situation. He feared that if peace was not made, it would be difficult to refuse the assistance of "the little Christian peoples (*les peuplades chrétiennes*)." They were, however, not ready for a war against the Porte. In the past Russia "had done nothing not only to assure . . . the eventual cooperation of these bellicose races" but had "even left them in a state of military destitution," which meant that they could not resist Ottoman oppression.[61]

The entire question of Balkan rebellion and the Russian attitude toward it was, of course, closely tied to the military planning. As

---

[60]Nesselrode to Meyendorff, St. Petersburg, December 2, 1853. Nesselrode, *Lettres et papiers*, X, pp. 307–10.
[61]Meyendorff to Nesselrode, Vienna, November 29/December 11, 1853. Meyendorff, *Briefwechsel*, III, pp. 100–4.

long as there was a possibility of a Danube crossing and as long as the Russian army remained in the Principalities, such events had to be considered. Although Russian support of a Balkan revolt was discussed in the spring, the increasingly hostile attitude of Austria endangered the entire Russian military position. Moreover, by June, as Nesselrode informed Meyendorff, the tsar had given up hope of seeing the Christians rise en masse.[62] The evacuation of the Principalities in August ended any possibility of using a Balkan revolt for Russian advantage.

It has been seen that during this period the Russian statesmen assumed that they had the support and friendship of the Balkan people and that they in some manner could speak for them, even without relying on the Treaty of Kuchuk Kainardji. Although undoubtedly in some regions still under direct Ottoman control, such as the Bulgarian lands, there was a great fund of support, that was certainly not true in the states under Russian protection. In Serbia and the Danubian Principalities, Russian intervention in internal politics had won the protecting power a great deal of ill will.

The situation was particularly tense in the Principalities, which had been evacuated by the Russian army only two years previously. At the beginning of the occupation the princes in office, Barbu Stirbei and Grigore Ghica, were caught between the Russian demand that they break relations with the Porte and the Ottoman directive, backed by Britain, that they leave their posts. Following the latter advice, they did indeed depart for Vienna. Thereafter, the two provinces were placed under a Russian military government, with General Andrei Fedorovich Budberg holding the office of president plenipotentiary. The boyar councils were filled with Russian supporters.

As previously, this military occupation, which lasted from July 1853 to August 1854, when the last units left, caused extreme discontent. Exerting strong control, the Russian authorities placed limits on public meetings, and a strict censorship was introduced. Once again, Russian requisitions of supplies and transport caused discontent. Even the Russian officers gave negative reports on the attitude of the population. General Michael Dmitrievich Gorchakov blamed the bad spirit of the inhabitants at least in part on the actions of "a revoltionary party" in Bucharest that he judged devoted to the

---

[62]Nesselrode to Meyendorff, St. Petersburg, June 9, 1854. Nesselrode, *Lettres et papiers*, XI, pp. 64–6.

Ottoman Empire.[63] He also formed a low opinion of the fighting spirit of the people. He reported that the Wallachian militia, which was integrated into the Russian forces, did not want to fight for or against Russia and that its officers were cowards.

Serbia, also under Russian protection, showed similar signs of discontent. This state was important in a time of crisis because of its strategic position in regard to both the Habsburg Empire and the eastern Balkan lands that could be the scene of any Russian march to Constantinople. Yet at this time Russian relations with Prince Alexander and his ministers were not good. In September 1852 Garašanin became premier and foreign minister, positions he was to hold until the Russian government forced his dismissal in March 1853. Nicholas I disliked him for his general policies and his ties with Polish and Hungarian revolutionaries. The Serbian minister was, as we have seen, a strong nationalist with a program aimed at the unification of ethnic and historical Serbian lands. No Panslav, he feared that a Russian domination of the Balkans would result in the absorption of Serbia by the great Slavic power. Russian opposition to his presence in the Serbian government caused him to write in August 1852:

And why should I care whether Russia can tolerate me or not? I eat bread not with Russian teeth but with my own and those of my forefathers; I am not a servant of Russia. When my father fought for the freedom of my country in the first and second uprisings and shed blood for it, he truly did not know that the Russians existed.[64]

With this attitude on the part of Serbia's chief minister, and with the general Russian conviction that the Orthodox Balkan people should be compliant and submissive, it is understandable why strong pressure was put on the Serbian government in the matter. During his mission in Constantinople, Menshikov visited Constantine Nikolajević, the Serbian representative, and conveyed the message that the tsar had instructed him to inform Prince Alexander that he should dismiss Garašanin. The Serbian minister, when he learned of the Russian intervention, refused to step down. In a letter to Nikolajević of March 6, 1853, he explained that should the Russian demands be met:

[63]General Gorchakov to the Military Ministry, Bucharest, November 4, 1853. Zaionchkovskii, *V.V.: Prilozheniia*, II, pp. 148–50. On the Wallachian discontent with the occupation see also Laurin to Buol, no. 72, Bucharest, May 21, 1854. *AGK*: I: 2, pp. 166–8.

[64]Quoted in MacKenzie, *Ilija Garašanin*, p. 124.

. . . Serbia would be transformed into a Russian province, and a poor and unfortunate one at that, resembling Moldavia or Wallachia. Our nationality would be laughed at subsequently by the Russians just as they now make fun of Moldavia and Wallachia, seemingly ignorant that they themselves are the cause of that people's misery and backwardness.[65]

However, by this time the Russian consul in Belgrade, Fedor Antonovich Tumanskii, had already issued a twenty-four-hour ultimatum, and Prince Alexander was forced to remove his minister from his important post. The Russian government did not like the prince or his other ministers either, regarding them as ungrateful and disobedient in their attitude toward their protector.[66] This heavy-handed Russian approach had its price. There were few signs of a spontaneous movement in favor of Russia, although there was a Russian party in Serbia that opposed the regime in power. Under these circumstances, and because it was not prepared to fight, the Serbian government adopted the policy of neutrality advised by the Porte, the Habsburg Empire, and the Western powers.[67] Garašanin too counseled the prince not to enter the conflict; he expected Russia to be defeated, and Serbia could gain no advantage from an active policy.

The Russian government also wished Serbia to remain tranquil. It was, as we have seen, very concerned about the Habsburg attitude. At the time when relations were still friendly, the tsar, as we have discussed previously, had suggested that Austria occupy Serbia. After the Habsburg government adopted a more hostile attitude, the Russian authorities did not want to provoke a military action. Moreover, they shared some of the Habsburg fears about the consequences of encouraging Balkan independence. In July 1853 Buol expressed to Meyendorff his fear that Serbia would declare its independence and that it would then become "the point of concentration of refugees and that this country would escape from the influence of

[65]Ibid., p. 132.
[66]See Radosavljević to Buol, no. 63, Belgrade, June 8, and Buol to Coronini, Vienna, July 18, 1853. *AGK*, I: 1, pp. 178–9, 258–60.
[67]The Habsburg government was also opposed to Garašanin and to Prince Alexander's government, since it regarded them as too close to France. It was also keenly aware of the unrest in the country. Both the Serbian and the Ottoman governments were thus advised not to take any precipitous actions. Serbia was cautioned to maintain a strict neutrality. See the despatches cited previously and Coronini to Buol, no. 144, Temesvar, July 16, 1853; Buol to Radosavljević, tel. Vienna, February 11, 1854; and Buol to Bruck, no. 1, Vienna, February 13, 1854, ibid., I: 1, pp. 252–3, 581, 587–8.

Russia and Austria in order to fall under that of France and England."[68] With similar feelings Meyendorff was concerned not only that a revolution would result in a declaration of Serbian independence, but that it would be under the influence of the radical left. Neither Russia nor the Habsburg Empire wished to see the increase in French influence that would result.

After Tumanskii died in July 1853, Feliks Petrovich Fonton, the chargé in Vienna, was sent to Belgrade to report on the situation and to ensure that the country remained calm. He urged the Serbian government to prepare to repel any Ottoman invasion, but not to act on its own. Even if the Russian military wished to use the Balkan people for a spring invasion, it certainly did not wish a premature uprising to occur. When in March 1854 plans to cross the Danube were abandoned, continued Serbian inactivity was obviously desired.

Among the Balkan people the Russian actions were greeted with the most approval in independent Greece.[69] The relations between the two countries were good; the reconciliation of the Patriarchate with the Greek church in 1850, in which Russia played a part, contributed to this feeling. Moreover, since the Greek nationalists did not know of Nicholas's aversion to the creation of a new Byzantine state, they could continue to feel that their best hope lay in gaining Russian support for the acquisition of additional territory. The Russian efforts in behalf of the Orthodox claims in the dispute over the Holy Places were also strongly approved. During 1854 there were indeed spontaneous uprisings in Thessaly, Epirus, and Chaldice, which did not have Russian backing.[70] Under public pressure the Greek government aided these revolts, and Greek troops entered Epirus.

Although the Greek actions did not significantly affect the military situation, they did arouse British and French suspicions that

[68]Meyendorff to Nesselrode, Vienna, July 12/24, 1853. Meyendorff, *Briefwechsel*, III, pp. 46–9.

[69]For Greek policy in this period see John A. Kofos, *International and Domestic Politics in Greece during the Crimean War* (Boulder, Colo.: East European Monographs, 1980).

[70]In a circular Nesselrode expressed the concern of the Russian government about the position of the Christians and declared that it was not pushing these people into bloody and unequal battles. This was also the attitude toward the Epirus uprising; Russia did not provoke it, and it regretted the possible consequence, that is, a violent repression. Nesselrode circular, March 2, 1854. Zaionchkovskii, *V.V.: Prilozheniia*, II, pp. 327–8.

the revolts were the result of Russian machinations. In May 1854 French and British warships arrived in Piraeus. Under their guns, the Greek government was forced to declare its neutrality. A new ministry was formed whose members were chosen from the British and French parties; the Western consuls exerted a strong influence on the government. Their warships did not leave until February 1857.

Once the Russian army was forced to leave the Principalities, it had, of course, no direct means of decisively defeating the Ottoman Empire and its Western allies. Thereafter, attention had to be turned to the difficult task of defending those areas that were open to attack by the sea powers, including the Baltic and Far Eastern coasts and the Black Sea area. After the Habsburg Empire and Prussia signed an agreement in April 1854, adhered to by the other German states, whose aim was to keep the war out of Central Europe, there were no obvious battlefields. The Crimea became the center of combat largely by a process of elimination: It was the one area where the sea powers could reach their enemy. In September 1854 French, British, and Ottoman forces were landed with the objective of capturing Sevastopol, the major Russian naval base. The allies won victories at the battles of the Alma (September), Balaclava (October), and Inkerman (November), but Sevastopol did not fall until September 1855. Meanwhile, Nicholas I had died on March 2. It was thus left to his son, Alexander II, to bring an end to a war that Russia was fighting without allies or even clear objectives.

The Peace of Paris of March 1856, whose terms were under negotiation during the entire war, served to meet the original Western intention of preserving the Ottoman Empire from destruction at Russian hands.[71] Most damaging for Russia was the provision that called for the demilitarization of the Black Sea, with both Russia and the Ottoman Empire forbidden to maintain warships or arsenals in the region. Russia was also compelled to cede a part of Bessarabia to Moldavia, an action that removed Russian control of the mouth of the Danube. The Russian protectorate over the Principalities and Serbia was replaced by a general great-power guarantee. The entire question of the relationship of the great powers to the Ottoman state and its Christian population was dealt with in two basically contradictory sections. In Article VII the Ottoman Empire was admitted to the concert of Europe; the signatory powers promised that they would "respect the independence and the territorial integrity of the

[71]The text of the Treaty of Paris is in Hertslet, *Map of Europe*, II, pp. 1250–65.

Figure 5. The Battle of Inkerman.

Ottoman Empire, guarantee in common the strict observance of that engagement, and . . . , in consequence, consider any act tending to its violation as a question of general interest." In Article IX the sultan announced his new reform decree, based on the assurance of the equal treatment of Christians and Muslims, and the powers stated that they recognized the value of the communication, but that it did not give them "the right to interfere, either collectively or separately, in the relations of His Majesty the Sultan with his subjects, nor in the internal administration of his Empire."

The announcement of the Porte's intention to introduce reforms allowed Alexander II in his manifesto of March 31, 1856 to "give thanks" that the "original and principal aim of the war" had been achieved and that "from now on, the future destiny and the rights of all Christians in the Orient are assured. The Sultan solemnly recognizes them, and in consequence of this act of justice, the Ottoman Empire enters into the community of European states! Russians! Your efforts and your sacrifices were not in vain. The great work is accomplished."[72]

Despite this optimistic summation, designed for public reassurance, the treaty was a disaster for Russian interests and a defeat for the major policies adopted in Eastern affairs during the century. Most important in Russian eyes were the sections calling for the demilitarization of the Black Sea. Not only did this clause limit Russian activities on its own soil, a national humiliation, but it also created a situation dangerous for the state's security. The sea powers, with the elimination of the Black Sea coastal fortifications as well as the Russian naval presence, would have the ability to strike more easily should another conflict arise. Although they too could not send warships into the Black Sea, the presence of their strong fleets in the Mediterranean assured them of an advantage. Moreover, although the Ottoman fleet also was denied access to the Black Sea, its ships could be stationed in the Straits. The threat offered by the combined, potentially hostile fleets affected Russian control not only over its Black Sea coast, but also over the Caucasian and, indirectly, the Central Asian lands. The loss of the possession of the mouth of the Danube similarly marked a strategic setback for the Russian position in the Balkans.

Two other basic elements in Russian policy during the century were also affected by the treaty: the relationship with the Porte and

---

[72]Quoted in Winfried Baumgart, *The Peace of Paris, 1856*, trans. by Ann Pottinger Saab (Santa Barbara, Calif.: ABC-Clio, 1981), p. 130.

the protectorship over the Balkan Christians. The demilitarization of the Black Sea area and the loss of prestige following the defeat signified, of course, that Russia could no longer use the threat of a land invasion or a naval operation directed against Constantinople to influence the Porte's decisions. For a period it would indeed be the voice of the victorious Western powers that would be paramount in the Ottoman capital.

The relationship with the Balkan Christians was even more deeply affected. The treaty specifically transferred the former Russian rights of protection in the Principalities and Serbia to the great powers collectively; the claims for a special relationship with the Orthodox were blocked by the section of the agreement concerning outside interference in the relations between the sultan and his subjects. Superficially examined, these stipulations would apparently place the great powers on an equal footing. In fact, they allowed France, Britain, and Austria to exert an increased influence in the Balkan peninsula. Moreover, the Ottoman promises of reform could be used by the Western powers in the same manner that Russia had previously exploited its ties with Balkan Orthodoxy. By insisting on the introduction of better political institutions, they could assume the role of the real protectors of Balkan national interests. As has been seen, Nicholas I had feared the possibility that Britain would take from him the role of the champion of the Balkan nationalities.

The signature of the Treaty of Paris ended an era of Russian–Balkan entanglements that had commenced with the rights and obligations contained in the Treaty of Kuchuk Kainardji. We have seen how in the next three-quarters of a century Russia was involved in three wars with the Ottoman Empire, with or without allies, that in some manner were related to treaty obligations or the relationship with Balkan Orthodoxy. Although throughout this period Russia, like the other great powers, would have preferred the maintenance of Ottoman territorial integrity, its government was repeatedly called upon to expend national energies on issues that arose from what was indeed a unique relationship with Balkan Christianity. What Russia won or lost by this situation will be briefly summed up in the Conclusion. Here it is sufficient to pose the question of what advantages could have been gained by the Russian nation at large had Alexander I and Nicholas I devoted the same expenditures to internal improvements such as roads, railroads, and better schools that they did to the Balkan campaigns, from which, with the defeat in 1856, they obtained nothing commensurate to the costs.

During this period the Russian active involvement in Balkan affairs, joined with their treaty rights, gave their representatives the opportunity to play a major role in the internal development of four states: Moldavia, Wallachia, Greece, and Serbia. In the Danubian Principalities they sponsored the introduction of the Organic Statutes, which did indeed mark an advance, but they thereafter stood as firm opponents to a further liberalization of the government or the national unification that was fast becoming the program of the politically active circles. In Greece the Russian influence was used to ensure the acceptance of an autocratic, monarchical government; in 1843 Nicholas I strongly criticized the events leading to the introduction of a constitutional system, to a great extent because they involved a revolt against a legitimate monarch. Because of its geographic situation, however, independent Greece was always to be more open to intervention from the Western sea powers than from Russia. As far as Serbia was concerned, although Russian diplomats did play a major role in gaining concessions from the Porte for the establishment of a truly autonomous relationship, they were[4] not able to control events in Belgrade as closely as they did those in Bucharest and Jassy.

Russian wars with the Ottoman Empire, of course, played a major role in enabling these four states to weaken and, in the case of Greece, to break the connection with the Ottoman Empire. Because of their sacrifices, Russian statesmen expected to be able to influence the internal affairs of the regions that, in their opinion, they had "liberated" from Ottoman bondage. Many also felt that they were bringing to backward Balkan people the advantages of their superior civilization and experience. When they met with resistance to their interference in domestic affairs, they tended to react with bitterness and to speak about ingratitude. The Russian expectation that aid to national advancement would be recompensed by a future willingness to follow directions from St. Petersburg was to remain a point of bitter controversy particularly two decades later, when Russia embarked upon another war against the Ottoman Empire, arising again from Balkan involvements.

CHAPTER IV

Balkan involvements continued: The Bulgarian question and the Russo–Turkish War, 1877–8

❧

The Crimean disaster, as could be expected, had a deep influence on subsequent Russian internal and foreign policy. Although the terms of the Treaty of Paris did not involve the life-or-death interests of the state as a great power, the defeat uncovered basic weaknesses in its political, economic, and social systems. Quite obviously its internal structure was not strong enough to support a military apparatus capable of defending its extensive territories; a serf state could not compete with nations organized on the Western system. Russia had been spared major losses because the German states had remained out of the conflict; another war might involve a different alliance configuration. The period of Great Reforms aimed not only at internal improvement, but also at introducing changes in institutions vital to Russian defense, particularly the military.

In 1855 Alexander II had ascended to the throne amid the difficult conditions of the war. At thirty-seven years of age, he had already had extensive experience in affairs of state. Although he was to support the reforms of the 1860s, he continued in the tradition of his predecessors, and he had faith in the autocratic system. In foreign affairs he was, however, to introduce a different style. As tsar he still made the final decisions, but he was to take a less commanding position than either Alexander I or Nicholas I, who had strong ideas and kept the control of foreign policy firmly in their own hands. Alexander II in the future worked primarily through the Foreign Ministry, but he consulted with and was influenced by a wider circle of advisers. His policy at least through the first two decades of his reign was to be primarily defensive, with the principal attention directed toward internal reform. As far as relations with

Figure 6. Alexander II.

Europe were concerned, he shared the general Russian disgust and disillusionment with Vienna, but he felt closely bound to Berlin. His relationship with his uncle, King William I, was strong.

During his reign Alexander II was to have but one foreign minister, Alexander Mikhailovich Gorchakov. Born in 1798, he was near sixty when he replaced Nesselrode in 1856. Entering the Foreign Ministry in 1821, he had subsequently attended the congresses of Laibach and Verona and had then held posts in London, Florence, Vienna, Stuttgart, Frankfurt, and finally again in Vienna in the crucial period of 1854–5. Although he was cosmopolitan in attitude and had wide international connections, his purely Russian background made him popular with those who tended to blame the Russian losses on the predominance of those of German lineage in the bureaucracy and the military.

Figure 7. Alexander Mikhailovich Gorchakov.

Gorchakov, with the support of Alexander II, was to introduce a diplomatic system different from that of Nicholas I and Nesselrode. At this time the Russian leaders recognized that it would be impossible to pursue an active European policy during a period of internal reform, when the resources and attention of the state had to be turned inward. Gorchakov thus was to follow the policy of *recueillement*, with an almost exclusive emphasis on domestic rather than external affairs. Whereas Nicholas I had been ready to intervene all over the map of Europe to defend conservative principles, his successor attempted to avoid involvement in external situations that might have dangerous consequences. A defensive and protective attitude was thus to characterize the Russian stance toward European affairs for twenty years.

Nevertheless, the Russian state could not remain completely apart from European events. Moreover, the government did have certain positive aims. First and foremost was the determination to secure the reversal of the terms of the Treaty of Paris, particularly Articles XI and XIII, calling for the neutralization of the Black Sea, and Article XX, providing for the cession of southern Bessarabia. Moreover, in view of the fact that the state would be in a period of relative weakness during the reforms and that certain European interests would have to be defended, the Russian leaders recognized that they could not remain isolated and that some sort of an alliance was necessary. After the war, Nesselrode had called for the reformation of the Holy Alliance, which he believed was the best combination to protect Russian conservative interests and the position in Poland. The reestablishment of this alignment, however, was to prove impossible, largely due to the intense Russian resentment of the Habsburg attitude in the previous years. Gorchakov instead introduced a policy that was in fact in contradiction to that of the previous reign. From 1856 to 1863, when the link snapped as a result of another Polish revolt, the Russian government sought to work with the France of Napoleon III, that is, with exactly the regime that had been so disliked by Nicholas I and that had played so large a part in initiating the crisis that led to the Crimean War.

The diplomatic reversal that occurred at this time was to have far-reaching implications. Nicholas I, it will be remembered, had been a strong advocate of the enforcement of treaty obligations and an outspoken opponent of revolutionary activities. Because the Russian government itself now wished to change treaty stipulations, it no longer was to be the defender of the map of 1815 or the treaty structure of Europe. In addition, whereas Nicholas I had acted as the "gendarme of Europe," Alexander II and his advisers were not in a position even to threaten to send Russian armies to preserve legitimate regimes. These changes themselves had a revolutionary significance for Europe. With the Russian restraining hand removed, and with the ill will against the Habsburg Empire remaining, France was able to assist in the unification of Italy and play a generally disruptive role in regard to other national movements, in particular the Polish.

Balkan involvements continued

RUSSIA'S BALKAN POLICY, 1856-75

In contrast to the attitude toward Western and Central Europe, Russian Balkan policy did not change so radically. Although in the Treaty of Paris the Russian protectorships were explicitly removed, these stipulations did not alter basic attitudes. As we will see, in the future the Russian statesmen, supported often by an enthusiastic public, continued to regard their nation as having a unique position in regard to the Balkan Orthodox, although the emphasis was to be increasingly on the Slavic people. In July 1856 Gorchakov sent an instruction to the Russian ambassador in Constantinople, Apollinarii Petrovich Butenev, clearly reflecting the continuity in policy. The foreign minister wrote that attempts had been made by Russia's enemies to persuade the clergy and the Orthodox people

that the only aim of our [the Russian] intercessions in favor of the church was political domination; that we were intending to bring the church and the populations under our influence with a view to conquest.

We do not need to say that this is not so. It is true that our political interests are, as they have always been and as they will never cease to be in the Orient, by the nature of the conditions themselves, tightly linked on those of Orthodoxy. Our adversaries know this perfectly. When they combat the church of the East, as well as when they pretend to protect it in order to better procure means of fighting it, it is not only from zeal for Catholic and Protestant propaganda, but also and above all with *arrière-pensée* against our influence.

Since the wars of Empress Catherine, the Orient has gone through a period of transition. Our great interest for ourselves is that it be able to emerge one day without losing the principal element of preservation and homogeneity that dwells there, living and powerful, for centuries, despite the vicissitudes to which it is a prey, despite the diversity of the races subjugated by the Ottoman conquest. It is an interest of the first order for us to have in our immediate neighborhood populations that are attached to us by the ties of the faith that brought Greece back to life and that will bring about progressively under our eyes the resurrection of the Slav and Romanian nationalities.

We do not hesitate to repeat that our interest in favor of our co-religionists of the East should not at all be concealed. It is based on two perfectly avowable principles: that of an intimate religious union and that of the conservation of the Ottoman Empire according to the sense of the Treaty of Paris.[1]

The withdrawal of the Russian restraining hand in international relations, combined with the encouragements sent out from Paris, opened the doors to the suppressed revolutionary movements. With their roots in the events of 1848-9, their leaderships came usually

[1]Gorchakov to Butenev, *réservé*, St. Petersburg, July 14/26, 1856. Russian Foreign Ministry documents on microfilm, State Archives, Bucharest. Cited hereafter as *RFM*.

from the left of the political spectrum, and they were willing to accept violent methods for the attainment of their aims. Some of the participants, in particular the Poles, Hungarians, and Romanians, saw autocratic Russia as their chief adversary. Until events proved that their territorial objectives conflicted, Germans, Italians, Poles, Hungarians, Romanians, Bulgarians, Greeks, and Serbs could cooperate against the powers that controlled them or blocked their national movements. In this group the Russian government was to find few friends. Even among the Orthodox, religion had lost, or was fast losing, its attractive powers. Mostly Western educated and oriented, the new generation was to remember Russia not as a power that had made sacrifices for Balkan Christianity, but as the representative of a form of government that its members despised.

The situation did not fit well into the Russian postwar policy of recueillement and the status quo. Throughout Europe able leaders sought radical change. Thus for a period, because of the reforms and its weak military establishment, the Russian government was forced to play a less active role in international affairs, and at a time when great events were occurring, in particular in the Italian and German lands.[2] The same policy was, of course, in effect in the Near East. The Russian influence in Ottoman affairs was for a period replaced by the dominating authority of the victor sea powers, especially France. Similarly in this period, France, Britain, and Austria all won influence in the governments of autonomous Romania and Serbia and of independent Greece. The previous Russian objective of being the sole great power to which the Balkan Orthodox turned was blocked. Moreover, particularly during the period of the French entente, major political changes took place in the Danubian Principalities, Greece, and Serbia, in which, contrary to the previous period, Russian representatives did not play a major role. They also did not show a great aversion to the use of force and violence to overthrow existing regimes. Instead, although often expressing regrets, they were to accept actions contrary to international agreements and to recognize rulers brought to power by military coups.

---

[2]In 1866 when the policy was reviewed, Gorchakov wrote:

> Our internal situation, the Great Reforms in the process of execution, impose upon us the duty of reducing to the least possible extent our action abroad and of avoiding all that can interfere with the great work that will be the glory of the reign of Our August Master and that is called upon to develop in Russia a strength which, once acquired, will give us all the alliances that we can desire. (Gorchakov to Ignatiev, secret letter, St. Petersburg, February 27/March 11, 1866, *RFM*)

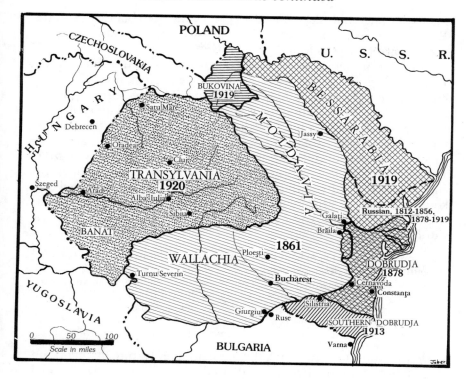

Map 6. The expansion of Romania, 1861–1920.

The most notable alterations in political status occurred in the Danubian Principalities, the region that, as we have seen, had previously been at the center of Russian concerns.[3] At this time, following the French lead, the Russian government accepted the double election of Alexander Cuza in both Wallachia and Moldavia in 1859 and, although with reluctance, the subsequent amalgamation of the administrations of the provinces in 1861 to form the unified Romanian state. The overthrow of Cuza and the election of Charles of Hohenzollern-Sigmaringen in 1866, carried through by revolutionary means, were also not opposed. These events, the most important in the formation of the Romanian national state, also

[3]Events in the Principalities are discussed in Barbara Jelavich, *Russia and the Formation of the Rumanian National State,* pp. 61–152, and *Russia and the Romanian National Cause, 1858–1859* (Bloomington: Slavic and East European Series, Indiana University Press, 1959).

marked a French diplomatic victory that was not regarded as in the Russian interest. Gorchakov believed that France was attempting to use the Principalities as a dam against Russia.

Although under the circumstances a strong French influence over Romanian political life was to be expected, Russian officials still could hope to have a say in church affairs. The Romanian government at this time, following the Greek and Serbian examples, wanted a national church free of the direct control of the Patriarchate. Once again Russian representatives, in particular the ambassador in Constantinople, Constantine Mikhailovich Basily (Bazili), wished to moderate a compromise. Following the policy of attempting to keep the unity of the Balkan Orthodox, he recommended that some changes in the relationship be made to reflect Romanian national individuality. As he recognized, the Russia position was difficult:

> We preach moderation to both sides. By encouraging the aspirations of nationality with a view to ecclesiastical autonomy we can provoke fatal complications for the future peace of the church of the East, above all in the present circumstances, and then we will see the natural enemies of the church of the East use the awakening of nationalities, by all sorts of secret and open means, in order to sow discord between them and to detach them from the common center which has guaranteed for centuries the unity of faith among the Christian nations of the East.[4]

Despite the Russian efforts, the Romanian government, after long negotiations with the Patriarchate, finally, in January 1865, declared the Romanian church autocephalous.

Even more important, in December 1863 the Romanian government secularized the lands of the Dedicated Monasteries, thus striking a strong blow at the financial basis of the Eastern Patriarchates. As elsewhere, the church controlled vast estates in the Principalities, a large proportion of which were in the possession of monasteries whose income went to the support of certain Holy Places and the Patriarchates. The export of funds to support foreign establishments had long been a source of resentment in the Principalities, and it formed a subject of discussion among the great powers. At a meeting in Constantinople of a commission set up to deal with Romanian affairs, Basily explained the importance of the question and mentioned some of the establishments supported by monastery funds:

The Orthodox church in all of the East has its principal resource in the Principalities. The ecclesiastical academy, the numerous schools, and the Greek and Arab press, all of the recent establishments of the patriarchate of Jerusalem, as well in

[4]Basily to Popov, no. 91, May, 1857, *RFM*.

Palestine as in Constantinople, the schools founded a few years ago in Alexandria, in Cairo, and in several other localities are maintained by this single revenue.[5]

The negotiations between the Romanian government and the Patriarchates never reached a successful conclusion. The weakness of Russian influence after the Crimean defeat was witnessed by the fact that in this crisis the Patriarchates accepted Britain as the main mediator. All of the powers, including Russia, wished the Patriarchates to agree to the secularization and accept an indemnity. As Gorchakov wrote: "The moment has come for them to see the light. . . . As for the warm sympathy of the emperor, that cannot be placed in doubt, but it is clear that neither Our August Master nor any of the sovereigns . . . will make war on Prince Cuza over that question."[6] The adamant refusal of the Patriarchates to accept the secularization meant that in the end they lost both the income from the monasteries and any indemnity.

Although the accession of a foreign prince in Romania was recognized with relatively few objections, the change of dynasty in Greece as a result of a military coup in 1862 did not bring such acceptable results.[7] During the Crimean War, it will be remembered, Greek support for Russia had manifested itself so enthusiastically that French and British warships had been sent to Piraeus. In the next years King Othon had to face the increasing criticism of the Western powers and the dissatisfaction of his subjects that no further moves had been made to advance Greek national objectives. The Russian government too was not happy about events in Athens. Its concern centered on its continued support of Orthodox interests. Othon did not have children; none of his Wittelsbach relatives in the direct line of succession appeared willing to abandon his Catholic faith. Yet the constitution of 1844 clearly stated that the next ruler should be Orthodox.

In October 1862 a military coup, much like that of 1843, occurred. This time, however, Othon did not attempt to save his throne, but instead left the country. Thereafter, the protecting powers, Britain, France, and Russia, immediately assumed the task of selecting the

[5]Protocols and reports of the European Commission, *Acte și documente*, VI, pt. 2, p. 637.
[6]Gorchakov to Novikov, May 10/22, 1864. Gerhard Hilke, "Russlands Haltung zur rumänischen Frage, 1864–1866," *Wissenschaftliche Zeitschrift der Martin-Luther-Universität Halle-Wittenberg* XIV:4 (1965), p. 199.
[7]This section is based on Barbara Jelavich, "Russia, Bavaria and the Greek Revolution of 1862–1863," *Balkan Studies* II:1 (July 1961), pp. 125–50.

next ruler. In this endeavor the Russian position was weakened by the lack of viable Orthodox candidates. Gorchakov would have accepted another Bavarian nomination, but none was forthcoming. Alexander II was concerned about the situation. He complained to the Prussian minister, Karl Friedrich von der Goltz, that he regretted

the revolution which had taken place in Greece as unjust and as an injury to conservative and monarchical principles in general, and in particular to the Christian interests in the East, for which the creation of the Kingdom served as a political base, and which was called upon to defend them and to develop them.[8]

The candidate finally chosen, Prince William of Denmark, who took the name George I, was to reign until 1913. He was not required to convert to Orthodoxy; this stipulation was postponed for another generation. Since he was the British candidate, the Greek government was able to secure the transference of the control of the Ionian Islands from Britain to Greece. British sea power at this time and in the future was to assure to London the major influence in Athens.

Yet Russian involvement in Greek affairs remained strong. In summer 1866 an uprising occurred on Crete; its diplomats and the Greek government both called for a cession of the island to Greece. In August the Greek leaders called upon the great powers to intervene, but only Russia was sympathetic to the Greek cause. Unable to act alone, its government called for an international action. Discussions over the question dragged on until 1868, when the revolt died out. The event demonstrated the Russian unpreparedness to face an Eastern crisis, and it damaged its influence among the Orthodox.

Although France did not offer the support in Greek affairs that Russia desired, the two governments, at least at first, followed the same policy in Serbia and approved a change of dynasty in Belgrade. In December 1858 Alexander Karadjordjević was overthrown in a military coup and Miloš Obrenović returned for a short second term. On his death in 1860, Michael Obrenović again ruled until his assassination in June 1868. For six years of his reign, until November 1867, Michael worked closely with Ilija Garašanin, whose resignation had been forced by the Russians when he served under Prince Alexander. By this time, however, Garašanin had mended his relations with the Russian officials. Both he and the prince had a similar attitude toward the great powers: They wished assistance in the attainment of their national goals, but they would not accept

[8]Quoted in ibid., p. 131.

domination. Garašanin believed that "Serbia . . . should never be allowed to become a tool of Russia or of any other power."[9] Good relations with other governments would serve to block an exclusive Russian influence.

Serbian policy in these years was directed toward the accomplishment of national aims similar to those previously enumerated in the Načertanije. Mistrustful of the influence of the great powers, the Serbian leaders now sought to bring the Balkan people together for the common purpose of ending Ottoman control. Agreements were concluded with Montenegro in 1866, with Greece in 1867, and with Romania in 1868. In line with its policy of promoting Balkan unity, the Russian government encouraged and aided in the formation of these alliances. At this time Serbia held the central position in its Balkan policy. In many fundamental ways, however, the Serbian actions were in contradiction to the Russian goal of preserving the peace. The purpose of the intra-Balkan agreements was to prepare for an uprising of the Balkan Christians, a war with the Ottoman Empire, and the eventual dissolution of that state, actions all in contravention to the Russian policy of disapproving "premature" rebellions, launched before Russia was strong enough to control the results. Russia wanted a Balkan alliance but not a Balkan war.

The Serbian government was also acting against Russian interests in establishing close links with the Italian, Hungarian, Polish, and Romanian revolutionary movements and in subsidizing and aiding exactly those Bulgarian revolutionary factions that St. Petersburg opposed. The attitude of the Serbian officials in this and other questions showed clearly the continued Russian inability to control this restless Balkan state.

In the end Michael's alliance policy failed. After his assassination in 1868, his thirteen-year-old nephew, Milan, succeeded him, with a regency at first in power. Without strong direction the alliance network collapsed. Although Michael did not attain his more exalted goals, he did secure certain Serbian objectives. In 1866 the Ottoman government agreed to the withdrawal of its soldiers from the six fortresses in Serbian territory that it still garrisoned. In addition, Michael recognized the need for a strong Serbian army. He introduced universal military service and organized his forces along modern lines. His minister of war was a French officer, Captain Hippolyte Mondain; the director of his artillery school was a Czech,

---

[9]Quoted in David MacKenzie, *Ilija Garašanin: Balkan Bismarck* (Boulder, Colo.: East European Monographs, 1985), p. 228.

František Zach, who had first visited Serbia in 1843 as an agent of the Hôtel Lambert and the Polish emigration. Before his death the prince was able to form an army of 90,000 men from a total population of 1,250,000. He also maintained good relations with Russia, which supplied him with arms. It was only in the last period of his reign that he turned away from the Russian orientation, based on the expectation of a Balkan war, to a possible agreement with Austria and an acquisition of territory by negotiation.

While these events were taking place in the Balkan lands, the unification of Italy had been accomplished. The next major transformation of the map of Europe was the creation of a united Germany under the leadership of Prussia.[10] This action was carried through by wars in 1866 against the Habsburg Empire and in 1870 against France. In both Russia supported the Prussian side. Although there was, of course, some hesitation about the wisdom of the policy, the decision was made on the basis of what were believed to be Russia's best interests, determined by the close connection with Berlin that had existed in the past and the apparent inevitability of the unification. As Gorchakov's associate, Alexander Genrikhovich Jomini, wrote in 1876:

. . . the weakness of Germany has always made it powerless to serve us while making it an instrument in the hands of our adversaries. The great Germany makes impossible today the coalition of 1854. Besides, Europe being broken up by the foolish Crimean War, that great Germany had to be made either by Prussia or by Austria. Between the two our choice could not be in doubt.[11]

The Franco–Prussian War, moreover, gave Russia an additional advantage, since it created conditions under which the government could achieve the first of its major foreign policy objectives after the Crimean War: the denunciation of the Black Sea clauses of the Treaty of Paris. On October 31, 1870, Gorchakov announced this decision. Although the British reacted strongly against the abolition of their major gain from the war, there was little that the government could do. To calm British objections, the Russian government

---

[10]The section on the Russian attitude toward German unification is based on Barbara Jelavich, "Russland und die Einigung Deutschlands unter preussischer Führung," *Geschichte in Wissenschaft und Unterricht*, XIX:9 (September 1968), pp. 521–38.

[11]Jomini to Giers, June 9, 1876. Charles Jelavich and Barbara Jelavich, eds., *Russia in the East, 1876–1880: The Russo–Turkish War and the Kuldja Crisis as Seen Through the Letters of A. G. Jomini to N. K. Giers* (Leiden: E. J. Brill, 1959), pp. 40–5.

agreed to a meeting of the signatories of the Paris treaty. This conference, which opened in January 1871, approved the Russian demand, but it also allowed the British representatives to present a statement condemning the unilateral denunciation of treaties.[12] The wording on the rules determining the closure of the Straits was also changed to allow the sultan to open the "Straits in time of peace to the vessels of war of friendly and allied powers, in case the Sublime Porte should judge it necessary in order to safeguard the execution of the stipulations of the Treaty of Paris of 30th March, 1856."[13] This alteration was at the time favored by Britain but not by Russia. The remilitarization of the Black Sea in theory allowed both Russia and the Ottoman Empire to construct arsenals and maintain fleets, but in fact neither power could afford a giant military or naval buildup in the area.

The unification of Germany and the modifications made in the Treaty of Paris brought to a high point the relationship between Berlin and St. Petersburg. Emperor William I telegraphed his appreciation to the tsar of the Russian attitude at the time of the Franco–Prussian War: "Prussia will never forget that she owes it to you that the war has not assumed extreme dimensions."[14] The new map of Central Europe and the fact that Russia had indeed paid Austria back for the humiliation of the Crimean War were to pave the way for the renewed cooperation of the three conservative courts. In the fall of 1872 Alexander II and Franz Joseph visited Berlin, the first sign of Russian–Austrian reconciliation since 1856. In the next years, meetings between the three monarchs laid the basis for the formation of the Three Emperors' Alliance, an alignment that carried the same themes of conservative policies and mutual cooperation of the previous Holy Alliance.

Although Russia was again allied with the Habsburg Empire, its partner had undergone a radical administrative reorganization that changed the nature of the state and was to affect their mutual relationship in the future. After the defeats suffered during the events connected with the unification of Germany and Italy, the Habsburg leaders accepted the necessity of coming to an understanding with their strongest and best-organized nationality, the Hungarians. In

---

[12]On the London Conference see Barbara Jelavich, *The Ottoman Empire, the Great Powers, and the Straits Question, 1870–1887* (Bloomington: Indiana University Press, 1973), pp. 25–84.

[13]Ibid., p. 188.

[14]Quoted in W. E. Mosse, *The European Powers and the German Question, 1848–1871* (Cambridge: Cambridge University Press, 1958), p. 355.

the *Ausgleich* or Compromise of 1867 the empire was divided into two sections, separated by the river Leitha. Franz Joseph ruled in both, holding the title of emperor in his western Austrian lands and king in the Kingdom of Hungary. Only three ministries – for foreign affairs, defense, and finance as related to the first two offices – had jurisdiction over the entire country. Delegations from both sections also met periodically to consider common problems. Almost all the other state affairs were handled separately in Vienna and Budapest; there was no common citizenship. Henceforth, the accepted designation for the monarchy was *Austria-Hungary*. The implications of this reorganization for Russian and Habsburg Balkan policy were to present serious dangers in the future.

Before proceeding to a discussion of the major theme of this chapter, the Russian policy toward the Bulgarian national movement, two other developments of crucial importance for the future must be mentioned: Russian expansion in Asia and the Panslav movement, both of which involved Russian Balkan policy. It is most important to note that during this period of retrenchment in Europe, Russia acquired a vast empire in Asia. At this time the Russian army began to move against the Central Asian khanates, an action successfully concluded by 1885 with the conquest of Khiva, Bokhara, and Tashkent, along with lands inhabited by Turkomen tribes. As far as policy toward China was concerned, the major agreement of the century, the Treaty of Peking of November 1860, gave Russia territory along the Amur and Ussuri rivers to the Pacific Ocean.

The Russian advances aroused enormous apprehension in London. British policy at this time called for the maintenance of Afghanistan, Persia, and the Ottoman Empire as buffers against Russian expansion toward India and the imperial lines of communication.[15] The opening of the Suez Canal in 1869 made the status of the Mediterranean of even greater importance. The British government feared that its opponent had embarked upon an active policy of penetration into both the Balkans and Central Asia. Should this indeed be the Russian policy, the Black Sea and the Straits would inevitably play a key role. Without a significant army, Britain relied on its navy to protect its world position. In a war with Russia, it thus needed the assurance that it could repeat the actions of the Crimean War, that is, sail through the Straits and attack Russia in the south. There were also hopes that the Caucasian people would rise against

---

[15]The British plans are discussed in Barbara Jelavich, "British Means of Offense against Russia in the Nineteenth Century," *Russian History*, I: 2 (1974), pp. 119–35.

the Russian occupier. This issue was, of course, of vital importance to the Russian government too. Not only was its southern Black Sea region open to attack, but the main line of communication with its Central Asian territories ran from Odessa across the Black Sea, then overland to the Caspian, then over that sea to the port of Krasnovodsk. With this situation in mind, it can be understood why the Russian government in the next crisis was so concerned about the status of the Straits and the ultimate disposition of the eastern Balkan lands bordering on the Black Sea.

Despite the enormous areas acquired in Central Asia and the Far East, these acquisitions do not appear to have stirred the imagination or awakened the enthusiasm of that small section of Russian society that was concerned with foreign policy issues and was in a position to make its influence felt. Many in this group, with their eyes on Europe, saw that Russia had apparently stood aside while France, Italy, and Germany, under the leadership of Napoleon III, Camillo di Cavour, and Otto von Bismarck, had remade the map of Europe and made great strides in their own national development. Moreover, although enormous changes had been introduced by the Great Reforms, many aspects had aroused discontent and unease. Since censorship was always stricter in matters of domestic than in foreign policy, those who were not happy with the course of Russian development could direct their frustrations against the official position in international relations.

The Panslav movement, which emerged against this background, had, of course, important historical antecedents. Although the emphasis in official policy had previously been on Orthodoxy, the Slavic element had also been present. The Slavophilism of Nicholas's reign had influenced some of those engaged in diplomatic activities. However, the major Russian interests, as we have seen, were before 1856 primarily involved with the affairs of the Greeks and Romanians, who were not Slavs.

Although the Panslav concept embraced many different ideas and was never formulated into a single easily stated ideology, we define it for this narrative as a program calling for the removal of the Orthodox Slavs from foreign control, their organization into separate states, and the establishment of a federation under Russian leadership. Panslavs were extremely critical of Catholic Slavs, in particular the Poles, and they certainly did not extend their liberating intentions to non-Great Russian people within the Russian empire, such as the Ukrainians and Belorussians. Their program could, of course, be used against the Habsburg as well as the Ottoman empires.

The Panslavs had among their numbers many talented authors and journalists, in particular Ivan Sergeevich Aksakov and Michael Nikiforovich Katkov, and one important organization. The Slavic Benevolent Society was founded in Moscow in 1858 in order to assist Slavic people, in particular the South Slavs of the Ottoman Empire. It is difficult to judge exactly what influence this group exerted. Some important individuals, including the heir to the throne, the future Alexander III, were sympathetic to its doctrines. However, most of the officials connected with the Foreign Ministry disliked its influence, since the Panslavs were calling for an active program when responsible statesmen believed that Russia could not afford foreign policy adventures in a time of reform.

As far as Russian relations with the Balkan people were concerned, the Panslavs provided the important service of directing public attention to the affairs of the peninsula. Their writers and journalists gave wide publicity to the events occurring there. Their shift in emphasis from the Orthodox as a whole to the Slavic people in particular was also to be significant for the future. In foreign relations they called for an alignment different from the Holy Alliance policies of Nicholas I. In their eyes the "German" states, in particular the Habsburg Empire, were the principal dangers to Russian interests and to the well-being of the non-Russian Slavic people. In their relations with these, their fellow Slavs, their attitude was heavily paternalistic. In fact, they believed that without the connection with the great mother nation, the Slavs had little to hope for in the future. As Aksakov wrote:

> The connection of the Slavic peoples with Russia, the feeling which attracts them to Russia, is a natural, organic, free feeling, which flows from the deepest depths of their popular essence. : . . Because they are called to a universal role, not as Czechs, Slovaks, Slovenes, and so on, separately, but *as Slavs and through Slavdom*: only by this aspect of their existence, only as parts of the universally significant Slavic tribe can they attain importance in the history of the world. When they are outside this common Slavic bond, or when they betray the idea of Slavdom, they are nothing.[16]

Panslav ideas were given an impetus when in the mid-1870s another crisis arose in the Balkan peninsula. The events that were to occur then opened the door for action to those who called for a more glamorous and glorious foreign policy or who wished to renew the crusade in the East.

---

[16]Quoted in Nicholas V. Riasanovsky, *Russia and the West in the Teaching of the Slavophiles* (Gloucester, Mass.: Peter Smith, 1965), p. 201.

In 1875 revolts broke out in Bosnia and Hercegovina that the Ottoman authorities were unable to suppress. The basic cause was the extreme discontent of the Christian South Slavic peasants who worked the lands of Slavic, but Muslim, landholders. Although the issues were primarily economic and social rather than national, the insurgents and their supporters called for the introduction of autonomous institutions for the provinces. The revolt inaugurated a three-year crisis, which once again brought the great powers into conflict over Balkan affairs.[17] In this discussion the events of 1875–8 will be considered primarily in relation to the manner in which they drew Russia into a deep involvement in the fortunes of yet another Balkan people.

RUSSIAN-BULGARIAN CONNECTIONS

So far in this narrative very little has been said about the Bulgarians, whose national movement had indeed not proceeded as fast as that of the Greeks, Serbs, and Romanians, to which the major attention has so far been given. Since the Bulgarian lands were situated so close to Constantinople, their political development could be more carefully monitored by the Porte. Moreover, during the period of Phanariot predominance in the Ottoman Empire, Greek cultural and religious control had been established there too. The first step in the national movement thus had to be the establishment of Bulgarian schools and a separate national church. Like the other Balkan people the Bulgarians also sought a foreign patron, and they had only one possible choice. They could not expect assistance from France, the Habsburg Empire, or Britain, largely because of their geographic location and the lack of historic involvement in the area by the Western powers. Russia was, therefore, the only state to which they could turn. The religious, ethnic, and linguistic ties were also important; because of the closeness of the languages, educated Bulgarians could also read Russian. Major difficulties, however, lay in the way of Russian–Bulgarian cooperation. As we have seen, during most of the century the Russian government had wished to maintain good relations with the Porte; it had also not wanted to endanger its

[17]For this study, see in particular David MacKenzie, *The Serbs and Russian Pan-Slavism, 1875–1878* (Ithaca, N.Y.: Cornell University Press, 1967); Richard Millman, *Britain and the Eastern Question, 1875–1878* (Oxford: Oxford University Press, 1979); and B. H. Sumner, *Russia and the Balkans, 1870–1880* (Oxford: Oxford University Press, 1937).

understandings with Britain or the Habsburg Empire unless a major issue arose. Before 1856 a strong stand had also been taken against revolutionary agitation.

Perhaps just as important was the fact that conditions were not all that bad in the Bulgarian lands; in fact, some groups benefited from their position in the Ottoman Empire. With the loss of the Black Sea lands and Egypt, the Ottoman government needed alternate sources of food supplies and raw materials. In 1826 a regular Ottoman army was organized; Bulgaria supplied wool for the uniforms and other basic necessities. With the end of the right of preemption in the Danubian Principalities after 1829, the provisioning of the city of Constantinople also was provided by these adjacent lands. These developments resulted in the establishment of a prosperous and influential merchant and manufacturing class in Bulgaria and the growth of merchant colonies in Constantinople and Bucharest.

Nevertheless, even among these groups there was a strong desire for political reform. The major causes for unrest were those that we have seen elsewhere. The central Ottoman government had a great deal of difficulty controlling its local administrators and containing the prevalent graft and corruption. Although reforms were introduced in 1839 and 1856, the Porte could not ensure that they would be carried out. Major discontent was also caused by the social and economic conditions of the time. The revolts that were organized in 1835, 1841, 1842, and 1850 arose more from these internal difficulties than as a result of national agitation seeking political goals.

Despite their preoccupation with the Danubian Principalities and Greece, Russian officials had previously come into direct contact with Bulgarians. Russian troops had operated in their lands in connection with the wars with the Ottoman Empire of 1806–12 and 1828–9. There had also been some colonization by Bulgarians in Russia. It will be remembered that after the acquisition of New Russia, the authorities had attempted to attract colonists to fill up the vacant lands. Where possible, they encouraged Muslim emigration into the Ottoman Empire and Christian immigration from the Balkans. After the annexation of Bessarabia, they had adopted a policy of expelling the Tatar population; they then attempted to attract Bulgarian settlers. Another wave of immigration came after the Treaty of Adrianople when some Bulgars had compromised themselves in assisting the Russian invasion. In the early 1860s another group arrived with Russian encouragement. Despite Russian efforts to keep them, many of the Bulgarians returned home. For many, conditions in fertile Bulgaria, even under Ottoman rule, were preferable to those in Russia, particularly before the abolition of serfdom. As a result, in contrast to the situation existing among the Greeks prior to the Greek revolution, the Bulgarian colonies in Russia did not become major centers of conspiracy.

Before 1856, of course, the Russian government was urging a policy of calm throughout the Balkans. In this period two major revolts took place – in Niš in 1841 and in Vidin in 1850.[18] After the first revolt, a Russian emissary was sent to report on conditions. The second rebellion, which the Porte incorrectly blamed on Russia, occurred at the time when the Russian army was in occupation of the Principalities as a consequence of the revolution of 1848. The Russian officials watched the development of the movement, but they certainly did not participate in its organization. In June 1850 General Alexander Osipovich Duhamel, the commander of the Russian army, reported to Leo Grigor'evich Seniavin on the events.[19] His long dispatch is particularly interesting, since it echoes the approach taken earlier by Russian officials toward events in Greece.

Describing the acts of violence, Duhamel wrote: "There has already been unhappily much blood spilled on both sides and the Turks, where they can, massacre without pity not only the insurgents taken with arms in their hands, but inoffensive inhabitants, women and children." He feared that if the revolt was not stopped, there would occur "the massacres and cruelties of which the Greek war of independence has given us such deplorable examples." The Turks, he claimed, ". . . made no distinction between the innocent and guilty. The rich are persecuted in order to seize their fortunes and the poor are terrorized in order to oblige them to surrender their children so that they can be converted by force to Islam."

Duhamel, it will be remembered, was in Wallachia to suppress a political revolution that his government had strongly denounced. He, however, justified the Vidin revolt because it was caused by "the truly intolerable impositions, which the Turkish authorities wished to impose upon the Christian populations, for besides a very stiff contribution in money, they have demanded from the Bulgars deliveries in kind for the provisioning of the Turkish garrisons of the fortresses of the Danube out of all proportion with the real needs of these garrisons."

---

[18]See Mark Pinson, "Ottoman Bulgaria in the First Tanzimat Period – the Revolts in Nish (1841) and Vidin (1850)," *Middle Eastern Studies*, XI: 2 (May 1975), pp. 103–46.

[19]Duhamel to Seniavin, no. 182, Bucharest, June 17/29, 1850, *RFM*.

In order to aid the victims, Duhamel proposed that refugees from the revolt be allowed to cross into Wallachia. In 1848 and 1849, he argued, refugees from Transylvania had crossed the border, and in 1849 the Ottoman government "had shown without exception sympathies toward the remains of the Magyar insurrection, although in the number of those who had come to seek refuge in Wallachia could be found the leaders of the Hungarian–Polish revolutionary party, which had raised the standard of revolt against its legitimate sovereign." Under these circumstances it seemed reasonable to give temporary asylum to "unfortunate inoffensive Christians" who were fleeing for their lives. However, when Duhamel presented his proposals to the Ottoman commissioner in the joint occupation, he was met with a refusal, and he did not press his demands.

Although aid was not given in this instance, in the future the Russian representatives in Bucharest continued to have a sympathetic attitude toward Bulgarian actions as long as they were devoid of a revolutionary imprint. In October 1851 the Russian consul, F. L. Khaltchinskii, reported favorably on the activities of Peter Beron, a man important in the development of Bulgarian education.[20] In a conversation with him concerning the formation of a society to aid in the establishment of Bulgarian schools, the consul warned that if "he or his associates attempted to diverge from the goal of charity that he proposed, I would be the first to demand the suppression of that association." In his report Khaltchinskii expressed the opinion that the society was indeed "exempt from any political tendency."

Although no basic change occurred in the official Russian attitude toward revolutionary activity, the Slavic Benevolent Society did much to inform Russian society about Balkan conditions, and it brought Bulgarian students to Russia for their education. Moreover, despite Russian efforts to keep the region tranquil, it could not be expected that the Bulgarian leadership would remain inactive, particularly after the establishment of independent or autonomous regimes in Greece, the Principalities, and Serbia. In fact, the danger now arose that these states would appropriate to themselves the Bulgarian-inhabited lands. The Bulgarian population thus had to organize to defend its own interests against its neighbors as well as to assert its national rights against the Ottoman suzerain.

Like the other Balkan nationalities, those involved in the national regeneration movement among the Bulgarians fell into two catego-

[20]Khaltchinskii to Titov, Bucharest, September 29/October 11, 1851, *RFM*.

ries. The more conservative, those holding traditional values, favored a slow pace of progress. Coming from the prosperous classes of merchants and notables, they established strong centers in Constantinople and Bucharest. In Romania their principal organization was the Benevolent Society, which was close to the Russian consulate.

The second group, recruited primarily from the educated youth, was much more radical and favored direct action. Since the Bulgarian lands lacked the presence of local military units, such as those that had played such a major role in the Serbian and Greek revolutions, some of these men supported the formation of small armed bands, or *chetas*, that could be sent into the Bulgarian countryside to incite rebellion. Wallachia became the center of such activities, which were carried on with the knowledge and often the support of the Romanian authorities.

The first such cheta action, organized in Braila in 1841 and led by Vladislav Tatich and Vasil Hadzivulkov, was a complete disaster. Similarly, the raids of Filip Totu and Panaiot Khitov in April and May 1867 and of Hadzhi Dimitŭr and Stephen Karadzha in July 1868 failed in their objective of inciting the Bulgarian population to revolt. In 1870 the major leaders on the left, including Liuben Karavelov, Vasil Levski, and Khristo Botev, formed in Bucharest the first major revolutionary organization, the Bulgarian Revolutionary Central Committee. Their subsequent efforts to arouse revolutionary enthusiasm across the Danube also brought nothing but repeated failures.

These activities by radical circles were opposed by the Russian government for the same reasons that had determined its attitude toward similar events in Greece, Serbia, and the Danubian Principalities. The revolutionary leadership was acting beyond Russian control, and it espoused doctrines dangerous to the Russian state. The Russian representatives thus put strong pressure on the Romanian government not to harbor these men. Before the Dimitŭr and Karadzha raid the Russia consul in Bucharest, Genrikh Genrikhovich Offenberg, thus warned the Romanian minister Ion Brătianu that "around a hundred individuals are gathered at Giurgiu and Zimnicea or are en route to go there; I believe that it would be in your interest as in that of peaceful men, who could be gratuitously compromised, that measures, swift and energetic, be taken in order to stop reprehensible and thoughtless acts."[21] Russian officials

---

[21]Démètre A. Sturdza, ed., *Charles Ier, Roi de Roumanie: Chronique-Actes-Documents* (Bucharest: Charles Göbl, 1899), I, p. 438.

delivered similar warnings until the great revolt of spring 1876 broke out.

The Russian interest in and knowledge about Bulgarian activities in Romania were shown in a long report that Offenberg sent to Nicholas Pavlovich Shishkin, the Russian consul-general in Belgrade, in November 1871. Here Offenberg criticized the revolutionary organizations and denied that they represented Bulgarian opinion:

The Bulgarians of the Principalities, and especially those of Bucharest form . . . amidst Romanian society a very united and very homogeneous group, which is animated by the same sentiments and which follows the same current of ideas. Outside of that compact mass, it is true that some young radicals of the modern school are active, but for reasons which I will try to elucidate, they are neither followed nor even understood by their compatriots.[22]

Since most of the politically active Bulgarians, Offenberg continued, were small merchants and manufacturers, who had achieved relative prosperity with difficulty, they were willing to make sacrifices only for a specific and obtainable goal. They had already organized in Romania "a national church, a school, a Slavic library, a press, a journal (*Otechestvo*) and several other institutions of the same nature." Their leadership, however, was endangered by the actions of those who supported "action at any price" and who were now seeking to win control of the Benevolent Society and its funds. The consul's judgment of Karavelov was strongly critical; he was "fundamentally hostile to Russia and in consequence also to the Orthodox church, which he considers as a docile instrument of our ambition and our covetousness."

Offenberg's conclusions and recommendations reflected his negative view of the revolutionary activities:

1.) There does not exist any more in Romania the Bulgarian party of action that appeared in 1866 and 1867. That party, which contained good elements, has faded away and left as residue a clique of ambitious and hungry malcontents, who do not have any community of ideas with the mass of their compatriots and who alienate from the common work the fearful spirits and the large fortunes by the violence of their language. 2.) It is not desirable that "Young Bulgaria" takes a too direct part in the affairs of the commune, where it immediately introduces disorder and discord. Its role should begin the day before and finish the day after an action. 3.) An organic development of the moral and material resources is possible only with the aid of the elements which are organized around the Committee of Assistance [the Benevolent Society], but it is essential to give to these elements a precise

[22]Offenberg to Shishkin, very confidential letter, October 25/November 6, 1871, *RFM*.

direction and a reviving impulsion. 4.) The most effective means to unite in a single and unique group all the individual forces would be the creation at Bucharest of a well directed Bulgarian journal, placed on the national ground and outside of personal questions and social doctrines.

Although Romania was to provide a haven for the organization of revolutionary conspiracies by the Bulgarian nationalists, Constantinople was the center of positive Russian efforts in their behalf. In 1864 Nicholas Pavlovich Ignatiev became the Russian minister to the Porte; his role was to be central for Bulgarian affairs through 1878.[23] An aggressive and independent diplomat with original and wide-ranging schemes, he represented the school of Russian thought that in the past had called for active intervention in Balkan affairs and a paternalistic relationship to the national movements. As long-range objectives he favored the breakup of the Ottoman Empire and the establishment of national states closely linked to Russia. However, he recognized that in the 1860s and 1870s his government was not in a position to determine the fate of the Balkan peninsula independently. Until such a situation developed, his goal was to secure for Russia the first voice in the councils of the sultan, another traditional Russian aim. Since by 1870 he had indeed been able to win this position, he did not want events to occur that would endanger his influence. In regard to the Balkan people, he favored Orthodox unity, but if that could not be obtained, then he sought at least cooperation between the South Slavs and Russia. The relationship was in no way to be equal: The Balkan leaders were to look to St. Petersburg for guidance. The Russian government would determine the timing and details of any future national manifestations; there were to be no premature uprisings.

The major problem connected with Bulgarian affairs that Ignatiev faced dealt with the question of the establishment of a Bulgarian church organization separate from the Patriarchate.[24] As we have seen, the formation of national religious institutions had been a major aim of the other Balkan people too. For the Bulgarians, who had been under Greek cultural as well as religious domination, the question was particularly important. In the subsequent complicated negotiations the Porte, the Patriarchate, the Greek government, and

---

[23]Ignatiev's activities in these years are discussed in Gisela Hünigen, *Nikolaj Pavlovič Ignat'ev und die russische Balkanpolitik, 1875–1878* (Göttingen: Musterschmidt-Verlag, 1968).

[24]See in particular Thomas A. Meininger, *Ignatiev and the Establishment of the Bulgarian Exarchate, 1864–1872* (Madison: The State Historical Society of Wisconsin, 1970).

Ignatiev all became involved. In compliance with previous Russian practice, Ignatiev wished to set himself up as the arbiter between the contending factions. His main personal interest was to maintain Orthodox unity, but his instructions directed him to obtain some concessions to the Bulgarian desires. The entire question was extremely sensitive, since the major issue was not the organization of an autonomous Bulgarian church as such but the territories over which it would have jurisdiction. It was generally assumed that they would be the lands that would some day form part of an independent or autonomous Bulgarian state. Athens and Belgrade, as well as St. Petersburg and Constantinople, were thus watching the developments with concern.

After long and complicated negotiations the Porte, in the interest of maintaining tranquility in its Bulgarian regions, took the decisive step. In 1870 a firman was issued establishing the Bulgarian Exarchate; it was given authority over a wide area, including Plovdiv, Varna, and lands to the Danube. The most controversial section was Article X, which provided that should two-thirds of the voters approve, any district could join the Exarchate. This provision was to be the major cause of the future cultural and religious strife among Bulgarians, Greeks, and Serbs over Macedonia.

The Bulgarian Exarchate was thus created by an Ottoman rather than a Russian action. However, the patriarch would not accept it. In March 1872 the first exarch, Antim I, declared the independence of his church, and the institution was immediately declared schismatic by the patriarch. This result, that is, another division within the Orthodox church, was exactly what Ignatiev had wished to avoid. He was finally able to secure the negotiation of a compromise and a recognition of the Bulgarian church by the Patriarchate.

Meanwhile, the Bulgarian revolutionary activities in Romania became more intense. In 1875 another revolt at Stara Zagora failed. Ignatiev, who strongly disliked these actions, which were, of course, not under Russian direction, urged the Porte "to attribute the least importance possible to these incidents and not to have the responsibility fall on the peaceful Bulgarian notables."[25]

In early 1876 the Russian consul in Bucharest, Ivan Alekseevich Zinoviev, reported in detail on the unrest among the Bulgarians in Romania; all the groups, young and old alike, considered that the

---

[25]Ignatiev to Alexander II, Buyukdere, October 2/14, 1875, *Osvobozhdenie Bolgarii ot turetskogo iga* (Moscow: Izdatel'stvo Akademii nauk SSSR, 1961), I, p. 127. Cited hereafter as *OBTI*.

situation was intolerable.[26] They differed only on the means to be used to meet the situation. The more conservative still preferred pacific paths, but they had no confidence in the Porte. They wished an outside intervention to ensure that the promised Ottoman reforms were indeed applied. The young revolutionaries, Zinoviev continued, still favored an armed uprising. They saw in the revolt in Bosnia and Hercegovina an example to be followed. The continued resistance there had attracted European intervention and had won outside support. A Bulgarian action could similarly force a European involvement.

Although Zinoviev knew about the growing unrest among the Bulgarian colony in Bucharest, he was not aware of the details of the specific actions being organized by the revolutionary circles. The largest rising of the Bulgarian movement started on May 2 in the towns of Koprivshtitsa, Panagiurishte, and Klisura.[27] Once again the revolutionary organization failed to produce an effective rebellion. What it did bring about, however, was a massive Ottoman retaliation. Because of the events in the western Balkans, the regular Ottoman army was concentrated in that part of the empire. The Porte thus used irregular troops (*bashi-bazuks*) to suppress the revolt. In the course of this action there were widespread massacres, with reports of the number of people killed varying from 3,000 to 100,000 according to the sources. Even the hope of the insurgents that a Bulgarian uprising would attract European attention was not immediately fulfilled. It was not until late summer and fall, when reports on atrocities filled the Western presses, that the events affected international diplomacy.

At the time of the rebellion Alexander II was in Ems, meeting with Franz Joseph and William I. He learned about the events directly from Ignatiev and Zinoviev. In the next months information on Bulgarian affairs continued to come chiefly from Constantinople. From this source the Russian officials received an erroneous impression of what exactly had occurred. Once again the Russian government suffered from its inability to obtain reliable information on internal conditions in the Balkans. The issue facing the tsar and his advisers was very similar to the one that arose at the beginning of the Greek revolution: Was this a revolution against a legitimate ruler or an unprovoked massacre of innocent Christians?

---

[26]Zinoviev to Gorchakov, no. 4, Bucharest, February 4/16, 1876. Ibid., I, pp. 177–8.
[27]This section is based on Barbara Jelavich, "Russia and the April Uprising," *Southeastern Europe*, IV: 2 (1977), pp. 217–32.

Because of his influential position in Constantinople, Ignatiev's reports on the uprising were bound to be read with care in St. Petersburg. His conclusions, however, were based on erroneous reports. He was thus not aware that the actions in Panagiurishte and Koprivshtitsa were directed by the Bulgarian Revolutionary Committee, although he was informed about the existence of secret organizations. He received his information from the Russian consulates, in particular from Plovdiv, which was closest to the central events. The Russian vice-consul here was Naiden Gerov, a Bulgarian by birth. His views coincided with those of the Bulgarians who opposed open rebellion and instead sought national advance through cooperation with the Ottoman government to achieve gradual reforms. In his reports Gerov repeatedly emphasized that there had been no real revolution, but only disorders caused by Ottoman misgovernment. He thus described the uprisings in Koprivshtitsa and Panagiurishte as minor disturbances provoked by police agents collecting taxes. The reprisals and the massacres were then portrayed as actions taken against an innocent population that had not participated in an armed rebellion; the Muslim irregulars had committed atrocities against a basically loyal and peaceful population. Gerov's reports also implied that the Ottoman government was using the opportunity provided by the reports of a revolt, which in fact had not occurred, to suppress and control the Bulgarian people.[28]

Prince Aleksei Nikolaevich Tseretelev, who was sent by Ignatiev to investigate the situation, reported in a similar manner. He described the massacres themselves in great detail, and he judged the initial Bulgarian actions as of minor significance. On June 5 he wrote that the uprising had been the result of either a conspiracy or "Moslem vexations; the facility itself of their repression proves that these disorders are of little importance and that several companies of regulars could without difficulty have dispersed people armed with stone guns and wooden canons."[29] A later report directly denied that a revolution had occurred: "It is false that there has been a civil war, the Bulgarians having everywhere laid down their arms except in cases of legitimate defense."[30]

Ignatiev's dispatches to the tsar and the Foreign Ministry reflected

[28]See Gerov's dispatches in Bŭlgarska akademiia na naukite, *Dokumenti za bŭlgarskata istoriia* (Sofia: Dŭrzhavna pechatnitsa, 1932), II, pp. 155–289.

[29]Tseretelev report, May 25/June 5, *OBTI*, I, p. 232.

[30]Tseretelev to Giers, no. 138, Plovdiv, July 22/August 3, 1876, *Dokumenti za bŭlgarskata istoriia*, II, p. 208.

these views. Despite his previous close association with events in the Balkans, the ambassador was obviously not aware of the extensive Bulgarian preparations preceding the revolt. Consequently, he too reported that the "disorders" were of a local character and were caused by Ottoman maladministration or, later, by the destruction caused by the irregular troops. The events were presented as representing another religious conflict on traditional Muslim–Christian lines, not as a national uprising against Ottoman rule.

As reports of the events arrived by official and unofficial channels, many Russians expressed strong feelings of sympathy for the Bulgarians and felt that something should be done for them. For instance, in June, Alexander Genrikhovich Jomini, who was with Gorchakov in Jugenheim, wrote to N. K. Giers, at this time head of the Asiatic Department of the Foreign Ministry: "We are here at a standstill (*en panne*). One can do nothing other than observe the horrors that are taking place in Turkey. And it is only the beginning! The ferocious beast has smelled blood."[31] In reply Giers wrote: "But what can be said about unfortunate Bulgaria – should it be abandoned to its sad fate? I assure you that this country interests me at this moment much more than the other provinces of Turkey."[32] The Russian ambassador in Vienna, Evgenii Petrovich Novikov, wrote in a similar vein: "All this splling of Christian blood is deeply grievous, especially in long-suffering Bulgaria where the peaceful inhabitants are perishing by the thousands for the cruel exploits of the Serbian 'Omladina.'"[33]

Despite these and other expressions of sympathy, the Russian government's attention remained directed primarily toward the western Balkans, where an international mediation was attempting to end the troubles in Bosnia and Hercegovina. Ignatiev himself urged the Ottoman government to send regular troops into Bulgaria to restore order. After the reports of the atrocities came in, he advised the Porte to investigate and punish the guilty, but he did not call for a European or Russian intervention. He regarded the Bulgarian situation as an internal Ottoman affair to be handled by the responsible officials.

---

[31] Jomini to Giers, Jugenheim, June 7/19, 1876. Jelavich and Jelavich, *Russia in the East*, pp. 16–17.
[32] Giers to Jomini, St. Petersburg, June 15/27, 1876, *ibid.*, p. 144.
[33] Novikov to Giers, Vienna, July 21, 1876. From the collection of private papers of N. K. Giers. Cited hereafter as NKG. The Omladina was a Serbian youth movement deeply involved in the revolutionary activities of the time.

THE RUSSO-TURKISH WAR
AND THE CONGRESS OF BERLIN

Moreover, Russian attention was soon diverted by the more dramatic events that took place elsewhere. At the end of July, Serbia and Montenegro went to war with the Ottoman Empire, without the knowledge or approval of the Russian government. Even though official circles had tried to maintain peace, Panslav organizations had worked in the opposite direction, enthusiastically involving themselves in Serbian affairs. Their actions, marking the height of the Panslav movement, resulted in the sending to Serbia of about 5,000 volunteers, including General Michael Grigor'evich Cherniaev, the hero of the Central Asian conquests, who went without official permission.

This outpouring of Russian sympathy did little to aid the Slavic cause. Once in Serbia, the Russian volunteers did not endear themselves to their hosts; the Russians, in turn, gained a low opinion of the Serbs as fighters. The causes of friction were well described in letters sent by the Russian consul in Belgrade, Andrei Nikolaevich Kartsov, to Giers. On September 8, 1876, Kartsov wrote:

> I am sorry for our youth which is involuntarily disillusioned here after two or three days in the Serbian army. Drawn by the desire to take part in a military affair, they see that they are not among orderly troops but in some caravan or group of boastful cowards; and those who come because of sympathy for the Slavonic brotherhood discover with bitter amazement to what extent his own skin is precious to this brother and how little he values the sacrifice and the very life of those of the same faith who arrive to spill blood for the Serbian cause.[34]

On the subject of the volunteers themselves, he was also extremely critical: "Believe me that here exists much not worthy of the Russian name, beginning with the disgraceful drunkedness of our officers and soldiers recruited by the Slavic Committee and ending with that about which I dare not express myself here. . . . Besides our own Guard Officers and the small number of others who came at their own expense . . . the rest of our compatriots really only disgrace the Russian name." Kartsov was also concerned about "the seeds of fiery socialism" that the returning Russians would bring home "from Serbian tobacco circles and disgraceful groups which carry the name of Russian troops."

The mutual recrimination increased when the Serbian soldiers and their Russian friends were soundly defeated by the Ottoman

---

[34]Kartsov to Giers, private letter, Belgrade, August 27, 1876, NKG.

army. In fact, in October the Russian government had to deliver an ultimatum to Constantinople to conclude an armistice in order to save Serbia. This action and the end of the fighting in no way solved the major problems. At the same time, the tsar and his ministers faced enormous public pressure to act in a decisive fashion.

Meanwhile, to protect its own security interests should war be necessary, the Russian government was already concluding agreements with Austria-Hungary that were to affect its future attitude toward Bulgaria. In July 1876 at Reichstadt, in a continuation of the established policy of acting within the framework of the Three Emperors' Alliance, Gorchakov met with the Habsburg foreign minister, Julius Andrassy, to determine a common attitude toward the Serbian–Turkish War that was going on. Although the versions of the understanding reached differ on some points, on the sections relating to Bulgaria the foreign ministers agreed that in the event of a Christian victory a Bulgaria and a Rumelia would be established, but that no large Slavic state would be formed. Just prior to the outbreak of the Russo–Turkish War, in January and March 1877, this pact was reaffirmed and its stipulations further defined. If Russia went to war, the signators agreed that Russia would not conduct military actions in the western Balkans, that is, in Bosnia, Hercegovina, Serbia, or Montenegro; Austria-Hungary would not act in Romania, Bulgaria, Serbia, or Montenegro. These delimitations, in fact, denoted political as well as military spheres of influence. The understanding was in accord with Russian strategic interests as a Black Sea power, and the lines of division followed similar tracings in the past.

Although these agreements did not make specific reference to the territorial limits of the Bulgarian provinces, another proposal did. Despite the enormous pressure in Russia for war, the government continued to favor an international solution. In December 1876 representatives of the powers met in Constantinople to try to negotiate a settlement. By this time, largely because of the Serbian defeat and the necessity of compromising with the Habsburg Empire, Russian interest had shifted to the Bulgarian lands. At the conference Ignatiev, as the chief Russian delegate, placed his emphasis on the establishment of a large Bulgaria, including not only the lands north and south of the Balkan Mountains but also Dobrudja and most of Macedonia, including the cities of Niš, Skopje, Ohrid, and Kastoria. Because of the strong British objections, the Russian delegates finally accepted a division of the large Bulgaria into eastern and western sections. Despite the agreement reached between the two traditional opponents, the conference failed when the Ottoman government rejected its decisions.

From the fall of 1876 to the spring of 1877 the Russian officials attempted to secure by negotiation an acceptable solution to the Eastern crisis, including the conclusion of peace treaties for Serbia and Montenegro and the enactment of reforms in Bosnia, Hercegovina, and Bulgaria. Within the Russian government there continued to be a strong difference of opinion on the question of war. The minister of finance, Michael Khristoforovich Reutern, for instance, sent a memorandum to the tsar in October 1876 opposing hostilities. He argued that such an action would cut off Russian access to foreign capital and would produce a situation "with which no crisis in the past could compare." The Russian financial position would be ruined and "decades, if not generations" would pass before the country could recover.[35]

On the other side, the long association with the Balkan Christians had created links that were hard for the Russian leaders to break. Despite the formal end of the protectorships in the Treaty of Paris, Russian statesmen, even those who were not Panslavs, felt that honor and national self-esteem demanded a continuation of the former associations. In February 1877 Alexander II, during a discussion with his ministers, although recognizing that a war at that time was not in the national interest, nevertheless declared: "In the life of states just as in that of private individuals there are moments when one must forget all but the defense of his honor."[36] Thus the web of past entanglements and obligations influenced the final decision to declare war on April 24, 1877. At the beginning of this fourth Russo–Turkish War of the century, the tsar issued a proclamation:

Our faithful and beloved subjects know the lively interest which we have always devoted to the destinies of the oppressed Christian population of Turkey. Our desire to ameliorate and guarantee their condition has been shared by the whole of the Russian nation, which shows itself ready to-day to make fresh sacrifices to relieve the condition of the Christians in the Balkan Peninsula.

The life and property of our faithful subjects have always been dear to us. Our whole reign testifies to our constant anxiety to preserve to Russia the benefits of peace. This anxiety did not cease to animate us at the time of the sad events which came to pass in Herzegovina, Bosnia, and Bulgaria. We made it pre-eminently our object to attain the amelioration of the condition of Christians in the East by means

---

[35]W. Reutern-Baron Nolcken, *Die finanzielle Sanierung Russlands nach der Katastrophe des Krimkrieges 1862 bis 1878 durch den Finanzminister Michael von Reutern* (Berlin: Georg Reimer, 1914), pp. 121–30.
[36]Ibid., pp. 140–41.

of peaceful negotiations and concerted action with the great European Powers, our allies and friends.

During two years we have made incessant efforts to induce the Porte to adopt such reforms as would protect the Christians of Bosnia, Herzegovina, and Bulgaria from the arbitrary rule of the local authorities. The execution of these reforms followed, as a direct obligation, from the anterior engagements solemnly contracted by the Porte in the sight of all Europe. Our efforts, although supported by the joint diplomatic representations of the other Governments, have not attained the desired end. The Porte has remained immovable in its categorical refusal of every effectual guarantee for the security of its Christian subjects. . . .[37]

Like previous wars, this Balkan campaign was costly for the Russian army. Moreover, during the fighting the responsible officials continued to worry about the attitudes of Britain and even of the Habsburg Empire despite its previous agreements. Finally, after the Russian capture of Plevna (Pleven) and Adrianople, the Ottoman government was forced to seek peace. An armistice was signed on January 31, 1878, whose terms were left purposefully vague by the Russian victors. Concerning Bulgaria, however, the document called for the establishment of a state whose boundaries would be determined by "the majority of the Bulgarian population, and which cannot, under any circumstances, be less than those described by the Constantinople Conference."[38]

Before the negotiations were commenced, the task of formulating draft proposals was assigned to Alexander Ivanovich Nelidov; Igna-

---

[37]Hertslet, *Map of Europe*, IV, 2598–9. A proclamation by the tsar to the Bulgarians, issued in June, carried a similar message:

My troops, having crossed the Danube, enter to-day upon your territory, upon which they have already several times fought for the amelioration of the condition of the Christian inhabitants of the Balkan Peninsula. Faithful to their ancient and historical traditions, ever gathering fresh strength from the intimate union which had for centuries united them to the Orthodox population, my ancestors succeeded by their influence and their arms in successfully securing the position of the Servians and of the Roumanians by summoning them to a new political existence. Time and circumstances have not altered the sympathies of Russia for her coreligionists in the East. She nourishes ever the same affection, the same solicitude towards all the members of the great Christian family of the Balkan Peninsula. I have confided to my army, commanded by my brother, the Grand Duke Nicholas, the mission of securing the sacred rights of your nationality, which constitutes the immutable condition of the peaceful and regular development of all civil existence. You have not acquired these rights by force or armed resistance, but at the cost of centuries of suffering, at the cost of the blood of martyrs with which for centuries you and your ancestors have soaked the soil of your country. (*Ibid.*, IV, pp. 2640–2)

[38]Hertslet, *Map of Europe*, IV, 2658–60.

Figure 8. The Battle of Plevna.

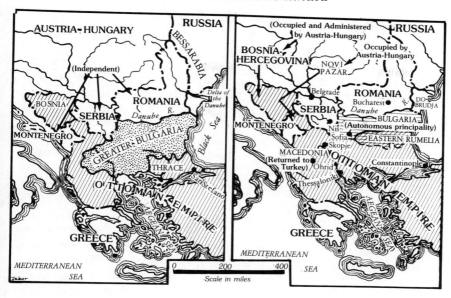

Map 7. The Treaty of San Stefano; the Treaty of Berlin.

tiev was appointed as the first delegate, with Nelidov as the second.[39] The heart of the Russian peace program was the creation of a large Bulgarian state consisting of the two provinces of the Constantinople Conference with the addition of Thrace, but without Dobrudja. During the negotiations, despite the strong Ottoman objections, Ignatiev was able to achieve this objective. The Treaty of San Stefano of March 3 thus provided, among other stipulations, for the creation of a Bulgaria whose size and situation guaranteed that in the future it would be the strongest Balkan state. In addition, other treaty conditions appeared to ensure Russia a controlling position. For instance, Russian officials were to supervise the organization of the administration of the autonomous province, and the army was to remain in occupation for two years.

The announcement of the terms of the treaty led immediately to a serious international crisis, with the objections centered largely on the Bulgarian question. Moreover, the settlement as a whole involved a change in international treaties and, of course, it was contrary to the previous agreements with Austria-Hungary. Faced

[39]This section is based on Barbara Jelavich, "Negotiating the Treaty of San Stefano," *Southeastern Europe*, VI: 2 (1979), pp. 171–93.

with a strong European reaction, Gorchakov was forced to concede that a European congress would have to be held to review the stipulations that contravened international accords. Nevertheless, European tension remained high until the opening of the Congress of Berlin in June. Both Britain and Austria-Hungary continued to direct their major attacks against the Bulgarian settlement. The Habsburg government rightfully argued that Bulgaria was the "large Slavic state" referred to in the previous agreements; it had also not received the compensation promised in these same understandings. The British statesmen were chiefly concerned that the erection of a dependent state, so close to the Straits and Constantinople and with an outlet on the Aegean, would henceforth allow Russia to dominate the Ottoman government.

It is interesting to note, given the controversies that were to occur later, that the great powers gave comparatively little attention to the ethnic composition of the large Bulgaria at this time. At the Constantinople Conference the delegates had recognized that the area designated as "Bulgarian" held a high percentage of other peoples, including Greeks, Serbs, and Turks, as well as Bulgarians. Dobrudja, included in the original plan, was seen as having a majority of Muslim Turks and Tartars. The possible existence of a separate Macedonian nationality did not form part of the discussions.

Aware that it could not defy Europe, the Russian government at the Congress of Berlin accepted a radical alteration of the San Stefano stipulations not only as regards Bulgaria, but in other questions as well. Most important, the San Stefano Bulgaria was divided into three sections. To the north Bulgaria proper was established as an autonomous tributary principality and assigned territories lying between the Balkan Mountains and the Danube, including the Sofia district and the major port of Varna. The Russian army was to remain in occupation for a limit of nine months. To the south another province, Eastern Rumelia, was given a semiautonomous administration with a Christian governor. The Macedonian lands were returned to direct Ottoman rule. Although the provision was not included in the treaty, the powers recognized that Russia would supervise the organization of the autonomous principality.

The Berlin settlement was a bitter blow for the Russian nationalists. Although Russia regained the region of southern Bessarabia lost in 1856, as well as some Asiatic territory, the major objective – the creation of a great Bulgarian state – had been blocked by British and Habsburg opposition. Moreover, the entire settlement was in violation of the principles held dear by strong nationalists and Panslavs in regard to the Balkans. Although many, like Ignatiev, would have preferred to have postponed a general crisis until Russia was strong enough to impose its own terms, the majority had enthusiastically supported the war in 1877. The Berlin treaty certainly did not represent a fulfillment of their hopes and expectations. Instead the Russian government had been forced to accept what was an implicit division of the peninsula into spheres of influence, a settlement that had been considered throughout the century but that it usually opposed. Austria-Hungary was now to occupy Bosnia, Hercegovina, and the Sanjak of Novi Pazar, and it also acquired the predominating influence in Belgrade. Habsburg ascendancy in the west thus balanced Russian control in Bulgaria. In addition, in the Treaty of Berlin, Montenegro, Serbia, and Romania were recognized as independent and given additional territory; Greece in subsequent negotiations acquired Thessaly. These benefits, however, were conferred by Europe in concert, not by Russia through bilateral negotiations with the Ottoman government. Again this result was in conflict with the previous Russian desire to pose as the single benefactor of the Balkan Christians. To make matters even worse, the peace conditions, in particular the Russian reacquisition of southern Bessarabia, in contradiction to previous assurances, caused bitter resentment in Bucharest, which had been an ally in the war. In the next years the Romanian government was to seek alliances with Germany and Austria-Hungary out of fear of further Russian encroachments.

Not only was the peace treaty a deep disappointment, but the war itself had been extremely expensive. The prizes of victory appeared not worth the cost. Like the Crimean War this conflict was followed by a period of internal unrest. The war again showed in a clear light the incompetence of the Russian administration; many blamed the domestic weaknesses for the difficulties of the army and the meager results obtained in the peace. Thus, as a Soviet authority wrote, the "senseless sacrifices near Plevna, massive abuses and graft, and the behavior of the tsar and his brothers in the military theater, could not but hasten the erosion of imperial authority."[40]

Not all of the Russian statesmen shared these negative opinions. Moderates such as Giers and the ambassador to Britain, Peter An-

---

[40]Peter A. Zaionchkovsky, *The Russian Autocracy in Crisis, 1878–1882* (Gulf Breeze, Fl.: Academic International Press, 1979), p. 5.

dreevich Shuvalov, understood that the settlement was necessary because Russia was not in a position to wage war against a European coalition. As Giers wrote to Jomini during the congress:

> The impossibility of obtaining more is recognized [and if the Black Sea port of Batum is acquired] we will be perfectly satisfied, and indeed with reason, for what war can be compared to this for results? The independence of three principalities, the creation of one Bulgaria only tributary and another autonomous . . . My God! would we not have treated as mad the man who would have dreamed of a similar result two years ago! And all that with the sanction of Europe.[41]

Nevertheless, disappointment with the results of the war remained strong. In the same manner that the Russian leaders had previously blamed the Habsburg Monarchy for the defeat in the Crimean War, they now placed the main burden for the disappointing peace on the shoulders of Germany, whose government, it was felt, had not given Russia strong enough support.

With the Three Emperors' Alliance in temporary shambles, Bismarck looked for alternative combinations. In October 1879 the Dual Alliance was concluded between Germany and Austria-Hungary. In 1882, with the addition of Italy, the Triple Alliance, which was to remain in effect until 1914, was completed. Meanwhile, however, the Russian government had recognized that it could not remain without allies. In June 1881 the Three Emperors' Alliance was renewed, this time in the form of a written agreement. Secret clauses provided that Russia could sponsor the unification of Bulgaria and Eastern Rumelia at a favorable time, and Austria-Hungary could annex Bosnia and Hercegovina.

Russian–Bulgarian relations, 1878–87

With its Balkan influence concentrated in the autonomous Bulgarian province, the Russian government naturally wished to establish as strong a base there as possible. It will be remembered that the Bulgarian lands were of great strategic importance in relation to the Ottoman capital, the Straits, and the balance of power in the Black Sea region. In turn, the Russian position in Central Asia depended on maintaining its lines of communication through the Black Sea safe from the British threat. In the first half of the 1880s Russian expansion toward the borders of Afghanistan continued, leading to a mounting crisis between Britain and Russia. At the end of March

[41]Giers to Jomini, St. Petersburg, June 23, 1878. Jelavich and Jelavich, *Russia in the East*, pp. 147–8.

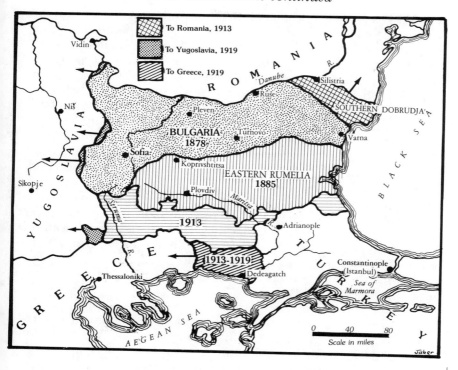

Map 8. Bulgarian territorial changes, 1878–1919.

1885 an incident at Penjdeh threatened to develop into a British–Russian war. Although the dispute was settled by September with a border agreement, the Russian government was made even more aware of the strategic significance of the Balkan and Black Sea regions in relation to its new Central Asian acquisitions.

As had previously been the case in the Danubian Principalities after 1829, the Russian officals in Bulgaria made great efforts to establish a strong and popular administration.[42] It is interesting to note that at this time they sponsored the introduction of the consti-

---

[42]See Cyril E. Black, *The Establishment of Constitutional Government in Bulgaria* (Princeton, N.J.: Princeton University Press, 1943), for the organization of the Bulgarian administration. Charles Jelavich, *Tsarist Russia and Balkan Nationalism: Russian Influence in the Internal Affairs of Bulgaria and Serbia, 1879–1886* (Berkeley: University of California Press, 1958), discusses the development of Russo–Bulgarian relations in these years.

tutional government and liberal institutions that were denied to the Russian people. Since the Russian period of occupation had been reduced to nine months, they were eager to have the new government in place as soon as possible. A draft constitution was prepared in November 1878 by the Russian commissioner, Prince Alexander Mikhailovich Dondukov-Korsakov. It was sent to Russia, where it was examined by the appropriate ministries and by a committee. The document was liberal in political direction in that more power was given to the legislative than to the executive branch. The Russian draft was then presented to a specially convened constitutional assembly with the assurance that it was only a suggestion and could be altered. The assembly, consisting of 231 members and meeting at Tŭrnovo, split along familiar lines into Liberal and Conservative parties. The Liberals, predominant in the assembly, were able to ensure that the legislature would have a strong position. The Conservatives, in general, came from the same group that before 1876 had stood for a gradual policy and that had been in touch with the Russian representatives. Their ideas were closer to those supported in St. Petersburg.

Although the Bulgarian representatives were given wide latitude in determining the content of their constitution, the great powers named as the ruler Alexander of Battenberg, a twenty-two-year-old prince of Hesse with almost ideal dynastic ties. The empress of Russia was his aunt; his family had close connections with the courts of Britain, Germany, and Austria-Hungary. Russian support was ensured at first because of the family relationship. As long as Alexander II was alive, relations between the prince and the tsar were relatively smooth. Problems, however, soon arose within Bulgaria that thoroughly tested the new ruler's abilities. Although the Russian army withdrew on schedule, it left behind General Peter Dmitrievich Parensov, who was appointed the Bulgarian minister of war and assigned the task of organizing and training a Bulgarian army. Russian interests were also defended by Alexander Petrovich Davydov, the consul-general in Sofia, who was the first diplomatic agent accredited to the autonomous principality. Very soon the prince, who had little sympathy with the constitution and its limitations on his power, came into conflict with the Liberal Party. The two Russian representatives entered into this internal political quarrel with vigor, but on opposite sides. Parensov supported the Liberals, while his colleague favored the prince and the Conservatives. Davydov thought that the constitution "was worth absolutely nothing" and that the prince was "the only good card that Bulgaria has in its game."[43]

Relations between Russia and its client state became even more complicated when Alexander III came to the throne in 1881 following the assassination of his father. His thirteen-year reign was a period of political reaction and of the suppression of national manifestations in domestic policy. In foreign relations the major crisis, and one that had a decisive influence on the Russian alliance system, came over Bulgarian affairs. A man who believed strongly in the autocratic system and was closely tied to Orthodoxy, the tsar had been attracted to Panslav and Russian nationalistic programs. After serving in the Balkans and witnessing directly the carnage of war, he lost his previous enthusiasms, but he did continue to read the Panslav press, in particular the writings of Katkov. In April 1881 the tsar commented:

> I understand only one policy. . . . To exact from every situation all that is needed by and is useful to Russia, to disregard all other considerations, and to act in a straightforward and resolute manner. We can have no policy except one that is purely Russian and national; this is the only policy we can and must follow.[44]

During his reign Alexander III had only one active foreign minister: Nicholas Karlovich Giers. Although Gorchakov kept the title until his death at the age of eighty-five in 1883, he was not able to carry on the duties of the office. A Lutheran of Baltic German-Swedish ancestry, married to a Romanian, Giers was an example of the service nobility that had played such a large role in the Foreign Ministry previously. He had an excellent background in Eastern affairs. His posts had been primarily in the Principalities, where he served during the crucial periods of the revolutions of 1848–9, the occupation of 1854, and the years of the double election of Alexander Cuza and the unification of the provinces. He had also gained experience in Egypt, in Persia, and in Western posts. An excellent restraining influence on the impulsive tsar, he consistently favored a German alliance and moderate policies. During his years in office he was under constant attack from those who wanted a more adventurous attitude and who opposed working with Berlin or Vienna. He had particular difficulties in connection with the Russian involve-

---

[43]Davydov to Giers, private letter, Bucharest, January 28/February 9, 1880. Charles and Barbara Jelavich, "Russia and Bulgaria, 1879: The Letters of A. P. Davydov to N. K. Giers," *Südost-Forschungen*, XV (1956), pp. 457–8.

[44]Quoted in Michael T. Florinsky, *Russia* (New York: Macmillan, 1960), II, p. 1088.

Figure 9. Alexander III.

ment in Bulgaria. There the tsar was to come into sharp conflict with the Bulgarian prince and his associates, who wanted to pursue an independent national policy.

Although Prince Alexander's relationship with his uncle, Alexander II, had been good, this condition did not characterize his feelings toward his cousin. At first there were few problems. On May 9, 1881, the prince suspended the constitution. Although he had not consulted the Russian agents before taking this action, the tsar supported the move. In the next years, however, conflicts between the Russian representatives and the Bulgarian officials increased. The Bulgarian officers in the new army resented the fact that all of the ranks from captain up were reserved for Russians; others objected to the overbearing attitude of some of the Russian

Figure 10. Nicholas Karlovich Giers.

representatives and their constant interference in the government. The opposition finally became so strong that in 1883 the Bulgarian political parties joined with the prince to form a front against Russian interference. At that time the prince, in order to conciliate the Liberals, restored the constitution. Prince Alexander, the Liberals, and the Conservatives thus faced the crisis that was about to arise joined by a common goal.

For the Bulgarian nationalist the great objective after 1878 was the eventual realization of the San Stefano Bulgaria. The next obvious action was the unification of Bulgaria and Eastern Rumelia.[45] The union was at first also supported by the Russian government; it was part of its understanding with Vienna and Berlin. The Russian officials assigned to Eastern Rumelia did what they could to encourage the Bulgarians to look forward to eventual unification. However, when the relations between the tsar and the prince became strained, the Russian attitude changed quickly. The Russian officials wanted any unification to take place under their auspices and under conditions that would ensure Russia a dominant position in the united state. By 1885 the tsar's disapproval of Prince Alexander had become so strong that the Russian government actively opposed unification, since it would, of course, strengthen his position. In August 1885 Giers met with the prince at Franzenbad. While urging a reconciliation, Giers nevertheless warned that the status quo should not be disturbed; the prince agreed.

However, by this time the unification movement in Eastern Rumelia had advanced beyond either the Bulgarian or Russian possibility to control. On the night of September 17 Rumelian revolutionary forces in Plovdiv took over the administration and announced unification with Bulgaria. Upon receiving this news, Prince Alexander was at first hesitant; he knew the Russian adverse opinion, and he was not sure of the reaction of the other powers, especially the Ottoman Empire. When his advisers warned him that

---

[45]The section is reprinted from Barbara Jelavich, "Tsarist Russia and the Unification of Bulgaria and Eastern Rumelia, 1885–1886," in Don Karl Rowney, ed., *Imperial Power and Development: Papers on Pre-Revolutionary Russian History* (Columbus, Ohio: Slavica Publishers, 1990), pp. 101–15. Three Bulgarian works are Andrei Pantev, *Angliia sreshtu Russiia na Balkanite, 1879–1894* (Sofia: Nauka i izkustvo, 1972); Elena Statelova, *Diplomatsiiata na kniazhestvo Bŭlgariia, 1879–1886* (Sofia: Izdatelstvo na Bŭlgarskata akademiia na naukite, 1979); and Elena Statelova and Andrei Pantev, *Sŭedinenieto na kniazhestvo Bŭlgariia i Istochna Rumeliia 1885 godina* (Sofia: Dŭrzhavno izdatelstvo Narodna Prosveta, 1985). In addition, the following articles also deal with the Russian attitude: W. N. Medlicott, "The Powers and the Unification of the Two Bulgarias, 1885," *English Historical Review*, LIV (1939), pp. 67–82, 263–84; Yono Mitev, "L'attitude de la Russie et de l'Angleterre à l'égard de l'union de la Bulgarie en 1885," *Etudes historiques* (Sofia, 1960), I, pp. 347–77; and three studies by Barbara Jelavich: "Russia, Britain and the Bulgarian Question, 1885–1888," *Südost-Forschungen*, XXXII (1973), pp. 168–91; "A Russian Diplomat's Comments on the Bulgarian Crisis, 1885–1888: The Letters of E. E. Staal to N. K. Giers," ibid., XXXIV (1975), pp. 247–74; and "The Bulgarian Crisis of 1885–1887 in British Foreign Policy," in Thomas Butler, ed., *Bulgaria: Past and Present*, (Columbus, Ohio: American Association for the Advancement of Slavic Studies, n.d.), pp. 65–70.

he had to accept union or abdicate, he assumed the leadership of the national movement and prepared to meet the consequences.

The union of Bulgaria and Eastern Rumelia accorded with the desires of the Bulgarian public, of much Russian opinion, and of many individual Russian officials. However, it occasioned a violent reaction from Alexander III, who, as we will see, henceforth devoted his attention to securing the expulsion of the disobedient prince. Personal passion aside, the Russian government had solid reasons to be concerned about the union and its implications. With the Bulgarian rejection of its tutelage, Russia had lost the major gain from the Russo–Turkish War. Russian prestige and power were damaged in the eyes of exactly those whom it was supposed to impress: the Ottoman government and the Balkan nationalities. Moreover, and most important, the Russian leaders did not want another Eastern crisis at this time; they had hardly recovered from the expenses and losses of the last war. They were well aware that the union, if allowed to stand, would bring demands for compensation from Serbia and Greece, probably for Ottoman Macedonian territory. At issue was not only the balance of power among the Balkan states, but the division of influence among the great powers and the territorial integrity of the Ottoman Empire.

At the time of the unification, the Russian leadership was dispersed. Alexander III was visiting his father-in-law in Copenhagen; Giers was in Meran. Thus Alexander Georgievich Vlangali, in charge of the Foreign Ministry in St. Petersburg, and Nelidov, now the ambassador in Constantinople, were the first to deal with the crisis. Many of the Russian agents in both Eastern Rumelia and Bulgaria – as well as part of the Russian press – at first expressed their support of the action. The official position was, of course, decided in Copenhagen. Here on September 21 Alexander III made his strong opposition known by denouncing the union, depriving the prince of his Russian army rank, recalling the Russian general who was the Bulgarian minister of war, and summoning home the Russian officers in command of the Bulgarian army.

The Russian attitude was thus made clear to both the Bulgarians and the great powers. Appeals for approval and protection from the prince and the Bulgarian assembly were rejected. A Bulgarian delegation, headed by Metropolitan Kliment of Tŭrnovo and including Ivan Geshov, representing the assembly, and Ivan Gerdzhikov, Dimitŭr Papazoglu, and Dimitŭr Tonchev of Eastern Rumelia, went to

Copenhagen, where they spoke with the tsar and Giers.[46] In a meeting held on October 2, Alexander III expressed his sympathy for the idea of union, but he refused to offer assistance as long as the present government was in power. The tsar appears to have believed that his strong stand would influence the Bulgarians to overthow their prince. He and other Russian diplomats at this time and later suffered from the illusion that the Bulgarian people as a whole would be eternally so grateful to their "liberator" that these sympathies would override their duties as Bulgarian citizens.

In order to carry out its Bulgarian policy, the Russian government turned to the other powers, in particular to its allies. It should be noted that in this crisis Russia could not and did not attempt an independent policy, nor did it consider a military intervention in Bulgaria. Without a common border with that country, a Russian army would have to pass through Romania, a nation that at this time was strongly anti-Russian and in alliance with Austria-Hungary. A landing by sea would be impossible because of the expected attitude of Britain. Instead the Russian officials took their stand on legality and treaty obligations and called for international cooperation.

The precise steps that the Russian government proposed were communicated to the powers in October: A conference should be convened in Constantinople, which would despatch a delegate to Plovdiv to inform Prince Alexander, in the name of Europe, that he should evacuate Eastern Rumelia. If he refused, he was to be told that the powers could no longer "protect the Bulgarians against the consequences of their acts." Thereafter, the powers should agree with the Porte on "measures of military execution." As a third and final duty, the conference should consider modifications in the provisions of the Treaty of Berlin concerning the province.[47]

The Russian proposals for the restoration of the status quo had at first the support of the Habsburg and German governments and, of course, the Ottoman Empire. Although some Habsburg statesmen could see advantages in the union, they recognized that there were grave dangers in the situation. As the protecting power of Serbia, the

---

[46]See the reports by Kliment and Geshov on these meetings in Ministerstvo na Vŭnshnite Raboti na NRB, *Vŭnshnata politika na Bŭlgariia: dokumenti i materiali* (Sofia: Nauka i izkustvo, 1978), I, pp. 586–8, 591–2.

[47]Communication of the Russian embassy in Paris, October 19, 1885. France: Ministère des affaires étrangères, *Documents diplomatiques français, 1871–1914* (Paris: Imprimerie nationale, 1934), series I, VI, p. 117; Freycinet circular despatch, Paris, October 23, 1885, ibid., pp. 131–2.

monarchy could expect King Milan to turn to it for assistance in gaining compensation. Since no power wanted another crisis over Ottoman Macedonian territory, such claims could only be satisfied at Bulgarian expense. The implications of this situation were well understood; the restoration of the status quo would remove the basis for the Serbian as well as the Greek demands.

The major obstacle to the achievement of the Russian desires in 1885 was, as in 1878, Britain. Its government, which had previously opposed a large Bulgaria when it seemed inevitable that it would be a Russian puppet, now had the opportunity to change the state into a barrier against Russian expansion southward. When the British prime minister, Lord Salisbury, heard of the union, he was at first skeptical. It was only after the anti-Russian nature of the action became clear and the Russian government supported the restoration of the status quo that the advantages for British policy became obvious. Therefore, although Germany and Austria-Hungary backed the Russian position, Salisbury refused to join with them. British policy became instead the acceptance of the personal union of the two provinces under Alexander of Battenberg, a course of action adopted, it will be remembered, at the time of the double election of Alexander Cuza. The unification carried through in this manner could be accommodated to the stipulations of the Treaty of Berlin.

In opposing the union of the Bulgarian provinces, the Russian government placed itself in a difficult position. Without the united support of all the powers, there was little chance that its policy could be carried out. Moreover, the situation soon disintegrated further. As the Russian government had foreseen, both Serbia and Greece demanded compensation. Expecting an easy victory, King Milan of Serbia sought to enforce his claims by an attack on Bulgaria on November 14. When the Serbian army met defeat at the battle of Slivnitsa, the Habsburg government was forced to intervene and impose an armistice. Greek demands, which endangered Ottoman territory, were opposed by a united action of the powers. A joint note was sent to Greece; upon its rejection an international force blockaded Greece until June 1886.

The decisive Bulgarian victory over Serbia had the important effect of forcing the Russian government to reconsider some aspects of its policy. Previously, Giers, who did not support the tsar's harsh treatment of Alexander, told a friend "that he had opposed as much as he could the stripping from the Bulgarian prince of the Russian rank and he considers that the position of [the Russian] government will become very delicate if that prince, degraded in the ranks by us, returns triumphantly from the war."[48] Even worse for the Russian foreign minister, the entire episode brought into question the value for Russia of the Three Emperors' Alliance that he so strongly supported. It was exactly those Panslav and nationalist elements that opposed a German connection that now were most strident in their attacks on Prince Alexander.[49] Although Giers regarded the alliance as "the fundamental base" of Russian policy,[50] he too was upset by certain Austrian actions, in particular the unilateral intervention in the Serbo–Bulgarian War, which had halted the Bulgarian army at the Serbian frontier. Despite these difficulties, he was, nevertheless, able to preserve the alliance, but he was not so successful in modifying the unforgiving attitude of the tsar, who in December declared:

> Prince Alexander of Bulgaria [is] the enemy of Russia, and so long as he rules there, his influence will always be hostile to us. It is certainly necessary to get rid of him sooner or later. To support him in the unification of Bulgaria which has been achieved under his sceptre or even the recognition of him only as governor-general of Rumelia would mean to reward him for all the measures which deserve not encouragement, but punishment.[51]

Although the Russian government was no longer to favor an Ottoman military intervention or to expect a full return to the status quo, the tsar insisted that the Russian officials continue to direct their efforts to blocking the unification or to attaching conditions to it that the prince could not accept. However, Alexander III did not wish the Bulgarian issue to lead to war, stating that "at the present time the interests of Russia demand that we should abstain from interfering in the affairs of the Balkan peninsula until such a time

[48]*Dnevnik gosudarstvennogo sekretaria A. A. Polovtsova* (Moscow: Izdatel'stvo nauka 1966), I, p. 351.

[49]M. N. Katkov wrote in September that "the union will be desirable when Russia will liberate Bulgaria from chaos, as not so very long ago she liberated her from the Turks." In October, K. P. Pobedonostsev, in a letter to Alexander III, referred to "the fantastic, mad, and outrageous act of the prince of Bulgaria." Aksakov and Ignatiev, however, were favorable to this advance in Bulgarian national interests. Boris Nolde, *L'Alliance franco–russe* (Paris: Librairie Droz, 1936), pp. 324–6.

[50]Giers wrote to Staal that for Russia it was essential "to maintain the agreement of the three empires, around which the other powers interested in preserving the continent from dangerous complications will gather. The more the English cabinet makes visible efforts to break that accord, the more we believe it urgent to conserve it. It is the fundamental base of our policy." Quoted in Nolde, *L'Alliance franco–russe*, p. 336.

[51]*Dnevnik Polovtsova*, I, p. 367.

that questions arise there which are more directly of concern to us."[52] The control of the Straits, or at least of the Bosphorus, remained the preeminent, although distant, goal.

In Constantinople, where the ambassadors met formally in conferences from November 5 to 25, 1885, and then for a final session on April 5, 1886, opposing stands were taken by the Russian ambassador, Nelidov, and his British counterpart, Sir William White, who was holding a temporary assignment in Constantinople.[53] At first, because of the firm support that his government was giving to the Ottoman position, Nelidov worked closely with the Turkish officials as well as with the German and Habsburg representatives. A strong adherent of an aggressive Russian Balkan policy, the Russian representative was regarded as a contender for Giers's post as foreign minister. Although he could uphold the first Russian demands with enthusiasm, he recognized the damage done by the Bulgarian victories on the battlefield. On December 3 he wrote to Giers that he regarded the situation in which Russia found itself as extremely difficult. The British were encouraging the Bulgarians to resist; an entrance of Ottoman troops into Eastern Rumelia could result in disasters that would arouse Russian public opinion. Despite his instructions, which he had just received, not to support an Ottoman occupation, he did not think that the Rumelians would give in without the use of force. Yet if the union were kept, Austria might act in the Serbian interest:

---

[52]Ibid.

[53]White's activities are described in Colin L. Smith, *The Embassy of Sir William White at Constantinople, 1886–1891* (London: Oxford University Press, 1957), and in H. Sutherland Edwards, *Sir William White* (London: John Murray, 1902). The second book contains lengthy extracts of the correspondence of White and Sir Robert Morier in St. Petersburg (pp. 228–38). The two diplomats held differing views on the crisis. Morier believed that Britain should not oppose all Russian interests in Europe in order to avoid problems in Asia. He wrote in November 1885: "I will say that our Asiatic concerns are for me *en première ligne* – our rivalry with Russia in Europe *en seconde ligne*, and very far behind" (pp. 230–1). White, although not advocating as strong a policy as Salisbury, believed that "we cannot shape our course in Europe by purely Asiatic considerations. Of course, our great interests are there; but we still have European duties and a European position, and even European interests" (p. 234). Morier's career is discussed in Agatha Ramm, *Sir Robert Morier* (Oxford: Oxford University Press, 1973). The protocols of the Constantinople conference are to be found in Gabriel Noradounghian, *Recueil d'actes internationaux de l'Empire Ottoman* (Nendeln, Liechtenstein; Kraus Reprint, 1978), IV, pp. 366–410.

It is a vicious circle, from which it is difficult to break out, and I hold to the idea that I have already once taken the liberty to express – hold back, let things alone, and only intervene at a decisive moment and in a decisive fashion.[54]

In the next months Nelidov could do little more than attempt to ensure that the settlement would be as disadvantageous to Prince Alexander as possible, and, to an extent, at least, he was successful in modifying the provisions of the agreement that was worked out between the prince and the Porte. During this period German support for the Russian position remained firm. Bismarck also put pressure on Vienna not to come into conflict with Russia.[55] The British government, in particular through its discussions with Ottoman representatives, however, continued its efforts to gain a settlement favorable to the prince. Thus in December 1885 Salisbury told the Ottoman ambassador, Rustem Pasha, that it seemed to be the "wish of the powers" that the Bulgarian question be settled by direct negotiation between the sultan and the vassal state. The foreign secretary gave assurances of British support for such an arrangement, but not for "any attempt to restore the original state of things."[56] On February 3, 1886, Rustem Pasha was able to give Salisbury the text of an agreement, which was also communicated to the other powers. According to its terms Prince Alexander was to be appointed governor-general of Eastern Rumelia on the basis of the Treaty of Berlin, that is, for five years, but his renewal would be determined by the sultan. In addition, both Bulgaria and Eastern Rumelia were to provide military assistance to the Ottoman Empire in case any of its territories were attacked. The other stipulations of the Treaty of Berlin were to remain in effect, but a commission was to be formed to consider possible administrative changes.[57] Salisbury

[54]Nelidov to Giers, private letter, Pera, November 21/December 3, 1885. This letter is from the *Hariciye Arshivi*, Istanbul.

[55]See *Denkwürdigkeiten des Botschafters General von Schweinitz* (Berlin: Verlag von Reimar Hobbing, 1927), II, pp. 312–13. In the interest of preserving the German–Russian alliance, Bismarck adopted a harsh attitude toward the prince. For instance, in 1884 he warned him: "If you wish to remain in Bulgaria you must submit to Russia for better for worse . . . I therefore advise you to seize every opportunity of making your peace with Russia." Egon Caesar Corti, *Alexander von Battenberg* (London: Cassell and Company, Ltd., 1954), p. 124.

[56]Salisbury to White, Foreign Office, December 24, 1885. *British and Foreign State Papers* (London: William Ridgway, 1892–3), LXXVI, pp. 1311–12.

[57]Said Pasha to Rustem Pasha, Constantinople, February 2, 1886, communicated to Salisbury by Rustem Pasha on February 3, 1886, ibid., LXXVII, pp. 616–18.

accepted the agreement and promised to attempt to secure its approval by the other powers.[58]

As could be expected, the Russian government made immediate objections, in particular in regard to the naming of Prince Alexander specifically, the renewal of his position without recourse to the powers, and the provisions for administrative reform in Eastern Rumelia.[59] The Russian leaders also could not accept the military clauses that obligated the Christian Bulgarians to fight for the Ottoman Empire; they certainly realized that the terms might involve Bulgarian soldiers joining with Ottoman and British troops against the Russian army. Despite the strong opposition of Prince Alexander,[60] the powers finally did agree to accept some of the Russian proposals for modifications in the original Bulgarian–Ottoman agreement. In its final form, not only was the term *prince of Bulgaria* rather than the name of Prince Alexander used, but his renewal in office was made subject to the approval of the powers. Although a Turko–Bulgarian commission would draw up new administrative regulations for Eastern Rumelia, its work would be submitted for examination to the ambassadors at Constantinople. No mention was made of Bulgarian military obligations.[61] On April 12, 1886, Prince Alexander, while maintaining his objections to the changes in the original agreement concerning the need for great-power approval for his reappointment, accepted the terms.[62] Nevertheless, despite the fact that the document maintained the division between Bulgaria and Eastern Rumelia intact, the prince soon joined the assemblies of the two provinces and proceeded to govern Bulgaria as a united state.

The acceptance of the personal union by Alexander II did not take Bulgaria out of the international limelight largely because of the

---

[58]Salisbury to White, Foreign Office, February 4, 1886, ibid., LXXVII, p. 619.

[59]Said Pasha to Rustem Pasha, Constantinople, February 12, 1886, communicated to Rosebery by Rustem Pasha on February 13, ibid., LXXVII, pp. 622–3.

[60]Prince Alexander did not like "the reestablishment of international sovereignty in Eastern Rumelia," on which he blamed the past difficulties in the province. Prince Alexander to Said Pasha, telegram, Sofia, March 19/31, 1886. *Vŭnshnata politika na Bulgariia*, p. 788.

[61]Protocol no. 8, meeting of March 24/April 5, 1886, of the Conference of Constantinople on Eastern Rumelia. Norodounghian, *Recueil d'actes internationaux de l'Empire Ottoman*, IV, pp. 408–10.

[62]Said Pasha to Rustem Pasha, Constantinople, April 12, 1886, communicated by Rosebery to Rustem Pasha on April 14. *British and Foreign State Papers*, LXXVII, p. 641.

deep resentment of the tsar toward the prince. What had been a victory for the latter had been a personal humiliation for the Russian ruler. At this time the Russian leaders recognized that they could not stand against the Bulgarian desire for national advancement, but they believed that they could force the abdication of the prince. They therefore attempted to demonstrate that the nation could expect no further gains without Russian support and that the presence of the prince was blocking further advances. The tsar's dislike of the prince was shared by other members of the Russian government. Zinoviev, in charge of the Asiatic Department and thus of Bulgarian affairs, described the prince as the "ulcer that had been grafted" on Bulgaria; he believed that the Bulgarians were "still children" who needed firm Russian guidance.[63]

This attitude on the part of Russia, which was still regarded abroad as the protecting power, caused concern within Bulgaria. Some were worried about the influence that Russia had been able to wield over the final form of the union. It appeared that without a reconciliation with Russia, the Bulgarian future was dark. The Russian agents within Bulgaria were able to work on the fears of these people, as well as on those who were unhappy with other aspects of the prince's rule.

Under these conditions conspiracies could flourish. As we have seen in other Balkan countries, the army in Bulgaria provided officers who were willing to take part in an action against their ruler. In the summer of 1886, with the cooperation of the Russian military attaché, these men prepared to act in the Russian interest. Despite all of the rumors that circulated at the time, Prince Alexander did not take adequate precautions to protect himself. The conspiracy was known to a large number of Bulgarian officials, including the prime minister, Karavelov, the foreign minister, Ilia Tsanov, and the minister of war, Constantine Nikiforov. In Russia the tsar, Giers, and the minister of war, General Nicholas Nikolaievich Obruchev, as well as others, all knew of the impending coup.

On the night of August 20, 1886, the conspirators forced their way into the prince's residence, took him prisoner, and then compelled him to sign an instrument of abdication. He was moved by his kidnappers to different locations in Bulgaria, then taken to Silistria, and finally released in Reni in Bessarabia. Thereafter he started to return to Germany. At first, it appeared that the Russian government had achieved success. A new government under the strongly

[63]Zinoviev to Giers, September 14/28, 1885, NKG.

Russophil Metropolitan Kliment was organized; Russia accepted this regime. The coup, however, did not have popular approval. Soon after the abdication, a counterrevolution, led by Stephen Stambolov, resulted in the formation of another government, which invited the prince to return.

On August 29, ten days after the revolt, the prince crossed the border back into Bulgaria. At that point he made a grave mistake. Seeing a Russian vice-consul in the crowd that had gathered to welcome him, he mistakenly interpreted his presence as a sign of Russian support. He therefore sent a telegram to the tsar that concluded with the statement: "As Russia gave me my crown, I am prepared to give it back into the hands of its Sovereign." Alexander III now had what he wanted: a clear means of getting rid of the prince. He therefore replied that he did not approve of his return, concluding: "Your Highness will understand what devolves upon you."[64] The prince had no choice but to abdicate. However, even with the departure of its opponent, the Russian government was not able to reassert its former influence. With a regency headed by Stambolov holding the executive power, the Bulgarian government maintained an independent attitude; elections were held for a national assembly to choose a new prince. Finally, in November, Russia broke diplomatic relations with its former protégé.

Despite its difficult international position, the assembly after numerous attempts was able in July 1887 to elect a prince, Ferdinand of Coburg, who would accept the headship of the state. Russo–Bulgarian relations did not return to normal until 1896. By this date Alexander III had died and Stambolov had been dismissed. At this time, with Russian approval, the powers officially recognized Ferdinand as prince and accepted the union of 1885 as permanent.

As could be expected, the entire Bulgarian episode left bitter feelings in St. Petersburg. Once again it appeared as if Russia had made sacrifices for a Balkan Christian cause and had suffered for it. In a conversation with the British ambassador, Sir Robert Morier, in July 1886, Giers well expressed these emotions:

We have submitted, and we are submitting, to the deepest humiliation. Can no one feel or understand what a Russian understands and feels, when he reflects that, having spent his best blood and half his treasure in rescuing the Christian populations of the Balkans from the Turkish yoke, and with that blood and treasure furnished the conditions for Bulgarian autonomy and well-being, all the fruits of his toil are being taken from him by others who have not stirred a finger to aid in

[64]Quoted in Charles Jelavich, *Tsarist Russia and Balkan Nationalism.* pp. 258–9.

the accomplishment of results for which they profess such sympathy, and show the true motives that actuate them by hounding on the Bulgarians to repudiate the obligations they are under to Russia, as if such repudiation were the act of patriots and heroes.[65]

The disillusioned Alexander III in 1885 reacted in direct terms: "The Slavs must now serve us and not we them."[66]

Certainly, aside from questions of pride and prestige, the Bulgarian crisis, which dominated European diplomacy in the 1880s, much as the Greek revolt had done in the 1820s, seriously weakened the Russian international position to the benefit of its chief rival – Great Britain. In 1885, at the beginning of the crisis, the Russian position had been favorable; Russia formed part of the strongest continental coalition, the Three Emperors' Alliance; Britain, at odds with France over Egypt, was isolated. However, at each stage of the Bulgarian crisis, Britain was able to improve its position. With the union of 1885 Russia lost its special influence in Bulgaria, its chief gain from the Russo–Turkish War. The second stage, the kidnapping of Alexander of Battenberg, broke the Three Emperors' Alliance. In February and March 1887 Austria-Hungary joined Britain, Italy, and Spain in the First Mediterranean Agreement, a consultative pact designed to preserve the status quo in the Mediterranean, Adriatic, and Black seas. When the Three Emperors' Alliance came up for renewal, both the Russian and Habsburg governments agreed that it should lapse. After the election of Ferdinand of Coburg a second Mediterranean agreement was signed in December that was specifically designed to meet a possible Russian occupation of Bulgaria. Previously, in June, Russia had signed the Reinsurance Treaty, a neutrality pact with a secret protocol ensuring German support of the Russian position on Bulgaria and the closure of the Straits. This agreement, however, was not renewed after the accession of a new emperor, William II, in Germany.

The breaking of the formal diplomatic connection with Germany, which had been a mainstay of Russian diplomacy for almost two decades, deeply disturbed Giers but not Alexander III, who did not regret the ending of the alliance. Russia was now isolated, a dangerous situation for any great power with wide strategic commitments. Since Britain was still perceived as the principal opponent, and

---

[65]Morier to Rosebery, no. 253 most secret, St. Petersburg, July 21, 1886 (Public Record Office, FO 65/1260), printed in Barbara Jelavich, "Bulgaria and Batum," *Southeastern Europe*, I: 1 (1974), pp. 74–9.

[66]"Zapiska A. I. Nelidova," *Krasnyi Arkhiv*, LXVI (1931), p. 180.

Germany and Austria-Hungary were out of consideration, only France remained as a possible partner. Although the discussions went slowly, in August 1891 an entente was negotiated and, finally, in January 1894 a strong alliance was concluded that brought together two governments whose relations in the previous century had often been difficult.

Although the French alignment ultimately had a major influence on Russian–Balkan relations, this result was not immediately apparent. In fact, after the accession of Nicholas II in 1894 a return was made to the previous policy of cooperation with Vienna. In April 1897 the tsar and Franz Joseph met and agreed upon the desirability of maintaining the status quo in the Balkan penisula. In the next years crises were to occur in regard to Crete and Macedonia and in connection with the Greek–Turkish War of 1897. In these events Russia cooperated with the other great powers to maintain peace and the status quo. The Russian leaders turned their chief attention to the Far East and embarked on new adventures, which were to lead to another military disaster.

The events covered in this chapter brought an end to many of the illusions and hopes that Russian officials had cherished earlier. Most significant, the tsarist government could in the future no longer act openly as a protecting power; its officials could not expect to move in and run Balkan administrations. The Bulgarian fiasco was a lesson at least for some Russian diplomats. In 1888 Jomini wrote to Giers:

> Let us rest on our *non possumus* and *laissons faire*. All things come to him who waits for the opportunity, prepares for it and seizes it. . . . It will be the same in Bulgaria. If we have had painful failures, it is we who have brought them upon ourselves in acting out of order. You will not make people like you by using force. It is time to finish with that system.[67]

Nevertheless, despite the realities of the situation, many Russians retained the belief that their country continued to have a unique relationship with the Balkan people, one shared by no other nation. They still tended to see acts of obstruction or resistance to Russian pressure by Balkan governments as the result of intrigues by other great powers. In fact, not only was this an illusion, but with the passage of time, Balkan political leaders became even more attracted to Western political models. As we have seen, Bulgarian, Serbian,

---

[67] Jomini to Giers, July 4, 1888, NKG.

and Romanian national organizations had previously cooperated with European revolutionary circles, and thus with Poles and Russian radicals deeply opposed to the Russian autocracy.

This period should also have shown the Russian leaders how difficult it was to establish an effective unity among the Balkan states and one that St. Petersburg could direct. Despite Ignatiev's concerns, Russia could not control the actions of Balkan nationalists or revolutionaries. Moreover, the events of the time indicated that once the new states succeeded in freeing themselves from Ottoman domination, they would direct their attention to competing among themselves for the control of territory and diplomatic advantage. The negotiations during Prince Michael Obrenović's reign and the Serbian attack on Bulgaria in 1885 provided examples of the difficulty of bringing these competitive peoples together. Neither Orthodoxy nor Slavdom could provide an effective alternative to rampant nationalism.

This period also clearly demonstrated the immense dangers faced by Russia in adopting a policy of intervention in Balkan affairs. The state came out of the Russo–Turkish War and the Bulgarian complications in a much worse strategic and diplomatic position than before. After the Congress of Berlin, Russia was isolated: The Three Emperors' Alliance was temporarily in disarray, Britain remained an opponent, and France was still too weak to provide alternate support. The situation deteriorated further in the 1880s. By 1890 the alliance relationship with Vienna and Berlin had been permanently broken and, despite the contributions that Russian military support had indeed given, the Russian government had no close friends among the Balkan states, with the possible exception Montenegro. The cool relationship with Romania and Bulgaria was a strategic problem for the Black Sea power; there was now no easy land road to Constantinople should another Eastern crisis occur. Facing these realities, the Russian government did for a time refrain from Balkan involvements, but in 1908 its leaders returned to a policy close to that which had previously led to disaster.

CHAPTER V

Final steps: The Belgrade link and the origins of World War I

The Congress of Berlin of 1878 in a sense marked a watershed in European and Balkan relationships. In the next years the great powers, with the exception of the Habsburg Monarchy, were to turn their attention away from Europe and to embark on new imperial enterprises. On the peninsula the independent states and autonomous Bulgaria placed their main emphasis in foreign relations on the acquisition of territory that they regarded as their national heritage but that was still under outside control. The intensification of European imperial drives and the competition over lands among the Balkan governments created an uneasy international atmosphere. The Russian leaders, involved deeply in these controversies and engaged in an aggressive policy in the Far East, had also to be concerned about an increasingly dangerous revolutionary situation at home.

The new tsar, Nicholas II, thus faced a combination of problems perhaps more difficult to solve than those with which his predecessors had dealt. Succeeding to the throne in October 1894 at the relatively young age of twenty-six after the unexpectedly early death of Alexander III, Nicholas II was not sufficiently prepared for his high office. He had not been entrusted previously with responsible positions, although he had traveled extensively in 1890 and 1891. Like other Russian rulers, he accepted his autocratic powers as divinely ordained and as intrinsically correct. When he became a constitutional monarch after the revolution of 1905, he was never comfortable in the position, and he insisted on retaining at least the title of autocrat. Nevertheless, despite his convictions about the inherent righteousness of divine right monarchy, he did not have a

Figure 11. Nicholas II.

commanding temperament. Generally judged to possess a sympathetic but weak character, he had the reputation of being easily influenced; some considered him childish. These characteristics were, of course, disastrous in a country where the ruler made the final decisions in foreign policy. Even after 1905 Nicholas II retained full control of Russian international relations until his abdication in 1917. This situation could have been ameliorated had he been served by competent ministers, perhaps not by a Bismarck or a Metternich, but at least by the equivalent of Nesselrode, Gorchakov, and Giers, who had been good administrators and had provided continuity and experience to Russian policy. Instead Nicholas II worked with seven ministers in addition to Giers, who died in 1895.[1]

---

[1]The Foreign ministers of Nicholas II were N. K. Giers to 1895, A. B. Lobanov-Rostovskii to 1896, M. N. Muraviev to 1900, V. N. Lamzdorf to 1906, A. P. Izvolsky

The policies of two, Alexander Petrovich Izvolsky and Sergei Dmitrievich Sazonov, will be discussed in greater detail later because of their importance for Balkan policy. In addition to the Russian diplomatic corps, the tsar was strongly influenced by his relatives and by other advisers and ministers. Although some were indeed competent, many were outright adventurers or charlatans, among whom Rasputin stands out.

Nicholas II inherited a relatively good international position. At his accession the major foreign policy commitment was the strong military and political alliance with France. The other alignments, the Dual Alliance of Germany and Austria-Hungary and the Triple Alliance of Germany, Austria-Hungary, and Italy, were not at the time a threatening presence. In fact, on a world scale, Great Britain was the major opponent of both Russia and France; their initial cooperation was directed more against that power than against their German neighbor. For Russia, Britain became even more of a danger when in 1902 its government broke its tradition of isolation to negotiate an alliance with Japan directed against Russian expansion in Asia.

During the first part of Nicholas's reign the Far East and Persia replaced the Balkans and continental Europe as the center of Russian attention. Russia had already, as has been previously noted, made extensive gains in territory in both Central Asia and the Far East; its frontiers in these regions had been established by agreements with Britain in 1887 and in the treaties of Aigun (1858), Peking (1860), and St. Petersburg (1881) with China. Nevertheless, like all the great powers, Russia's ambitions extended further. For Russia the major competition was with Japan for predominance in Manchuria and Korea, a struggle that culminated in the Japanese attack on Port Arthur in February 1904.

The Russo–Japanese War, the only conflict since 1815 that did not arise over the Eastern Question, was to have, nevertheless, a profound influence on future Russian policy in the Near East. The war was a disaster on both land and sea. In March 1905 the Russian army was defeated, but not annihilated, at the Battle of Mukden. The record at sea was even more dismal. At the beginning of the fighting, the Japanese quickly eliminated Russian naval power in the Pacific. Since the Straits agreements prevented the use of the Black Sea fleet, the Russian government was forced to send its Baltic squadrons on

to 1910, S. D. Sazonov to 1916, B. V. Sturmer to 1916, and N. N. Pokrovskii to 1916–1917.

the long journey to the Pacific, where they were wiped out at the battle of Tsushima in May 1905. Despite these successes, the Japanese leaders realized that they would be at a disadvantage in a long war. Similarly apprehensive, the Russian government, influenced by the defeats, the problems associated with fighting a war in the Far East, and the rise of revolutionary activity at home, joined with Japan in accepting a U.S. mediation. The peace treaty, signed at Portsmouth, New Hampshire, on September 5, 1905, handed over to Japan most of the recent Russian gains in China and the southern half of the island of Sakhalin. Thereafter, learning from experience, the Russian government reversed its previous policy. Instead of continuing the confrontation with Japan, it negotiated agreements, of which the most important was signed in 1910, that settled the lines of the Russian and Japanese spheres of influence in Manchuria and Mongolia. With these settlements, backed by a colonial agreement with Britain in August 1907, the Russian leaders were free to turn their full attention to events in the Near East.

The situation at home, however, could not be settled so easily. The first ten months of 1905 were filled with strikes, riots, and peasant revolts in the countryside. Fearful of a complete collapse of the political system, Nicholas II in the October Manifesto announced his intention to introduce wide reforms, including a guarantee of civil liberties and a representative assembly. The details of some of the changes were announced in the manifesto of February 20, 1906. Russia at this time was given a parliament of two houses. The upper chamber, the Council of State, had an appointed membership. The lower, the Duma, had its members chosen through electoral colleges. After the failure of the first and second Dumas, the franchise was changed to ensure that more representatives from the right and center-right were chosen. For Balkan affairs, the reactions of the third Duma, meeting in 1907, and the fourth, chosen in 1912, were to be of particular significance.

RUSSIA AND THE BALKANS AFTER 1905

In Chapter 1, a discussion of the general Russian position at the beginning of the nineteenth century and the ties with the Balkan peninsula was given. Although some of these generalizations remained relevant, the changes that had taken place by the end of the century make another review necessary. As before, the topics discussed will be economic interests, geopolitical considerations, and ideology.

Belgrade link and origins of World War I

Economic interests

At the beginning of the nineteenth century, as we have seen, Russia had an agrarian economy and an enserfed peasantry. Since similar conditions existed in neighboring states, this situation was not in itself a point of weakness. Only Britain had experienced an industrial revolution. As the century progressed, the Western economies underwent basic changes. Germany, France, and the United States became industrial powers. After the Crimean War the Russian government had ended serfdom because it recognized that a modern state could not compete in the world arena with an unfree peasantry. In the same spirit Russian leaders in the 1890s supported the industrialization of the country. The aim of economic policy was thus the enhancement of state power. In this endeavor the Ministry of Finance was to play a leading role, particularly during the term as minister of Sergei Iulievich Witte from 1892 to 1903. Since native capital was not available, the Russian leaders recognized that they needed foreign investments and loans. Russian economic problems will be considered here only where they link with foreign policy decisions.

In seeking trading partners and investors, the Russian government could expect interest in three major capitals – Paris, Berlin, and London. As far as trade was concerned, the closest relationship was and remained with Germany, which in 1901 took 23 percent of the Russian exports and provided 35 percent of its imports. Britain stood in second place. German money also held first place in foreign investment in Russian enterprises, but other European countries were deeply involved in various industries, as is shown in the following quotation:

The share of foreign capital in total productive expenditure in Russia reached almost 55 percent between 1908 and 1913 (1,420 million rubles). . . . Foreign investors had always concentrated on the railways, heavy industry and other developing sectors. Mining, smelting, metallurgy and machine-building attracted French and Belgian investors in particular. In the spring of 1917, 54.1 per cent of these shares were in foreign hands, while 45 per cent of the chemical industry and as much as 61.8 per cent of construction companies and municipal services were owned by foreigners. The involvement of international capital reached its peak with the monopoly production and sale of oil. In 1914 about 55 per cent of total investment in this branch of industry came from outside Russia, 37 percent from Great Britain alone. The electrical industry was dominated by subsidiaries of the German companies Siemens and AEG, and in 1914 Russian capital held less than a 15 per cent share.[2]

[2]Dietrich Geyer, *Russian Imperialism: the Interaction of Domestic and Foreign Policy, 1860–1914* (New Haven, Conn.: Yale University Press, 1987), p. 266.

For the Russian government, however, the chief need was to secure foreign capital for domestic purposes, such as the building of railroads, armaments, and internal improvements, and here Paris provided the necessary financial support. French loans to Russia assumed serious proportions after 1887, when Bismarck closed the German market for political reasons. Thereafter French banks handled government loans as well as investments in Russian enterprises, in particular the railroads; by 1895 "more than half of all Russian securities handled on financial markets were in French hands."[3] By 1914 about a quarter of the French foreign investments were made in Russia.[4]

These economic relationships have inevitably brought up the question of dependency, or who was in fact exploiting whom.[5] Russian interests were aided by the fact that the French banks were aggressive in promoting the sale of Russian securities. As a result, not only was the necessary money raised, but thousands of middle-class Frenchmen gained a stake in Russia's survival as a great power and, in addition, in the tsarist regime. The Franco–Russian alliance thus had a strong underpinning in the popular interest that the alignment aroused. On the negative side, the French government often attached conditions to the loans. For instance, it used its influence to press at times for the construction of railroads that had strategic rather than economic value, a policy that also had the support of the Russian military. The Russian leaders were well aware of the political implications of the loans, and they made efforts not to be trapped into commitments that were not in their own interest. This financial dependence of Russia on France, it should be emphasized, although it did affect the relationship in certain questions, did not play a major role in Balkan controversies. For both states their great-power strategic interests, not their economic involvements, chiefly influenced their policy decisions.

The imperial world of international finance did, nevertheless, introduce another element that weakened Russian–Balkan links. The independent governments, like the Russian, were also the delighted recipients of European loans and investments.[6] Most of the

[3]Ibid., p. 173.

[4]James Joll, *The Origins of the First World War* (London: Longman, 1984), p. 129.

[5]See D. W. Spring, "Russia and the Franco–Russian Alliance, 1905–1914: Dependence or Interdependence?," *The Slavonic and East European Review*, LXVI: 4 (October 1988), pp. 564–92.

[6]John R. Lampe and Marvin R. Jackson, *Balkan Economic History, 1550–1950: From Imperial Borderlands to Developing Nations* (Bloomington: Indiana Uni-

money was used for railroad building, armaments, state expenses, and, later, for the servicing of the loans themselves. Here again France held the predominant position, followed by Britain, Germany, and Austria-Hungary. Some funds were also invested in economically advantageous projects, such as ports, irrigation projects, and roads. The French financial stake in the economic stability and prosperity of both the Balkan states and the Ottoman Empire often caused conflicts with Russian political goals, but these differences did not lead to a major crisis or an open breach in the relationship between the allies. Russian interests were primarily political and strategic; France, it should be noted, with the largest financial investment in the region, was to exert perhaps the least political influence over Balkan developments among the great powers.

In addition to the predominant position of French financial interests, the Western and Central European states were also the principal trading partners of the Balkan states, to the almost complete exclusion of Russia. The Romanian grain, Serbian livestock, and Greek olives, raisins, and tobacco had natural markets in the industrial states, which could in return send products in demand among Balkan buyers. In contrast, Russia had little to offer; in 1909 it "provided only 2.7 per cent of Romanian, 3.9 per cent of Bulgarian and 2.4 per cent of Serbian imports."[7] Although the relationship was not equal, and many local artisans and manufacturers were indeed forced out by European competition, it was based on economic realities, which continued to exist throughout the century. The lack of an economic base in the Balkans to back its political pretensions was a point of weakness for the Russian government.

Geopolitical considerations

After 1878 the Russian government had to deal not only with the new imperial expansion, but also with the consequences of the unification of Germany. Russian support of Prussia, it will be remembered, had been given in order to maintain the balance of power and to prevent the recurrence of the Crimean situation. As

versity Press, 1982), pp. 202–36. For the French financial interests see also Peter W. Reuter, *Die Balkanpolitik des französischen Imperialismus, 1911–1914* (Frankfurt: Campus Verlag, 1979), and Ljiljana Aleksić-Pejković, *Odnosi Srbije sa Francuskom i Engleskom, 1903–1914* (Belgrade: Izdanje Istorijskog instituta, 1965).

[7] Alan Bodger, "Russia and the End of the Ottoman Empire," in Marian Kent, ed., *The Great Powers and the End of the Ottoman Empire* (London: Allen & Unwin, 1984), p. 84.

long as Bismarck remained in office, Russian hopes for German cooperation were usually not disappointed; alliance with Russia was the basis of his diplomatic system. In 1890 the connection was broken on the German, not the Russian, initiative. The subsequent alliance with France rested on the common interest of both states in maintaining the continental balance of power. Germany at this time was not only the strongest single military power, but by the end of the century it was also an industrial giant. Under these circumstances Russia could not allow Germany to defeat France in another war; Russian interests everywhere would suffer dangerously if Germany had clear hegemony in Europe. From this defensive point of view, Russian and French opinion coincided. On other matters, chiefly involving changes in the status quo, the allies pursued separate paths. For instance, France did not always support the Russian position on questions concerning the Straits or the Balkan peninsula; Russia was largely indifferent to the fate of Alsace-Lorraine. Nevertheless, the alliance stood on firm ground. Close cooperation between the general staffs ensured that should war break out the armies would be prepared for joint action.

The defeat by Japan, like the Crimean debacle, forced the Russian leaders to embark upon another period of military reform. In the past Russia had been primarily a land power; the navy was destroyed at the battle of Tsushima. Nevertheless, at this time it was decided that the Russian navy should be rebuilt and brought up to world standards. Russians, like Germans and others, shared the conviction that great powers needed to be mighty sea powers. Moreover, the state did have three coasts to defend: the Baltic, the Black Sea, and the Pacific. Emphasis on naval affairs logically drew more attention to the issue of the closure of the Straits. During the war with Japan the Black Sea fleet had been prevented from joining the Baltic squadrons. Although the closure probably saved the ships from destruction, the action had implications for the future. Among these was the obvious fact that the resources of the southern Russian region could not be used for the building or maintenance of the fleet. Warships built there would be confined to the Black Sea.

In addition, after the beginning of the twentieth century Russian statesmen were more aware than ever of the importance of the Straits for Russian economic development. In order to meet the heavy obligations connected with modernization and industrialization, a policy inaugurated primarily during the ministry of Witte, the Russian government had to ensure a favorable balance of trade, a condition that was dependent on grain exports. Between 1903 and

1912, 37 percent of Russian exports went through Black Sea ports; 50 percent of the grain exports traveled by this route. When the Straits were closed, as happened in 1806–12, the 1820s, 1853–5, 1877, and 1911, the Russian economy suffered. Despite the Russian concern over the significance of the Straits for commerce, it must be emphasized that other factors were even more important in securing the free flow of trade. For instance, Russia did not have a significant mercantile fleet. Thus its goods were carried in foreign ships; the share of the carrying trade was: Britain 40 percent, Greece 18 percent, and Austria-Hungary 9 percent. The markets were in Western Europe, and the British navy controlled the seas.[8] Thus, in the same manner that Russia depended on French loans, the state also relied on Britain for the protection of its sea routes and its markets. The military significance of the Straits as the *defense* of Russia's Black Sea coast thus outweighed all other considerations in regard to this problem.

In the past the Russian government had generally preferred the solution adopted in 1841, that is, that the Straits should be closed to ships of war when the Ottoman Empire was at peace. This arrangement was satisfactory, however, only as long as the Ottoman government was either under firm Russian control or at least not under the direction of another power. Previously, the main contenders had been France and England. However, at the end of the nineteenth century the British government shifted its center of concern from the Straits to Egypt and the Suez Canal. At the same time, German influence in Constantinople increased. The Russian officials had now to fear that they would meet German military power not only on their western border, but also at the Straits and in the Near East.

Under these circumstances, the question of the status of the Straits assumed a place in Russian strategic planning even greater than it had enjoyed before. Various solutions were discussed up to 1914 and, of course, after the outbreak of World War I. Thus the Russian ambassador in Constantinople, A. I. Nelidov, in 1882, 1892, 1895, and 1896 proposed that Russia seize the Straits or at least the Bosphorus. As in previous years when this solution was considered, the responsible officials rejected it as impractical, since Britain and France, in particular, would not allow it. Moreover, they recognized

---

[8]On the economic significance of the Straits see Marlene P. Hiller, *Krisenregion Nahost: Russische Orientpolitik im Zeitalter des Imperialismus, 1900–1914* (Frankfurt: Peter Lang, 1985), pp. 90–6, and Bodger, "Russia and the End of the Ottoman Empire," pp. 82–4.

that the area could not be held unless Russia controlled a large European and Asian hinterland, probably including Constantinople, and the Aegean islands dominating the entrance to the Dardanelles. They knew, however, that such a radical alteration in the balance of power in the area could be achieved only in connection with a major war. As such, the Russian leaders adopted what they regarded as a compromise solution and attempted to obtain the approval of the other powers to the opening of the Straits for the warships of the Black Sea powers only. Under no condition did they want a full opening or a neutralization of the Straits.

Russian policy toward the Straits was in important ways in contradiction to its general Balkan policy. If complete control over the Straits could not be won, the Russian government desired at least a close tie with the Porte, if possible a return to the Unkiar Iskelessi relationship. This policy, in turn, called for the protection of Ottoman interests and the territorial status quo in the Near East. In contrast, Russian patronage of the Balkan governments involved the opposite: These states wanted Russian military support for further gains at Ottoman expense. In the 1890s and even until 1912, this contradiction caused no difficulties. After 1905, deeply committed to solving the problems connected with the defeat in the war with Japan and the subsequent revolution, the Russian leaders were determined to maintain peace and the status quo in the Near East.

Ideology and politics

Of the three themes of the Orthodox religion, autocratic political principles, and national interests that in one form or another have received emphasis before, only the third had retained its original power in foreign relations. By the end of the nineteenth century the Orthodox church remained certainly a basic element in Russian life; the great majority of the population in all sectors of society were believers in its doctrines. In foreign relations, however, the role of Orthodoxy as a bond between Russia and the Balkan people had weakened. This trend reflected in part the disillusioning experiences of the Russian government with Romania, Bulgaria, and Greece.

The nature of the autocracy also changed after 1905 and in a manner that indirectly affected foreign policy. The tsar was still in control of foreign relations and the military, but the influences that could affect policy decisions had become more complex and varied. As before, the tsar relied on his ministers and friends for advice and information. They, however, found themselves faced with a barrage of criticism and protest. Foreign policy was discussed in the Duma, among members of the political parties, and in the newspapers and other publications. Although previously journalists such as Katkov and Aksakov had been able to influence opinion, their successors had access to a much wider audience. In 1913 there were 856 daily newspapers; *Novoe Vremia*, the most influential, had a circulation of 150,000.[9] In general, the press was anti-German, anti-Austrian, and pro-Slav. Both the newspapers and the major political parties – the Octobrists, the Kadets, and the Nationalists – were supporters of this line and thus also approved an alignment with France and Britain. They were also interested in an active Balkan policy.[10] The difficulties of the weak tsar and his ministers in meeting this public pressure will be shown throughout the rest of this narrative.

The weakening of the autocracy had another implication important for foreign affairs and for the Balkan relationship. Although previously fears about revolutionary agitation had been constantly present in the minds of the Russian leadership, the actual occurrence of a revolution was to affect policy even more deeply. From 1905 to 1914 Russian officials were in constant fear that their actions would lead to another upheaval. Their reactions were often contradictory. For instance, in regard to Balkan affairs they were concerned that a European war, arising from events in the Near East, would open the door to another revolution at home, but they were similarly apprehensive that the appearance of weakness in regard to support for the Slavic people would cause a public reaction dangerous to the regime.

Similar contradictions were to be found in connection with the position of the minority nationalities. Although Great Russians constituted less than half of the total population at the end of the nineteenth century, the government adopted increasingly repressive policies toward the other nationalities. Previously, as we have seen, the government had simply ignored this situation and in domestic and international affairs acted as if Russia was a unitary national state. The successful national movements in the rest of Europe were bound to affect the Russian situation. Beginning with the reign of

[9]D. C. B. Lieven, *Russia and the Origins of the First World War* (New York: St. Martin's Press, 1983), pp. 119, 131.
[10]On the press and the parties see also ibid., pp. 118–38; and Geoffrey A. Hosking, *The Russian Constitutional Experiment: Government and Duma, 1907–1914* (Cambridge: Cambridge University Press, 1973), pp. 215–42.

Alexander III the government commenced a policy of Russification directed against the Poles, Jews, Ukrainians, Muslim Tartars, Baltic Germans, Finns, and others. Although the nationalities made some gains in 1905, attempts were made immediately to resume the Russification drive. One of the major supporters of this effort was Peter Arkadievich Stolypin, the extremely influential minister of interior from 1906 to 1911. Regarding Russia as a unitary national state, like France or Italy, he took further measures against the minorities. His attitude was shown, for instance, in a Duma debate in November 1907, when in answer to complaints from the representative of a Polish district, he explained that the Poles had no university because they would not accept Russian as the language of instruction and that they should: "First of all come over to our point of view . . . admit that the greatest blessing is to be a Russian citizen, bear this name with the same pride with which once the Romans bore their citizenship, and then you will call yourselves first-class citizens and you will receive all your rights."[11] This approach won general approval from Russian public opinion, that is, among the literate small percentage of the population, concentrated in St. Petersburg and Moscow, that concerned itself with foreign and domestic affairs.

Despite the negative attitude toward minorities, including the Slavs, within the Russian empire, the government and the public continued its strong interest in Slavs who were citizens of other states. Although most of the previous Panslav myths on the relationship of Russia to the other Slavic peoples remained, another movement, Neoslavism, attracted attention for a short time. This doctrine called for the union of all the Slavic peoples, regardless of religious differences, on an equal basis. Each was to have a separate political, cultural, and economic development, but they would cooperate among themselves. Neoslavism, primarily of Czech origin, enjoyed some support among the political parties, including the Kadets and the Octobrists, but it ran against the prevailing Russian attitude toward the other Slavs, which remained paternal, superior, and anti-Catholic. This attitude was well expressed in a letter published in a Czech newspaper in 1901 written by General Alexander Fedorovich Rittikh of the St. Petersburg Military Academy and a member of the Slavic Benevolent Society:

[11]Quoted in Hugh Seton-Watson, *The Russian Empire, 1801–1917* (Oxford: Clarendon Press, 1967), p. 665.

I came from the far Slav East, from the slumbering forests of the icy North, and from the boundless steppes of the Black Sea region. I came to bring you proof of our Russian love and to inform you that you can depend entirely upon the might of Russia. But I have to tell you something of even greater importance; you must study and become acquainted with this vast Russian-Slav country. In it you Czechs will find all that you seek, and that you hope for. . . . Until you have learned to know Russia, you Czechs will not realize the source of Slav strength. In this sign you will conquer! . . . Trust and believe in the God of Russia – He is great – for He created our Slavonic Russia.[12]

The Neoslav program, like other similar plans, involved the Slavs of the Habsburg Monarchy as well as the Ottoman Empire. Since responsible Russian statesmen did not want to contribute to the breakup of the Habsburg Empire at this time, these concepts could not win official endorsement. Also, a Russian regime that was suppressing Slavic, that is, Polish, Ukrainian, and Belorussian, movements within the empire could not well stand for the liberation of all Slavs on a general basis. Because of this, as before, both official and public attention became almost exclusively focused on the South Slavs, particularly those who were still under Ottoman rule.

Despite the costs of the war of 1877–8 and the disillusionment suffered in the Bulgarian experience, it is interesting to note that the illusions of the 1870s about Russian–Balkan relations were alive in the twentieth century. The same rhetoric about "historic missions" and the "Ottoman yoke" remained, even though conditions had changed drastically. There were at this time, after all, organized Balkan states, none of which showed much eagerness to accept Russian direction except in return for concrete material assistance, preferably military. Yet the new Panslavs were in effect again involving themselves in the lives of Balkan people, whose material circumstances could be far superior to those of their Russian peasant counterparts, whose taxes were supporting the Russian armies that might operate in the Balkans. An authority on Russian public opinion has commented:

After the defeat suffered in the Far East the participation of Russia in the solution of the Balkan questions was the touchstone for the maintenance of great-power status. It is difficult to determine what concrete political and religious motive hid behind the often used code-words (*Chiffre*) of the "historic mission," of

[12]Paul Výsný, *Neo-Slavism and the Czechs, 1898–1917* (Cambridge: Cambridge University Press, 1977), p. 26. On Neoslavism see also Caspar Ferenczi, "Nationalismus und Neoslawismus in Russland vor dem ersten Weltkrieg," *Forschungen zur osteuropäischen Geschichte*, XXXIV (1984), pp. 7–127.

the "historic task," but it is not difficult to ascertain that these conceptions were so deeply rooted in Russian society, that a disinterest in the events in the Balkan peninsula was impossible.[13]

It is also important to note that attention to Balkan affairs drew together all sides of the Russian political scene – liberals, conservatives, nationalists, Neoslavs, and Panslavs alike. Despite the fact that it was generally recognized that Russia was not prepared for an adventurous foreign policy, and that it might be best to return to the *recueillement* of Gorchakov's days, Balkan issues exerted such an emotional hold on Russian sympathies and imaginations that a crisis might once again compel Russian intervention

RUSSIAN–BALKAN RELATIONS, 1894–1914

During the years when Russian attention was concentrated on the Far East, the government had every interest in maintaining peace and calm in the Near East, a policy similarly favored by all the great powers, whose eyes were also turned in other directions. Nevertheless, in the 1890s crises arose in three areas: the Armenian lands of the Ottoman Empire, Crete, and Macedonia. All of these in some manner involved the question of Ottoman territorial integrity and the status of the Straits. In each instance the great powers cooperated to maintain calm and prevent the occurrence of a major international conflict.

Like the other national groups the million Armenian inhabitants of the Ottoman Empire wished an amelioration of their political condition, preferably by the grant of autonomous institutions. Similar to their Balkan counterparts, the Armenian nationalists had among their numbers revolutionary groups who resorted to violent tactics. In actions that recalled the earlier situation in Bulgaria, the Ottoman authorities reacted with extreme reprisals. Reports on massacres in 1895–6 again aroused public opinion, particularly in Britain. Although the European diplomats concerned themselves with the situation, they could not organize an effective intervention. The Russian government, which was introducing Russification measures among its own Armenian population, could not be enthusiastic about this national movement. In November 1896, Nelidov drew up plans for a Russian seizure of the Bosphorus should Britain

---

[13]Caspar Ferenczi, *Aussenpolitik und Offentlichkeit in Russland. 1906–1912* (Husum: Matthiesen Verlag, 1982), p. 152.

take action against the Porte. The immediate crisis, however, subsided, although the Armenian problem remained.

The island of Crete similarly became a center of attention in the 1890s. It will be remembered that Crete had been placed under Egyptian control from 1824 to 1840, when it was returned to the Ottoman Empire. Always a center of unrest, the island witnessed notable uprisings in 1841, 1858, and 1866–8. The social and economic status of the Christian Greek population caused the major discontent. As in other areas of the Balkans, the great powers attempted to calm the situation by pressing reform measures on the Porte. Such actions were, however, doomed to failure. The Cretans wanted not a better Ottoman administration, but union with their co-nationals. They also received encouragement and material support from independent Greece.

The fate of the islanders aroused enormous sympathy in Greece. Thus, when in February 1897 yet another revolt broke out, there was great pressure on the government to intervene. Prince George, King George's second son, led a volunteer military unit to the assistance of the rebels. The great powers once again demonstrated their divided positions over Mediterranean questions. With a strong position at Constantinople and effective influence with the government, the Russian diplomats supported the Ottoman stand. In contrast, the British government, with equal interests in Greece, opposed the establishment of a blockade to stop Greek aid to the rebellion.

The situation deteriorated sharply in April 1897 when Greek troops crossed into Ottoman territory. At this time the Greek government was forced by public pressure into a war for which it was not prepared. The Ottoman army was easily victorious over the Greek forces. They, in turn, received no help from the other Balkan states. The Russian government firmly advised Serbia and Bulgaria to remain out of the affair. Because of the universal desire to contain the crisis, the powers finally cooperated in imposing a settlement that was really to the ultimate Greek advantage. The state was required to pay only a small indemnity and to surrender some land. Crete, however, received an autonomous regime and Prince George became the governor. The way was thus prepared for the ultimate union of the island with Greece in 1913.

Both the Armenian and the Cretan questions involved primarily the conflicting aims of Russia and Britain. Meanwhile, Russian relations with Austria-Hungary, the other possible rival in Balkan affairs, were good, again largely because of the preoccupation of the powers with other questions. The desire of both states to maintain the status quo and avoid conflicts was shown when Franz Joseph and his foreign minister, Agenor Goluchowsky, visited St. Petersburg in April 1897. The agreement made at that time repeated the pattern that we have seen in other Russian understandings: The two governments agreed to work together to maintain the status quo and thus the territorial integrity of the Ottoman Empire. Should that, however, prove impossible, then the general lines of yet another partition of influence were agreed upon. Russia, for its part, received the assurance that the closure of the Straits would be maintained, thus "prohibiting . . . access to the Black Sea to foreign war vessels."[14] As far as Habsburg gains were concerned, and according to the Austrian interpretation, that government reserved the right to annex Bosnia, Hercegovina, and Sanjak of Novi Pazar. The agreement also provided for the establishment of an Albanian state should the Ottoman Empire lose its Balkan lands. The Russian government modified and limited the understanding on these points in a note of May 17, 1897 stating:

. . . we deem it necessary to observe that the Treaty of Berlin assures to Austria-Hungary the right of military occupation of Bosnia and Herzegovina. The annexation of these two provinces would raise a more extensive question, which would require special scrutiny at the proper times and places. As to the Sanjak of Novibazar, there would also be the necessity to specify its boundaries, which, indeed, have never been sufficiently defined.

It seems to us that points . . . having regard to the eventual formation of a principality of Albania and to the equitable partition of all the territory to be disposed of between the different small Balkan States, touch upon questions of the future which it would be premature and very difficult to decide at present.[15]

Both powers agreed further that although the Ottoman territory would be divided among the Balkan states, they would avoid "every combination which would favor the establishment of a marked preponderance of any particular Balkan principality to the detriment of the others."[16] With this understanding, whose provisions paralleled similar agreements made in the 1870s and 1880s, the Russian government was free to concentrate its attention on the Far East. The policy of cooperation with Austria-Hungary endured until 1908 and kept the peace in the Balkans even though the Macedonian question in these years repeatedly created a situation of crisis.

[14]Alfred Franzis Pribram, *The Secret Treaties of Austria-Hungary* (Cambridge, Mass.: Harvard University Press, 1920), I, pp. 185–91.
[15]Muraviev note, St. Petersburg, May 5/17, 1897, ibid., I, pp. 191–4.
[16]Ibid., I, pp. 189–91.

Although the problem of the union of Crete with Greece was on the way to a satisfactory solution, the major issue of the control of Macedonia, still under Ottoman administration, was never to achieve a similar settlement. Instead it was to remain the major cause of division and dispute among the Balkan states and, in particular, hinder Russian attempts to bring at least the Slavic nations together. With the ultimate Ottoman demise widely assumed, the three states immediately affected by the long-awaited division of the heritage – Serbia, Greece, and Bulgaria – all prepared for the coming event. Romania too intended to benefit, since it expected compensation for territorial additions given to other states.

The intensification of the struggle among the nations and of partisan activities within the lands forced the Russian government to devote attention to the area despite its prior interest in the Far East. Previously, when the question of the partition of Macedonia had arisen, the Russian government had favored the Bulgarian claims. At the Constantinople Conference and in the terms of the Treaty of San Stefano, the Russian representatives had given their support to the concept that the Bulgarians were at least a plurality in Macedonia, a view that coincided with the opinion of most observers at the time. The division of Bulgaria at the Congress of Berlin had aroused deep resentment in St. Petersburg, since the Russian statesmen had considered the San Stefano state as their major achievement in the Russo–Turkish War. The eventual union of Bulgaria and Eastern Rumelia was made part of the agreements of the Three Emperors' Alliance. The Russian views changed only when it became apparent that the new Bulgarian state would not be under predominant Russian influence. After the break between Alexander III and Alexander of Battenberg occurred, Russia opposed further Bulgarian gains. As we have seen, the Russian government denounced the union of the two provinces in 1885 and, after the abdication of Alexander of Battenberg, it did not recognize the new prince, Ferdinand of Coburg. Realizing that he needed Russian help in gaining Macedonian lands, Ferdinand took steps to appease Russia. In 1896 relations were reestablished, but certainly not on the basis that the Russian government had envisaged when in 1878 it gave such strong support to Bulgarian territorial claims.

Even without Russian sponsorship the Bulgarian government continued to consider the boundaries of the Treaty of San Stefano as the correct limits of its national state. It thus made great efforts to attract the Slavic inhabitants of Macedonia to its side, and it had an effective instrument in the Exarchate. It will be remembered that

Article X of the firman establishing this institution provided that if two-thirds of a district voted favorably, it could join the Exarchate. As could be expected, neither the Serbian nor the Greek government accepted the Bulgarian position. They hastened to form their own organizations and to try to win converts for themselves in the disputed lands. Although most of the efforts were educational and cultural, some involved terror and violence. Rival national groups established competing armed bands that were used to enforce their claims. The best known among these was the Internal Macedonian Revolutionary Organization, or IMRO, which at first stood for the organization of an independent state. The Ottoman authorities were unable to maintain order in these troubled lands; Bulgarians, Serbs, Greeks, Albanians, and Turks all took arms against each other. The mounting unrest and violence culminated in the Ilinden Uprising of 1903. Until 1908 the Macedonian question was in the eyes of foreign observers the major Balkan problem.[17]

The revival of national struggles in the Balkans was, naturally, strongly detrimental to Russian policy at this time. As before, the Russian government wanted no Balkan revolts that it could not control and that could cause a dangerous international crisis at a time when it was involved elsewhere. In October 1903 Nicholas II and his foreign minister, at this time Vladimir Nikolaevich Lamzdorf, met with Franz Joseph and Goluchowsky at Mürzsteg. Here the statesmen agreed upon a program of reforms for Macedonia that provided for a strong European intervention. The region was also to be divided into districts along ethnic lines, a provision that, as could be expected, was to cause an intensification of the fighting among the rival groups. In November, Sultan Abdul Hamid II accepted the plan with great reluctance, but he delayed its application.

Although the defeat by Japan and the revolution of 1905 weakened Russian foreign policy, the events caused the Russian government to redirect its attention back to Europe and forced a reexamination of its commitments. The alliance with France had been of little value in the war against Japan. In 1904 Britain and France had settled their colonial conflicts and established the so-called Entente Cordiale. During the Russo–Japanese War the French government had thus seen its partner, Russia, at war with Japan, a British ally. Desiring to end the conflict between the alliance systems, the French diplomats were most eager to secure a settlement between Russia and

---

[17]On Macedonia see Duncan M. Perry, *The Politics of Terror: The Macedonian Liberation Movements, 1893–1903* (Durham, N.C.: Duke University Press, 1988).

Britain. In 1907 these two powers signed a treaty that settled the last major disputes involved in the "great game in Asia." The heart of the agreement was the division of Persia into three spheres, with Russia dominant in the north, Britain in the south, and a neutral zone in the center. In addition, Tibet was recognized as being under Chinese sovereignty and Afghanistan was to remain a British protectorate. The Triple Entente of France, Britain, and Russia was thus established, with the Russo–French alliance as the strongest component of an otherwise loose alignment.

Although the alliance system with which Russia entered World War I had now been formed, it was clear to St. Petersburg that only in certain circumstances would it function in favor of Russian Balkan interests. It was perfectly obvious, for instance, that France would not go to war to further a predominantly Russian program in the area. Although Britain had made agreements settling Asian conflicts, disagreements remained over questions connected with the regime of the Straits and Ottoman territorial integrity. In contrast, as in the previous century, Russian relations with the Habsburg Empire, rather than with France or Britain, were usually of more importance for Balkan affairs. The cooperation of the two powers was becoming increasingly difficult due to the national agitation in the Habsburg Empire and, to a lesser extent, the measures taken against the nationalities in Russia.

By the beginning of the twentieth century the national principle had triumphed in Western and Central Europe; national revolutions had also led to the formation of the Balkan states. If national states were indeed the inevitable wave of the future, then the next two empires destined for partition were obviously the Habsburg and the Russian. As we have seen, Hungarian national pressure had resulted in the splitting of the monarchy in the Ausgleich of 1867. Subsequent changes in the franchise in the Austrian section had given a stronger voice to the Polish and Czech inhabitants in particular. In contrast to the relative progress there, the political situation in Hungary had become more difficult. After the conclusion of the Ausgleich the Hungarian government in 1868 enacted an agreement, the *Nagodba*, which gave Croatia-Slavonia certain autonomous rights, including the use of the Croatian language in local administration. In addition, the Nationalities Law of 1868, if it had been implemented, would also have given other Hungarian minorities significant cultural advantages. However, in the next decades state policy, instead of seeking the conciliation of the nationalities, became increasingly directed toward the assertion of Hungarian supremacy and the Magyarization of all of its citizens. The failure of the Hungarian government to recognize the claims of its divergent nationalities, or even to extend the franchise, created a great amount of discontent and political agitation in that part of the Dual Monarchy.

After the turn of the century it was, however, the South Slav problem that was to have the greatest effect on international relations. Serbs, Croats, and Slovenes lived in both sections of the empire, but primarily in Hungary. The Croats and Slovenes were Catholic, the Serbs Orthodox; the Croats and Serbs shared a common literary language. In the nineteenth century various programs of national emancipation were developed for these people. Obviously, many Serbs looked toward an eventual union with independent Serbia and Montenegro; some Croats favored the creation of a Greater Croatia, including Croatia-Slavonia, Bosnia-Hercegovina, and Dalmatia. For international relations, however, the more important programs were those that called for the unification of all of the South Slavs. Such a state could, of course, be formed by the breakup of the Habsburg Empire and the unification of the Habsburg Slavs with Serbia, either as a federation or with full central control from Belgrade, but another possibility also existed. Those who supported the program of Trialism proposed that the monarchy be reorganized to allow the formation of a South Slav unit, which might eventually even attract independent Serbia. It will be noted that in all of these alternatives, the attitude of the Serbian government would be of major importance.

What is interesting here is that the Russian leaders do not appear to have been aware of the depth or significance of the Habsburg national problems for foreign policy. Although there was indeed a great deal of loose talk about the breakup of the Habsburg Empire in Neoslav and Panslav circles, the significance of such a development for the European balance of power or Russian basic interests was seldom seriously considered. For the most part in the past responsible Russian statesmen had been aware that the maintenance of the monarchy was to the Russian advantage. Moreover, they opposed Trialism or any plan that would increase the Slavic position in the monarchy, fearing that should the Habsburg Empire become a Slavic state or have an administration appealing to Slavs in general, it would become a point of attraction to their own Poles, Ukrainians, and Belorussians. This issue was, of course, complicated by the role that the Slavic question played in Russian public opinion and the Russification policies adopted by the tsarist regime against its own minorities.

Despite these problems the Russian–Habsburg entente established in 1897 survived through the period of the Russo–Japanese War and the immediate postwar years. In 1906, however, both the Habsburg Empire and Russia acquired ambitious foreign ministers. In St. Petersburg, A. P. Izvolsky joined an administration headed by Stolypin as premier and minister of interior and including Vladimir Nikolaevich Kokovtsev as minister of finance. In Vienna, Count Alois Lexa von Aehrenthal became foreign minister, thus holding one of the three joints posts in the Dual Monarchy. Both men were experienced diplomats, but Izvolsky had previously served primarily in Western European missions – the Vatican, Munich, and Copenhagen – with only a year in Belgrade. In contrast, Aehrenthal had just returned from a successful term as ambassador in St. Petersburg from 1899 to 1906. Like Aehrenthal, Izvolsky favored a continuation of the past relationship. Recognizing that Russia was in no condition to risk a war, he preferred a policy of balance between the two European alliance systems, rather than an exclusive reliance on the ties with France and Britain, states that offered little support in Balkan crises.

Although the agreement of 1897 still held, by 1908 strains had appeared in the relationship. There was some disagreement over aspects of the Macedonian reforms and over the construction of railroads. Serbia and Russia at this time opposed an Austrian-supported plan to build a railroad through the Sanjak of Novi Pazar and favored an alternate Danube–Adriatic proposal. Nevertheless, both foreign ministers had objectives that they believed they could best achieve through cooperation. These involved a change in the status quo on the peninsula, the protection of which had been the original basis of the understanding. The Habsburg government was willing to consider annexing Bosnia-Hercegovina; Izvolsky wished to alter the Straits agreements.

Well aware of the increased significance of the Straits for Russian commerce and defense, Izvolsky attempted to implement a policy that was a compromise between the extremes of accepting the closing and seizing the waterway. What he hoped to secure was the agreement of the powers to the opening of the Straits, but only for the warships of the Black Sea states. Previously, as we have seen, the major opposition to an alteration in the Straits settlement had come from Britain, but the policy of that power had changed. Moreover, during the negotiations that preceded the 1907 agreement, there had been some indication that the British government would accept a new arrangement. Similarly, Izvolsky received further encouragement during the conversations held on naval affairs at Reval in June 1908. In fact, during these discussions the British diplomats appear to have been chiefly interested in avoiding direct answers in order not to hurt the relationship with St. Petersburg. With this false impression of British goodwill in mind, Izvolsky turned to the task of gaining the approval of the other powers.[18]

With this objective the Russian minister on July 2 sent a memorandum to the Habsburg government that dealt with the questions of Macedonian reform and the railroads, but whose most significant section contained the offer of a bargain involving Russian recognition of the Habsburg annexation of Bosnia-Hercegovina and the Sanjak of Novi Pazar in return for Austrian approval of an alteration of the regime of the Straits; it stated that

the question of the modification of the conditions established by article XXV of the Treaty of Berlin, that is to say the annexation of Bosnia, Hercegovina, and the Sanjak of Novipazar, has an eminently European character and is not of a nature to be regulated by a separate entente between Russia and Austria-Hungary. We are ready, on the other hand, to recognize that the same reserve applies to the question of Constantinople, of the adjacent territory, and of the Straits. Nevertheless, in view of the extreme importance for these two countries to see that the two above-mentioned questions be regulated in conformance to their reciprocal interests, the Imperial Government would be ready to accept a discussion of them in a spirit of friendly reciprocity.[19]

The memorandum did not awaken any marked enthusiasm in Vienna. The Habsburg officials believed that they had already secured a Russian agreement to an eventual annexation in the secret arrangements of the past years.[20] It is interesting to note that Izvolsky

---

[18]For Russian policy during the Bosnian crisis see in particular I. V. Bestuzhev, "Borba v praviashchikh krugakh Rossii po voprosam vneshnei politiki vo vremiia bosniiskogo krizisa," *Istoricheskii Arkhiv*, V (September–October 1962), pp. 113–47, and Francis Roy Bridge, "Isvolsky, Aehrenthal, and the End of the Austro-Russian Entente, 1906–1908," *Mitteilungen des österreichischen Staatsarchivs*, XXIX (1976), pp. 315–62. This article contains an English translation of almost all of the documents in the previous article.

[19]Izvolsky memorandum, St. Petersburg, June 19/July 2, 1908. Ludwig Bittner and Hans Uebersberger, eds., *Osterreich-Ungarns Aussenpolitik von der bosnischen Krise 1908 bis zum Kriegsausbruch 1914* (Vienna: Osterreichischer Bundesverlag, 1930), I, p. 9–11. (This series is cited hereafter as *OA*.)

[20]The Habsburg position in Bosnia and Hercegovina had been defined in agreements with Russia in 1876 (Reichstadt), 1877 (Budapest), 1881 (Three Emperors' Alliance), and 1897 (Russo-Austrian understanding on the Balkans). On this subject see Michael Aleksandrovich Taube, *La Politique russe d'avant-guerre et la fin de l'empire des tsars, 1904–1917* (Paris: Librairie Ernest Leroux, 1928), pp. 194–201.

was not aware of these obligations; he evidently did not learn of the terms until his return to St. Petersburg after the annexation crisis had broken out. He thus believed that he was indeed offering a fair exchange, whereas the Habsburg officials, delaying an answer, did not see what they would gain. Their attitude changed, however, when in July a revolution broke out in Constantinople. The sultan was forced to put into effect a constitution that had been formulated in 1876. For a period there was great confusion over the significance of the event and, for Vienna, of the effect that it would have on Bosnia-Hercegovina, still under Ottoman sovereignty. On August 19 a conference of ministers meeting in Vienna decided that the two provinces would be annexed, but that the Sanjak would be returned to full Ottoman control. Despite the fact that this action would involve the breaking of the Treaty of Berlin, the Habsburg government decided to handle it as an internal matter; the powers were to be notified only a few days before the annexation. On August 27 the Foreign Ministry sent a reply to Izvolsky's memorandum; it expressed agreement on the points covered, took note of the Russian assurance that an annexation would be regarded with "a benevolent and friendly attitude," should it become necessary, and accepted the proposal "for a confidential and friendly exchange of views" on the Straits.[21]

In order to clarify the points under negotiation, Izvolsky and Aehrenthal met on September 16 at Buchlau in Moravia.[22] Convinced that the monarchy intended to annex Bosnia-Hercegovina and that Russia could not stop it, the Russian minister wished to gain compensation for his country and for the Balkan states. Unaware of the previous arrangements, he saw the transaction as a straight bargain: the Straits for Bosnia-Hercegovina. After the meeting was concluded, Aehrenthal drew up a memorandum on the decisions reached;[23] a similar Russian document was never sent to

[21]Memorandum for the Russian government, August 27, 1908. *OA*, I, pp. 59–61.
[22]For the comments of Russian participants in the Bosnian affair see the following memoirs: Taube, *La Politique russe*, pp. 85–201, 224–31; Nicholas Valerievich Charykov (Tcharykow), *Glimpses of High Politics: Through War and Peace, 1855–1929* (New York: Macmillan, 1931), pp. 268–72; Vladimir Nikolaevich Kokovtsov, *Out of My Past* (Stanford, Calif.: Stanford University Press, 1935), pp. 214–18; Alexander Aleksandrovich Savinskii (Savinsky), *Recollections of a Russian Diplomat* (London: Hutchinson & Co., n.d.), pp. 147–54; and Nicholas Nikolaevich Shebeko (Schebeko), *Souvenirs: Essai historique sur les origines de la guerre de 1914* (Paris: Bibliothèque diplomatique, 1936), pp. 81–4.
[23]Aehrenthal memorandum on the Buchlau meeting of September 16, 1908. *OA*, I, pp. 86–92.

Vienna.[24] Izvolsky's reactions can, however, be judged from the reports that he sent back to the assistant foreign minister, Nicholas Valerievich Charykov. Judging from his first account, Izvolsky was satisfied with the results of his day of "very stormy negotiations."[25] In this account and in another report sent the next day, he presented his accomplishments in a very favorable, if misleading, light.[26] Here he claimed to have overridden Aehrenthal's arguments and forced him to admit that Russia and the Balkan states should have guarantees and compensation, including a Habsburg renunciation of the Sanjak, independence for Bulgaria, a change in the regime of the Straits, an end to the restrictions on Montenegro in regard to the Adriatic, and other accommodations, most of which the Habsburg government had independently already determined to implement. Obviously pleased with the transaction, Izvolsky believed that the surrender of the Sanjak would block a further move forward by the Habsburg Empire and that Russian prestige among the Balkan states would be strengthened: "The Balkan governments will of course understand that we shall not go to war on account of Bosnia and the Herzegovina, but it is necessary to show them that we shall not cease to look after them, and that if they receive even only insignificant advantages, then they owe them entirely to us."[27]

In the controversies that arose subsequently over what had been decided at Buchlau, two questions were of particular importance: the timing of the annexation and the means by which it would receive international recognition. As far as the date of the event was concerned, Izvolsky, both in his telegram and in his report to Charykov, expressed the opinion that it would occur at around the time of the meeting of the Delegations, that is, around October 6 to 8. In his memorandum of the meeting Aehrenthal also mentioned the first days in October, but stated that he would give Izvolsky a previous timely (*rechtzeitig*) notice. On the second issue, Izvolsky's accounts did not mention a discussion of a conference, but Aehrenthal's memorandum noted that a meeting might be necessary simply to register the fact of the annexation, perhaps an ambassadorial conference in Constantinople. Since the Habsburg action involved

---

[24]A draft memorandum on the negotiations was prepared but not sent. Draft of a memorandum to the Austro-Hungarian government, September 19/October 2, 1908, in Bridge, "Izvolsky, Aehrenthal," pp. 358–60.

[25]Izvolsky to Charykov, Buchlau Castle, September 3/16, 1908, ibid., 348–351.

[26]Urusov to Charykov, Vienna, September 4/17, 1908, transmitting a report of Ignatiev, ibid., p. 348.

[27]Izvolsky to Charykov, Buchlau Castle, September 3/16, 1908, ibid., pp. 348–51.

the Treaty of Berlin of 1878, a conference of the signatories should have been held to accept or block the annexation before it occurred. The Habsburg leaders were determined to prevent the holding of such a meeting, where they might be outvoted. The first suggestion for a conference came, in fact, from Charykov, who wrote to Izvolsky after receiving an account of the Buchlau conversations. Charykov argued that such a congress could discuss all of the "outdated" sections of the Berlin treaty. Moreover, the tsar favored "the idea of replacing the Treaty of Berlin of evil memory with another document."[28] In reply, Izvolsky argued that Russia should wait until after the annexation and then suggest a conference where "we indeed will come forward in the role of defenders of the interests of the Balkan states, and even of Turkey itself."[29]

Despite the initial enthusiastic reception of the Buchlau agreement by the tsar and Charykov, difficulties soon arose. In negotiating with Aehrenthal, Izvolsky did not have plenipotentiary powers, but he did have the full approval of the tsar at every step. Although he acted on his own authority, without notifying the other ministers, he had not violated any rules, since foreign affairs were indeed completely in the tsar's control. Nevertheless, he did instruct Charykov to inform his colleagues. When they learned about the Buchlau transaction in early October, Stolypin and Kokovtsev, in particular, were extremely upset, especially by the fact that Russia was consenting to the surrender of two Slavic provinces.[30] Charykov joined them, and together they persuaded Nicholas II to reverse his position. Thus, even before the annexation took place, the Russian leadership had repudiated Izvolsky's negotiations with Aehrenthal.

With the timing determined by domestic pressures, the Habsburg government on October 6 announced the annexation,[31] having informed the other governments, including Russia, only a short time previously. On October 5 Ferdinand declared Bulgaria independent and took for himself the title of "tsar." This action, taken in close cooperation with Austria-Hungary, aroused great displeasure in St. Petersburg, since the Russian leadership still looked upon Bulgaria as a wayward child that should accept guidance and rewards

[28]Charykov to Izvolsky, St. Petersburg, September 6/19, 1908, ibid., pp. 351–2. Charykov to Izvolsky, Standart Roads, Yacht "Neva," September 8–9/21–2, 1908, ibid., pp. 352–5.
[29]Izvolsky to Charykov, Egern/Tegernsee, September 11/24, 1908, ibid., pp. 355–8.
[30]Kokovtsov, *Out of My Past*, pp. 214–18.
[31]Instruction to Paris, Berlin, London, Rome, and St. Petersburg, October 3, 1908. *OA*, I, pp. 123–4.

only from Russian hands. It was the annexation, however, that produced the largest outburst of public protest. Russian public opinion, expressed through the newspapers and the declarations of the political leaders, was outraged. Having no knowledge of the previous secret understandings or of the policies of the tsar and his foreign minister, national leaders could easily see in the annexation just another example of Habsburg–German machinations at the expense of the Slavs.

Izvolsky, in Paris at the time of the event, received no direct prior notice, although St. Petersburg did. On October 6 he visited Rudolf von Khevenhüller, the Habsburg ambassador, and he argued for what was now the official Russian position. Russia would not oppose the annexation, but it would propose the convening of a conference to consider a revision of the Treaty of Berlin.[32] The question of a conference was also discussed by Charykov and the Habsburg ambassador in St. Petersburg, Leopold Berchtold. From this time on Izvolsky and the Russian diplomats argued that at Buchlau the minister had insisted that the annexation had a European character, that the question had to be submitted to a congress, and that other powers might demand compensation. The Habsburg government remained with its original position that it would obtain a recognition of the action by direct bilateral negotiations with the other powers, and it would not submit the question to international jurisdiction.

Izvolsky's position became even more difficult when it became clear that he could not gain the assent of Britain and the Ottoman Empire to his proposed changes in the Straits regime. Even the French ally would not agree. As far as relations with the Porte were concerned, the Russian government wanted more than its assent to a change in the regime of the Straits. It now sought once again the reestablishment of the relationship of Unkiar Iskelessi, including close diplomatic cooperation and an assumed if not directly stated Russian guarantee of Ottoman territorial integrity. In October a draft agreement was drawn up.[33] At the time of the annexation Izvolsky spoke with Naum Pasha, the Ottoman ambassador in Paris, about the action and the Russian insistence that a conference be called. He assured Naum that other Ottoman territory was not in

---

[32]Khevenhüller telegrams no. 29 and 30, Paris, October 6, 1908, ibid., I, pp. 141–2.
[33]Project of an entente between the imperial government and the Ottoman government, September 23, 1903. Branko Pavićević, *Rusija i aneksiona kriza, 1908–1909* (Titograd: Crnogorska Akademija nauka i umjetnosti, 1984), I, pp. 458–9.

question and that "neither Serbia nor Montenegro will be allowed to advance their claims on any part whatsoever of Turkish territory." He then presented the Russian case for a change in the status of the Straits and declared the Russian "wish to return to the principles which regulated the relations between Russia and Turkey at the time of the Treaty of Unkiar Skelessi."[34] After his arrival in London, Izvolsky argued along the same lines in his conversations with Rifat Pasha, the Ottoman ambassador to Britain. Rifat reported to his government that the Russian minister "let me understand in courteous terms that what he asks of us today in a friendly manner Russia can demand by force the day when she feels herself strong enough to do it." Izvolsky also informed him that Nicholas II was "ready to conclude an alliance with us in exchange for the opening of the Straits. He insists only that this alliance be held secret."[35]

More important for the attainment of Izvolsky's objectives, however, was to be the attitude of the British government, and here the minister received what for him was an apparently unexpected rejection. Sir Edward Grey, the foreign secretary, expressed again the basic British position against the opening of the Straits for the riparian powers alone. Britain, at this time as before, would have accepted an arrangement allowing full freedom of passage for all warships, exactly the settlement that the Russian government most disliked.

Returning to St. Petersburg after his ill-fated journey, Izvolsky continued to call for a conference and to argue that this had been his policy all along. Since such a congress would have opened the entire Eastern Question, none of the powers supported his proposal. The Habsburg diplomats, meanwhile, were attempting to secure the recognition for the annexation through a bilateral exchange of notes. On February 26 , 1909, Austria-Hungary and the Ottoman Empire reached an agreement that gave the Porte an indemnity in return for its acceptance of the loss of the provinces. In April a similar settlement, in which the Russian government played a major and constructive part, secured the Ottoman recognition of Bulgarian independence.

With these important questions settled, the Habsburg diplomats, nevertheless, still had to secure the acceptance of the powers, in

[34]Quoted in Barbara Jelavich, *The Ottoman Empire, the Great Powers, and the Straits Questions, 1870–1887*, (Bloomington: Indiana University Press, 1973), pp. 164–5.
[35]Ibid., p. 167.

particular Russia. The negotiations between Vienna and St. Petersburg, which continued throughout the winter, dealt also with the Serbian demands for territorial compensation, which will be discussed in the next section and which received Russian backing. The Bosnian episode assumed crisis proportions when on March 21 the German government, in an action in aid of its ally, delivered a note to St. Petersburg that the Russian officials regarded as an ultimatum. It stated that Russia should accept the abrogation of Article XXV without any reserve and that "any evasive, conditional, or unclear response" would be regarded as a refusal: "We would then withdraw and let events take their course."[36] Since the Russian leaders had already recognized that a war was impossible, and since they did not have the backing of their French ally, they accepted the humiliating demand and recognized the annexation. They also could give no support to Serbia, whose strong reaction to the situation will be discussed subsequently. This state, under great-power pressure, thus agreed to a statement that had been approved beforehand by Vienna:

> Serbia recognizes that its rights have not been impaired by the *fait accompli* carried out in Bosnia-Hercegovina and that it will consequently conform to whatever decision the powers will take in regard to Article 25 of the Treaty of Berlin. Accepting the councils of the Great Powers, Serbia promises from now on to abandon the attitude of protest and opposition that it has observed in regard to the annexation since last autumn and promises besides to change the course of its present policy toward Austria-Hungary in order to live henceforth with the latter on the basis of good neighborliness.[37]

As a result of the Serbian and Russian backdown the Central Powers did indeed achieve a paper victory, but at an ultimately high cost. The Russian government and public opinion in general considered that they had suffered a "diplomatic Tsushima." The policy of accord with Austria-Hungary, established in 1897, came to an end. Most Russian leaders were now convinced that the German powers, the Habsburg Empire in particular, were embarked on an

---

[36]Bülow to Pourtalès, Berlin, March 21, 1909. Johannes Lepsius, Albrecht Mendelssohn Bartholdy, and Friedrich Thimme, *Die Grosse Politik der Europäischen Kabinette, 1871–1914* (Berlin: Deutsche Verlagsgesellschaft für Politik und Geschichte, 1925), XXVI: 2, pp. 693–5. (cited hereafter as *GP*).

[37]In Cartwright to Grey, telegram no. 88, Vienna, March 22, 1909. G. P. Gooch and Harold Temperley, *British Documents on the Origins of the War, 1898–1914* (London: His Majesty's Stationery Office, 1928), V, pp. 718–19. (cited hereafter as *BDOW*).

aggressive policy aiming at the domination of the Balkans and of the Ottoman government. With little understanding of the domestic problems of the Dual Monarchy, they felt that they had to take active measures to halt what some perceived as an Austrian drive towards Thessaloniki. The Russian government was also concerned over the situation in Constantinople, where, after the Young Turk Revolution, it appeared that German influence was increasing.

The new regime in Constantinople, although it came to power with the goal of modernizing and strengthening the state, could not halt the decomposition of the empire. Moreover, it was apparent that Russia would not act to protect the status quo, as it often had in previous years. In fact, the Russian government aided in the accomplishment of the next surrender of territory. Not only the Serbian but also the Italian government felt that it was entitled to compensation after the Habsburg annexation despite the Triple Alliance agreements to the contrary. Angry with Vienna, the Russian leaders were willing to aid the Italian effort. In October 1909 Nicholas II and Victor Emmanuel III met at Racconigi. Here the Russian leaders agreed to accept the Italian claims in Tripoli in return for support for the opening of the Straits to Russian warships. The subsequent Italian war with the Ottoman Empire in 1911 not only ended in a further loss of territory for the Porte, but it also rekindled the ambitions of the Balkan states in regard to Macedonia.

After the Bosnian disaster Izvolsky remained as foreign minister for a year and a half, largely because of the lack of an obvious successor. During this period his policies were dominated by his strong anti-Austrian feelings and, in particular, his personal resentment against Aehrenthal. In 1910 he became ambassador in Paris, where he was to continue to play a major role in foreign policy. His successor, S. D. Sazonov, the brother-in-law of Stolypin, entered upon his new duties with inadequate experience. He had entered the Foreign Ministry in 1883 and thereafter had held subordinate posts in London, Washington, D.C., and Rome. From 1906 to 1909 he was the Russian minister at the Vatican. He then returned to become Izvolsky's assistant in May 1909; in October, 1910 he was appointed foreign minister. After Izvolsky's Bosnian failure, Stolypin played an increasingly important role in the formulation of foreign policy, working first with Charykov and then with Sazonov. Following Stolypin's assassination in September 1911, Sazonov assumed a more independent position, but he cooperated with Kokovtsov. However, he did not provide strong leadership. He has been de-

Figure 12. Sergei Dmitrievich Sazonov.

scribed personally by such adjectives as simple, modest, good-
natured, and weak, attributes that also characterized his policies.[38]
An indecisive tsar thus had to rely on a foreign minister of a similar
temperament in a period of increasing foreign and domestic danger.

[38]Sazonov was judged severely by his colleagues. Taube wrote that he was "simple,
modest, affable, upright in character, with a perfect personal disinterestness, very
aware of moral questions and profoundly religious, very orthodox and very
Russian, . . . [a good candidate for] the post of procurator general of the Holy
Synod, or even for that of a high prelate of the Russian church." Taube, *La
Politique russe*, pp. 248–9. Andrei Dmitrievich, Kalmykov, a diplomat who served

At the beginning of his term in office Sazonov accompanied Nicholas II to Potsdam to meet with the German leaders. As before, many Russians, including the tsar, wished to maintain good relations with Berlin and not become completely dependent on the Triple Entente. No general accord was reached, but an agreement was made concerning Ottoman railroads. During much of 1911 Sazonov was seriously ill, so the important decisions were made by men in lesser positions, such as the new assistant foreign minister, Anatol Anatolevich Neratov; Charykov, appointed in May 1909 as ambassador in Constantinople; Izvolsky; and the representatives in Sofia and Belgrade.

The Bosnian episode affected not only the Russian position on Ottoman affairs, but also that of all of the Balkan states. These governments, with active and independent foreign policies, wished to use the apparent Ottoman weakness to their own advantage.[39] They had in the past strongly disliked agreements among the powers that decided their fate without their participation, such as the Russian–Austrian understanding of 1897 and the Buchlau accord. Although they realized that they needed to come to an agreement among themselves, they also knew that they needed great-power sponsorship. As in the past the best choice appeared to be Russia, whose government might also be able to bring French and British support behind Balkan national aims in a time of crisis. Moreover, should the Balkan states in alliance suffer a defeat, Russia was still the best hope for eventual military support.

The Russian policy of cooperation with the Balkan states adopted

in Skopje as consul-general during the Balkan Wars, was even more critical. He described the foreign minister as "modest, well-meaning, sensitive, and touchy . . . lacking in talent and experience," and without energy, character, or initiative. Sazonov told Kalmykov that "Balkan affairs were entirely new to him"; the consul agreed, commenting that "Sazonov himself knew nothing about the Balkans, as I understood from my talk with him, and had only an instinctive feeling of distrust." Andrei Dmitrievich Kalmykov, *Memoirs of a Russian Diplomat: Outposts of Empire, 1893–1917* (New Haven, Conn.: Yale University Press, 1971), pp. 214–17.

[39] For Russian policy in this period and in the Balkan Wars see Ernst Christian Helmreich, *The Diplomacy of the Balkan Wars, 1912–1913* (Cambridge, Mass.: Harvard University Press, 1938); Iu. A. Pisarev, *Velikie dershavy i Balkany nakanune pervoi mirovoi voiny* (Moscow: Izdatel'stro nauka, 1985); Andrew Rossos, *Russia and the Balkans: Inter-Balkan Rivalries and Russian Foreign Policy, 1908–1914* (Toronto: University of Toronto Press, 1981), and Edward C. Thaden, *Russia and the Balkan Alliance of 1912* (University Park: The Pennsylvania State University Press, 1965).

at this time thus was bound to receive a favorable reception. With the collapse of the Habsburg entente and the obvious fact that the Western allies could not be counted on unreservedly to back its Balkan interests, the Russian government naturally looked to these governments for diplomatic support. The initiative came from two sources. Shortly after the end of the Bosnian affair, Izvolsky inaugurated a policy of attempting to bring the Balkan states together under Russian guidance. In Constantinople, Charykov sought to maintain close relations with the Porte, on the one hand, and to forward the formation of a Balkan confederation, including the Ottoman Empire, on the other. It should be strongly emphasized that the Russian goals at this time were defensive. Recognizing that their army was not ready to face a military showdown in the Balkans, the responsible leaders did not want any precipitate actions on the part of the Balkan states; again they opposed premature uprisings.

The difficulties of implementing such a policy were obvious. The goal of the Balkan states was the partition of the remaining Ottoman possessions in Europe; the purpose of cooperation with Russia was to forward this aim. Moreover, the Russian leadership itself was divided in its actions. Izvolsky's support of the Racconigi arrangements and the Italian plans for the acquisition of Ottoman territory were bound to arouse Balkan desires for similar annexations. Russian agents in the Balkan capitals were also to play a major part in stimulating an active and aggressive policy in the states to which they were assigned.

In any attempt to form a Balkan front, the Russian emphasis was bound to be on Serbia and Bulgaria. This choice also reflected Slavic sentiments at home. The inclusion of the Ottoman Empire in a Balkan alliance system, although considered, was finally rejected as impractical. The Russian objective remained the establishment of a protective wall against further German penetration, whether by Austria-Hungary or Germany, or both together, and the maintenance of the status quo until Russia was better prepared to act decisively and unilaterally. This policy was to be carried out by two energetic agents: Nicholas Genrikhovich Hartwig arrived in Belgrade in the fall of 1909; Anatol Vasil'evich Nekliudov was appointed to his post in Sofia in February 1911.

Of the two men, Hartwig plays the major role in this narrative. A strong Russian nationalist despite his German name and grandfather, he had already had much experience in the Russian service before he came to Serbia. He was the director of the Asiatic Department during the Lamzdorf ministry; subsequently, he served as minister in Persia from 1906 to 1909. As the Russian representative in Belgrade from 1909 to 1914, he was able to exert a strong influence on the Serbian government, and he intervened constantly in internal affairs. Acquiring a reputation for deviousness, he did not always inform his government of his activities. At this time he believed that Serbia should be the base of Russian Balkan policy. Since that country was in a weaker position geographically than Bulgaria, it needed Russian support all the more, and its loyalty was thus assured.

Nekliudov in Sofia was to prove a more cautious and careful agent.[40] Realistically appraising the situation, he at first did not believe that Russia should actively forward the formation of a Balkan alliance system. He also opposed the suggestion that the Ottoman Empire be brought into the Balkan front. He expected that state to dissolve soon, and he fully realized the extent of the Balkan territorial ambitions. In the same manner that Hartwig supported the Serbian aims, Nekliudov was sympathetic to the Bulgarian objectives, but he was more critical in his reporting of the actions of the government and its leaders than his colleagues in Belgrade.

Active negotiations had been carried on between Serbia and Bulgaria since the beginning of the century. Treaties of friendship and alliance in April 1904 and a tariff agreement of 1905 had failed to be effective because of Habsburg opposition and changes in the Bulgarian government. After 1909 Serbia took the initiative in reviving the discussions. As in the past, the major issue separating the two South Slav states was their deep disagreement over the fate of Macedonia. The Bulgarian government, expecting eventually to acquire the entire area, supported a program calling for autonomy for the region as a unit; the Serbian diplomats, in contrast, favored a partition. At this time, however, they were chiefly interested in securing access to the Adriatic, which involved the acquisition of territory inhabited primarily by Albanians, most of whom were Muslims or Catholics under Habsburg protection.

Serious negotiations for an alliance were carried on between Serbia and Bulgaria from September 1911 to March 1912, with the full participation of the Russian representatives. The major obstacle to an agreement was, as before, the division of the Macedonian lands.

[40]For Nekliudov's policies see his memoirs: Anatolii Vasil'evich Nekliudov, *Diplomatic Reminiscences before and during the World War, 1911–1917* (New York: E. P. Dutton and Company, 1920).

Finally, on March 13, 1912, secret military and political agreements were concluded, both clearly directed against the Ottoman Empire.[41] The political treaty had an annex specifying the division of the Ottoman lands and naming the tsar as the arbiter for the disputed regions. The military convention assigned the tasks for the respective armies, with the main enemy clearly designated as the Ottoman Empire, but with preparations also made for a war against Austria-Hungary.

These agreements, aggressive in nature, were clearly in preparation for a conflict with the Ottoman Empire with the aim of obtaining Macedonia. They thus did not reflect the official Russian policy of the maintenance of the status quo and the formation of a front against the Habsburg Empire. The dangers in the situation were recognized by Nekliudov and by Michael Nikolaevich Giers, appointed the Russian ambassador in Constantinople in March 1912. Giers feared that the Balkan states could not stand up against the Ottoman army, despite the fact that the war with Italy was still in progress.[42] The other Russian officials, however, apparently trusted in the wording of the first article of the annex of the political agreement, which stated:

If an agreement about a military action should take place, then Russia is to be informed about it, and if the latter puts no obstacles in the way, then the allies will proceed to the agreed upon military operations . . . if an agreement is not reached, the question will be submitted to Russia for judgment. The decision of Russia is binding on both alliance contracting parties.[43]

This stipulation did not, however, obligate the other states that were now to enter into the anti-Ottoman alignment. In the subsequent negotiations that widened the Balkan front, the Russian government was aware of the discussions but not of their details. In May 1912, Greece and Bulgaria concluded an agreement; in October Montenegro signed similar pacts with Serbia and Bulgaria. The Balkan League was thus complete.

Meanwhile, the European governments were becoming increas-

---

[41] The texts of the two conventions are in Miloš Bogićević (Boghitschewitsch), *Die auswärtige Politik Serbiens, 1903–1914* (Berlin: Brückenverlag, 1928), I, pp. 208–13 (cited hereafter as *APS*).

[42] Nekliudov, *Diplomatic Reminiscences*, pp. 94–5. Giers was also worried that the Bulgarians would attempt to seize Constantinople, a possibility that would threaten the Russian "historical ideal." Giers to Neratov, very confidential message, August 16/29, 1912. B. von Siebert, ed., *Graf Benckendorffs Diplomatischer Schriftwechsel* (Berlin and Leipzig: Walter de Gruyter & Co., 1928), II, pp. 441–2.

[43] *APS*, I, pp. 208–9.

ingly aware that a dangerous situation was developing. Although they did not have the texts of the agreements, they knew of their general purpose. The Russian officials too were worried that events might occur that they could not control, but they were reluctant to make the Balkan controversies a matter of international negotiation. However, they knew that Russia could not wage a major war at the time, and they realized that their French and British friends would not support the Russian Balkan program with arms. This condition was made very clear when President Raymond Poincaré visited St. Petersburg in August 1912. There, seeing the texts of the Bulgarian–Serbian agreements, he recognized that they were indeed war alliances.[44] He warned that French public opinion would not countenance a war over Balkan issues unless German actions were such that the alliance stipulations were called into effect. The terms of the Russo–French agreement did not apply to a conflict between Russia and Austria-Hungary alone.

By September all of the powers had become deeply concerned about the dangerous situation. In an attempt to forestall a crisis, the Russian government sent direct warnings to the Balkan capitals and entered into discussions with the other great powers. Thus, in a meeting with General Stephen Paprikov on September 16, 1912, Sazonov bluntly told the Bulgarian representative: "What do you expect of Russia?" Russia had done enough for the Balkan Slavs; they should not expect more.[45] At the same time, similar warnings were delivered by the Russian representatives in Greece, Serbia, and Montenegro. Sazonov also sent another clear indication of Russian disapproval to the Bulgarian and Serbian governments:

> In the event that in spite of our warnings the two states decide now to employ their alliance to launch a joint attack on Turkey . . . and to expose their territorial integrity and independence to a ruinous ordeal, then we deem it our duty to warn them in advance that in such a case we will be guided solely by our concern for the direct and immediate interests of Russia.[46]

After protracted discussions the powers finally came to an agreement that the Russian and Austro-Hungarian governments in the name of Europe should warn the Balkan states. The statement promised that the powers would take action to press for Macedonian reforms, but "if, nevertheless, war should break out between the

---

[44]Poincaré's reaction to the events is given in his memoir: Raymond Poincaré, *The Origins of the War* (London: Cassell and Company, Ltd., 1922), pp. 115–20.
[45]Quoted in Rossos, *Russia and the Balkans*, pp. 64–5.
[46]Quoted in ibid., p. 65.

Balkan states and the Ottoman Empire, they will tolerate at the end of the conflict no modifications of the territorial status quo in Turkey in Europe."[47] A collective note was also sent to the Porte calling for action on the reforms.[48] The joint Russian–Austrian declaration was delivered to the Balkan capitals only on October 8, the day Montenegro declared war. Bulgaria, Greece, and Serbia joined in on October 18.

Russian official policy had thus failed. Although the public and the Panslavs greeted the subsequent Balkan victories with jubilation, these, in fact, placed the government in an awkward situation. As we have seen, the Russian leaders had not wanted to make the Balkan controversies an international issue. They had wished to postpone any decisive changes in the peninsula until Russia was strong enough to determine, perhaps unilaterally, the fate of the peninsula. The Balkan precipitate actions at this time made great-power intervention inevitable. During this crisis the Russian government attempted both to localize the conflict and to limit the great-power role as much as possible.

This objective was, however, difficult to achieve. The crushing defeat of the Ottoman army made it clear that drastic changes would be made in the Treaty of Berlin and that all the signatories would be involved. In December 1912 a conference of ambassadors in London was called into session to discuss the question. Henceforth the major decisions would be reached through negotiations among the powers rather than by the representatives of the Balkan states themselves under benevolent Russian guidance. The outbreak of the Second Balkan War in June 1913, involving Bulgaria in a conflict with Serbia, Greece, Romania, Montenegro, and the Ottoman Empire, did not affect this great-power participation, but the final peace was signed in Bucharest, not London.

The Balkan victories and the great-power intervention thus faced the Russian government with difficult immediate decisions. The original intention of preserving the status quo was soon abandoned, but the partition of highly disputed territories among the victorious belligerents still had to be settled. In his instructions to the Russian ambassador in London, Alexander Konstantinovich Benckendorff, Sazonov told the Russian representative to ensure that the Balkan

---

[47]Berchtold to Rome, Berlin, St. Petersburg, etc., telegram, October 6, 1912. *OA*, IV, pp. 558–9.

[48]Pallavicini telegram no. 461, Constantinople–Pera, October 10, 1912, ibid., IV, p. 596.

governments gained the greatest possible advantages from their victories; these states, "called into life" by Russia, were its natural allies in Europe.[49] The Russian task, Sazonov continued, was not limited to protecting Balkan interests against the great powers, but "true to its traditions Russia must understand the interests of these states wider and deeper than they themselves do." The Russian representatives should thus advise them to cooperate among themselves, since their disunity would only aid their common opponents. They would place in jeopardy the fruits of their sacrifices "if they in mad delusion fell upon each other." The Russian objective was thus to hold together the prewar Balkan alliances, an aim that was, of course, impossible to achieve after the Second Balkan War.

The major problem facing the Russian diplomats was that they had to balance the rival claims of states, all of which they wished to please: Serbia, Bulgaria, Greece, Romania, Montenegro, and even the Ottoman Empire. In essence, the problems involved chiefly lands claimed by Bulgaria and its national goal of the re-creation of the San Stefano state. At the time of the First Balkan War the Russian government insisted on two Bulgarian sacrifices. First, it feared that the Ottoman defenses of Constantinople would collapse. Under no condition would it allow Bulgaria to control the city. Preparations were made for a naval action in case such an event threatened. The successful Ottoman defense, however, halted the Bulgarian advance. Second, at this time, with much success, the Russian diplomats were attempting to win Romania away from its ties with the Triple Alliance. Thus, when the Romanian government insisted on compensation, despite the fact that it did not enter the war, the Russian representatives pressed the Bulgarian government to cede Silistria and some other border territories. After the Second Balkan War, Romania gained its major objectives.

The chief controversies, however, revolved around the division of Macedonia and Thrace, areas where the Greek, Serbian, and Bulgarian national myths collided. The situation was made worse when the great powers decided on the creation of an Albanian state and denied to Serbia an outlet on the Adriatic, a matter that will be discussed in the next section. Faced with a loss of its first objective, the Serbian government, whose armies were in occupation of the disputed territories, sought to acquire more than their original share in the Macedonian partition, a demand that met a strong Bulgarian

---

[49]Sazonov to Benckendorf, no. 848 very confidential, November 30/December 12, 1912. Siebert, *Benckendorff*, II, pp. 529–35.

refusal. The subsequent Bulgarian military collapse in the Second Balkan War, however, allowed all of its neighbors to expand their claims and to acquire territory whose loss was never to be accepted by the Sofia government.

The map of the Balkans of 1914, although it showed gains for all of the Balkan states, even Bulgaria, and limited the Ottoman possessions to a small area around Constantinople, failed to satisfy the contradictory aspirations of the Balkan governments. Greece, Serbia, and Montenegro opposed the creation of the new Albanian state despite its clearly Albanian ethnic basis; they would have preferred a partition of its territories. Serbia had not obtained its major goal of access to the sea. Bulgaria, a defeated state, was in the worst position of all. Far from achieving the San Stefano boundaries, it received a smaller share in the Macedonian and Thracian partition than its Greek and Serbian rivals. In addition, it was forced to cede a large section of Dobrudja to Romania. The settlement, producing massive resentment and discontent, provided a poor foundation for a peaceful future.

During this period the Russian government, including the military authorities, continued to seek a change in the status of the Straits. With the continuing decline of Ottoman prestige and power, some Russian officials became increasingly worried about its ability to act as the guardian of this vital waterway. With these concerns in mind Neratov, in charge of the Foreign Ministry during the absence of Sazonov, in September 1911 instructed Charykov to initiate negotiations with the Porte.[50] On October 12, 1911, the ambassador presented to the Ottoman government a draft agreement that again resembled the Unkiar Iskelessi arrangement.[51] The terms included the improvement of mutual relations, the protection of the status quo in the Balkans, and a change in the regime of the Straits. Once more, as repeatedly in the past, such an arrangement met the opposition of the other powers, in particular Russia's entente partners. Sazonov disavowed the negotiations in December; in March 1912 Charykov was recalled and retired.

The extreme sensitivity on the issue was again shown during the Balkan Wars in the Russian fear that the Bulgarian army might

---

[50]Neratov to Charykov, letter no. 617, October 2/September 19, 1911. *Mezhdunarodnye otnosheniia v epokhu imperializma* (Moscow: Gosudarstvennoe sotsial'no-ekonomicheskoe izdatel'stvo, 1938), series II: 2, pp. 58–60 (cited hereafter as *MO*).

[51]The text is in André N. Mandelstam, "La politique russe d'accès à la Méditerranée au XXe siècle," Académie de droit international, *Recueil des cours*, XLVII (1934), p. 694.

attack and occupy Constantinople. The establishment of full Young Turk control over the Ottoman government in January 1913 caused other problems. Since Germany in the past had been the single European great power that had not directly threatened its territorial integrity, the Ottoman government naturally was attracted to a policy of cooperation. In May 1913 it asked for German military assistance in the reform of its army. The mission was headed by General Otto Liman von Sanders, who, as part of his assignment, was given the command of the First Army Corps in Constantinople. The Russian government made immediate strong objections, although it accepted the presence of a similar British naval mission. After much discussion, the general was promoted in rank and given a higher position in the Ottoman army, one that did not directly involve the Straits. The crisis passed, but the Straits issue remained under consideration. In February 1914 a ministerial council discussed the question of the seizure of the Straits. Here the decision was reached that Russia "did not possess the means to take swift and decisive action, and that years would elapse before we were in a position to execute the plans we had in view."[52]

For the Russian government Near Eastern affairs by 1914 were in a far from satisfactory condition. Its goal after 1909 had been to bring the Balkan states together to protect the status quo against the Central Powers and to ensure Russia a predominant position in the region. Instead in 1913 it faced a shattered Balkan alliance, and it was forced to accept a great-power settlement for the peninsula. The Russian public tended to regard the results of the wars as a defeat for its national interests and a victory for the Central Powers. It was true that Russian relations were better with Greece and, in particular, with Romania, but Bulgaria was in the enemy camp. The Slavic powers were thus divided. In fact, in 1914 in some Russian eyes, only Serbia could be counted as a reliable ally. The Russian involvement with that state was to bring the government into another dangerous entanglement, this time leading to a major disaster.

RUSSIA AND SERBIA

In the past Russian relations with Belgrade had not followed a steady course. Despite the protectorate established in 1826, the Russian government was never able to exert the type of control in

---

[52]Serge Sazonov, *Fateful Years* (New York: Frederick A. Stokes Company, 1928), p. 126.

Belgrade that it did in Bucharest or Sofia. Nevertheless, here as elsewhere, Russian agents worked not only to secure a favorable attitude on foreign policy issues but also to ensure that the internal regimes served Russian interests. Despite the efforts made to maintain a predominant position, the Russian leadership recognized that Serbia's geographic position opened the state to Habsburg influence and also gave that government a legitimate interest in developments there. Thus, for instance, during the Crimean War and afterward a Habsburg primacy in the region was accepted under certain circumstances.

The Russian policy of abstention from adventurous policies adopted after the Crimean War also affected relations with Belgrade. The former protectorate, of course, had been replaced by the great-power guarantee in the Treaty of Paris. At this time the Russian government, weakened by the military defeat, could not interfere in Balkan affairs, nor could it offer assistance to the national movements. Recognizing this situation, Michael Obrenović, as we have seen, attempted to organize an alliance of Balkan states that could act independently. Although many plans were drawn up and negotiations carried on, Michael's assassination in June 1868 cut these efforts short.

During the first part of the reign of his successor, Milan Obrenović, relations with Russia were good. In this period international relations were dominated by the problems associated with the last stages of German unification. Russia subsequently became a member of the Three Emperors' Alliance, an alignment that limited its ability to carry out an independent Balkan policy. In fact, at this time the priority of Habsburg interests in the western Balkans was accepted. When the revolts in Bosnia and Hercegovina broke out, Gorchakov agreed that Vienna should be the center of negotiations. We have also seen how in 1876, during the war between the Ottoman Empire and the two Slavic states, the Russian government, in the discussions over the Reichstadt agreement, failed to support the Serbian aims in Bosnia.

The worst period in Serbian–Russian relations occurred after the Serbian defeat. Although the Russian government did intervene to force the Ottoman Empire to sign an armistice, Russian efforts subsequently were devoted to furthering Bulgarian claims. The Serbian government, with no other great-power protector, nevertheless still turned to St. Petersburg for assistance and hoped through Russian intervention to gain Bosnia and territories to the southwest, referred to as Old Serbia. The Russian representatives, however, consistently favored the Bulgarian position. At the Constantinople Conference of December 1876 Ignatiev asked only for a return to the status quo before the war for Serbia. In contrast, one of the two Bulgarian states agreed upon at that time was assigned Niš, Prizren, and Skopje. In February and March 1877, before entering the war with the Ottoman Empire, the Russian government again surrendered Serbian interests to the Habsburg Empire. In secret agreements Russia confirmed the territorial provisions of the Reichstadt Convention and agreed not to carry on military operations in the western Balkans.

At the outbreak of the Russo–Turkish War in April 1877 the Serbian government thus found itself in a difficult position. The previous January it had made peace with the Ottoman Empire; the Serbian army was in no condition to fight. At first, the Russian government, confident of victory, rejected any military assistance from the Balkan states. After the failure to take the fortress city of Plevna in the summer, the Russian position was reversed; strong pressure was exerted on the Balkan states to join in the conflict. Although Romania entered the war almost at once, the Serbian decision was delayed until December 13, a few days after the fall of Plevna. In the subsequent fighting Serbian troops took Niš, Pirot, and Vranja. An armistice was signed between Russia and the Ottoman Empire on January 31, 1878.

In the negotiations over the peace terms, the Russian diplomats made it perfectly clear that their main interests lay in the Bulgarian lands. The Serbian representatives were told bluntly that they should rely on Vienna for support for their claims. Certainly, in the negotiations leading to the conclusion of the Treaty of San Stefano, Ignatiev put the Russian emphasis first on Bulgaria and second on Montenegro. In the treaty Serbia acquired only 150 square miles of territory; Montenegro received 200 square miles. The large Bulgarian state was awarded Macedonian territory that the Serbs regarded as rightfully theirs.

Although the Treaty of Berlin gave Serbia some advantages, it marked the beginning of a period when Belgrade fell under the control of Vienna. Serbia received about 200 square miles of territory, including Niš, Pirot, and Vranja. The awarding of Bosnia, Hercegovina, and the Sanjak of Novi Pazar to the Habsburg Monarchy, however, caused great bitterness. Nevertheless, because of the Russian attitude and because no other alternative existed, the Serbian ruler, Milan Obrenović, was forced to establish close economic and political ties with the Habsburg Empire. In return for a trade treaty and a political understanding that reduced Serbia to a protectorate of Vienna, Milan was able to declare himself king, and he received a promise of support for Serbian southward expansion. He also had to accept the Habsburg control of Bosnia and Hercegovina and to give assurances that he would suppress intrigues directed against the monarchy.

The Russian attitude toward Serbia changed in 1885 when it became clear that Bulgaria would not accept Russian direction. The dissolution of the Three Emperors' Alliance in 1887 also formally ended an alignment that was based on a partition of influence in the Balkans. At this time, however, Russia had no interest in exploiting the Balkan conditions. Moreover, in 1896 relations with Bulgaria were reestablished.

In 1889 King Milan abdicated because of domestic political difficulties. The reign of his successor, his thirteen-year-old son, Alexander Obrenović, was to be short and dominated by scandal. In 1900 a major controversy arose over the desire of the young monarch to marry Draga Mašina, a thirty-six-year-old widow with a doubtful reputation. By this time, however, relations with Russia had improved. Nicholas II was in fact the best man by proxy at the wedding. This period also was marked by the rise of the political influence of the pro-Russian Radical Party, led by Nikola Pašić. The Radicals were able to dominate the government until 1914 almost without interruption. However, despite its good relations with St. Petersburg, Serbia could not expect assistance in furthering its national goals as long as Russia was involved in the Far East. The agreement between Russia and Austria-Hungary in 1897 also served to put Balkan affairs "on ice," as the contemporary expression put it.

In 1903 Alexander was assassinated in a military coup that brought to the throne Peter Karadjordjević of the rival dynasty. Although the British government, horrified by the event, refused to recognize the new regime, the Russian and Habsburg governments accepted it almost at once. King Peter was regarded as pro-Russian; the Radical Party remained in control. Although the dangers in the situation were at first not clear, this leadership was to stand for a program in foreign policy that was bound to lead to another Balkan crisis. King Peter, coming to the throne at the age of almost sixty, had spent the previous portion of his life in exile; he was thus not closely acquainted with or in control of Serbian domestic politics. Owing his position to the army, he could also not act against military interests. The army, joined by most of the influential political parties and leaders, stood at this time for an aggressive national program, and they took the previous Italian and German unification movements as their ideal. Similar to their Bulgarian neighbors, who sought the re-creation of the San Stefano state, and the Greeks, with their Great Idea of the revival of Byzantium, the Serbian nationalists had a vision of a future state based not on ethnic foundations, but on past history and national mythology.[53] Looking south, they thus saw as the proper boundaries of their state those that had constituted the empire of Tsar Dušan in the thirteenth century, lands occupied in 1903 by Albanians, Bulgarians, and Turks but only a minority of Serbs. Their western and northern claims were even more controversial. Adopting the attitude that Catholic Croats and South Slav Muslims were in fact Serbs who had betrayed their original Orthodox faith, many Serbian leaders claimed as "Serbian lands" Bosnia, Hercegovina, Dalmatia, Istria, Croatia, and Slavonia. As will be shown, the Russian statesmen and the tsar accepted this position without criticism. In addition, both Serbs and Russians regarded the Montenegrins as Serbs. Throughout the century there had been various proposals to unite the two countries. The rivalry of the Montenegrin Petrović dynasty with the Serbian Obrenović and Karadjordjević royal families and

[53] Because of the enormous importance of the concept of "Serbian lands" in Russian and Serbian foreign policy in this period, a study of the nationality statistics in the areas claimed is of importance. The figures for the Habsburg Empire based on the 1910 census are reliable and have been accepted by most scholars. These give the following numbers for the Serbian population in the regions in question: (1) Croatia-Slavonia, 25 percent Serbian, 65 percent Croatian; (2) Dalmatia, 16 percent Orthodox (Serb), 82 percent Catholic (predominantly Croatian); (3) Bosnia-Hercegovina, 44 percent Orthodox (Serb), 22 percent Catholic (Croatian), 33 percent Muslim (claimed by both the Serbs and Croats, but after 1945 representing a separate nationality). There was no appreciable Serbian population in Istria or the Slovene-inhabited provinces. Other statistics are more difficult to verify. Before 1914 Montenegro was regarded by its inhabitants and by most Europeans as Serbian. The great problem arises with the population of the lands still under Ottoman control at the turn of the century, in particular Macedonia, inhabited by Bulgarians, Greeks, Turks, Albanians, Serbs, Vlachs, Jews, Gypsies, and people who simply identified themselves with their locality. After 1945, in what was possibly the best solution to the nationality problem at that time, Yugoslavia was divided into six sections: Bosnia-Hercegovina, Croatia, Macedonia, Montenegro, Serbia, and Slovenia. Serbia acquired two autonomous provinces: Vojvodina, with a strong Serbian plurality but a considerable Hungarian, Romanian, and other populations, and Kosovo, the heart of Old Serbia, which has an 85–90 percent Albanian majority against only 10–15 percent for the Serbs. For a discussion of how the Serbs and Croats identified their national lands see Charles Jelavich, *South Slav Nationalisms – Textbooks and Yugoslav Union before 1914* (Columbus: Ohio State University Press, 1990).

the opposition of Vienna had prevented a political union, although, as we have seen, the two states usually supported each other in foreign affairs.

The Greater Serbian program, involving the annexation of lands inhabited not only by Serbs, but also by Croats and Slovenes, commanded the support of few Habsburg South Slavs. No Croatian party or leader of consequence called for the outright annexation of these lands by Serbia; even among the Habsburg Serbs there was disagreement over Greater Serbian ideals. As far as the primary Serbian national territorial goal, Bosnia-Hercegovina, was concerned, the majority of the population was made up not of Serbs, but of Catholic Croats and Muslims with a South Slav ethnic background. Neither of these peoples called for a direct unification with their Orthodox neighbor. The annexation was in fact accepted with favor by the Croats, since it strengthened the position of those who wished to create a Croatian national unit within the monarchy, and by the Slovenes, Czechs, and Poles because it increased the percentage of Slavs in the state. Previously, the Germans and Hungarians had opposed annexation for precisely these reasons.

Nevertheless, despite this situation the Habsburg authorities were concerned about the political activities of their South Slav citizens, who were certainly not content with their status in the dual system and who made their grievances known. Increasing efforts were also made by both Serb and Croat leaders to bring the two peoples together and to strengthen the ties with Serbia. In 1905 the Serb and Croat parties in Dalmatia and the Croatian kingdom joined together to form the Croatian–Serbian Coalition. This successful political front was able to win elections, but it was in no sense a revolutionary organization. Its goals were to win political influence and to improve the conditions of the monarchy's South Slavs.

Alongside this perfectly legal activity, however, some groups did use a vocabulary and support programs that caused apprehension among Habsburg officials. By the early twentieth century the Yugoslav movement, based on the idea that the Serbs, Croats, and Slovenes were one people, had made considerable headway, in particular among students, teachers, and other intellectuals. At the same time the cultural links between the Habsburg Slavs and Serbia were increased; students and teachers of both groups exchanged visits and issued fiery declarations of mutual support and affection. These and other activities, considered together with the irredentist slogans issuing from Belgrade, gave many Habsburg leaders what were in fact unjustified concerns about the loyalty of their South Slav population.

As a result, particularly after 1903, relations between Serbia and the Habsburg Empire declined precipitously. Worried about the political ambitions of its southern neighbor and increasingly frustrated by the national antagonisms in the monarchy, the Habsburg leadership watched with concern anything that looked like an increase of Serbian power. The formation of a large South Slav state, presumably a Russian ally, had long been a Habsburg fear. For this reason the government strongly opposed the economic agreement signed between Bulgaria and Serbia in 1905, and it initiated a tariff war with Serbia that lasted from 1906 to 1911. Since it involved a Habsburg embargo on Serbian livestock, it was known as the Pig War. The controversy made even clearer to the Serbian government its economic dependency on the monarchy and forced it to seek other markets. This endeavor in turn increased its desire to have communications with the outside world that did not depend on the monarchy, in particular an Adriatic port and direct connections to it. These commercial concerns also determined the Serbian opposition, backed by Russia, to the Habsburg plan to build a railroad through the Sanjak of Novi Pazar to the Aegean, thus skirting Serbian territory. Serbia and Russia proposed instead an alternate Danube–Adriatic line, which would have given Serbia access to the sea.

The Habsburg annexation of Bosnia-Hercegovina struck at the heart of the Serbian national program, since these lands were its next objective. The intensity of the Serbian feeling about these provinces was certainly not understood by Izvolsky, as is evidenced by his words at this time. In 1908 Serbia was governed by a Radical Party ministry, with Pera Velimirović as prime minister and Milan Milovanović as foreign minister, but it did not include such leading Radicals as Nikola Pašić and Stojan Protić. The crisis faced this government with difficult choices. The enormous public outcry made some action necessary. Moreover, the Bulgarian declaration of independence had an effect on the Balkan balance of power; Serbia could claim compensation here too.

Two alternate approaches were argued to deal with the situation. Milovanović, who had prior warning of the annexation, adopted a moderate and realistic solution, arguing that Serbia should use diplomatic channels to obtain compensation. In contrast, another group, including the heir, Prince George, and Pašić, insisted upon a strong stand, arguing that Serbia's maximum demands should be presented, that the state should prepare for war, and that the annexation should not be accepted. Instead Serbia should demand autonomy for the two provinces, refuse compensation, and attempt to cooperate with the Ottoman Empire. This position would preserve the image of Serbia as the leader of the Balkan peoples, in particular the South Slavs.

This defiant attitude was not adopted; the Serbian government instead sought to gain some compensation. In order to present the Serbian position, Milovanović traveled to Rome, Berlin, and London, while Pašić went to St. Petersburg. As compensation the Serbian representatives asked for a stretch of land running through Bosnia-Hercegovina and connecting Serbia with Montenegro and the sea. They also requested either land or a right of way for a railway line through the Sanjak. All of the proposals met with a negative reception. In London, Izvolsky told the Serbian minister, Slavko Gruić, that the provinces were lost to Serbia even before the annexation.[54] They could be won only by a war, but that would be suicide for the state. The Russian minister promised only to protect Serbian interests in the wider sense and to attempt to obtain some kind of compensation, but not including territorial additions. After his return to St. Petersburg, Izvolsky spoke in the same manner in a conversation with Pašić on October 29.[55] Russia, the minister declared, was not ready for war; his government had wished the annexation discussed at a conference, but the Habsburg Empire, backed by Germany, had refused. Serbia could expect only diplomatic, not military, aid. Izvolsky also warned that the Serbian attitude of defiance was only making a settlement more difficult to achieve.

In this conversation Pašić adopted an approach that he was to repeat later; he in effect threatened that Serbia might act alone, thus forcing a Russian action. The minister emphasized how deeply Serbian feelings had been aroused and that outbreaks of violence could occur. Moreover, he declared, "if it is a question of the existence, the honor, and the dignity of the people," then they would risk everything. In the future, some Serbs and other Balkan leaders believed that if they took a provocative action that led to a Habsburg or an Ottoman invasion, then Russia would be forced to come to their defense because of public pressure. In this regard, Izvolsky was

[54]Gruić to the Foreign Ministry, London, September 30/October 13, 1908, *APS*, I, pp. 15–17.
[55]Pašić to the Foreign Ministry, telegram, St. Petersburg, October 16/29, 1908, ibid., I, pp. 25–30. Other Pašić reports on his visit to St. Petersburg are on pp. 33, 36–7, 44. See also Izvolsky to Maksimov, St. Petersburg, November 3, 1908. Pavićević, *Rusija i aneksiona kriza*, I, pp. 570–1.

well aware that the Serbs could appeal to Russian public opinion. In this conversation he told Pašić that his government should not interfere in Russian internal affairs; it was not 1875 and 1876.

Despite Izvolsky's disclaimer, the situation was in fact similar to, if not worse than, that existing before the Russo–Turkish War of 1877–8. Both the Russian and Serbian leaders knew that the same pro-Slav public opinion was at work. At the height of the crisis in March 1909, Izvolsky scolded Demeter Popović, the Serbian minister, about his government's attitude, saying, "You have already from the beginning been an obstruction to my policy; there are people among you who believe that the Russian government can be forced into war through agitation in Russian public opinion."[56] Izvolsky, however, added another consideration to the effect that Serbia lost nothing by agreeing to the Habsburg demands; they had been extracted by force and thus were not binding.[57]

Both Popović and another Serbian representative, Radovan Košutić, received similar advice from other sources: Serbia should give up its demand for territorial compensation, accept the decisions of the powers, and await a better future. Thus General Michael Aleksandrovich Taube, formerly the military attaché in Belgrade, argued with Popović that Russia was not ready for war, but that after it had increased its military power, it could adopt a policy more in accord with its traditions and greatness; Serbia should thus have patience.[58] Košutić reported that Izvolsky had told some Duma members that Russia would not go to war even if Austria-Hungary occupied Serbia, but he expected the monarchy eventually to fall apart.[59] When that happened, Russia would solve the Serbian question.

The Russian pressure on Serbia to accept the declaration demanded by Austria-Hungary in 1909 has been noted. As could be expected, both Russian and Serbian public opinion was shocked by the outcome of the Bosnian crisis. Very few people, after all, knew that the Russian government had previously acquiesced repeatedly to Habsburg control of Bosnia and Hercegovina and that Izvolsky had indeed made the provinces a pawn in his game to win the

[56] Popović to the Foreign Ministry, St. Petersburg, March 5/18, 1909, *APS*, I, pp. 77–8.
[57] Ibid. See also Izvolsky to Sergeev, St. Petersburg, March 4/17, 1909, Siebert, *Benckendorff*, I, 77–8.
[58] Popović to the Foreign Ministry, Petersburg, January 14/27, 1909, *APS*, I, p. 49.
[59] Košutić to the Foreign Ministry, telegram, St. Petersburg, February 25/March 10, 1909, ibid., I, pp. 68–9.

Straits. In a broad sense, however, Serbia had won by the outcome. Although the provinces were lost, the Russian government from this time on made Belgrade the center of its Eastern policy; individual statesmen apparently felt somehow obligated to support Serbian interests. This attitude was buttressed by the widely held belief that the premises of the Greater Serbian program were correct and that "oppressed Serbs" did indeed form the majority of the population in the areas claimed.

The subsequent attempts of the Russian government to counter what it regarded as a humiliating defeat by the establishment of a Balkan alliance system were immensely aided by the appointment of Hartwig to Belgrade in 1909. An ardent supporter of Slavic causes, he advocated a policy of opposition to both Austria-Hungary and Britain but friendship with Germany. His association with Pašić, clearly the most influential Serbian politician, was so close that foreign observers often commented that he was in fact in control of the Serbian government. Although an advocate of the official Russian policy in the Balkans, Hartwig often acted in an independent manner and did not carry out his government's instructions, nor did he always faithfully report his own activities. He also played a part in internal Serbian politics far greater than his position as a Russian representative warranted.

In the negotiations among the powers about the issues in the Balkan Wars, the Russian government was deeply involved not only in the division of Macedonia, but also in the settlement of the Serbian and Montenegrin demands, most of which were opposed by Austria-Hungary, usually backed by Italy and Germany. Three major controversies arose: the Serbian demand for an Adriatic port, the Montenegrin seizure of Shköder (Scutari), and the Habsburg ultimatum to Serbia to evacuate northern Albania. All of these involved the larger issue of the creation of an Albanian state.

In addition to its objectives in Macedonia, Serbia's major wartime aims included the acquisition of an Adriatic port, namely Durrës (Durazzo). Aware that this claim was strongly opposed by Austria-Hungary and Italy and not supported by another power, the Russian government after November 1912 realized that this acquisition was out of Serbian reach. However, as had been the case in regard to the annexation of Bosnia-Hercegovina, the Serbs were difficult to convince that they could not obtain the port without fighting and that a war for what the Russians regarded as a secondary objective could not be considered. In regard to this question and the other related controversies, Sazonov had difficulties with Serbia, Hartwig, and Russian public opinion. As far as the Serbian attitude was concerned, Sazonov wrote in his memoirs: "My problem was still further complicated by the fact that even in Serbia, in spite of the sincere and ardent solicitude for her felt by the Russian Government, I did not always find that self-control and sober estimate of the dangers of the moment which alone could avert a catastrophe." He considered Hartwig a major cause of the problem: "To my mind the Serbian attitude was partly accounted for by the fact that M. Hartwig, our Minister in Belgrade, preferred the agreeable rôle of countenancing the exaggerated attitude adopted by Government and social circles in Belgrade, to the less grateful one which he should have adopted in the true interests of Serbia . . . Hartwig interpreted Russian policy in Belgrade according to his own taste, and thereby greatly added to my difficulties."[60] The dangerous pressure of public opinion was also felt in this issue:

> At the beginning of 1913, public sympathy with Serbian aspirations became so strong that it inspired in me a certain fear lest the Government should find itself unable to control the course of political events. In society circles . . . which were in close touch with certain Court and military centres, there was a rooted conviction that a favourable moment was approaching for settling with Austria-Hungary for the sins of the Aehrenthal policy.[61]

The Russian government had similar problems when Montenegro took Shköder against the protests of all of the great powers in April 1913. It agreed that the city should be awarded to Albania, although it did not join in the blockade that was imposed. On May 5 Montenegrin troops left the city. A similar position was taken in October 1913 when the Habsburg Monarchy delivered an ultimatum to Serbia to evacuate northern Albania; the Russian government advised a withdrawal. On the wider question of the boundaries of Albania, Russian support did aid in the attainment of some Serbian objectives. With a general policy of "the Balkans for the Balkan people," the Russian government could not oppose the creation of the Albanian state, but it did aid in securing a frontier that gave Serbia important territorial gains, including the cities of Dibra and Djakovo, which the Russian diplomats also recognized as ethnically Albanian.

Despite the final favorable solution, the Russian government during the negotiations continued to have problems with Serbia. Neither the

[60]Sazonov, *Fateful Years*, p. 80.   [61]Ibid., p. 78.

Serbs nor the Greeks recognized the Albanians as a nationality with rights; they wished to divide the land between themselves. When told that Russia would not fight for Djakovo, Pašić adopted a heroic stance:

> No one in Serbia will agree without a fight that Djakovo and Dibra are Albanian. If Serbia is defeated on the battlefield, then at least it will not be despised by the world, for the world will esteem highly a people which would not living enter the servitude of Austria.[62]

This attitude certainly concerned Sazonov; he told Popović that he could not sleep at night because of the Albanian question.[63]

During the First Balkan War and, in particular, after the Second, the Russian government was concerned about the adamant Serbian attitude toward the partition of Macedonia. Although obviously the Balkan front had been broken, St. Petersburg attempted to lessen the tension between Serbia and Bulgaria; there was concern about future ties between Sofia and Vienna. Although a clear statement of preference for Serbia was given, that government was urged to be moderate in its attitude toward the settlement with Bulgaria. In the discussions with Serbian diplomats, the Russian representatives argued that Serbia should look to the future for its greatest gains, which would obviously be at Habsburg expense. Thus on December 27, 1912, Sazonov told Popović that the Serbs should content themselves "with what they had received and I regard this only as a stage, for the future belongs to us."[64] Similarly, on February 13, 1913, the Russian minister declared that Serbia should accept the settlement offered and organize for the future "in order later when the time has come to cut out the Austro-Hungarian ulcer which today is not as ripe as the Turkish. A nation that shows such outstanding characteristics as the Serbian must be victorious."[65]

Similar sentiments were expressed in Sazonov's letter to Hartwig on May 6, in which he urged a Serbian–Bulgarian understanding. While emphasizing that the Serbs were the most sympathetic of all the Slavic peoples, he pointed out:

[62]Pašić to Popović, Belgrade, January 27/February 3, 1913, *APS*, I, 294–5.
[63]Popović to the Foreign Ministry, telegram, St. Petersburg, February 26/March 5, 1913, ibid., I, pp. 308–9.
[64]Popović to the Foreign Ministry, telegram, St. Petersburg, December 14/27, 1912, ibid., I, pp. 279–80.
[65]Popović to the Foreign Ministry, St. Petersburg, January 31/February 13, 1913, ibid., I, pp. 298–9.

Serbia has however passed through only the first stage of its historic road and in order to reach its goal it must still endure a frightful struggle, in which its entire existence could be brought into question. Serbia's promised land lies in the lands of the present Austria-Hungary and not there where it now aspires and where the Bulgarians stand in its way.[66]

Although time was indeed working in its favor, Sazonov argued, Serbia should preserve its alliance with Bulgaria. Such arguments did appeal to the Serbian representatives. When on May 12 Sazonov spoke in the same manner with Popović, the Serbian minister answered, partly in jest, that his country would gladly give Bitola (Monastir) to Bulgaria in return for Bosnia and other Austrian lands.[67]

In Sofia, Nekliudov spoke along identical lines in his discussions with the Serbian minister, Miroslav Spalajković:

. . . one must look to the future. The Bulgarians will have nothing more to gain, whereas the Serbians will have all their historic goals before them. These goals are situated in the west. Sooner or later, the Serbians will aspire to unite all Serbian lands, and then, if successful, they will possess a splendid coast, inhabited by Serbians of the purest race, and who have been experienced sailors, from father to son, whereas, in this respect, the Bulgarians have to depend on Greeks and Turks.[68]

Even after the outbreak of the Second Balkan War and the great increase in enmity between the Serbs and Bulgarians, the Russian diplomats continued to use the argument that if the intention was to "unite all Serbs," then Serbia needed Bulgarian support. Other Russian politicians acted to bring the representatives together. In December 1913, through the initiative of the Octobrist Party leader, Alexander Ivanovich Guchkov, Popović met with the Bulgarian minister in St. Petersburg, Ratko Dimitriev.[69] The latter suggested a territorial bargain that could be made: Bulgaria had aspirations that it could not give up in Dobrudja, Thrace, and a part of Macedonia; Serbia wanted Bosnia, Hercegovina, Dalmatia, Croatia, and Slavonia. All this would have to be decided in the future.

Although these Russian declarations may have been made to calm

---

[66]Sazonov to Hartwig, St. Petersburg, April 23/May 6, 1913, ibid., II, pp. 408–10.
[67]Popović to the Foreign Ministry, telegram, St. Petersburg, April 29/May 12, 1913, ibid., I, p. 331.
[68]Nekliudov, *Diplomatic Reminiscences*, p. 138. Nekliudov was obviously unaware that the Dalmatian coast, to which he was referring, was inhabited overwhelmingly by Catholic Croats and not by Orthodox Serbs.
[69]Popović to Pašić, personal, very confidential, St. Petersburg, December 8/21, 1913, *APS*, I, pp. 403–6.

the immediate situation, they were certainly irresponsible when delivered to the representatives of a state enthusiastically embarked upon a course of national expansion and with goals that quite clearly could lead to war with a great power. How little the Russian leadership understood what was going on in the South Slav lands was clearly shown during Pašić's conversation with Nicholas II on February 2, 1914.[70] Throughout this narrative examples have been given of how the Russian government was drawn into dangerous situations because the responsible statesmen did not know much about the people or issues with which they were dealing. In this episode the tsar gave clear evidence that he did not understand the South Slav problem. Speaking with Pašić for an hour, the tsar asked him how many "Serbocroats"[71] lived in Austria and what they wanted. The Serbian minister replied that there were 6 million, and he explained where they lived. He also discussed the Slovenes, who, he declared, were gravitating toward the "Serbocroatians" and their language because their "dialect" was bad, and they had long ago lost their national independence. He also declared that there had been a change in the attitude of the Habsburg Slavs. Those who before had looked to Austria now saw only Russia or Serbia as their salvation. He also declared that he could obtain as many soldiers from these lands as he had weapons. After hearing this slanted, Serbian-national explanation, Nicholas II commented that Austria treated the Slavs very badly, ignoring for a moment his own problems with the Poles, Ukrainians, and Belorussians.

RUSSIA, SERBIA, AND THE ORIGINS OF WORLD WAR I

Although there were certainly few signs in January 1914 that the year would end in total disaster, the Russian position after the Balkan Wars was certainly not as favorable as it had been before

---

[70]Pašić report to King Peter, St. Petersburg, January 20/February 2, 1914, ibid., I, pp. 414–21.

[71]Shortly before the outbreak of World War I, influenced by the Yugoslav movement in the Habsburg Empire, some Serbian statesmen used terms such as *Serbo-Croatian* or *Yugoslav* and recognized the close affinity of the two peoples. However, most of those who accepted the national identity of Serbs, Croats, and Slovenes and supported the creation of a Yugoslav state conceived it as organized by Serbia and run from Belgrade, as indeed happened after 1918.

Map 9. The Balkan states, 1914.

the conflict.[72] The territorial settlement made it inevitable that Bul-

[72]No attempt is made to cite all of the relevant books and documentary collections available on Russia and the origins of World War I. The reader is, however,

garia would gravitate toward the Habsburg Empire; the new Albanian state, if it could be established on a firm footing, would obviously be in the Habsburg and Italian camp. Although Russian relations with Romania were much better, it was probable that this state and Greece would remain, at best, neutral in any conflict. As far as Russia's great-power allies, Britain and France, were concerned, they had failed to provide unhesitant support to Russia's Balkan objectives, and they had opposed the attempts to change the Straits settlement. This situation signified that in Balkan affairs Serbia might indeed be Russia's only reliable friend. In the first months of 1914 the Russian diplomats devoted considerable effort to attempt to bring Serbia into a closer relationship with Montenegro in order to strengthen the position of both states against the Habsburg Empire.

The relationship with Serbia, however, involved certain dangers for Russia. We have seen how Russian representatives had given tacit approval to the Serbian national program and vague assurances about support in the future. It has also been repeatedly demonstrated that throughout the previous century the Serbian statesmen had done what St. Petersburg told them to do only when it was to their clear advantage. Other problems were also to arise from the Belgrade connection. As we have seen, Russia had been involved in serious crises and even wars through its direct or indirect association with revolutionary movements over which it had no control and whose origins it could only deplore. For instance, the Greek crisis of the 1820s and the Bulgarian uprising of 1876 began with underground revolutionary conspiracies of a type that official Russia strongly disapproved, yet because of the Orthodox and Slavic implications it could not afford to ignore. Certainly, in 1914 the Russian leadership continued for the most part to hold the same fears of the "revolution" that had influenced its predecessors since the beginning of the nineteenth century. Yet the relationship with Serbia was by 1914 to link the Russian government indirectly, and without the knowledge of its responsible representatives, with underground activities that

referred to two books concerning Russian policy: D. C. B. Lieven, *Russia and the Origins of the First World War*, already cited; N. P. Poletika, *Vozniknovenie pervoi mirovoi voiny* (Moscow: Izdatel'stvo sotsial'no – ekonomicheskoi literatury mysl', 1964); and Vladimir Dedijer, *The Road to Sarajevo*, 2 vols. (New York: Simon & Schuster, 1966). This section is based on two articles by Barbara Jelavich: "Official Russia and the Balkan Slavic Connection," *Canadian Review of Studies in Nationalism*, XVI: 1–2 (1989), pp. 209–26, and "When Diplomats Fail: Austrian and Russian Reporting from Belgrade, 1914," Occasional Paper, East European Program, Wilson Center, Washington, D.C.

were, in turn, directed toward overturning conditions that were favorable to Russian interests.

Despite the fact that the Balkan Wars resulted in major Serbian territorial acquisitions, this national victory led in fact to a dangerous crisis that threatened the internal stability of the state. Ever since the army coup of 1903, which had been carried out by about 120 junior officers, there had been a continual conflict between the military and the civilian leadership. International pressure had compelled King Peter to exclude the major conspirators from important posts, but they were able to influence public opinion, and they remained in a strong position in the army. Highly nationalistic, they participated in underground military activities, such as the formation of the armed bands that fought in Macedonia to protect Serbian interests against similar Bulgarian, Greek, and Albanian units. For Serbian–Habsburg relations the most important secret society was *Narodna Odbrana* (National Defense), which was organized during the Bosnian annexation crisis. The society at first intended to organize volunteer armed bands to operate in Bosnia after the Macedonian example. However, after Habsburg pressure forced the Serbian government to end such activities, Narodna Odbrana became ostensibly a cultural society, although many of its members continued their underground associations.

The leading role in conspiratorial activities was subsequently assumed by a new organization, *Ujedinjenje ili Smrt* (Union or Death), known by its enemies as the Black Hand, founded in May 1911. Under the leadership of Colonel Dragutin Dimitrijević (also called Apis, the bull, after the Egyptian god) and Major Vojin Tankosić, who had been active in the Macedonian conflicts, the society had as its major goal, as stated in its constitution, the unification of all Serbs, including those under Habsburg as well as Ottoman control. The emphasis was on revolutionary rather than cultural means, but it worked closely with Narodna Odbrana, many of whose members also joined the Black Hand. Its activities included the smuggling of arms into Bosnia. The victorious conclusion of the Balkan Wars added greatly to its prestige and influence, since the high-ranking officers in the army were probably Black Hand members. Although the organization was in theory secret, its activities were known to the public and the press in Serbia and abroad. Its newspaper, *Pijemont* (Piedmont), openly propagated its Greater Serbian and anti-Habsburg goals.

In addition to its program for the acquisition of what it defined as Serbian lands, the society sought domestic political influence, and it came into direct conflict with Pašić and his supporters. The major crisis, which took place in spring 1914, involved the administration of the newly acquired lands. As a result of the Balkan Wars Serbian territory had increased from 48,300 to 87,300 square kilometers. Since the majority of the population of the area was not Serbian and consequently resisted Serbian control, the army felt compelled to adopt violent measures. At the same time, the military and the civilian authorities came into conflict over who should administer "New Serbia." The so-called Priority Question, the major issue in Serbian politics from May to the end of June 1914, brought into the open the sharp differences between the military and the Pašić government. The situation became dangerous when the premier's political opponents joined with the army. As a result, Pašić was forced to resign on June 2, but, with the backing of Hartwig, he returned to power on June 11. The assembly was dissolved on June 24. At this time King Peter handed over his powers to his son Alexander, who became regent.

During this period of political crisis the conspiracy was organized that culminated in the assassination of the heir to the Habsburg throne, Franz Ferdinand. At this time three young Bosnian students were given arms and were trained by Major Tankosić, with the approval of Dimitrijević, who was now chief of army intelligence as well as the head of the Black Hand. On the night of June 1 the students were smuggled into Bosnia, where for the next weeks they were assisted by those with connections with Narodna Odbrana and the Black Hand. Although Pašić was deeply involved in the domestic crisis, he learned through his contacts in Narodna Odbrana that the students had crossed the border with arms, and he was perhaps aware of their intentions. He discussed the situation with some of his associates, and he ordered an investigation of the border conditions. He did not, however, directly or indirectly warn any Habsburg official, nor did he discuss the matter with Hartwig. The Russian military attaché, Colonel Viktor Alekseevich Artamonov, was on vacation in Europe at this time, so he was not involved in the conspiracy or the domestic quarrel.

Although the news of the assassination of Franz Ferdinand and his wife in Sarajevo on June 28 was a shock to the Russian leaders, as to those of the other European states, there was little apprehension at first about the possible consequences of the event. Until the delivery of the Austrian ultimatum to Serbia on July 23, the grave danger facing all the European states was not fully realized. During this period the Russian officials judged the situation primarily on the basis of the reports from their representatives in Belgrade and Vienna and on the information provided by the Serbian and Austro-Hungarian agents in St. Petersburg.

As could be expected, Hartwig's reports supported the Serbian denial of any responsibility. Although he had always prided himself on his great influence over and his knowledge about Serbian politics, the information that Hartwig sent his government on the details of the domestic situation were sparse and in a sense misleading. At this time, as previously, he gave his full support to Greater Serbian objectives, and he stressed Pašić's outstanding abilities and his loyalty to Russia. For instance, in February he reported that the Serbian minister on returning from his visit to Russia had declared:

> In each word of your tsar . . . I felt, besides, the special benevolence of his imperial highness for Serbia . . . the tsar's kindness serves also in our eyes as a pledge for the bright future of Serbia, which, of course, without the powerful moral support of Russia cannot succeed in overcoming the difficulties created for it at each step by the neighboring monarchy, always with a hostile attitude in [its] relations with Serbia.[73]

Hartwig's reporting on the June crisis was certainly not of a kind that would contribute to an understanding in St. Petersburg of Serbian events. His first account was contained in a telegram of June 2, where he wrote that the political opposition had forced Pašić to resign.[74] In a despatch of June 16, he gave more details and placed the blame for the crisis on "senseless obstruction" and the jealousy of other political leaders. On the same day he reported further on the Priority Question and the Black Hand.[75] Dismissing the first as a minor affair, he similarly denied the importance of the conspiratorial society, declaring that it never had the smallest sympathy in the army, "which does not intervene in internal affairs," a statement that he must have known was false. At this time he gave his approval of the assumption of power by Prince Alexander, who, he noted, was a supporter of Pašić and appreciated "the careful and wise policy of the first Serbian statesman."[76]

After the assassination in his reports of the Serbian reaction, Hartwig accepted the government's explanation: There had been no

[73]Hartwig to Sazonov, no. 6, Belgrade, February 11/24, 1914, *MO*, series III; 1, pp. 410–11.
[74]Hartwig to Sazonov, telegram no. 160, Belgrade, May 20/June 2, 1914, ibid., III: 3, pp. 172–3.
[75]Hartwig to Sazonov, nos. 33 and 34, Belgrade, June 3/16, 1914, ibid., III: 3, pp. 327–30.
[76]Hartwig to Sazonov, no. 37, Belgrade, June 17/30, ibid., III: 4, pp. 62–4.

official involvement, and the act was the direct result of the Habsburg maladministration of Bosnia-Hercegovina. He emphasized the correct reaction of the Serbian officials and public: "All Serbia expresses itself sympathetically on the occasion of the misfortune that has befallen the neighbor state and condemns the criminal act . . . strongly."[77] Hartwig further reported that Pašić agreed that a strong response should not be given to the attacks that were appearing in the Habsburg press and that Serbia would not react to the "unworthy" Austrian provocation.[78] He also described the effect on Serbian opinion caused by the actions taken in Bosnia by Muslim and Croatian crowds against Serbian individuals and their property, an aspect of the crisis that was to have an important place in both Serbian and Russian diplomatic reporting.

Hartwig's career was soon, however, to come to a sudden end. On July 10, in a moment of high drama, he died of a heart attack in the Habsburg consulate in the arms of the Austrian representative, Baron Wladimir Giesl von Gieslingen.[79] A popular figure, Hartwig was sincerely mourned by the Serbian government and public. Rumors soon circulated in Belgrade that he had been murdered by the Austrians, perhaps poisoned by a cigarette or coffee, or, as Giesl overheard, by an electric chair brought from Vienna.[80] His body was buried in Serbia with great honor by a government and public that were convinced that his Panslav and pro-Serbian opinions were indeed those of official Russia.

After Hartwig's death Vasilii Nikolaevich Shtrandtman, the chargé d'affaires, continued to write in the same spirit as his predecessor: The Serbian government was avoiding provocative acts; it was attempting to calm the press; and it depended on Russia for support and military supplies. Throughout this period the Serbian leaders assured the Russian diplomats that the assassination was an event dangerous for the existence of their kingdom and that it brought all of their plans into disarray. The danger now existed that the monarchy would use this time when Serbia was militarily unprepared, because of the losses in the Balkan Wars, to settle accounts. The Russian representatives were assured that Serbia would accept any Habsburg demands that were compatible with its independence.

[77]Hartwig to Sazonov, no. 40, Belgrade, June 17/30, 1914, ibid., III: 4, pp. 64–5.
[78]Hartwig to Sazonov, telegram no. 187, Belgrade, June 26/July 9, 1914, ibid., III: 4, p. 199.
[79]Shtrandtman to Sazonov, letter, July 1/14, 1914, ibid., III: 4, pp. 263–7.
[80]Wladimir Giesl von Gieslingen, *Zwei Jahrzehnte im Nahen Orient* (Berlin: Verlag für Kulturpolitik, 1927), pp. 260–1.

Throughout the crisis Pašić kept in close touch with the Russian embassy and continually emphasized Serbian dependence on St. Petersburg.

In contrast to the Serbian attitude, the reaction of the Habsburg government was to arouse Russian apprehensions about its true intentions. After the assassination the Habsburg leaders decided that decisive measures would be taken against Serbia, either in the form of military intervention or insistence on the acceptance by its government of humiliating terms. The relationship with Belgrade had been in a condition of crisis for a decade and had certainly presented problems ever since the establishment of the autonomous and then independent state. Viewing the problem as a matter between Vienna and Belgrade alone, the Habsburg government intended to reject all outside interference. At this time it could not submit its grievances against Serbia to a conference of great powers, since it could have as adversaries not only the Russian friends, France and Britain, but also Italy. The support of Germany was requested and given, but Berlin was not consulted on the precise terms to be presented to Serbia. It should be noted that the decision to settle the Serbian problem was made *before* assurances of German support were received. Whether a German negative reply would have affected the Habsburg actions can only be surmised. However, given the general situation and the attitude toward Serbia held by the leading Habsburg statesmen, it was probable that, no matter what the diplomatic situation was, they intended to have a decisive confrontation with their southern neighbor. What is difficult to explain, however, is why they made no attempt to negotiate immediately after the assassination with Russia on what steps should or would be taken, a policy that was in strong contrast to that pursued throughout most of the nineteenth century. Instead, as one scholar has written, they "acted as if Russia did not exist."[81]

Faced with this attitude, the Russian ambassador in Vienna, Nicholas Nikolaevich Shebeko, could not obtain a clear statement of Habsburg intentions. Until the delivery of the ultimatum the Austrian standpoint was that the conspiracy had been organized in Serbia with official involvement, that it was one of a series of similar actions, and that these, together with Panserb propaganda, endan-

---

[81]Samuel E. Williamson, Jr., "Vienna and July 1914: The Origins of the Great War Once More," in S. R. Williamson, Jr., and Peter Pastor, eds., *Essays on World War I: Origins and Prisoners of War* (New York: Social Science Monographs, Brooklyn College Press, 1983), p. 26.

gered Habsburg *internal* stability. Because the Serbian actions affected the monarchy's domestic conditions, the matter was to be handled on a bilateral, not an international, basis. Since the Habsburg officials were determined not to make the conditions that they intended to present to Belgrade a matter of negotiation with Russia, Shebeko had little concrete information to send to St. Petersburg. He reported that when asked what they intended to do, the Habsburg diplomats usually replied that they would decide on their future actions after the investigation of the assassination was concluded.[82] The ambassador, however, did advise his government that it should warn Vienna that it would not accept the imposition of demands on Serbia that would compromise its independence or integrity.[83] Although Shebeko heard rumors that the Habsburg government intended to take strong measures, neither he nor the other European representatives expected a major crisis. In fact, on July 21 Shebeko left Vienna for a vacation in St. Petersburg.

Under these circumstances it can be understood why the harsh Habsburg ultimatum, delivered to Serbia on July 23 and carrying a forty-eight-hour time limit, caused such concern in diplomatic circles.[84] The document, designed to be rejected, accused the Serbian officials of violating the March 1909 declaration and presented them with a series of demands all directed toward changing the relationship between the two countries and securing the suppression of anti-Habsburg agitation and propaganda. The sections that were most controversial dealt with the charge that "the murder at Sarajevo was conceived at Belgrade" and with its investigation. The Serbian government was:

5. to agree to the cooperation in Serbia of the organs of the Imperial and Royal Government in the suppression of the subversive movement directed against the territorial integrity of the Monarchy,

[82]See the declarations of Tisza in Shebeko to Sazonov, no. 45, Vienna, July 3/16, 1914, *MO*, III: 4, pp. 312–13.

[83]Shebeko to Sazonov, telegram no. 88, Vienna, July 3/16, 1914, ibid., III: 4, p. 299. On July 9/22 Sazonov instructed Shebeko to warn Berchtold in a friendly but decisive manner that Austria-Hungary should not take any steps of a character damaging to the dignity of Serbia. Sazonov to Shebeko, telegram no. 1475, July 9/22, 1914, ibid., III: 4, pp. 381–2. In addition to Shebeko's dispatches the Russian government had the excellent report written by Michael Anatolevich Gagarin, the second secretary of the Vienna embassy, who was sent to Sarajevo. Gagarin doubted that there had been official Serbian involvement in the conspiracy, but he also saw few signs of oppression in Bosnia. Enclosure in Shebeko to Sazonov, no. 44, July 3/16, 1914, ibid., III: 4, pp. 299–311.

[84]The text of the ultimatum is in *OA*, VIII, pp. 515–18.

6. to institute a judicial inquiry against the participants in the conspiracy of the twenty-eighth of June who may be found on Serbian territory; agents delegated by the Imperial and Royal Government will take part in the investigations relative to it.

From the point of view of the Russian government, as well as that of other states, the demand for the participation of Habsburg officials represented a violation of Serbian independence. From the Serbian side, their leaders could, of course, not allow an outside investigation that might uncover all the steps leading to the assassination and also confirm many of the other charges.

With his knowledge of Serbian events based primarily on the reports from Vienna and Belgrade, as well as on the reassuring statements of Friedrich Szápáry, the Habsburg ambassador in St. Petersburg, Sazonov naturally was surprised and dismayed by the terms of the ultimatum. Szápáry reported his violent reaction: "You want to make war on Serbia. . . . You set Europe on fire. It is a great responsibility that you assume; you will see the impression that this will make here and in London and Paris and perhaps also elsewhere. They will consider that as an unjustified aggression."[85] Certainly, there had been no warning to St. Petersburg of the Habsburg intentions to take such strong steps. In their conversations with Russian representatives, the Habsburg diplomats had primarily emphasized the common interest of the two countries in opposing conspiracies against established governments. They had also given assurances that it was not the Habsburg intention to humiliate the Serbian government, take any of its territory, or change its relative power position. The goal was simply to end the threat to Habsburg territorial integrity.

These arguments made little impression in St. Petersburg, in particular when the Habsburg authorities, even after a thorough investigation of the actions of the conspirators in Sarajevo, failed to come up with convincing evidence implicating the Serbian government directly in the assassination. Without strong evidence of complicity, they could not expect the Russian leaders to accept their arguments. Certainly, the Russian government was sensitive on questions of political terrorism. In a meeting with the Habsburg councillor of embassy, Otto Czernin, on June 30, Sazanov recognized the threat of revolutionary actions and the common interest of monarchical states "to control this plague."[86] On July 3 he com-

[85]Szápáry to Berchtold, telegram, St. Petersburg, July 24, 1914, ibid., VIII, pp. 645–6.
[86]Czernin to Berchtold, telegram no. 131, St. Petersburg, June 30, 1914, ibid., VIII, pp. 224–5.

mented that "the struggle against treacherous weapons will become more and more a common interest of the monarchies."[87] He and the other Russian diplomats, however, demanded proof of specific Serbian official involvement in such actions. Thus, when on July 19 Szápáry brought up the question of the use of terrorist revolutionary methods, Sazonov replied that "proof of the tolerance of such machinations on the part of the Serbian government" could not be demonstrated.[88]

The same demand for proof arose when Szápáry delivered the terms of the ultimatum to Sazonov. The foreign minister declared that the monarchy was using the opportunity offered by the assassination to make war on Serbia, and "the monarchical idea has nothing to do with that."[89] He also asked for the dossier containing proof of the allegations that the Habsburg officials had previously promised but had not delivered. At this time and again on July 27 he made the same request, but Szápáry was forced to admit that he did not have it.[90] Once more, on July 29, Sazonov asked for this material, arguing that once war started, it would be too late to examine it.

After the reception of the ultimatum the Serbian government turned immediately to St. Petersburg for support. Already on July 21, before the delivery of the ultimatum, Spalajković, now the Serbian representative in St. Petersburg, had presented an urgent request for assistance, emphasizing the peaceful and conciliatory attitude of Serbia and its "willingess to fulfill all the international duties incumbent upon every European state" and expressing concern about the possibility that Austria-Hungary would deliver demands whose acceptance would be a humiliation for the country.

> The danger is there, and the Serbian government has the honor to request the imperial government to take the point of view and the just cause of Serbia under its high protection, and to do, in the name of peace, what it will judge necessary in order that the present situation, due to the tenacity of the Austro-Hungarian schemes, and weighing so heavily on Serbia and the Serbs, give way to better dispositions, so necessary to the pacification of spirits and to the consolidation of good relations between neighboring states.[91]

---

[87]Czernin to Berchtold, no. 31A, St. Petersburg, June 20/July 3, 1914, ibid., VIII, pp. 282–3.

[88]Szápáry to Berchtold, telegram no. 146, St. Petersburg, July 19, 1914, ibid., VIII, p. 495.

[89]Szápáry to Berchtold, telegram no. 157, St. Petersburg, July 24, 1914, ibid., VIII, pp. 646–7.

[90]See Szápáry to Berchtold, telegram no. 160, July 24, and telegram no. 165, July 27, 1914, ibid., VIII, pp. 648–9, 804–6.

[91]Memorandum from Spalajković to Sazonov, confidential, July 9/22, 1914, *MO*, series III: 4, pp. 374–7.

A similar appeal was sent by Prince Regent Alexander to the tsar after the delivery of the ultimatum, whose terms were declared "incompatible with the dignity of Serbia as an independent state and needlessly humiliating." The message concluded:

We are not able to defend ourselves; for that reason we entreat Your Majesty to aid us as soon as possible. Your Majesty has given us so many proofs of his valuable benevolence and we firmly hope that this appeal will find an echo in his Slavic and generous heart. I am the interpreter of the sentiments of the Serbian people who, in these difficult moments pray Your Majesty to consent to interest himself in the destinies of Serbia.[92]

Prince Alexander also visited the Russian consulate, where he denounced the terms of the ultimatum, whose fulfillment he considered impossible "for a government having the smallest feeling for its own dignity." He "placed all his hopes on His Majesty the emperor and Russia, whose commanding word alone could save Serbia."[93]

These appeals were difficult to resist. In the preceding weeks the Russian officials had urged the Serbian government to maintain a calm and moderate attitude, but not to accept conditions damaging to its prestige and independence. The Russian government thus had assumed certain obligations toward its protégé. Moreover, in the absence of proof to the contrary, it did appear that the Habsburg Empire, a great power, with the backing of Germany, without adequate provocation was about to launch an attack upon a small state, Serbia, and was refusing to inform St. Petersburg about its exact intentions. Obviously, given the past history of Serbian–Russian relations, the Russian leaders could not be indifferent to the fate of this nation. They were also not satisfied with the Habsburg explanations and justifications. The assurance that no Serbian territory would be annexed by the monarchy was of little significance; Serbia could be severely weakened by assigning part of its territory to Albania and Bulgaria. The Russian representatives were also aware that either the acceptance of the Habsburg ultimatum or a military defeat would result in the overthrow of the pro-Russian Karadjordjević dynasty and its replacement by an Austrian-oriented ruler. This drastic overturn of the balance of power in the Balkan peninsula could not be accepted by the Russian government.

In addition to the effect that Habsburg control of Serbia would

---

[92]Transmitted in Shtrandtman to Sazonov, telegram no. 215, Belgrade, July 11/24, 1914, *MO*, III: 5, pp. 54–5.
[93]Shtrandtman to Sazonov, telegram no. 212, Belgrade, July 12/25, 1914, ibid., III: 5, pp. 92–3.

have on Russian political-strategic interests and prestige, the Russian leadership had to take into account that influential section of public opinion that had been influenced to a greater or lesser extent by Neoslav, Panslav, and nationalist ideas, as well as those expressed by Duma party leaders.[94] The concepts basic to these programs emphasized the inevitability of a Slav–German conflict and the Russian responsibilities to other Slavs. Their predictions about the future now appeared to be approaching fulfillment. Even Sazonov, who previously had shown little sympathy for the "Slavic idea" as such, viewed the crisis in 1914 in similar terms. In his public declarations and later in his memoirs he placed full blame on Germany, not on Austria-Hungary or Serbia.

His position was made clear in the important meeting of the Council of Ministers held on July 24 to discuss the response to the ultimatum. Here he called for a firm policy and the support of Serbia, declaring that Russia, which had made "immense sacrifices" for the Slavic people, should continue "her historic mission" or "she would be considered a decadent state and would henceforth have to take second place among the powers . . . Russian prestige in the Balkans [would] collapse utterly."[95] His views reflected those of his colleagues, who also saw Germany as the main opponent and who, although realizing that their country was not ready for war, did not think that concessions would ensure peace. Thus Alexander Vasil'evich Krivoshein, the influential minister of agriculture, argued: "All factors tended to prove that the most judicious policy Russia could follow in present circumstances was a return to a firmer and more energetic attitude towards the unreasonable claims of the Central European powers." Peter Lvovich Bark, the minister

[94]The influence of the parties has been aptly described: "The Octobrists, the Progressists, the Kadets, and often also the Moderate Rights/Nationalists were seeking a foundation for their own political standing. . . . And of course they found it in the Russian 'people,' a source of authority to which they could always appeal. Persistent reference to the 'people' led them in foreign policy and nationality questions to take up attitudes which were (with the regular exception of certain Kadets) both Russian nationalist and Pan-Slav, and which helped to create the climate of opinion wherein war against Germany and Austria-Hungary appeared an acceptable and indeed necessary instrument of policy." Hoskins, *The Russian Constitutional Experiment*, p. 215.

[95]Quoted in Lieven, *Russia and the Origins of the First World War*, p. 142, from the unpublished memoirs of Peter Bark. For the meeting of the Council of Ministers see ibid., pp. 141–4, and the journal of the Russian Council of Ministers for July 11/24, 1914, *MO*, Series III: 5, pp. 38–40.

of finance, similarly opposed yielding, "since the honour, dignity and authority of Russia were at stake."[96] In general agreement, the ministers decided that Serbia should be supported, that Russian policy should be firm, and that the possibility of war had to be faced. In addition, they agreed to request the Habsburg government to extend the time limit of the ultimatum to allow the other powers to investigate the charges. Serbia was to be advised to accept the conditions that did not endanger its independence and, should Austria-Hungary attack, not to respond but to appeal to the great powers. Agreement was also reached on a possible partial mobilization. Nicholas II accepted these recommendations.

The decisions in regard to Serbia were communicated by Sazonov to Spalajković, who reported them back to Belgrade in terms that could only strengthen Serbian resolve.[97] Sazonov, the minister wrote, denounced the ultimatum, which he believed contained demands that a state could not accept without committing suicide. Although Serbia could "unquestionably" count on Russian support, its form had yet to be determined. The tsar would decide, and France would be consulted. This encouraging message, which was received in Belgrade when the Serbian leaders were discussing the answer to be delivered to the ultimatum, may or may not have influenced the decision not to agree to all the demands. On July 25, after the Serbian government refused to accept the Habsburg ultimatum unconditionally, Giesl broke diplomatic relations and departed for Vienna; on July 28 the Habsburg Empire declared war on Serbia.

During this time of acute crisis the Serbian government remained in close touch with St. Petersburg. On July 27 Nicholas II replied to Prince Alexander's previous appeal for assistance.[98] While advising the Serbian government to try to avoid war, but also to safeguard "the dignity of Serbia," he concluded:

As long as there is the least hope of avoiding an effusion of blood, all our efforts should be turned toward that aim. If, in spite our most sincere desire we do not succeed in this, His Highness can be assured that in any case Russia is not disinterested in the fate of Serbia.

[96]Lieven, *Russia and the Origins of the First World War*, p. 43.
[97]Spalajković to Pašić, telegram no. 56, St. Petersburg, July 11/24 1914. *Dokumenti o spoljnoj politici Kraljevine Srbije* (Belgrade: Srpska Akademija nauka i umetnosti, 1980), VII: 2, pp. 648–9.
[98]Nicholas II to Prince Alexander, July 14/27, 1914, ibid., VII: 2, pp. 691–2.

In his answer, written on July 30 when his country was already at war, Alexander touched on the Slavic theme.

This extremely painful moment can only reaffirm the bonds of the profound attachment that unite Serbia to Holy Slavic Russia and the sentiments of eternal recognition for the aid and protection of Your Majesty will be piously conserved in the soul of every Serb.[99]

Although assurances were sent to Belgrade, the Russian leaders, even after the Habsburg declaration of war on Serbia, continued to attempt to find a peaceful resolution to the crisis, either through international negotiations or by direct Russian–Austrian discussions. Neither Nicholas II nor his advisers wanted a war for which Russia was not yet adequately prepared. When the tsar, with extreme reluctance, agreed to full mobilization on July 30, he and the other Russian officials did not expect the action to lead directly to war, but they recognized the danger. On August 1 Germany declared war on Russia, with Austria-Hungary joining in combat on August 6.

The outbreak of World War I found the Russian officials and the public in agreement. The fact that Germany took the decisive step, of course, made the situation clearer. However, even before, the responsible Russian leaders shared a similar point of view on the ultimatum and the Habsburg action against Serbia, which they, like the tsar, regarded as "an ignoble war" on a "weak country."[100] The reactions of Shebeko and Sazonov, as recorded in their memoirs and their official reports, reflected the general beliefs. Thus on July 30 Shebeko told Berchtold, now the Habsburg foreign minister, that "the attack on little Serbia by a powerful empire such as Austria, supposedly in order to defend its own existence, cannot be understood by anyone in my country; it has been considered simply as a means of delivering a death-blow to Serbia."[101] Sazonov, convinced of the "innocence" of the Serbian government "from any complicity in the Sarajevo murders," and with faith in Pašić's "firmness and wisdom,"[102] saw the events as the result of a conspiracy between Germany and Austria-Hungary to destroy Serbia and eliminate Russian influence from the Balkan peninsula. As he wrote: "The absurd accusation of complicity in the murder of the only Habsburg who showed any interest in the fate of the Slavonic subjects of the Dual Monarchy was obviously but a pretext for destroying the

[99]Prince Alexander to Nicholas II, Niš, July 17/30, 1914, ibid., VII: 2, p. 745.
[100]Nicholas II to William II, telegram, July 15/28, *MO*, series III: 5, p. 181.
[101]Schebeko, *Souvenirs* (Paris: Bibliothèque diplomatique, 1936), pp. 255–7.
[102]Sazonov, *Fateful Years*, pp. 151, 177.

Serbian state, over whose ruins Austria-Hungary hoped to join hands with her protégé, Ferdinand of Coburg." Habsburg domination over the peninsula would "deliver the Slavonic East, bound hand and foot, into the power of Austria-Hungary, to exclude once for all from the Balkans the influence of Russia – the legacy of a century and a half of effort and sacrifice on behalf of the Balkan nations."[103]

Although Russia was again drawn into a war because of its Balkan commitments, in contrast to the situation in 1828, 1853, and 1877, the state was not fighting alone. In this account of the assassination crisis the position of the Russian Entente allies, France and Britain, has not been discussed because, in fact, their views played a very small part in influencing Russian decisions. As we have seen, although sharing similar interests in preserving the continental balance of power against Germany, Russia and its allies did not have the same policies in the Near East. In 1914, as previously, France, with its enormous financial investment in the Ottoman Empire and the Balkan states, opposed changes in the status quo, although the French president, Raymond Poincaré, wished to strengthen the bonds of the alliance.[104] As events unfolded, however, France was drawn into the war because of circumstances that its leaders could not control.

As in other European capitals, there was little awareness in Paris that the assassination would lead to a general catastrophe. As a result, Poincaré, accompanied by the foreign minister, René Viviani, and the political director of the foreign ministry, Pierre de Margerie, left for a state visit to St. Petersburg on July 15, returning to Paris only on July 29, a day after Austria-Hungary declared war on Serbia. Although the threatening situation was discussed in St. Petersburg, there is no indication that French opinion played a part in determining the Russian decisions. In fact, there was no formal consultation about the Russian mobilization, as was required by the alliance agreement. In this crisis the French government gave its Russian ally the same degree of unqualified support that Germany offered to Austria-Hungary. The German declaration of war on Russia, of course, brought into effect the alliance obligations. Although the British position was at first not clear, that state entered the conflict

[103]Ibid., pp. 178–9.
[104]For French policy see John F. V. Keiger, *France and the Origins of the First World War* (New York: St. Martin's Press, 1983).

after the German invasion of Belgium. The Russian alliance system thus did function in a time of crisis.

The outbreak of the war did not, however, end the difficulties experienced by the Russian government in its relations with the Balkan states. Only Serbia and Montenegro were at first on the Russian side; Greece, Romania, and Bulgaria, as well as the Ottoman Empire, remained neutral. Albania did not have an organized government until the postwar period. In November the Ottoman Empire joined with the Central Powers, thus cutting direct communications between Russia and its Western allies. Thereafter the acquisition of the Straits and Constantinople became a principal Russian war aim. Following negotiations over territorial compensation in Macedonia, Bulgaria entered the war in September 1915 on the side of the Central Powers, a move that doomed the Serbian resistance; after a military disaster, its government and the remnants of its army moved to Corfu. Subsequently, Romania in 1916 and Greece in 1917 joined the Entente. After the abdication of Nicholas II in March 1917, the Provisional Government attempted to continue the war, a policy that was reversed after the October Revolution. The denunciation of the wartime agreements by the Bolsheviks and their break in relations with the ultimately victorious Western powers meant that Russia had little to say about the territorial settlements after the war.

This final period in the relations of tsarist Russia with the Balkan nations made evident the difficulties and contradictions in the situation. At this time the Russian government had to deal with independent states, each with aggressive national programs involving territorial expansion. Unfortunately for all concerned, their governments had overlapping objectives, with the Greek–Serbian–Bulgarian conflict over Macedonia being the most difficult problem. The struggle over disputed lands made it impossible for the Russian government to achieve its aim of bringing the states together under its leadership or to implement a policy of the "the Balkans for the Balkan people" to oppose Habsburg influence. Moreover, the national movements continued, as before, to involve dangers for the Russian state. Previously, as we have seen, Russian connections with the Balkan Christians had led to wars with the Ottoman Empire and in 1854 also with the great powers, France and Britain. The situation in 1914 was to be even more complex, but at this time the Russian government once again came to the support of a Balkan nationality with a program whose intricacies were not fully understood in St. Petersburg. However, once Serbia became its major ally in the

Balkans and the declarations of its leaders were believed, the Russian statesmen could not see that state fall under Habsburg control. On July 27, 1914 Sazonov told Szápáry that "he had no feeling for the Balkan Slavs." They were a "heavy burden" and Russia had "had to suffer on account of them already."[105] Nevertheless, it was this Orthodox and Slavic tie, continuing into the twentieth century, that drew Russia into its fifth Balkan war since the beginning of the nineteenth century.

[105]Szápáry to Berchtold, telegram no. 165a, St. Petersburg, July 27, 1914, *OA*, VIII, pp. 804–6.

A century of Balkan involvement:
Gains and losses

This survey has covered over a century of the relationship of tsarist
Russia with the Balkan national movements, with the emphasis on
the special relationship that existed between the Russian government and the Orthodox and Slavic peoples of the region. As we have
seen, by 1914, at least in part because of the wars between Russia and
the Ottoman Empire, six independent states – Albania, Bulgaria,
Greece, Montenegro, Romania, and Serbia – had come into existence. Despite this fact, at the time of the outbreak of World War I
only Serbia and Montenegro could be regarded as firm Russian
friends. In the next years, the other Balkan states joined the camp
that could offer the best rewards or exert the strongest pressure. Thus
one of the great Russian illusions of the nineteenth century, that
liberated national states would provide faithful allies, was effectively
shattered.

If the war offered few examples of Russian–Balkan mutual support,
the Bolshevik revolution broke decisively the remaining connections,
at least on the official level. The Russian withdrawal from the war, the
Allied intervention, and the very nature of the Russian revolution
created a breach between East and West after 1918, with the Balkan
nations, as well as the Habsburg succession states, cooperating with
France, or Italy, and, finally, some with Germany. The extent of the
estrangement is shown by the fact that Greece recognized the Bolshevik regime in 1924, but Albania, Bulgaria, and Romania only in
1934. Yugoslavia, due partly to the former close dynastic ties, delayed
until 1940. At the time of the invasion of the Soviet Union in 1941,
both Romania and Bulgaria were German allies, although Bulgarian
troops did not participate in the action. Thus, when Soviet troops in

1944 entered Romania, Bulgaria, Yugoslavia, and, indirectly, gained control of Albania, they were resuming a relationship, of course under entirely different circumstances, that had been interrupted for over a quarter of a century.

In considering the attitude of tsarist Russia toward the Balkan peninsula, it is important to remember that the region had a major geopolitical significance for wider imperial policy. In the nineteenth century the status of the Straits and the defense of the Black Sea were vital concerns for a state with extensive frontiers to defend. During most of this period the Russian leadership identified Britain as its principal adversary on the world scene and France as its major opponent in Europe. Since the Russian southern frontiers, the lands in the Caucasus, and the communications with Central Asia were vulnerable to attack from the sea, the attitude of the naval powers had to be watched carefully. The diplomatic alignment of Romania and Bulgaria, also Black Sea powers, was also similarly important. When the alliance with France became the mainstay of Russian diplomacy, the allegiance of the Balkan states became even more significant. Not only did they possess useful armies, but they could provide valuable assistance by opening a third front against the Central Powers and by drawing Habsburg troops from the Galician frontier. In 1914 the Russian government thus had a strong military interest in preserving its influence in Serbia, and it had hopes of winning Romania away from the Triple Alliance.

General security and strategic considerations did indeed play a role in involving Russia, in one manner or another, in the five wars under discussion. This account, however, has attempted to emphasize other motivations as being perhaps primarily responsible for drawing Russia into conflicts that, in the wider view, were disasters for the economic development of the state and certainly complicated its relationship with other powers. Throughout this text the declarations issued by the tsars before each war have been extensively quoted. Allowing for the rhetorical exaggeration of such documents, they did express what the Russian leadership felt at the time. Although responsible officials in each crisis acted to prevent war, there was indeed a strong current of support for Slavs and Orthodox Christians, all of whom were popularly believed to be suffering innumerable horrors under Ottoman and Habsburg rule. To a surprising degree the defense of these people remained part of Russian national mythology even after the decline of Panslavism as a political program. In addition, before the Crimean War the Russian relationship to the Balkan Christians had been defined in treaties with the Ottoman Empire. Their maintenance thus involved Russian honor, an important concept in the nineteenth century.

The Russian military excursions in the peninsula, although gaining that state few lasting advantages, did give the Balkan national movements needed assistance at crucial times. Thus Romanian autonomy and then independence were a result of successful Russian wars; the organization of autonomous Bulgaria in 1878 came about after a Russian victory. The Russian campaigns of 1828 and 1829 created the situation that enabled the powers to establish an independent Greece. Similarly, Russian military and diplomatic efforts made possible the widening of Serbian autonomy and its achievement of independence. Russian backing of the Balkan League in 1912 allowed the member states to divide the rest of the Ottoman territories in Europe. Certainly, the repeated Russian claims that their blood and money had created these states had some justification.

The attitude of the Balkan leaders was quite different. As we have seen, they were willing to use a quite subservient vocabulary in their appeals to St. Petersburg. Typical of this approach was the declaration of Alexander Ipsilanti in March 1821 at the commencement of the Greek revolution:

> Do not disregard, Sire, the prayers of ten million Christians, who, faithful to our divine Redeemer, are at the same time stirred by hatred for their tyrants. Save us, Sire, save religion from its persecutors; restore our churches and our altars that from the great nation which you govern the divine light of the Gospel may shine forth. Deliver us, Sire, purge Europe from the bloody monsters and deign to add to all the great titles which Europe already gives you that of Liberator of Greece.[1]

Similar statements at later times have been cited, including Regent Alexander's appeals during the assassination crisis to Nicholas's "Slavic and generous heart" and "Holy Slavic Russia." Although many of the authors of such declarations might indeed have been expressing their true feelings, it can be safely assumed that in general they were simply using the forms and vocabulary best suited to winning Russian assistance.[2] Unfortunately, many Russian officials

---

[1] Quoted in Charles A. Frazee, *The Orthodox Church and Independent Greece, 1821–1852* (Cambridge: Cambridge University Press, 1969), p. 17.

[2] The Russian authorities may also have expected this approach. In his memoirs Nekliudov commented: "In our country everyone was so accustomed, when addressing the Monarch, to using a semi-biblical, semi-servile language, taken from the litanies of the Church, that a similar style was expected of the Slav and Orthodox *clientèle* of the Great Empire and the 'White Tsar' when addressing him." A. V. Nekliudov, *Diplomatic Reminiscences: Before and during the World War, 1911–1917* (New York: E. P. Dutton and Company, 1920), p. 173.

took such words seriously, a situation that led to later misunderstandings.

The major cause of future tension was, as we have seen, not the Russian military assistance, but the fact that Russian officials after the victories often refused to leave. The role of the Russian government in the establishment of the political institutions of the new states has been explained. It has also been emphasized that, in general, the Russian efforts were well-meaning. Instead of attempting to transplant Russian autocracy into the Balkans, Russian administrators took what they regarded as advanced European institutions as their models and thus in fact introduced Western forms of representative government into the Balkans.

The basic problem was the different approaches of the Russian statesmen and the Balkan leaders to their mutual relationship. With an attitude often characterized by heavy-handed benevolence, the Russian officials serving in the Balkans expected the local regimes to follow their leadership and treat their commands with respect and gratitude. In other words, they wished the Balkan leaders to accord to them the same degree of docile obedience, even servility, that, at least in theory, governed their own relations with the autocratic tsar. Unfortunately for the success of their policies, no Balkan regime or political leader looked upon Russia, its tsar, or its representatives in this manner.

In fact, the reaction was often quite the opposite. Accustomed to resistance to political authority, whether exerted by the Porte, a Russian representative, or their own officials, Balkan populations were consistently critical in their judgments of the Russian presence in the peninsula. Perhaps even more important, most Balkan leaders, certainly by the middle of the nineteenth century, had direct experience with life in Western and Central Europe. In comparison, they found little to admire in tsarist Russia. Paris, not St. Petersburg or Moscow, approached their model of an ideal city.[3]

Nevertheless, the political leaders correctly judged that Russia was the great power from which aid could most easily be obtained. Once

---

[3]Some Russian diplomats recognized this situation. Roman Romanovich Rosen, formerly ambassador to the United States and an opponent of Balkan involvements, wrote a memorandum for the tsar in 1912, stating: "As far as material culture is concerned, Russia stands in as little need of Slavdom as Slavdom does of Russia. Culture in the Slav countries of Austria stands by no means on a lower plane than in Russia, and in Bohemia, for instance, one might say on a higher one." Baron Rosen, *Forty Years of Diplomacy* (London: Allen & Unwin, 1922), p. 93.

Russian military and financial resources had been utilized, however, they wanted the benefactor to go home. They did not consider the fact that most debts, whether private or national, usually must be paid. The Balkan attitude was well expressed by Liuben Karavelov in 1870: "If Russia comes to liberate, she will be received with great sympathy; but if she comes to rule, she will find many enemies."[4]

The reaction of the Balkan governments in rejecting Russian control caused enormous disappointment in St. Petersburg. The wars were waged at a huge cost in casualties and money. In more than a century of warfare against the Ottoman Empire, Russia had won extensions of territory on its Asiatic borders, but only Bessarabia in Europe, which was gained in 1812 but lost after World War I. For these meager rewards the state paid a high price, most obviously in military casualties. In 1828–9 the Russian army lost 40,000 men, in the Crimean War 450,000, and in 1877–8 120,000, figures far overshadowed by the 3,000,000 killed and wounded in World War I.

The economic aspects of these wars are more complicated and require an examination of more than the direct costs of the military operations. During this entire period the backward economic conditions in Russia made it difficult for the state to maintain its position as a great power even in peacetime. The wars thus greatly strained the resources of the state. The wartime expenses were usually met by the imposition of extra taxes, but principally by domestic and foreign borrowing and, most important, by printing money. Throughout the century Russian finance ministers regularly expressed concern about the instability of the Russian currency and its adverse effect on the economy. With their attention devoted to promoting internal prosperity and later industrial development, they naturally opposed a foreign policy that might lead to war, and they tried to cut down military costs. This in 1828 Egor Frantsevich Kankrin, the finance minister, sought to reduce the estimates for the coming war with the Ottoman Empire, arguing that "the more cheaply we fight, the more we raise the might of Russia."[5] Although this conflict caused no major economic problems, the Crimean War was another matter. An authority has written: "The bad state of Russian finances during almost all of the second half of the nineteenth century has thus its

---

[4]Quoted in Charles Jelavich, *Tsarist Russia and Balkan Nationalism: Russian Influence in the Internal Affairs of Bulgaria and Serbia, 1876–1886* (Berkeley: University of California Press, 1958), p. vii.
[5]Quoted in John Shelton Curtiss, *The Russian Army under Nicholas I, 1825–1855* (Durham, N.C.: Duke University Press, 1965), p. 55.

source in the Crimean War."[6] The financing of the conflict proved a definite problem. London banks, previously the chief source for loans, could not, of course, be used. The Russian government thus relied primarily on the printing press and internal loans. The number of paper rubles in circulation doubled, and the national debt rose from 108 million rubles in 1853 to 533 million in 1856.[7]

The entire issue of economic advancement as against foreign wars was thoroughly discussed in the debates preceding the war of 1877. In October 1876 M. K. Reutern, the minister of finance, it will be remembered, sent a memorandum to Alexander II strongly opposing war.[8] His pessimistic predictions were to prove well founded. When the war commenced, the government could not obtain adequate loans abroad, and since neither an increase in taxes nor domestic borrowing could meet the needs, the printing presses were again put to work. The official estimate on the cost of this war was 910 million rubles, but this figure does not include the losses connected with the depreciation of the Russian currency.[9] After the war the value of the paper ruble of 100 kopeks fell to 69 gold kopeks, signifying a 31 percent depreciation.[10]

The exact degree to which the wars over Balkan affairs impeded Russian economic development, a question far more important than the exact monetary cost of the campaigns, is difficult to assess. One writer has commented: "In the long run an active foreign policy not only affected Russia's finances, but tended indirectly to perpetuate the backwardness of her economy, as all potential savings were skimmed off by taxation and absorbed by the budget for military and other mainly unproductive expenditures."[11] Certainly, those most concerned with Russian economic advancement at the time shared this opinion.

---

[6]Bertrand Gille, *Histoire économique et sociale de la Russia du moyen âge au XXe siècle* (Paris: Payot, 1949), p. 158.

[7]See ibid., pp. 157–9, and Olga Crisp, *Studies in the Russian Economy before 1914* (New York: Barnes and Noble, 1976), pp. 96–7.

[8]W. Graf Reutern-Baron Nolcken, *Die finanzielle Sanierung Russlands nach der Katastrophe des Krimkrieges 1862 vis 1878 durch den finanzminister Michael von Reutern* (Berlin: Georg Reimer, 1914), pp. 121–30.

[9]Frederick Martin, *The Statesman's Year-Book: 1879* (London: Macmillan and Co., 1879), p. 377.

[10]Roger Portal, "The Industrialization of Russia," in H. J. Habakkuk and M. Postan, eds., *The Cambridge Economic History of Europe* (Cambridge: Cambridge University Press, 1966), VI, p. 815.

[11]Olga Crisp, *Studies in the Russian Economy before 1914*, p. 97. See also Walter Pintner, "Inflation in Russia during the Crimean War Period," *Slavic and East European Review*, XVIII: 1 (February 1959), pp. 81–7.

They particularly disliked the depreciation of the currency associated with the wars. Successive finance ministers throughout the century, all interested primarily in internal development, believed that a stable currency and a balanced budget were needed to attract the foreign capital that they considered essential for Russian economic advancement. The military ventures, which had made this prerequisite difficult to attain, thus in their eyes retarded the pace of development.[12]

Russian diplomats, as well as those concerned with economic affairs, were also quite aware of the relationship of war and internal reform. In September 1877, in the midst of the fighting, Jomini wrote to Giers, who was at that time in charge of the ministry in St. Petersburg:

> The emancipated brother Slavs will astonish us with their ingratitude . . . I continue to think that instead of pursuing these Slavic fantasies, we should have done better to have taken care of our own Christian Slavs. If the emperor wished to descend from official heights and splendors and play Haroun al Rashid, if he wished to visit incognito the suburbs of Bucharest and his own capital, he would be convinced of all that there was to do to civilize, organize and develop his own country and he would be convinced that a crusade against drunkedness and syphilis was more necessary and profitable to Russia than the ruinous crusade against the Turks for the profit of the Bulgarians![13]

This situation, the fact that the Russian government did wage wars that benefited Balkan nations, and that those states, once established, insisted upon acting independently, caused a reaction in Russian diplomatic circles that was in a sense unique among the great powers. A theme of ingratitude runs not only through their commentaries on the Balkan attitudes but also through the accounts of other relationships. Thus Russian policy toward the Habsburg Empire after 1856 was deeply influenced by the idea of "betrayal," that is, that the monarchy had not repaid the "debt" owed because of the Russian intervention in Hungary in 1849. Similar charges were made against Germany after 1878; that state had failed to repay the Russian favorable attitude toward the Prussian unification of Germany. The criticisms of the Balkan states were bound to be even more severe. Responsible Russian statesmen, often completely for-

---

[12]See Haim Barkai, "The Macro-Economics of Tsarist Russia in the Industrialization Era: Monetary Developments, the Balance of Payments and the Gold Standard," *Journal of Economic History*, XXXIII: 2 (June 1973), pp. 339–71.

[13]Jomini to Giers, September 1, 1877. Charles Jelavich and Barbara Jelavich, eds., *Russia in the East, 1876–1880: The Russo–Turkish War and the Kuldja Crisis as Seen Through the Letters of A. G. Jomini to N. K. Giers* (Leiden: E. J. Brill, 1959), pp. 59–60.

getting that the national movements were in fact initiated by the Balkan leaders, were convinced that it was their efforts alone that had brought victory and that sufficient gratitude for this achievement had not been shown. Thus two words, "blood" and "treasure," were often repeated. Examples of this attitude have been quoted previously, but the reaction was perhaps best expressed by Giers in his frequent comments on the Bulgarian actions in the 1880s. In November 1885 he told the British ambassador in St. Petersburg, Sir Robert Morier, that Russia had received "a lesson we can never forget and which is most wholesome for us – Never again to go forth making moral conquests with our blood and money but to think of ourselves and our interests only."[14]

In October 1886 he continued on the same theme, believing that the answer to the problem was

a total abandonment by Russia of Bulgaria, and all her concerns, as a country deep dyed in ingratitude, against which the Slav mother should shake off the dust of her feet.[15]

He expressed similar feelings in July 1887:

The dominant feeling . . . is one of disgust at the ingratitude of the Bulgarian people, and at the folly which made Russia shed so much blood and waste so much treasure on such people.[16]

Despite the recurrent disillusionment, Russian preoccupation with Balkan affairs, as we have seen, remained constant. It is both tragic and ironic that in 1914 the tsarist regime entered a war that brought its own downfall as a result of its support of a cause that involved principles it had spent a century denouncing. From the reign of Alexander I the Russian leadership had consistently opposed underground conspiracies, particularly those originating in military circles, and it had certainly acted decisively against national manifestations in its own lands. Russian officials had also resented foreign interference in these matters, such as French concern over Polish affairs. Moreover, as far as the Balkan national programs were concerned, they had not previously approved those with imperial goals, such as the Greek Great Idea, that involved territory

[14]Morier to Rosebery, no. 384c, secret and confidential, St. Petersburg, November 11, 1885. Great Britain. Foreign Office, Political Despatches, 65/1219.
[15]Morier to Iddesleigh, FO 65/1262, no. 366 most confidential, St. Petersburg, October 13, 1886.
[16]Morier to Salisbury, FO 65/1297, no. 260 confidential, St. Petersburg, July 26, 1887.

inhabited by a mixed population. At San Stefano the Russian negotiators did indeed create a large Bulgaria, but its boundaries were very similar to those agreed upon by the powers at the Constantinople Conference of 1876.

Yet in 1914, after a century of acting as a restraint on Balkan imperial romantic-national goals, Russia gave its support to Serbia, where a secret organization, with perhaps a controlling influence in the army, took part in a conspiracy, whose aim was known to at least some high officials. It resulted in the assassination of the heir to the Habsburg throne, an action that involved monarchist as well as revolutionary principles. Moreover, at this time Russian statesmen gave encouragement to the Serbian irredentist program, aimed at the eventual weakening or breakup of the Habsburg Empire, without, it appears, any responsible consideration of the alternatives to the Habsburg organization of Danubian Europe.

The Russian ministers and the tsar, of course, did not know the details of the conspiracy, nor did they understand the complex relationship of the Habsburg nationalities. As far as Serbia was concerned, they had been consistently misinformed, if not openly lied to, not only by the Serbian officials but also by their own representative, Hartwig. Without understanding the situation, and in the face of the failure of the Habsburg government to make its motives clear or to agree to discuss the crisis on an international basis, the Russian leaders naturally fell back on the assumptions of the previous century. The conviction that Russia, having "called into life" the Balkan states, was somehow responsible for their defense remained strong. As in previous crises, the frequently repeated phrases about responsibilities and "historic missions" were bound to continue their hold on Russian minds. Thus, for instance, in a conversation with Grey in August 1914, the Russian ambassador, Benckendorff, compared Britain's role in Belgium and Holland to that of Russia in the peninsula: "we have assumed in the Balkans the protection of the small states that owe their existence to treaties just as England has done the same in the north of Europe. To each his duty."[17]

The combination of the concepts of honor, duty, and the connection with the Balkan people were all expressed by Nicholas II in his

---

[17]Benckendorff to Sazonov, telegram no. 249, London, July 22/August 4, 1914. *Mezhdunarodnye otnosheniia v epokhy imperializma* (Moscow: Gosudarstvennoe sotsial'no-ekonomicheskoe izdatel'stvo, 1938), series III; 5, pp. 407–8.

manifesto of August 3, 1914 which thus forms a fitting conclusion to
this narrative:

> By the grace of God, we, Nicholas II, Emperor and Autocrat of all the Russians,
> King of Poland, and Grand Duke of Finland, etc., to all our faithful subjects make
> known that Russia, related by faith and blood to the Slav peoples and faithful to
> her historical traditions, has never regarded their fates with indifference.
>
> But the fraternal sentiments of the Russian people for the Slavs have been
> awakened with perfect unanimity and extraordinary force in these last few days,
> when Austria-Hungary knowingly addressed to Servia claims inacceptable for an
> independent State. . . .
>
> Today it is not only the protection of a country related to us and unjustly
> attacked that must be accorded, but we must safeguard the honor, the dignity, and
> the integrity of Russia and her position among the great powers.[18]

---

[18]*The New York Times Current History: The European War*, I, (1915), p. 358. On
October 11 Georgii Petrovich Bakhmetev, the ambassador to the United States,
offered a similar opinion: "The whole situation in a nutshell is that Germany
entered the war from racial hate and motives of commercial greed, while Russia
drew her sword out of motives of humane and kindly sympathy for a small and
oppressed nation of her own kindred. Germany had been grabbing and wished to
grab more; Russia rose in arms to stand by and protect her 'little brother.'" Ibid..
p. 364.

Bibliography

Because of the large number of books available on European diplomatic history in the century discussed here, all of which deal in some manner with Russian policy, this bibliography has been limited to a listing primarily of material cited in the footnotes. Articles and archival sources are not included.

Published documents

Baumgart, Winfried, ed. *Akten zur Geschichte des Krimkriegs: Osterreichische Akten zur Geschichte des Krimkriegs*. Series I, 3 vols. Munich: R. Oldenbourg Verlag, 1979–1980.

Bittner, Ludwig, and Hans Uebersberger, eds. *Osterreich-Ungarns Aussenpolitik von der bosnischen Krise 1908 bis zum Kriegsausbruch 1914*. 9 vols. Vienna: Osterreichischer Bundesverlag, 1930.

Bogićević, Miloš. *Das auswärtige Politik Serbiens, 1903–1914*. 3 vols. Berlin: Brückenverlag, 1928–31.

Bulgaria: Ministerstvo na Vŭnshnite Raboti na NRB. *Vŭnshnata politika na Bŭlgarii: dokumenti i materiali*. Sofia: Nauka i izkustvo, 1978.

Bŭlgarska akademiia na naukite. *Dokumenti za bŭlgarskata istoriia*. 6 vols. Sofia: Dŭrzhavna pechatnitsa, 1931–51.

Dokumenti o spoljnoj politici Kraljevine Srbije. Vols. V–VII. Belgrade: Srpska Akademija nauka i umetnosti, 1980–5.

France: Ministère des affaires étrangères. *Documents diplomatiques français, 1871–1914*. 41 vols. in 42. Paris: Imprimerie nationale, 1929–59.

Gooch, G. P., and Harold Temperley, eds. *British Documents on the Origins of War, 1898–1914*. 11 vols. London: His Majesty's Stationery Office, 1926–38.

Great Britain, Foreign Office. *British and Foreign State Papers*. Vols. LXXVI, LXXVII. London: William Ridgway, 1892–3.

Hertslet, Edward. *The Map of Europe by Treaty*. 4 vols. London: Butterworths, 1875–91.

Hurewitz, J. C. *Diplomacy in the Near and Middle East*. Vol. I. Princeton, N.J.: D. Van Nostrand Company, Inc., 1956.

Institutul de Istorie Nicolae Iorga. *Revoluţia din 1821 condusă de Tudor Vladimirescu: documente externe*. Bucharest: Editura Academiei Republicii Socialiste România, 1980.

Jelavich, Barbara. *Russia and Greece during the Regency of King Othon, 1832–1835: Russian Documents on the First Years of Greek Independence*. Thessaloniki: Institute for Balkan Studies, 1962.

Bibliography

Lepsius, Johannes, Albrecht Mendelssohn Bartholdy, and Friedrich Thimme. *Die Grosse Politik der Europäischen Kabinette, 1871–1914.* 40 vols. in 54. Berlin: Verlagsgesellschaft für Politik und Geschichte, 1922–7.

Mezhdunarodnye otnosheniia v epokhu imperializma. Series 2 and 3. Moscow: Gosudarstvennoe sotsial'no-ekonomicheskoe izdatel'stvo, 1931–8.

Ministerstvo inostrannykh del SSSR. *Vneshniaia politika Rossii XIX i nachale XX veka: Dokumenty Rossiiskogo ministerstva inostrannykh del.* Vols. I–XIV. Moscow: Izdatel'stvo nauka, 1960–5.

Noradounghian, Gabriel, ed. *Recueil d'actes internationaux de l'Empire Ottoman.* 4 vols. in 3. Nendeln, Liechtenstein: Kraus Reprint, 1978.

Osvobozhdenie Bolgarii ot turetskogo iga. 3 vols. Moscow: Izdatel'stvo Akademii nauk SSSR, 1961–7.

Pavićević, Branko. *Rusija i aneksiona kriza, 1908–1909.* Vol. I. Titograd: Crnogorska Akademija nauka i umjetnosti, 1984.

Pervoe serbskoe vosstanie 1804–1813 gg. i Rossiia. 2 vols. Moscow: Izdatel'stvo nauka, 1980–3.

Pribram, Alfred Franzis. *The Secret Treaties of Austria-Hungary, 1879–1914.* 2 vols. Cambridge, Mass.: Harvard University Press, 1921–2.

Prokesch-Osten, Anton von. *Geschichte des Abfalls der Griechen vom Türkischen Reiche im Jahre 1821 und der Gründung des Hellenischen Königreiches.* 6 vols. Vienna: Carl Gerold's Sohn, 1867.

Sturdza, Dimitri A. *Acte și documente relative la istoria renascerei României.* 9 vols. Bucharest: Carol Göbl, 1900–9.

Memoirs, letters, diaries

Basily, Nicholas Aleksandrovich, *Memoirs.* Stanford: Hoover Institution Press, 1973.

Charykov, Nicholas Valerievich. *Glimpses of High Politics: Through War and Peace, 1855–1929.* New York: Macmillan, 1931.

Chichagov, Paul Vasil'evich. *Mémoires de l'Amiral Tchitchagoff, 1767–1849.* Leipzig: A. Franck'sche Verlags-Buchhandlung, 1862.

Giesl von Gieslingen, Wladimir. *Zwei Jahrzehnte im Nahen Orient.* Berlin: Verlag für Kulturpolitik, 1927.

Hoetzsch, Otto, ed. *Peter von Meyendorff: ein russischer Diplomat an den Höfen von Berlin und Wien: Briefwechsel.* 3 vols. Berlin and Leipzig: Walter de Gruyter & Co., 1923.

Hübner, J. A. von. *Neuf ans de souvenirs d'un ambassadeur d'Autriche à Paris, 1851–1859.* Paris: Librairie Plon, 1905.

Isvolsky, Alexander Petrovich. *Recollections of a Foreign Minister.* Garden City, N.Y.: Doubleday, Page, & Company, 1921.

Jelavich, Charles, and Barbara Jelavich, eds. *The Education of a Russian Statesman: The Memoirs of Nicholas Karlovich Giers.* Berkeley: University of California Press, 1962.

Russia in the East, 1876–1800: The Russo-Turkish War and the Kuldja Crisis as Seen through the Letters of A. G. Jomini to N. K. Giers. Leiden: E. J. Brill, 1959.

Kalmykov, Andrei Dmitrievich. *Memoirs of a Russian Diplomat: Outposts of Empire, 1893–1917.* New Haven, Conn.: Yale University Press, 1971.

Bibliography

Kokovtsov, Vladimir Nikolaevich. *Out of My Past*. Stanford, Calif.: Stanford University Press, 1935.

Korff, Sergei Aleksandrovich. *Russia's Foreign Relations during the Last Half Century*. New York: Macmillan, 1922.

Lamzdorf, Vladimir Nikolaevich. *Dnevnik V. N. Lamzdorfa, 1886–1890*. Moscow: Gosudarstvennoe izdatel'stvo, 1926.

Dnevnik, 1891–1892. Moscow: Academia, 1934.

Meyendorff, A. *Correspondance diplomatique de M. de Staal, 1884–1900*. 2 vols. Paris: Librairie des sciences politiques et sociales, 1929.

Nekliudov, Anatolii Vasil'evich. *Diplomatic Reminiscences: Before and during the World War, 1911–1917*. New York: E. P. Dutton and Company, 1920.

Nenadović, Prota Matija. *The Memoirs of Prota Matija Nenadović*. Oxford: Oxford University Press, 1969.

Nesselrode, A., ed. *Lettres et papiers du chancelier comte de Nesselrode*. 11 vols. Paris: A. Lahure, 1904–11.

Poincaré, Raymond. *The Origins of the War*. London: Cassell and Company, Ltd., 1922.

Polovtsov, Alexander Aleksandrovich, *Dnevnik gosudarstvennogo sekretaria A. A. Polovtsova*. Moscow: Izdatel'stvo nauka, 1966.

Rosen, R. R. *Forty Years of Diplomacy*, 2 vols. New York: Knopf, 1922.

Savinskii, Alexander Aleksandrovich. *Recollections of a Russian Diplomat*. London: Hutchinson & Co., 1927.

Sazonov, Sergei Dmitrievich. *Fateful Years, 1909–1916*. New York: Frederick A. Stokes, 1928.

Shebeko, Nicholas Nikolaevich. *Souvenirs: Essai historique sur les origines de la guerre de 1914*. Paris: Bibliothèque diplomatique, 1936.

Schweinitz, Hans Lothar von. *Denkwürdigkeiten des Botschafters General von Schweinitz*. 2 vols. Berlin: Reimar Hobbing, 1927.

Siebert, B. von, ed. *Graf Benckendorffs diplomatischer Schriftwechsel*. 3 vols. Berlin and Leipzig: Walter de Gruyter & Co., 1928.

Simpson, J. Y., ed. *The Saburov Memoirs*. Cambridge: Cambridge University Press, 1929.

Sturdza, Démètre A. ed. *Charles Ier, Roi de Roumanie: Chronique-Actes-Documents*. 2 vols. Bucharest: Charles Göbl, 1899–1904.

Taube, Michael Aleksandrovich. *La politique russe d'avant-guerre et la fin de l'empire des tsars, 1904–1917*. Paris: Librairie Ernest Leroux, 1928.

Witte, Sergei Iulievich. *The Memoirs of Count Witte*. Garden City, N.Y.: Doubleday, Page & Company, 1921.

Zaionchkovskii, P. A., ed. *Dnevnik D. A. Miliutina*. 4 vols. Moscow: Biblioteka SSSR imeni V. I. Lenina, 1947–50.

Books

Aleksić-Pejković, Ljiljana. *Odnosi Srbije sa Francuskom i Engleskom, 1903–1914*. Belgrade: Izdanje Istorijskog instituta, 1965.

Anderson, M. A. *The Eastern Question, 1774–1923*. New York: St. Martin's Press, 1966.

Arsh, G. L. *Eteristskoe dvizhenie v Rossii*. Moscow: Izdatel'stvo nauka, 1970.

I. Kapodistriia i grecheskoe natsional'no-osvoboditel'noe dvizhenie, 1809–1822. Moscow: Izdatel'stvo nauka, 1976.

Bibliography

Atkin, Muriel. *Russia and Iran, 1780–1828*. Minneapolis: University of Minnesota Press, 1980.

Baumgart, Winfried. *The Peace of Paris, 1856*. Santa Barbara, Calif.: ABC-Clio, 1981.

Bestuzhev, I. V. *Bor'ba v Rossii po voprosam vneshnei politiki, 1906–1910*. Moscow: Izdatel'stvo Akademii nauk SSSR, 1961.

Beyrau, Dietrich. *Russische Orientpolitik und die Entstehung des deutschen Kaiserreiches, 1866–1870/71*. Wiesbaden: Harrossowitz, 1974.

Black, C. E. *The Establishment of Constitutional Government in Bulgaria*. Princeton, N.J.: Princeton University Press, 1943.

Clogg, Richard, ed. *The Struggle for Greek Independence*. Hamden, Conn.: Archon Books, 1973.

The Movement for Greek Independence, 1770–1821: A Collection of Documents. London: Macmillan, 1976.

Corti, Egon Caesar. *Alexander von Battenberg*. London: Cassell and Company, Ltd., 1954.

Crisp, Olga. *Studies in the Russian Economy before 1914*. New York: Barnes and Noble, 1976.

Curtiss, John Shelton. *Church and State in Russia: The Last Years of the Empire, 1900–1917*. New York: Columbia University Press, 1940.

The Russian Army under Nicholas I, 1825–1855. Durham, N. C.: Duke University Press, 1965.

Russia's Crimean War. Durham, N. C.: Duke University Press, 1979.

Dakin, Douglas. *The Greek Struggle for Independence, 1821–1833*. London: B. T. Batsford, Ltd., 1973.

Dedijer, Vladimir. *The Road to Sarajevo*. New York: Simon & Schuster, 1966.

Djuvara, T. G. *Cent projects de partage de la Turquie, 1281–1913*. Paris: Librairie Félix Alcan, 1914.

Dostian, I. S. *Rossiia i Balkanskii Vopros*. Moscow: Izdatel'stvo nauka, 1972.

Driault, Edouard. *Histoire diplomatique de la Grèce de 1821 à nos jours*. 5 vols. Paris: Les presses universitaires de France, 1925–6.

Druzhinina, E. I. *Kiuchuk-Kainardzhiiskii mir 1774 goda*. Moscow: Izdatel'stvo Akademii nauk SSR, 1955.

Edwards, H. Sutherland. *Sir William White*. London: John Murray, 1902.

Efremov, P. N. *Vneshniaia politika Rossii, 1907–1914 gg*. Moscow: Izdatel'stvo Instituta mezhdunarodnykh otnoshenii, 1961.

Fadeev, A. V. *Rossiia i vostochnyi krizis 20kh godov XIX veka*. Moscow: Izdatel'stvo Akademii nauk SSR, 1958.

Ferenczi, Caspar, *Aussenpolitik und Offentlichkeit in Russland, 1906–1912*. Husum: Matthiesen Verlag, 1982.

Florinsky, Michael T. *Russia*. 2 vols. New York: Macmillan, 1960.

Frazee, Charles A. *The Orthodox Church and Independent Greece, 1821–1852*. Cambridge: Cambridge University Press, 1969.

Georgiev, V. A. *Vneshniaia politika Rossii na Blizhnem Vostoke v kontse 30-nachale 40-kh godov XIX v*. Moscow: Izdatel'stvo Moskovskogo universiteta, 1975.

Georgiev, V. A., N. S. Kiniapina, M. T. Panchenkova, and V. I. Sheremet. *Vostochnyi vopros vo vneshnei politike Rossii konets XVIII-nachalo XX v*. Moscow: Izdatel'stvo nauka, 1878.

Bibliography

Geyer, Dietrich. *Russian Imperialism: The Interaction of Domestic and Foreign Policy, 1860–1914.* New Haven, Conn.: Yale University Press, 1987.

Gille, Bertrand. *Histoire économique et sociale de la Russie du moyen âge au XXe siècle.* Paris: Payot, 1949.

Grimsted, Patricia Kennedy. *The Foreign Ministers of Alexander I, 1801–1825.* Berkeley: University of California Press, 1969.

Grosul, V. Ia., and E. E. Chertan. *Rossiia i formirovanie rumynskogo nezavisimogo gosudarstva.* Moscow: Izdatel'stvo nauka, 1969.

Habakkuk, H. J., and M. Postan, eds. *The Cambridge Economic History of Europe.* Cambridge: Cambridge University Press, 1966.

Hann, Hans Henning. *Aussenpolitik in der Emigration: die Exilpolitik Adam Jerzy Czartoryskis, 1830–1840.* Munich: R. Oldenbourg Verlag, 1978.

Helmreich, Ernst C. *The Diplomacy of the Balkan Wars, 1912–1913.* Cambridge, Mass.: Harvard University Press, 1938.

Hiller, Marlene P. *Krisenregion Nahost: Russische Orientpolitik im Zeitalter des Imperialismus, 1900–1914.* Frankfurt: Peter Lang, 1985.

Holland, Thomas Erskine. *A Lecture on the Treaty Relations of Russia and Turkey from 1774 to 1853.* London: Macmillan and Co., 1877.

Hosking, Geoffrey A. *The Russian Constitutional Experiment: Government and Duma, 1907–1914.* Cambridge: Cambridge University Press, 1973.

Hünigen, Gisela. *Nikolaj Pavlovič Ignat'ev und die russische Balkanpolitik, 1875–1878.* Göttingen: Musterschmidt-Verlag, 1968.

Ignat'ev, A. V. *Vneshniaia politika Rossii v 1905–1907 gg.* Moscow: Izdatel'stvo nauka, 1986.

Ingle, Harold N. *Nesselrode and the Russian Rapprochement with Britain.* Berkeley: University of California Press, 1976.

Institute for Balkan Studies. *Les relations gréco-russes pendant la domination turque et la guerre d'indépendance grecque.* Thessaloniki: Institute for Balkan Studies, 1983.

Jelavich, Barbara. *Russia and the Romanian National Cause, 1858–1859.* Bloomington: Slavic and East European Series, Indiana University Press, 1959.

Russia and the Greek Revolution of 1843. Munich: R. Oldenbourg, Verlag, 1966.

The Habsburg Empire in European Affairs, 1814–1918. Chicago: Rand McNally & Company, 1969.

The Ottoman Empire, the Great Powers, and the Straits Question, 1870–1887. Bloomington: Indiana University Press, 1973.

St. Petersburg and Moscow: Tsarist and Soviet Foreign Policy, 1814–1974. Bloomington: Indiana University Press, 1974.

History of the Balkans: Eighteenth and Nineteenth Centuries. New York: Cambridge University Press, 1983.

Russia and the Formation of the Romanian National State, 1821–1878. New York: Cambridge University Press, 1984.

Jelavich, Charles. *Tsarist Russia and Balkan Nationalism: Russian Influence in the Internal Affairs of Bulgaria and Serbia, 1876–1886.* Berkeley: University of California Press, 1958.

South Slav Nationalisms – Textbooks and Yugoslav Union Before 1914. Columbus: Ohio State University Press, 1990.

Jelavich, Charles, and Barbara Jelavich. *The Establishment of the Balkan National States, 1804–1920.* Seattle: University of Washington Press, 1977.

Bibliography

Jewsbury, George F. *The Russian Annexation of Bessarabia, 1774–1828: A Study of Imperial Expansion*. Boulder, Colo.: East European Monographs, 1976.

Joll, James. *The Origins of the First World War*. London: Longman, 1984.

Jomini, Alexander Genrikhovich. *Etude diplomatique sur la guerre de Crimée*. 2 vols. St. Petersburg: Librairie de la Cour Impériale H. Schmitzdorff, 1878.

Keiger, John F. V. *France and the Origins of the First World War*. New York: St. Martin's Press, 1983.

Kennan, George F. *The Decline of Bismarck's European Order: Franco-Russian Relations, 1875–1890*. Princeton, N.J.: Princeton University Press, 1979.

Kent, Marian, ed. *The Great Powers and the End of the Ottoman Empire*. London: Allen & Unwin, 1984.

Kofos, John A. *International and Domestic Politics in Greece during the Crimean War*. Boulder, Colo.: East European Monographs, 1980.

Lampe, John R., and Marvin R. Jackson. *Balkan Economic History, 1550–1950: From Imperial Borderlands to Developing Nations*. Bloomington: Indiana University Press, 1982.

Lieven, D. C. B. *Russia and the Origins of the First World War*. New York: St. Martin's Press, 1983.

MacKenzie, David. *The Serbs and Russian Panslavism, 1856–1878*. Ithaca, N.Y.: Cornell University Press, 1967.

Ilija Garašanin: Balkan Bismarck. Boulder, Colo.: East European Monographs, 1985.

Martin, Frederick. *The Statesman's Year-Book: 1879*. London: Macmillan and Co., 1879.

Medlicott, William N. *The Congress of Berlin and After: A Diplomatic History of the Near Eastern Settlement, 1878–1880*. London: Methuen & Co., Ltd., 1938.

Meininger, Thomas A. *Ignatiev and the Establishment of the Bulgarian Exarchate, 1864–1872: A Study in Personal Diplomacy*. Madison: State Historical Society of Wisconsin, 1970.

Meriage, Lawrence P. *Russia and the First Serbian Revolution, 1804–1813*. New York: Garland Publishing, Inc., 1987.

Millman, Richard. *Britain and the Eastern Question, 1875–1878*. Oxford: Oxford University Press, 1979.

Mosely, Philip E. *Russian Diplomacy and the Opening of the Eastern Question in 1838 and 1839*. Cambridge, Mass.: Harvard University Press, 1934.

Mosse, W. E. *The European Powers and the German Question, 1848–1871*. Cambridge: Cambridge University Press, 1958.

Nikitin, S. A. *Slavianskie komitety v Rossii v 1858–1876 godakh*. Moscow: Izdatel'stvo Moskovskogo universiteta, 1960.

Nolde, Boris. *L'Alliance franco-russe*. Paris: Librairie Droz, 1936.

Pantev, Andrei. *Angliia sreshtu Russiia na Balkanite, 1879–1894*. Sofia: Nauka i izkustvo, 1972.

Pavlowitch, Stevan K. *Anglo-Russian Rivalry in Serbia, 1837–1839: The Mission of Colonel Hodges*. Paris: Mouton, 1961.

Perry, Duncan M. *The Politics of Terror: The Macedonian Liberation Movements, 1893–1903*. Durham, N.C.: Duke University Press, 1988.

Petrovich, Michael Boro. *The Emergence of Russian Panslavism, 1856–1870*. New York: Columbia University Press, 1956.

A History of Modern Serbia, 1804–1918. New York: Harcourt Brace Jovanovich, 1976.

Bibliography

Pisarev, Iu. A. *Velikie derzhavy i Balkany nakanune pervoi mirovoi voiny.* Moscow: Izdatel'stvo nauka, 1985.

Poletika, N. P. *Vozniknovenie pervoi mirovoi voiny.* Moscow: Izdatel'stvo sotsial'no-ekonomicheskoi literatury mysl', 1964.

Puryear, Vernon J. *England, Russia and the Straits Question,* Berkeley: University of California Press, 1931.

Ramm, Agatha. *Sir Robert Morier.* Oxford: Oxford University Press, 1973.

Reuter, Peter W. *Die Balkanpolitik des französischen Imperialismus, 1911–1914.* Frankfurt: Campus Verlag, 1979.

Reutern, W. Reutern-Baron Nolcken. *Die finanzielle Sanierung Russlands nach der Katastrophe des Krimkrieges 1862 bis 1878 durch den Finanzminister Michael von Reutern.* Berlin: Georg Reimer, 1914.

Riasanovsky, Nicholas V. *Nicholas I and Official Nationality in Russia, 1825–1855.* Berkeley: University of California Press, 1959.

Russia and the West in the Teaching of the Slavophiles. Gloucester, Mass.: Peter Smith, 1965.

Rich, Norman. *Why the Crimean War? A Cautionary Tale.* Hanover, N.H.: University Press of New England, 1985.

Roider, Karl A., Jr. *Austria's Eastern Question, 1700–1790.* Princeton, N.J.: Princeton University Press, 1982.

Rossos, Andrew. *Russia and the Balkans: Inter-Balkan Rivalries and Russian Foreign Policy, 1908–1914.* Toronto: University of Toronto Press, 1981.

Runciman, Steven. *The Great Church in Captivity: A Study of the Patriarchate of Constantinople from the Eve of the Turkish Conquest to the Greek War of Independence.* Cambridge: Cambridge University Press, 1968.

Saab, Anne Pottinger. *The Origins of the Crimean Alliance.* Charlottesville: University Press of Virginia, 1977.

Saul, Norman E. *Russia and the Mediterranean.* Chicago: University of Chicago Press, 1970.

Schiemann, Theodor. *Kaiser Nikolaus.* 4 vols. Berlin and Leipzig: Walter de Gruyter & Co., 1908–19.

Schroeder, Paul W. *Metternich's Diplomacy at Its Zenith, 1820–1823.* Austin: University of Texas Press, 1962.

Austria, Great Britain, and the Crimean War. Ithaca, N.Y.: Cornell University Press, 1972.

Schütz, Eberhard. *Die europäische Allianzpolitik Alexanders I. und der griechische Unabhängigkeitskampf, 1820–1830.* Wiesbaden: Otto Harrassowitz, 1975.

Seton-Watson, Hugh. *The Russian Empire, 1801–1917.* Oxford: Oxford University Press, 1967.

Sheremet, V. I. *Turtsiia i Adrianopol'skii mir 1829g.* Moscow: Izdatel'stvo nauka, 1975.

Osmanskaia imperiia i zapadnaia Evropa vtoraia tret' XIX v. Moscow: Izdatel'stvo nauka, 1986.

Shparo, O. B. *Osvobozhdenie Gretsii i Rossiia, 1821–1829.* Moscow: Izdatel'stvo mysl', 1965.

Smith, Colin L. *The Embassy of Sir William White at Constantinople, 1886–1891.* London: Oxford University Press, 1957.

Stählin, Karl. *Geschichte Russlands.* 4 vols in 5. Graz: Akademische Druck, 1961.

Stanislavskaia, A. M. *Rossiia i Gretsiia v kontse XVIII nachale XIX veka: Politika Rossii v Ionicheskoi respublike, 1789–1907 gg.* Moscow: Izdatel'stvo nauka, 1976.

Bibliography

Statelova, Elena. *Diplomatsiiata na Kniazhestvo Bŭlgariia, 1879–1886.* Sofia: Izdatel'stvo na Bŭlgarskata akademiia na naukite, 1979.

Statelova, Elena, and Andrei Pantev. *Sŭedinenieto na kniazhestvo Bŭlgariia i Istochna Rumeliia 1885 godina.* Sofia: Dŭrzhavno izdatel'stvo "Narodna Prosveta," 1985.

Sumner, B. H. *Russia and the Balkans, 1870–1880.* Oxford: Oxford University Press, 1937.

Tarle, Evgenii Viktorovich. *Krymskaia voina.* 2 vols. Moscow: Izdatel'stvo Akademii Nauk SSSR, 1950.

Temperley, Harold. *England and the Near East: The Crimea.* London: Longmans, Green and Co., Ltd., 1936.

The Foreign Policy of Canning, 1822–1827. London: Frank Cass, 1966.

Thaden, Edward C. *Russia and the Balkan Alliance of 1912.* University Park: Pennsylvania State University Press, 1965.

Uebersberger, Hans. *Osterreich zwischen Russland und Serbien.* Cologne: Verlag Hermann Böhlaus Nachf., 1958.

Vinogradov, V. N. *Rossiia i ob'edinenie rumynskikh kniazhestv.* Moscow: Izdatel'stvo nauka, 1961.

Velikobritaniia i Balkany ot Venskogo Kongressa do Krymskoi Voiny. Moscow: Izdatel'stvo nauka, 1985.

Vinogradov, V. N., et al., eds. *Mezhdunarodnye otnosheniia na Balkanakh, 1815–1830 gg.* Moscow: Izdatel'stvo nauka, 1983.

Mezhdunarodnye otnosheniia na Balkanakh, 1856–1878 gg. Moscow: Izdatel'stvo nauka, 1986.

Mezhdunarodnye otnosheniia na Balkanakh, 1830–1856. Moscow: Izdatel'stvo nauka, 1990.

Vyšný, Paul. *Neoslavism and the Czechs, 1898–1914.* Cambridge: Cambridge University Press, 1977.

Webster, Charles. *The Foreign Policy of Castlereagh, 1815–1822.* London: G. Bell and Sons, Ltd., 1947.

Woodhouse, C. M. *Capodistria: The Founder of Modern Greek Independence.* London: Oxford University Press, 1973.

Zaionchkovskii, A. M. *Vostochnaia voina.* 4 vols. in 5. St. Petersburg: Ekspeditsiia zagotovleniia gosudarstvennykh bumag, 1908–13.

Zaionchkovskii, P. A. *The Russian Autocracy in Crisis, 1878–1882.* Gulf Breeze, Fla.: Academic International Press, 1979.

Index

Abdul Hamid II, 190, 214, 219
Abdul Mejid, 96, 116, 125, 126, 140
Aberdeen, Lord, 113, 115
Act of Submission, 70
Aehrenthal, Alois Lexa von, 217, 219–21, 225, 245
Afghanistan, 27, 156, 178
Aksakov, Ivan Sergeevich, 93, 158, 207
Albania, 14, 34, 56, 120, 212, 214, 229, 234, 239, 244, 245, 249, 251, 259, 264, 266, 267
Alexander I, tsar of Russia, 32, 90, 141, 273; life and character, 42–6; and the Greek revolution, 48, 51–4, 57, 58, 60–4, 68, 71, 73, 75, 87, 88; and the Serbian revolution, 11–13, 16, 17, 20–2; and the wars of the French revolution and Napoleon, 6–8
Alexander II, tsar of Russia, 32, 34, 138, 140, 151, 152, 155, 182, 271; and the Bulgarian question, 167, 180; life and character, 143–6
Alexander III, tsar of Russia, 158, 197, 207, 208, 213; and the Bulgarian question, 181, 182, 184–6, 188, 191–4
Alexander of Battenberg, prince of Bulgaria, 180–94, 213
Ali Pasha of Janina, 56, 61
alliances
  1814: Quadruple Alliance, 44, 45, 60
  1815: Holy Alliance, 45, 67, 96, 109, 115, 117, 127, 146, 155, 158
  1872, renewed 1881: Three Emperors' Alliance, 155, 171, 178, 188, 194, 196, 213, 218, 236, 238
  1879: Dual Alliance, 178, 199
  1882: Triple Alliance, 178, 199, 225, 267
  1887: Reinsurance Treaty, 194
  1894: Franco-Russian Alliance, 195, 199, 202, 204, 214, 215
  1902: British–Japanese Alliance, 199

  1904: Entente Cordiale, 214
  1907: Triple Entente, 215, 227, 263
Andrassy, Julius, 171
Antim I, Exarch, 166
Arsenije III Crnojević, 10
Arsenije IV Crnojević, 10
Artamonov, Colonel Victor Alekseevich, 252
Ausgleich (Compromise) of 1867, 155, 156, 215
Austria, see Habsburg Empire

Bagot, Sir Charles, 62, 64
Bakhmetev, Georgii Petrovich, 275n
Bark, Peter Lvovich, 260, 261
Basily, Constantine Mikhailovich, 150
battles
  1805: Austerlitz, 13
  1807: Friedland, 16
  1821: Drăgășani, 54
  1827: Navarino, 82, 83
  1832: Konya, 95
  1853: Sinope, 126
  1854: Alma, 138, Balaclava, 138, Inkerman, 138, 139
  1855: Sevastopol, 138
  1877: Plevna, 173, 174, 177, 237
  1885: Slivnitsa, 187
  1905: Mukden, 199
  1905: Tsushima, 200, 204, 224
Bavaria, 87, 106, 108, 152
Belgium, 97, 117, 201, 264, 274
Belorussians, 157, 209, 216, 248
Benckendorff, Alexander Konstantinovich, 232, 233, 274
Berchtold, Leopold, 222, 262
Beron, Peter, 162
Bessarabia, 1, 5, 7, 44, 51, 52, 87, 138, 146, 160, 176, 177, 270
Bismarck, Otto von, 47, 157, 190, 198, 202–4

Black Sea, 3, 26–8, 30, 32, 51, 54, 58, 66, 87, 88, 100, 126, 138, 140, 141, 146, 154, 155, 157, 160, 171, 178, 179, 204–6, 212, 217, 267
Bosnia and Hercegovina, 5, 14, 18, 30, 31, 85, 120, 128, 130, 159, 167, 169, 171, 172, 177, 178, 212, 216–20, 224, 225, 228, 236, 237, 239–41, 243, 244, 247, 251, 252, 254, 256n
Bosphorus, *see* Straits
Botev, Khristo, 163
Brătianu, Ion, 163
Brunnow, Filipp Ivanovich, 97, 115, 119
Budberg, General Andrei Fedorovich, 134
Bukovina, 31
Bulgaria, 5, 28, 30, 34, 114, 119, 120, 129, 134, 148, 153, 197, 206, 210, 211, 213, 214, 220, 236–9, 264, 266, 268, 273, 274; in the Balkan Wars, 228–34, 246, 247; the declaration of independence, 221, 223; and Serbia, 236–9, 241, 251; Russia and the Bulgarian national movement, 159–78, 250; Russia and the autonomous principality, 178–96, 209; and World War I, 259, 264
Buol-Schauenstein, Karl Ferdinand von, 125, 136
Butenev, Apollinari Petrovich, 103, 147
Byron, Lord, 66
Byzantium, 5, 35–8, 86, 107, 113, 114, 137, 239

Canning, George, 66, 73, 74
Cantemir, Dimitrie, 2, 41
Capodistrias, Ioannis, 46n, 47–9, 52, 54, 59, 62–5, 85, 105
Castlereagh, Lord, 61–3, 66
Catherine the Great, 3, 5, 8, 29, 36, 41, 42, 51, 58, 147
Catholic church in the Ottoman empire, 22; and the Crimean War, 116–18; French interest in, 31; Habsburg attitude to, 30
Caucasus, 1, 3, 5, 28, 127, 132, 140, 156, 157, 267
Caulaincourt, Armand de, 17
Cavour, Camillo di, 157
Charles of Hohenzollern-Sigmaringen, prince of Romania, 149
Charles X, king of France, 94
Charykov, Nicholas Valerievich, 220–2, 225, 227, 228, 234
Cherniaev, Michael Grigor'evich, 170
Chichagov, Paul Vasil'evich, 17, 18
China, 27, 156, 199, 200

conferences and agreements
  1830: London Protocol, 87
  1871: London Conference, 154, 155
  1876: Constantinople Conference, 171, 173, 175, 176, 213, 237, 274
  1876: Reichstadt agreement, 171, 218, 236, 237
  1887: Mediterranean agreements, 194
  1897: Russian–Habsburg agreement, 195, 212, 217, 224, 227, 238
  1903: Mürzsteg agreement, 214
  1908: Buchlau agreement, 219–21, 227
  1909: Racconigi agreement, 225, 228
congresses
  1815: Vienna, 21, 27, 48
  1820: Troppau, 53
  1821: Laibach, 53, 54, 58
  1822: Verona, 65
  1856: Paris, 138, 140, 141
  1878: Berlin, 176, 177, 196
constitutions
  1829–34: Organic Statutes, Danubian Principalities, 99, 102
  1835: Presentation Constitution, Serbia, 102
  1838: Turkish Constitution, Serbia, 103
  1844: Greek Constitution, 108
  1876: Turkish Constitution, 219
  1879: Tŭrnovo Constitution, Bulgaria, 180
Crete, 5, 67, 70, 95, 107, 114, 152, 195, 210, 211
Crimea, 1, 3, 138
Croatia-Slavonia, kingdom of, 10, 215, 216, 239, 240, 247
Croats, 10, 18, 215, 216, 239, 240
Cuza, Alexander, 149, 151, 181
Czartoryski, Prince Adam, 12, 94
Czechs, 153, 158, 215, 240, 247
Czernin, Otto, 257

Dalmatia, 13, 15, 18, 216, 239, 240, 247
Danubian Principalities of Wallachia and Moldavia, 26, 28–30, 34, 37, 38, 94; and the Crimean War, 120, 122, 125, 128–32, 134–6, 138, 141, 142; and the Greek revolution, 50, 52–4, 56, 58–61, 63, 65, 70, 72, 75, 76, 79–81, 85–9, 160; relations with Russia until 1812, 2–12, 14–17, 41; Russia and the autonomous principalities, 98–101, 105, 108, 110, 111, 114, 119, 168 (*For events after 1859 see* Romania)
Dardanelles, *see* Straits
Davydov, Alexander Petrovich, 180, 181

Index

Dedicated Monasteries, 150, 151
Dibich, General Ivan Ivanovich, 62, 85
Dimitriev, Ratko, 247
Dimitrijević, Colonel Dragutin, 251, 252
Dimitŭr, Hadzhi, 163
Dobrudja, 171, 175, 234, 247
Dolgoruki, Vasilii Andreevich, 103
Dondukov-Korsakov, Prince Alexander
    Mikhailovich, 180
Drouyn de Lhuys, Edouard, 128n
Duclos, A., 103
Dudley, Lord, 84
Duhamel, Alexander Osipovich, 161,
    162
Dušan, Stephen, 239

Eastern Rumelia, 171, 176, 178, 183-7,
    189-91, 213
Egypt, 5, 6, 67, 68, 73, 74, 92, 96-8, 112-14,
    117, 160, 181, 194, 205, 211
Ermolov, General Aleksei Petrovich, 62
Esterházy, Count Valentin Ladislaus, 131
Exarchate, 165, 166, 213, 214

Ferdinand of Coburg, 193, 194, 213, 221,
    262, 263
Ferdinand I, king of the Two Sicilies, 53
Ficquelmont, Karl Ludwig von, 92, 113
Fonton, Feliks Petrovich, 137
France, 2, 4-6, 26-34, 48, 91, 105, 108, 109,
    111, 146, 148-54, 194, 196, 266, 267;
    and the alliances with Russia, 195,
    199, 201-205, 207, 208, 214, 215, 222,
    224, 227, 231; and the Crimean War,
    115-20, 124-6, 128, 130, 137, 138; and
    the Egyptian crisis, 95-8; and the
    Greek revolution, 54, 67, 71, 73, 75,
    81, 83-5, 87, 88; and the origins of
    World War I, 255, 263; the wars of the
    French revolution and Napoleon, 13-
    19, 42
Franz Ferdinand, 252
Franz Joseph, 110, 118, 128, 131, 155, 156,
    167, 195, 212, 214
Frederick William III, king of Prussia, 90
Frederick William IV, king of Prussia, 109,
    126n, 131n
Fuad Pasha, 116, 119

Gagarin, Michael Anatolevich, 256n
Garašanin, Ilija, 104, 135, 136, 152, 153
Gennadius, Patriarch, 35
George I, king of Greece, 152, 211
George, prince, Greece, 211
Gerdzhikov, I, 186, 187

Germany, 26, 30, 34, 44, 105, 148, 155, 199,
    201-5, 207, 266, 272; and the origins of
    World War I, 222, 224, 225, 227, 228,
    231, 235, 242, 244, 255, 259, 260, 262,
    263; and the Bulgarian crises, 167, 176-
    8, 180, 184, 187-90, 192, 194-6
Gerov, Naiden, 168
Geshov, Ivan, 185, 186
Ghalib Effendi, 18
Ghica, Grigore, 76, 134
Giers, Michael Nikolaevich, 230
Giers, Nicholas Karlovich, 33, 169, 170,
    177, 178, 181, 184-9, 192-5, 198, 272,
    273
Giesl von Gieslingen, General Wladimir,
    254, 261
Goderich, Lord, 82
Golovkin, Iurii Aleksandrovich, 62
Goltz, Karl Friedrich von der, 152
Goluchowsky, Agenor, 212, 214
Gorchakov, Alexander Mikhailovich, 33,
    144-7, 150-2, 169, 171, 176, 198, 210,
    236
Gorchakov, General Michael Dmitrievich,
    134
Great Britain, 4, 26-32, 34, 44, 45, 91, 100,
    105, 108, 109, 111, 148, 151, 152, 155,
    156, 199-201, 203, 205-7, 267, 274; and
    the Bulgarian question, 159, 160, 176,
    180, 186, 187, 189-91, 194, 196; and
    the Crimean War, 112-15, 117, 119,
    121, 124-6, 128, 131, 137, 138, 141; and
    the Egyptian crisis, 95, 97; and the
    Greek revolution, 54, 61-4, 66-75, 81-
    8; and the origins of World War I,
    210, 211, 214, 215, 217, 222, 223, 227,
    231, 235, 244, 255, 263
Great Reforms, Russia, 143, 148, 157
Greece, 2, 4, 5, 10, 34, 37, 38, 40, 41, 148,
    150-2, 157, 203, 205, 206, 213, 214,
    251, 264, 266, 268; and the Bulgarian
    question, 159-63, 165, 166, 176, 177,
    185, 187; and the Balkan Wars, 230-5;
    and the Crimean War, 120, 137, 138;
    the Greek revolution, 49-89, 112, 250;
    the independent government, 105-9,
    142
Greek Project of Catherine the Great, 5, 29,
    51
Grey, Sir Edward, 223, 274
Grigorios, Patriarch, 56-8
Gruić, Slavko, 242
Guchkov, Alexander Ivanovich, 247
Gülhane decree, 1838, 117
Gurev, Dmitrii Aleksandrovich, 46, 62

Index

Habsburg Empire, 1, 2, 5, 42, 44, 46, 92, 109–11, 146, 148, 154–6, 197, 199, 203, 205, 207, 209, 211, 212, 214, 230, 231, 267, 272; and the annexation of Bosnia–Hercegovina, 217–25, 227, 241–4; and the Bulgarian question, 159, 160, 167, 171, 175–8, 180, 184, 186, 187, 189, 194–6; and the Crimean War, 112–15, 117, 118, 120, 125, 127–31, 134–8, 141; and the Egyptian crisis, 96, 97; and the Greek revolution, 53, 54, 60–4, 66, 68, 71–3, 75, 81, 83, 85, 88; and the origins of World War I, 249, 251, 253–63; and its position in Russian foreign policy, 26–34; and Serbia, 101–3, 236–48; and the Serbian revolution, 9–13, 17–19; and the South Slav question, 215–24, 228, 239

Hadzivulkov, Vasil, 163

Hartwig, Nicholas Genrikhovich, 228, 229, 244–6, 252–4, 274

Hercegovina, *see* Bosnia and Hercegovina

Hodges, George Lloyd, 103

Holy Places, 38, 115, 118, 120, 137, 150

Hôtel Lambert, 94, 154

Hübner, Joseph Alexander von, 128n, 129n

Hungary, 18, 92, 110, 111, 132, 135, 148, 153, 156, 162, 215, 216, 240, 272

Ibrahim, 73, 74

Ičko, Peter, 15

Ignatiev, Nicholas Pavlovich, 165–9, 171, 173, 175, 177, 196, 237

Inzov, General Ivan Nikitich, 52

Ionian Islands, 6, 11, 44, 48, 51, 152

Ipsilanti, Alexander, 51, 52, 268

Ireland, 28

Italinskii, Andrei Iakovlevich, 11, 13, 19, 20, 22, 76, 77

Italy, 30, 34, 44, 60, 65, 75, 128–30, 132, 146, 148, 153–5, 178, 194, 199, 208, 225, 228, 244, 249, 266

Ivan III, tsar of Russia, 36

Izvolsky (Izvolskii), Alexander Petrovich, 198, 199, 217–23, 225, 227, 228, 241–3

Japan, 199, 200, 206, 214

Jeremias II, Patriarch, 37n

Jomini, Alexander Genrikhovich, 154, 169, 178, 195, 272

Joseph II, 5

Jovanović, Metropolitan Peter, 103

July Monarchy, 109

Kalmykov, Andrei Dmitrievich, 227n

Kankrin, Egor Frantsevich, 270

Karadjordje Petrović, 11, 16, 17, 19, 21, 24, 100

Karadjordjević, Prince Alexander, 104, 135, 136, 152

Karadjordjević, Alexander, Prince Regent of Serbia, 252, 253, 259, 261, 262, 268

Karadjordjević, Prince George, 241

Karadjordjević, King Peter, 238, 251, 252

Karadzha, Stephen, 163

Karavelov, Liuben, 163, 164, 192, 270

Kartsov, Andrei Nikolaevich, 170

Katacazy, Gabriel A., 106, 108

Katkov, Michael Nikiforovich, 158, 181, 188n, 207

Khaltchinskii, F. L., 162

Khevenhüller, Rudolf von, 222

Khitov, Panaiot, 163

Kiselev, General Paul Dmitrievich, 62, 99

Kliment, Metropolitan, 185, 186, 192, 193

Kokovtsev, Vladimir Nikolaevich, 217, 221, 225

Košutić, Radovan, 243

Krivoshein, Alexander Vasil'evich, 260

Lamzdorf, Vladimir Nikolaevich, 198, 214, 228, 229

Langeron, General Alexander Fedorovich, 52

Leontije, Metropolitan, 11, 15, 19, 21

Leopold of Saxe-Coburg, Prince, 87

Levski, Vasil, 163

Lieven, Khristof Andreevich, 62, 63, 65, 73, 74, 84, 104

Liman von Sanders, General Otto, 235

Lobanov-Rostovskii, A. B., 198

Louis Philippe, king of France, 94, 97, 109

Ludwig I, king of Bavaria, 87

Macedonia, 17, 120, 166, 171, 176, 195, 210, 212–14, 217, 218, 225, 229, 230, 231, 233, 237, 244, 246, 247, 264

Mahmud II, 17, 67, 80, 83, 96

Marashli Ali Pasha, 24

Margerie, Pierre de, 263

Mašina, Draga, 238

Matuszewicz, Adam Fadeevich, 84

Maurer, Georg von, 106

Mehmet Ali, 67, 72, 73, 82, 92, 94–7, 101

Menshikov, Alexander Sergeevich, 118–20, 122–4, 135

Metternich, Clemens von, 46, 47, 53, 58, 61–4, 68, 75, 83, 109, 198

Index

Meyendorff, Peter Kazimirovich, 121, 122, 133, 134, 136, 137
Mihanović, Antun, 103
Military Frontier, 10
Milovanović, Milan, 241, 242
Minciaky, Matvei Iakovlevich, 72, 73, 78
Moldavia, *see* Danubian Principalities of Wallachia and Moldavia
Mondain, Captain Hippolyte, 153
Montenegro, 14n, 15, 18, 34, 117, 127, 130, 170-2, 177, 196, 220, 230-2, 234, 237, 239, 242, 244, 250, 264, 266
Morier, Sir Robert, 189, 193, 194, 273
Muraviev, Michael Nikolaevich, 198

Nagodba, 215
Napoleon I, 1, 6, 7, 11, 16, 17, 27, 42, 116
Napoleon III (Louis Napoleon), 111, 115-17, 146, 157
national organizations
    Benevolent Society, Bulgaria, 163, 164
    Black Hand (Union or Death) Society, 251-3
    Bulgarian Revolutionary Central Committee, 163, 168
    Internal Macedonian Revolutionary Organization (IMRO), 214
    Narodna Odbrana (National Defense), 251, 252
    Omladina (Serbian youth organization), 169
    Philike Etairia, 51, 52, 54
    Slavic Benevolent Society, 158, 162, 170, 208
national programs (Balkan)
    Greater Serbian program, 239, 240, 244, 255, 256
    Great Idea (Megali Idea), 107, 239, 273, 274
    Načertanije, 104, 153
    Trialism, 216
    Yugoslav movement, 240
Naum Pasha, 222, 223
Nedoba, Teodor Ivanovich, 21
Nekliudov, Anatol Vasil'evich, 228-30, 247, 247n
Nelidov, Alexander Ivanovich, 173, 175, 185, 189, 190, 205, 210, 211
Nenadović, Prota Matija, 9, 11, 12, 21
Neoslavism, 34, 208-210, 216, 260
Neratov, Anatol Anatolevich, 227, 234
Nesselrode, Karl Vasil'evich, 21, 33, 39, 40, 46, 47, 62, 69, 71, 73-9, 81, 86, 87, 91, 108, 111, 114, 117, 118, 121, 125, 127, 132-4, 137n, 144-6, 198

Nicholas I, tsar of Russia, 32, 34, 107, 108, 112, 138, 141, 142, 145, 146, 158; and the Crimean War, 113, 114-19, 124, 127-9, 131-5; and the Egyptian crisis, 95-7; and the Greek revolution, 73, 74, 82, 84, 86, 88; life and character, 90-4; and the revolutions of 1848-9, 109-11
Nicholas II, tsar of Russia, 32, 195, 200, 225, 238, 248, 264; and the Bosnian crisis, 221, 223; life and character, 197-9, 206, 207; and the origins of World War I, 259, 261, 262, 268, 274, 275
Nicholas, Grand Duke, 173n
Nikiforov, Captain Constantine, 192
Nikolajević, Constantine, 135
Novikov, Evgenii Petrovich, 169
Novi Pazar, Sanjak of, 177, 212, 217, 218-20, 237, 241, 242

Obrenović, King Alexander, 238
Obrenović, Prince Michael, 104, 152, 153, 196, 236
Obrenović, King Milan, 153, 186, 187, 236-8
Obrenović, Prince Miloš, 19, 24, 76-8, 100-4, 152
Obruchev, General Nicholas Nikolaevich, 192
October Manifesto, 1905, 200
Offenberg, Genrikh Genrikhovich, 163, 164
Orlov, Aleksei Fedorovich, 95, 118, 129
Orthodox church; as issue in Crimean War, 115-26, 133, 141; the church in Greece, 106-7; the church in the Habsburg Empire, 10, 11; the church in Serbia, 9, 10, 102, 103; provisions in favor of in the Treaty of Kuchuk Kainardji, 3-5; Russian attitude toward Balkan Orthodox, 22, 34-40, 49-51, 58-61, 87, 92, 147, 158, 165, 166, 172, 173, 206, 267, 268 (*See also* Partiarchate of Constantinople; Partiarchate of Peć; Dedicated Monasteries; Exarchate; Holy Places)
Othon, king of Greece, 87, 105-9, 151
Ottoman Empire, 26-31, 34-6, 38, 39, 90, 99, 101, 103, 104, 110, 111-15, 153, 155-7, 203, 205, 209, 237, 242, 243, 246, 264, 267, 268; and the Bulgarian question, 159-63, 165-78, 185-7, 189-91; and the Crimean War, 115-32, 134, 136n-8, 140-2; end of the empire in Europe (1894-1913), 210-35; and the

Index

Ottoman Empire (*continued*)
   Greek revolution, 48-51, 54-64, 66-89;
   and Mehmet Ali, 94-8; and the
   Serbian revolution, 9-24, 40; and the
   wars of the eighteenth century, the
   French revolution, and Napoleon, 1-8
   (*See also* battles; revolts and
   revolutions; treaties; wars)

Paleologus, Zoe, 36
Palmerston, Lord, 95, 124
Panslavism, 34, 93, 135, 157, 158, 170, 172,
   177, 181, 188, 208-10, 216, 232, 254,
   260, 267
Papazoglu, Dimitŭr, 185, 186
Paprikov, General Stephen, 231
Parensov, Peter Dmtrievich, 180
Pašić, Nikola, 238, 241-4, 246, 248, 251-4,
   262
Paskevich, Field Marshal Ivan Fedorovich,
   131
Pasvanoglu Osman Pasha, 6
Patriarchate of Constantinople, 10-12, 36-9,
   50, 77, 102, 106, 107, 123, 137, 150,
   151, 165, 166
Patriarchate of Peć, 10, 102
Paul, tsar of Russia, 1, 5, 6, 8, 42, 46
Paulucci, Filipp Osipovich, 15, 16
Peel, Sir Robert, 113
Peloponnesus, 3, 50, 54, 56, 67, 70, 73, 82,
   83, 85
Penjdeh incident, 178, 179
Persia, 1, 85, 156, 181, 215
Peter the Great, 2, 9, 36, 41, 93
Phanariots, 2, 8, 10, 13, 38, 50, 56, 76, 99,
   159
Pharmakidis, Theocletos, 106
Philhellenism, 59, 66, 81, 85, 87
Philotheus, 37
Piedmont, 126, 127
Pobedonostsev, Constantine Petrovich, 188n
Poincaré, Raymond, 231, 263
Pokrovskii, N. N., 199
Poland, 27, 34, 92, 100, 101, 104, 105, 110,
   127, 132, 135, 146, 148, 153, 154, 157,
   162, 196, 208, 209, 215, 216, 240, 248,
   273; Congress Kingdom of Poland, 44,
   94; Duchy of Warsaw, 44
political parties
   British, French and Russian parties in
   Greece, 108, 109
   Conservative Party, Bulgaria, 180, 183
   Constitutionalist Party, Serbia, 103, 104
   Croatian-Serbian Coalition, 240
   Kadets, Russia, 207, 208, 260n

Liberal Party, Bulgaria, 180, 183
Octobrist Party, Russia, 207, 208, 247,
   260n
Radical Party, Serbia, 238, 241
Popović, Demeter, 243, 246, 247
Portugal, 53, 66
Pozzo di Borgo, Karl Osipovich, 62
Priority Question, 252, 253
Protić, Stojan, 241
Prussia, 1, 17, 27, 28, 44-6, 53, 60, 68, 71,
   75, 81, 88, 90, 96, 97, 125, 138, 154,
   155, 203, 272 (*See also* Germany)

Rasputin, G., 199
Reutern, Michael Khristoforovich, 172, 271
revolts and revolutions
   1789: French revolution, 1, 27, 31, 42, 116
   1804: Serbian revolution, 8, 9-24
   1820: revolutions in Spain, Portugal,
      Kingdom of the Two Sicilies, 53
   1821: Greek revolution, 26, 39, 49-75, 89,
      91, 92, 94, 121, 133, 161, 194, 250, 268
   1821: revolt in the Danubian
      Principalities, 52, 54
   1825: Decembrist revolt, 73
   1830: revolutions in France, Belgium,
      and Poland, 94, 101
   1841: Niš revolt, 161
   1843: revolution in Greece, 108
   1848-9: revolutions of, 94, 109-11, 115,
      127, 128, 147, 148, 161
   1850: Vidin revolt, 161
   1862: revolution in Greece, 106, 151
   1866: revolt in Romania, 149
   1875: Stara Zagora revolt, 166; revolt in
      Bosnia and Hercegovina, 159, 167
   1876: Bulgarian revolt (April Uprising),
      167, 250
   1885: revolt in Eastern Rumelia, 184, 185
   1903: revolt in Serbia, 238; Ilinden
      uprising, 214
   1905: Russian revolution, 197, 200
   1908: Young Turk revolution, 219, 225,
      235
   1917: Bolshevik revolution, 264, 266
Ribeaupierre, Alexander Ivanovich, 72, 101
Rifat Pasha, Mehmed, 223
Rifat Pasha, Sadik, 119
Rittikh, General Alexander Fedorovich,
   208, 209
Rodofinikin, Constantine Konstantinovich,
   16, 17
Romania, 153, 157, 159, 203, 206, 213, 237,
   264, 266-8; and the Balkan Wars, 232-
   4; and Bulgaria, 163-5, 171, 186, 195;

Index

unification of the Principalities, 148–51 (*See also* the Danubian Principalities of Wallachia and Moldavia)
Rosen, Roman Romanovich, 269n
Rumiantsev, Nicholas Petrovich, 17
Rustem Pasha, 190

Samarin, Iurii Fedorovich, 93
Salisbury, Lord, 187, 190, 191
Sazonov, Sergei Dmitrievich, 199, 225, 227, 231, 233, 234, 244–7, 257, 258, 260–2, 265
Second Empire, 115
Selim III, 11
Seniavin, Leo Grigor'evich, 161
Serbia, 5, 8, 26, 30, 34, 38, 72, 148, 150, 159, 203, 211, 213, 214, 217, 266, 274, 275; and the Balkan Wars, 228–34, 244–7; and the Bosnian crisis, 222, 224, 241–4; and the Bulgarian question, 162, 163, 166, 170–3, 176, 177, 185–90, 195, 196; and the Crimean War, 119, 120, 122, 128–30, 134–8, 141, 142; Russian relations with, 75–81, 86, 88, 89, 94, 100–5, 108, 111, 114, 235–48; the Serbian revolution, 9–24, 40; and the origins of World War I, 248–64
Seymour, Sir Hamilton, 114
Shebeko, Nicholas Nikolaevich, 255, 256, 262
Shishkin, Nicholas Pavlovich, 164
Shtrandtman, Vasilii Nikolaevich, 254
Shuvalov, Peter Andreevich, 177, 178
Slavophilism, 34, 93, 157
Slovaks, 158
Slovenes, 10, 158, 216, 239, 240
Spain, 53, 65, 66, 75, 97, 194
Spalajković, Miroslav, 247, 258, 261
Sremski Karlovci (Karlowitz), 9, 10, 13, 103
Staal, Egor Egorovich, 188n
Stambolov, Stephen, 193
Stirbei, Barbu, 134
Stolypin, Peter Arkadievich, 208, 217, 221, 225
Straits (Turkish), 3, 6, 26, 28, 57, 79, 95–7, 126, 155, 157, 189, 204–6, 215, 217, 219, 222, 223, 225, 234–5, 243, 244, 264, 267
Strangford, Lord, 56, 67, 71, 72
Stratford Canning (Lord Stratford de Redcliffe), 119, 120
Stroganov, Grigorii Aleksandrovich, 53–60, 62, 65
Sturdza, Ioan, 76

Sturdza, Michael, 110
Sturmer, B. V., 199
Suez Canal, 27, 156, 205
Syria, 5, 29, 95, 97, 117
Switzerland, 65
Szápáry, Friedrich, 257, 258, 265

Tankosić, Major Vojin, 251, 252
Tatich, Vladislav, 163
Tatishchev, Dmitrii Pavlovich, 62, 63, 65, 66
Taube, Michael Aleksandrovich, 243
Theodore I, tsar of Russia, 36
Tonchev, Dimitŭr, 185, 186
Totu, Filip, 163
Tsanov, Ilia, 192
Transylvania, 127, 162
treaties
    1699: Karlowitz, 31
    1774: Kuchuk Kainardji, 2–5, 7, 41, 51, 57, 58, 120–5, 134, 141
    1792: Jassy, 5, 7
    1805: Pressburg, 13
    1807: Tilsit, 7, 16, 17, 29
    1812: Bucharest, 1, 7, 18–22, 40, 41, 49, 77, 78, 80, 87, 88, 101, 109
    1815: Vienna, 1, 2, 22, 27, 40, 44, 87
    1826: Convention of St. Petersburg, 74, 75, 81, 82, 84
    1826: Akkerman, 80–3, 88, 101
    1827: London, 81–4, 86
    1828: Turkmanchai, 85
    1829: Adrianople, 85, 86, 88, 100, 101, 109, 118, 119, 122, 125
    1830: London Protocol, 87, 105
    1833: Kutahia, 95
    1833: Unkiar Iskelessi, 95, 97, 206, 222–4, 234
    1833: Münchengrätz, 96, 112
    1833: Berlin Convention, 96
    1841: Convention of the Straits, 97, 111
    1849: Convention of Balta Liman, 110
    1856: Paris, 138, 140, 141, 143, 146, 154, 155, 172, 236
    1858: Aigun, 199
    1860: Peking, 156, 199
    1878: San Stefano, 175, 176, 183, 213, 233, 234, 237, 239, 274
    1878: Berlin, 176, 177, 186, 190, 196, 197, 212, 213, 218–22, 224, 232, 237
    1881: St. Petersburg, 199
    1905: Portsmouth, 200
    1913: Bucharest, 232
Tseretelev, Prince Aleksei Nikolaevich, 168
Tumanskii, Fedor Antonovich, 136, 137

Index

Ukraine, 157, 209, 216, 248
United States, 200, 201

Vashchenko, Gerasim, 103, 104
Velimirović, Pera, 241
Victor Emmanuel III, king of Italy, 225
Victoria, queen of England, 121
Vienna Note, 1853, 125, 126, 129
Viviani, René, 263
Vladimirescu, Tudor, 52-4, 56
Vlangali, Alexander Georgievich, 185

Wallachia, see Danubian Principalities of
    Wallachia and Moldavia
wars
    1768-1774: Russo-Turkish War, 3
    1806-12: Russo-Turkish War, 14-18
    1828-9: Russo-Turkish War, 75-89, 90,
        270
    1831-3: Ottoman-Egyptian War, 95
    1839-40: Ottoman-Egyptian War, 96, 97
    1853-6: Crimean War, 25, 80, 115-41,
        151, 154, 156, 178, 201, 203, 204, 236,
        267, 268, 270, 271
    1870-1: Franco-Prussian War, 154, 155
    1876: war of Serbia and Montenegro
        against the Ottoman Empire, 170-2

    1877-8: Russo-Turkish War, 172, 173,
        185, 194, 196, 213, 237, 243, 270
    1885: Serbo-Bulgarian War, 186-8
    1897: Greek-Turkish War, 195
    1904-5: Russo-Japanese War, 199, 200,
        214, 217
    1906-11: Pig War, 241
    1911-12: Italian-Turkish War, 225
    1912-13: Balkan Wars, 227n, 232-4, 244,
        247, 248, 251, 252, 254
    1914-18: World War I, 205, 215, 263-6,
        270
Wellington, Duke of, 74, 79, 82
White, Sir William, 189
William, king of the Netherlands, 94
William I, king of Prussia, emperor of
    Germany, 144, 155, 167
William II, emperor of Germany,
    194
Witte, Sergei Iulievich, 201, 204

Yugoslavia, 239n, 266, 267

Zach, František, 153, 154
Zinoviev, Ivan Alekseevich, 166, 167,
    192